A DESCRIPTION

OF

ANCIENT AND MODERN COINS,

IN THE

CABINET COLLECTION

AT THE

MINT OF THE UNITED STATES.

PREPARED AND ARRANGED UNDER THE DIRECTION OF

JAMES ROSS SNOWDEN,

DIRECTOR OF THE MINT

PHILADELPHIA:
J. B. LIPPINCOTT & CO.
1860.

PREFACE.

The collection of coins and medals at the National Mint was formally commenced in June, 1838; but for many years previously to that time master coins of the Mint, that is to say, fine specimen pieces struck from new and polished dies, had been preserved, and also specimens of foreign coins, which were received as deposits, were withheld from the melting-pot, to be used, in the event of the establishment of a conservatory, at a future day.

The first appropriation was made by Congress March 3d, 1839, as follows: "For specimens of ores and coins to be reserved at the Mint, one thousand dollars." During subsequent years an annual appropriation of three hundred dollars has been made to this object. A larger amount would, doubtless, have been granted if asked for, but it was deemed expedient "to set an example of moderation in a pursuit which has its temptations to extravagance and excess;"* besides, we possess great facilities in increasing the collection without incurring much expense, by occasionally making exchanges to supply deficiencies, and by obtaining from deposits coins and ores at their intrinsic value, when such specimens are interesting and worthy of preservation.

Under these influences the collection has gradually increased, and especially has it been enlarged and enriched within the last few years, in specimens of modern coins, medals, and minerals.

In view of the extent and value of this collection, and the increasing public taste for coins and medals, a full descriptive catalogue has been prepared; it contains also a brief dissertation on money and coins, with some notice of the coinage of the various countries, ancient and modern, embraced in the Mint collection. This has been prepared and arranged by Mr. George

---

* "A Brief Account of the Collection of Coins belonging to the Mint, more especially the Antique Specimens, by Wm. E. Dubois, Assistant Assayer U. S. Mint. 1846."

Bull, recently in charge of the Cabinet, who has received valuable advice and assistance from Mr. Wm. E. Dubois, Assistant Assayer of the Mint.

This publication will be followed by another volume containing a full description, with *fac-simile* illustrations of the medallic memorials of Washington, which have recently been added to the collection, and a descriptive catalogue of the national and miscellaneous medals in the Cabinet, with some notices of the ores and minerals which are placed therein.

We wish to remind the reader that this work was originally intended to be merely a descriptive catalogue of the coins in the Cabinet of the Mint; more than this we have neither the time nor the skill to accomplish. But to make the book more interesting to the general reader, and perhaps to the collector of coins, it was deemed advisable to say a few words on the coinage of the several countries embraced in the collection; and for the purpose of making it useful to the man of business and to the traveler, the value of the principal modern coin in our money is stated; our chief object, however, is to present a catalogue of the coins in the Cabinet of the National Mint, and thus supply a want which has heretofore existed.

J. R. S.

Mint of the United States,
Philadelphia, August, 1860.

The Plates.—The peculiar kind of plates used in illustrating this work, which, we believe, are a novelty on this side the Atlantic, having never before appeared in any American book, were produced by E. Ketterlinus & Co., of Philadelphia. Commendation on our part is unnecessary, as the beauty and accuracy of the plates will be seen by an inspection of them.

LIST

OF

DIRECTORS OF THE MINT,

FROM ITS ORGANIZATION

TO THE YEAR 1858.

David Rittenhouse, (the eminent philosopher, formerly Treasurer of Pennsylvania,) July, 1792, to July, 1795.

Henry William De Saussure (vice Mr. Rittenhouse resigned,) July 11th, to October 28, 1795, (afterwards and for many years Chancellor of South Carolina.)

Elias Boudinot (in place of Judge De Saussure resigned,) October, 1795, to July, 1805. (Previously President of Congress under the confederation.)

Robert Patterson (on the resignation of Dr. Boudinot), July, 1805, to July, 1824. (Vice-Provost of the University of Pennsylvania, and President American Philosophical Society.)

Dr. Samuel Moore (in place of Mr. Patterson deceased,) July, 1824, to July, 1835. (Member of Congress from Bucks County, Pa.)

Dr. Robert M. Patterson (on the resignation of Dr. Moore,) July, 1835, to July, 1851. (Professor of Natural Philosophy in University, Virginia, and President of American Philosophical Society.)

Dr. Geo. N. Eckert (vice Dr. Patterson resigned,) July, 1851, to April, 1853. (Member of Congress from Lebanon County, Pa.)

Thos. M. Pettit (in place of Dr. Eckert resigned,) April to June, 1853. (Judge District Court, Philadelphia.)

The present incumbent, James Ross Snowden, (previously Speaker of the Pennsylvania House of Representatives, Treasurer of Pennsylvania, and Treasurer of the Mint,) was appointed in June, 1853, in place of Judge Petit, who died on the 31st of May, in that year, having held the office of Director but a few weeks.

INTRODUCTION.

THE condition of man as an inhabitant of the earth, and the relations and intercourse of men as members of a common community, must of necessity involve the existence of a circulating medium. At different periods in the world's history this medium of exchange has been represented by various commodities and articles, which at the present day would be the very objects of barter. Thus, if we go back to an early period, we find that the ancient Greeks, who lived in small communities, separated by the many mountains which intersect the face of the country, and whose commercial transactions were consequently limited, used the cattle which grazed upon their land as currency. And it seems very natural that such should be the case. Their facilities for transportation were few; they had neither canals nor railroads, and probably no vehicles by which articles could be transported with ease over a mountainous country; and an article to be well adapted to the purposes of currency, which must be continually passing from one person to another, and often carried to great distances, must be something which requires the smallest expense and the least labor to move. Cattle required not to be carried, but could transport themselves, the only labor attending the transaction being that expended in driving or leading the animal to its place of destination; and, as the value of cattle varied but little, they naturally became the standard by which other commodities of a more variable character were regulated. Homer mentions the use of cattle as a medium of exchange in his episode of Glaucus and Diomed, where the former is represented as having given his golden armor, worth a *hundred oxen*, for the brazen armor of the latter, worth only *nine*.* The fact that they used cattle and other commodities as currency, however, must not lead us into the error of supposing that the

* Gillies's Ancient Greece, vol. i. p. 11.

precious metals were unknown to the Greeks; on the contrary, *talents of gold* are often mentioned by Homer. "They were proposed as prizes to combatants, and were used as dedications in temples, but were too valuable to serve as current specie;"† the Greeks being then a rude and barbarous people, whose uniform transactions required no such nicety of refinement as the use of the precious metals would indicate.

But as Grecian society began to assume a more tangible form, and commerce to develop itself, we find the Greeks introducing the precious metals as a substitute for cattle, and also adopting therefor a certain standard of fineness, at which it was made current in certain sums. And we may here presume that, as a unit upon which to base their money transactions, they used the term "oxen," or "cattle." The price of the precious metals having been regulated by the value of the cattle before used, that being the standard of value most universally known; and this may account for the statement of Plutarch, which we shall take occasion to notice presently.

It is very natural that the people, having become sufficiently civilized to appreciate the value of the precious metals as a medium of exchange, should very soon thereafter have increased their mercantile transactions to such an extent as to render it necessary, in order to facilitate trade, to give some definite form to their currency; and with this object in view, the use of stamped bars, and afterward of rings, was commenced: these were adjusted to a certain standard, both in weight and fineness, and were evidently intended as a species of *coin.* But this object was partially defeated, for the reason that the people of that time had as little confidence in the integrity of their neighbors as we of the present day, no one being willing to receive a piece of silver or gold, in payment of a debt, merely because his debtor averred that it was worth "one oxen," or "one shekel," without first ascertaining for himself that such was the case. For this reason we find that the ancients, notwithstanding the fact that they had rings, and pieces of metal of various sizes, all adjusted to a certain standard, never abandoned the practice of paying and receiving such money by weight until it was supplanted by an actual coinage, executed by authority; and even then it was the practice, for a long time, to weigh the coins whenever any large amounts were paid or received.

This brings us down to the time when actual coins were used, and to the time when the *art of coinage* had its origin. This period

† Gillies, quoting Homer and Heroditus.

would appear to be slightly shrouded in mystery, but the best authorities of the present day place the time at about seven centuries before the Christian era. There is some dispute also as to the exact locality, some authorities attributing the origin of the art to the little Island of Ægina in Greece, while others contend that coins were first struck at the City of Miletus, in Ionia, Asia Minor. Plutarch, however, throws some doubt upon the whole matter, both as regards time and place. In speaking of Theseus, the founder of Athens, he says: "To his money he gave the impression of an ox, either on the account of the Marathonian bull, of Minos's general Taurus, or because he wished to encourage the citizens in agriculture. Hence came the expression of a thing's being worth ten or a hundred oxen." This statement of Plutarch, however, seems to stand entirely alone, being considered as extremely doubtful testimony by most historians; and when we come to consider the fact that Theseus flourished about twelve centuries and a half before the Christian era, and also that Plutarch wrote at a time when historians were apt to place great reliance in legendary tales, often attributing the success or defeat of any great enterprise to the influence of the gods, we may be excused for not coinciding with him in the belief that Theseus had a mint.

If we concede the point that Plutarch is not sufficient authority in such a matter, we are reduced to the necessity of acknowledging that the authorities before mentioned are correct as regards the time. The only doubt remaining, therefore, is in regard to the place, and this we look upon as a matter of little consequence in this particular instance. The Greeks had visited and planted colonies in Asia Minor long before a coinage was thought of. In fact, the whole colony of Ionia appears to have been composed of Greeks who had spread themselves along the coast of that country: therefore, as it must be admitted that the origin of the art is purely Grecian, whether it was first used in Ægina, and from thence was carried across to the continent of Asia, to be imitated by their brethren in Ionia, or whether it originated with the people of the latter place, and then found its way back to the mother country, we do not propose to debate. It is certain that the coinage of both places, of which there are still specimens extant, were so near alike as regards execution, as to place them both very near the origin of the art. The coin of Ægina to which we refer was a silver *didrachm*, and had on its obverse the rude emblem of a tortoise (see No. 4 in the first division of Greek Coins), while on its

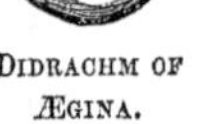

DIDRACHM OF ÆGINA.

reverse it bore merely the indentation of the punch. That of Miletus was a gold stater, and had on its obverse a lion's head, while the reverse was distinguished by the punch-mark as before. There is one fact, however, to which antiquarians appear to attach but little importance in discussing this question, to which we would incidentally call attention: the punch-mark found on the reverse of the stater of Miletus is very different in form to that found on the *first* coins of Ægina, while it bears a striking resemblance to the mark found on those coins of Ægina which are conceded to be of a later date than the *first;* and this, coupled with the fact that the lion's head of Miletus is much more artistic in execution than the first tortoise of Ægina, would seem to have some significance. There is little danger, however, in setting down the Miletus stater as being the *first gold coin of the world.*

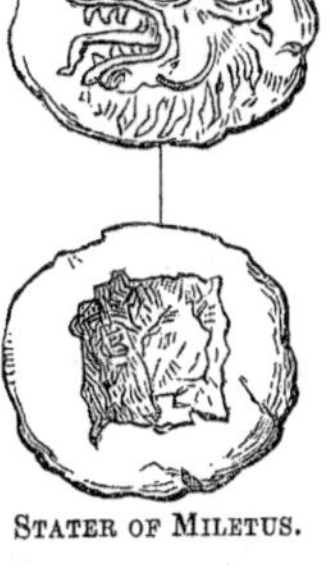

STATER OF MILETUS.

The pleasure derived from the study of the history of the art of coinage is greater than is generally thought. The comparison of the present state of the art with what it was, furnishes a gratification to the student of the present day which amply compensates for the time and trouble attending the research. When the coinage of Ægina was executed, the coiners possessed no "steam-coining presses," by which the most beautiful and artistic coins could be produced at the rate of eighty-five or ninety impressions per minute. Their "coining-press" probably consisted merely of a block of wood, upon which the die, or piece of hardened metal containing the sunken impressions, was placed, a hammer and punch; and these were worked by hand. The piece of metal to be coined was first fashioned into a semi-bullet shape; this having been placed upon the face of the die, the punch was applied to it and struck with a hammer. This constituted the coining operation in the earliest history of the art of which we have any account; and we have no doubt, from the appearance of the coins themselves, was the first process ever known or used.

It is a curious fact that the process by which money was coined made but little advance from this rude and imperfect apparatus, until the introduction of the mill and screw in the sixteenth century of the present era. The art, however, as far as it regards improvement in the type of the coin itself, continued to advance; and it is from this improvement in the execution that the relative ages of the most ancient coins are ascertained.

Thus we find that the earliest coins of the world, or such as belong to the *first epoch of time* in the history of the art, had no device upon the reverse, but merely the mark or indentation made by the punch. This mark, however, had a definite form, which was evidently designed and not accidental; being an irregular circle divided into several sections, of which the number varies.* But in discriminating between the *first* and *last* coins of this epoch, as well as the subsequent periods into which we propose to divide the most ancient coins, we are obliged to examine still more minutely into both the design and workmanship; and in so doing, we find that the *earliest* coins of the *first* epoch, and consequeutly the first known coins of the world, were extremely rude, bearing no letters or symbols other than the one device upon the obverse by which they can be distinguished. Afterward, as we draw toward the close of the period, symbols begin to make their appearance on the obverse, and then the initial letter of the country to which they belong, and in some cases the entire name appears.......The coins of the *second* period begin to display the first attempts at a device in relief for the reverse. These devices, however, are contained in a concavity, which is divided into four squares; the symbols or devices being disposed within the squares. The coins of this period, as well as those of a later time, always bear a legend, which, though sometimes much abbreviated and often indefinite, is a guide by which the country and date can be ascertained in a much more satisfactory manner than in the coinage of the former period.......The coins of the *third* division are concave on the reverse as before, but have a square compartment within the concavity which is bisected with bars, and contains symbols in relief as in the coins of the previous period; the legend generally appearing outside of the square.......In the earlier stages of the *fourth* division, the concavity still exists, but contains only a single device in relief. But as we approach the latter end of the period, the depression shows signs of diminishing in depth, and upon such coins as date near the end of the epoch, is scarcely visible. This has given some numismatists another division; but for our present purpose we find that the confining of the two divisions in one is sufficiently precise.......In the *fifth* division we find the most marked change of style; the obverse having the figures and symbols in relief, while on the reverse they are all in concave, and are often *facsimiles* of those on the obverse.......In the *sixth* division the concave devices disappear from the reverse of the coin, and in their stead we find figures in relief as on the obverse; but not copied

* If we concede the coins of Ægina to be the first.

therefrom. The legends are in the very ancient style of Greek characters.

This last division brings us down to the time at which the art first began to develop itself into the most finished style of execution to which the coins of Greece ever attained. The time over which the six epochs (into which we have divided the subject) extended was a period of from three to four centuries, beginning at about seven to eight centuries before Christ; consequently we have now arrived at the time of Philip and Alexander, of Macedon. Under these monarchs the coinage of Greece attained its greatest perfection, as will be amply attested by an examination of the gold staters both of Philip and Alexander, as well as the silver tetradrachms of the latter.

It was at this period in the history of the art that the coinage first began to exhibit an actual human portrait. The tetradrachm of Alexander the Great is thought to bear the features of the great Macedonian conqueror. If this be true, it would seem that he is clothed with the character of Hercules, and does not appear simply and boldly as Alexander. The successors of Alexander, however—those powerful lieutenants who, out of the fragments of his empire, erected for themselves independent kingdoms—did not hesitate to displace the effigies of the gods from the coins and substitute their own, though at first always under some pretense of deification—Lysimachus as a descendant of Bacchus, Seleucus of Apollo, etc.*

As Greece had now passed the highest pinnacle of her grandeur and commenced her course downward to almost utter extinction, we find her coinage declining with her until it loses its Grecian character and is entirely swallowed up in the coinage of her Roman conquerors. Of the coinage of the latter empire but little can be said in favor of any advance in the art as displayed in their execution. It is true, that down to the time of Constantine, the coins of Rome remained in a very good condition, but from that time to the end of the empire we witness a gradual but certain decline. It is remarkable that so little attention should have been bestowed upon this subject by the Roman emperors, especially when we consider the fact that in the height of its power the empire comprised the entire world as then known to the Romans. Thus we find that Joseph and Mary undertook the journey "from Galilee, out of the City of Nazareth, into Judea, unto the City of David, which is called Bethlehem (because he was of the house and lineage of David) to be taxed," in conse-

* Humphrey.

quence of a decree from the Emperor Cæsar Augustus "that *all the world should be taxed.*" (See Luke, ii.) Therefore, as we are unable to find any very commendable features in the Roman coinage other than the extreme prodigality with which the coins were disseminated, we pass over any further mention of the Roman art, referring the reader to a subsequent article devoted to that particular subject.

We find upon an examination of the first *modern* coins, or those immediately subsequent to the extinction of the Western Empire, that a still further decline in the appearance of the coinage is exhibited. And this is easily accounted for: upon the dissolution of the Roman Empire the whole of Europe was overrun by the various barbaric nations inhabiting the northern extremity of the continent, the Goths, Lombards, Huns, Vandals, and others, who, conquering the feeble remnants of the people, and establishing their own barbaric laws and customs, entirely crushed out the coinage instituted by the Kings of the West, and reduced it to their own rude standard. From this time, however, dates the final healthy and continued growth of the art, which has brought it to its present perfection. As soon as the savage tribes began to improve in civilization, or were driven back by the more enlightened inhabitants, the coins began to show a marked change for the better. We find them improving not only in form, but in type. They become more uniform in shape, the edge presenting a more perfect circle, and the impressions are stamped upon a more flat and even surface, being no longer of the bullet-shape observable in the coins of Greece and Rome, rendering the process of piling them one upon another (which is now considered an essential property in coins) no longer difficult or impracticable. Through the different grades of perfection which the art of coinage has experienced from that time to the present, we do not propose to follow, having neither the space nor inclination to warrant the prosecution of such a task; in fact, it would be entirely unnecessary in the present instance, the main portion of the following pages being devoted to a detailed description of the modern coins of all countries.

As we have before intimated, the implements used in the manufacture of coins continued in a very rude and imperfect state up to the time of the introduction of the mill and screw. We do not mean, however, to say that there was *no* advance from the crude condition in which we have before represented it; on the contrary, the coins themselves show that many improvements were made in this apparatus, by which it was enabled to produce much more perfect coins. The principles involved in its construction, however, were the same, until the introduction of the peculiar implement which we illustrate in the annexed engraving. At what particular time this instrument was invented we are unable to say with certainty, but probably not

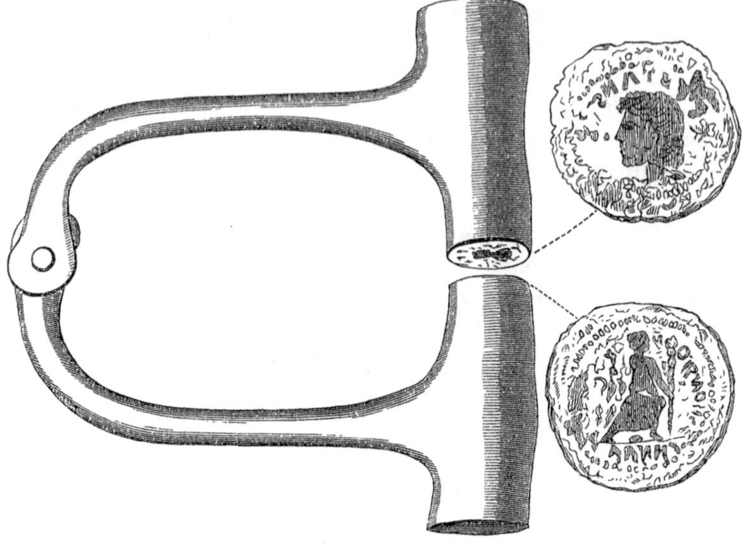

AN ANCIENT "COINING-PRESS."

earlier than the time of Constans (A.D. 337 to 350). The one which we here represent was used in the time of that emperor. "It was discovered at Beaumont-sur-Oise, and presented to the French cabinet by the maire of that commune. On the obverse die the letters S T A N S are still visible. The reverse has a victory, with a trophy and a palm branch."* The legend on the reverse is almost entirely effaced, the only visible portion being the letters......D. N...... The use of this instrument, it would appear, was discontinued, as we find that coins were struck by the old process long after the time of Constans.

The mill and screw was of French origin, the invention of which is ascribed to one ANTOINE BRUCHER, an engraver, who first used such a machine in the palace of Henry II., in 1553, for the purpose of stamping counters. It was continued in use until 1585, when it is said to have been laid aside, as it was found much more expensive than the old hammer process. We find no mention of its having been used after this time until the year 1623, when BRIOT, a French artist, unable to pursuade his own government to adopt it again,

* Akerman.

passed over to England, where it was immediately put in practice at the Royal Mint, under the direction of Briot himself, who was appointed chief engraver.* Here it was again discontinued, for the same reason as before, and a resort had to the old hammer and punch system. But when the Commonwealth was established, Cromwell, being anxious to improve the coinage, which was falling much behind that of many of the continental kingdoms, invited PIERRE BLONDEAU, a Frenchman, who had carried the most approved modes of stamping coins by the mill and screw to great perfection, to take charge of the coining operations at the English Mint. Upon his arrival Blondeau succeeded in coining half crowns by this process, which, for the first time, presented a legend upon the edge. "His first pattern half crown bore on the edge 'TRUTH AND PEACE, 1651, PETRUS BLONDEUS;' another, 'IN THE THIRD YEARE OF FREEDOME BY GOD'S BLESSING RESTORED.' The shillings and sixpences were beautifully grained on the edge, and the pieces were brought to their true weight with the utmost exactness."† Blondeau, notwithstanding his ingenuity, and his good services to the State, appears to have been badly used by the authorities of the Commonwealth, and was at last superseded by other artists, although his process of the mill and screw was continued. In 1662, however, Blondeau was taken into favor by the newly restored monarch Charles II., and appointed to superintend the operations at the Mint as before.

The mill and screw was continued in use until a very recent period. In fact, the screw-press is *now* used for striking medals which require a high relief, as it is found to be the only apparatus yet invented of sufficient power to bring up the impressions. The first steam coining-press was invented in 1833 by Thonnelier, a Frenchman, and was soon put in practice at the French Mint. It was first introduced into the Mint of the United States in March, 1836, the old screw-press having been used here up to that time. This invention (the operation of which we shall describe presently), with some modifications, is the press now in use, and is probably the nearest approach to perfection, as regards accuracy and speed, that we shall ever witness.

It is a matter worthy of comment that France has thus produced *two* of the greatest inventions ever known to the art of coining—the mill and screw, and the steam coining-press, both of which events furnish two epochs in the history of the art which shed much luster upon the inventive skill of the French people.

---

* Encyclopedia Britannica. † Humphrey.

In the preceding pages we have endeavored to convey to the mind of the reader some idea of the rise and progress of the art; we feel sensible, however, that we have been exceedingly indefinite upon a subject which contains substance enough to fill an entire volume; but it must be evident to any candid mind that it would be impossible to compress even the outlines of the history of the art within the space to which we are limited, without omitting many points which are of great interest, and as our object has merely been to give a few general remarks of an introductory character, we feel constrained to refer the reader to works devoted more particularly to this branch of the subject. But before we close, an explanation of the process of coining the precious metals as prosecuted at the mint will doubtless be interesting as well as instructive.

In the time of the Roman Empire the manufacture of coins was a laborious operation, requiring many artists and workmen. "They had first the OPTIO, or Director; then the EXACTORES, or NUMMULARII, Assayers; SCALPTORES or CŒLATORES, Engravers of the dies, who were, usually Greek artists; CENARII, Refiners; FUSARII or FLATUARII, Melters; EQUATORES, Adjusters of weight, and SIGNATORES, who certified the same; SUPPASTORES, who put the pieces on the die, and MALLEATORES, who struck the blow. The whole body constituted a corporation in law, and so numerous were they that, on one occasion, under the Emperor Aurelian (A.D. 274), they were excited to a revolt, and killed *seven thousand soldiers* before they could be subdued, from which incidental fact it is plausibly inferred that they themselves must have been at least seven thousand strong."* The process was briefly as follows: The metal, having been assayed and refined, was cast by the melters into bullets, this form of planchet being necessary in order to assist in producing the high relief which we have before mentioned. This casting was placed between the dies and submitted to repeated blows from a sledge or heavy hammer, which made the impression, and, at the same time, flattened the pieces out into that peculiar shape which is anything but a true circle, there being no *collar* used, as at the present time, to confine the piece and prevent it from *spreading.* It would seem that in some cases a large stone was made to drop upon the piece, and so produce the impression.†

This, therefore, appears to have been the ancient system of mintage; the system of the present day, although much more multifarious

---

* Manual of Coins and Bullion, quoting Pinkerton and Mongez.

† Pinkerton, from Manual of Coins and Bullion.

in its details than the ancient process, requires no such army of employees; the whole force employed in the United States Mint, including officers, does not exceed one hundred and seventy.

Bullion is brought to the mint in every form; amalgamations from the ore, coins, both foreign and domestic, bars, plate, jewelry, etc., and these present many grades of quality, some being nearly pure; the remainder representing all the grades of fineness from that down to three thousandths. Some of it is perfectly ductile and easily worked, while a portion is brittle and requires to be toughened. A deposit of gold is often found to contain a large portion of silver which requires to be separated by chemical agents; all these facts are ascertained by the investigations of the assay department.

The process is as follows: The deposit, upon being received, is weighed by the proper officers, and then sent to the deposit melting room, where the deposit is melted in a mass and cast into a bar; this bar is numbered, and a slip cut from it and sent to the assay department; here, by assaying this slip, the amount of pure metal contained in the entire deposit is ascertained. To do this with exactness requires a very careful and accurate manipulation. The operations of this department are intricate, and as they require an extended description for which we have not sufficient space, we are compelled to omit it and return again to the deposit. Its value having been ascertained by the assay, it is ready for the refining process. This is not strictly a mint operation; in some countries these preliminary processes have to be performed by private refiners. But at the Mint of the United States, departments have been provided in which the silver is separated from the gold, the refining and standarding of the metals, and the casting them into ingots or small bars from which the coins are to be made, are performed. The bars or ingots thus produced are about twelve inches long, half an inch thick, and from one to two-and-a-half inches in width, according to the size of the coin for which they are intended. These bars, before being wrought, have to be assayed, in order to test their fineness, and those which are found to be either above or below the legal limits in fineness are returned to the melting room to be remelted and cast at the proper rate.

The ingots, having been approved, are first brought to a red heat in order to anneal and render them sufficiently ductile to be rolled with facility; they are then passed between hardened steel rollers, driven by a steam-engine, which are so arranged that they can be adjusted with the greatest nicety in order to reduce the bar very nearly to the exact thickness required for the coin. In this form they are taken to the *drawing bench*, driven by the same engine, in which the strip is drawn slowly through the *drawing dies*, or plates of the hardest steel accurately adjusted to reduce the strips to their proper thickness. The strip, thus prepared, is next passed through the *cutting press*, also moved by steam, and pieces or *planchets* of the proper size are cut from it. The punch moves with such rapidity that one hundred and sixty pieces on an average are cut out in one minute. At the completion of this part of the process, which leaves the strip full of holes, it is folded up and returned to the melting pot.

The planchets are now carried to the coining room, where, in order to raise the edge of the planchet to protect the surface of the coin, they are passed through the *milling machine*. The planchets are fed to this machine through an upright tube, and as they descend from the lower aperture, they are caught upon the edge of a revolving wheel and carried about a quarter of a revolution, during which the edge is compressed and forced up—the space between the wheel and the rim being a little less than the diameter of the planchet. This apparatus moves so nimbly, that five hundred and sixty half dimes can be milled in a minute; but for large pieces the average is about one hundred and twenty.

The planchets are next to be cleaned, annealed, and whitened; after which, in the case of the gold, they are adjusted in their weight, piece by piece;* the silver pieces, however, having been tested by samples from each strip, are allowed to pass until after coinage, when their weight is proved in bulk.

The planchets are now ready to receive the last impression which is to render them a perfect coin. This most important office is performed by the *coining-press*, which we have before mentioned. This machine receives the planchets in a tube from the hand of a workman; as the coin reaches the bottom of the tube it is seized between a pair of fingers and carried forward and deposited within a steel collar between the dies; and while the fingers are expanding and returning for another planchet, the dies close upon the one within the collar, and by a rotary motion are made to impress it silently but powerfully. The fingers, as they again close upon a planchet at the mouth of the tube, also seize the coin, and while conveying a second planchet on to the die, carry the coin off, dropping it into a box provided for the purpose—and this operation is repeated *ad infinitum*.

---

* At the French mint this is done by the aid of an ingenious machine of French invention, a sample of which now stands in the Cabinet of the United States Mint. At our mint this is done entirely by hand.

These coining-presses are of various sizes to suit the different denominations of coin. The usual speed of striking is sixty pieces per minute for the half dollar; seventy-five for the quarter dollar; and ninety for the dime and half dime.

STEAM COINING-PRESS.

The coining dies, it will be necessary to state, are prepared by engravers specially maintained at the mint for the purpose. The process of engraving a die consists in cutting the devices and legends in soft steel, those parts being depressed which in the coin appear in relief. This having been finished and hardened, constitutes an "*original die;*" which being the result of a tedious and difficult task is deemed too precious to be directly employed in striking coins, but is used for *multiplying dies.* It is first used to impress another piece of soft steel, which then presents the appearance of a coin, and is called a *hub.* This hub being hardened, is used to impress other pieces of steel in like manner, which being exactly like the original die, are hardened and used for striking the coins. A pair of these will, on an average, perform two weeks' work.

ABBREVIATIONS, Etc.

G.—Gold.

S.—Silver.

C.—Copper.

B.—Bronze, or brass.

B.S.—Base Silver under 750 fine.

Obv.—*Obverse,* or principal side.

Rev.—*Reverse,* or nether side.

Exerque.—Space beneath the device or field, and divided therefrom by a sectional line.

Legend.—An inscription encircling the field.

Inscription.—Letters or words occupying the field of either side.

R.—Rare.

R.R.—Very rare.

R.R.R.—Exceedingly rare.

(......)—Used to denote a break in the legend, or a disconnection in the parts of a legend.

A DESCRIPTION

OF

ANCIENT AND MODERN COINS.

ANCIENT COINS.

GREEK.

THE first general division of this work will embrace a catalogue of the ancient or *antique* coins, Grecian and Roman—the former taking precedence of the latter, as being the first in point of time. We believe, as we have before intimated, that the art of coinage is of Grecian origin, the time of its introduction being approximated at seven centuries B.C. Consequently there must have been an interval of over one thousand years, in which the precious metals were known and used, before the ingenuity of man was able to apply them to the uses of coinage—a fact which we gain from sacred writ, where it is recorded, that as long ago as 1860 years before Christ, *three thousand seven hundred and twenty years ago*, when Abraham was in search of a burying-place for his dead wife Sarah, he desired to purchase the cave of Macphelah from its proprietor, Ephron, the Hittite. "Ephron answered Abraham, saying unto him, My lord, hearken unto me: the land is worth four hundred shekels of silver; what is that betwixt thee and me? bury therefore thy dead. And Abraham hearkened unto Ephron; and Abraham *weighed* to Ephron the silver, which he had named in the audience of the sons of Heth, four hundred shekels of silver, *current money with the merchant.*" (Gen. xxiii. 14–16.)

Having in the introductory article detailed, as accurately as was deemed expedient for our present purpose, the history of the origin of the art of coinage, together with the steps leading thereto, and taken a hasty glance at the gradual development of the art, it will be unnecessary to recapitulate here.

It often strikes the minds of modern antiquarians with wonder, when they enter upon the study of ancient coins, to find how common such relics are at the present day. Many of the antique coins do not begin to compare with some specimens of our own series of national coins in rarity. The ancient inhabitants of the world derived their subsistence and wealth from the soil which they cultivated. They paid no attention to financial concerns. They knew nothing of railroad corporations, canal companies, or banks, other than that from which they gathered their annual crops, and it was in the latter that they placed their trust. When the husbandman had sold his produce, and received in payment therefor a bag of silver tetradrachms or gold staters, he immediately deposited them in an earthen vessel and buried them beneath the floor of his little hut for future use. But anon the spoiler came. The invading host swept over his humble habitation, obliterating it and its inmates, like shadows, from the face of the earth. Two thousand years elapse, and the earth at last yields up its hidden treasure to the plowshare or spade of the modern farmer. Thus it is, that in the countries of the East these valuable antiquities are continually coming to light. And it is only recently that we have had revealed to us a whole history through the discovery of a series of Greco-Syrian coins.

Under the head of Greek coins, we comprise not only those of Greece and her colonies, but those countries which were overrun by the Macedonian conqueror, and over which Greek generals established themselves and their successors. Hence they include Greece proper, Sicily, Southern Italy, and more western points in Europe, and Asia Minor, Syria, Egypt, Persia, and Bactria, during all that time when the Grecian name was the most illustrious in the world, and the Roman was preparing to supplant it.

They are easily subdivided into the REPUBLICS and MONARCHIES.

Of the first sort there are known to have been no less than *one thousand* cities, colonies, and petty States, who coined their own money, and left an endless, perhaps useless, study for modern antiquarians. Many of these are exceedingly interesting not only to the numismatist, but to the historian; but we consider them sufficiently represented in our moderate collection. The order of arrangement in this division is not chronological, the coins being arranged alphabetically by the names of the states, cities, etc., in which they were coined. This arrangement will be sufficiently satisfactory to the numismatist, but may not meet the approbation of the general reader and searcher after ancient lore. But we have followed the example set by most numismatists, in this respect, considering it the only safe arrangement, from the fact that it is impossible to state the dates with any degree of accuracy.

In the second class, it has been found necessary to include a few which are not inscribed with Greek characters, and which are not, in any sense, Grecian; such as the *daric*, the shekel, the "fire-worship" series of Persia, and the barbarian coins of Bactria: they were not sufficient in number, nor sufficiently congruous, to form a third general division.

We have ventured to depart from numismatic usage in one particular, of no great importance. The coins of Greek cities, of a date subsequent to their incorporation into the Roman empire, and bearing little else than the imperial head and titles, have been withdrawn from the department of Greek republican coins, and placed with the Roman, under their respective emperors. Their proper position would be a nice point to argue, if it were worth an argument. But (without summing up the reasons) we apprehend that the democratic taste will justify a distinction between the potin of Antioch and the silver of Athens.

The collection contains a small number of acknowledged counterfeits, nearly all of imperial Roman coins, and all from the manufactory of Mr. Becker, of Berlin. This eminent amateur of coins conceived and effected the project of supplying collectors with *copies* of such pieces as by their rarity and high price were hardly to be procured; and for this purpose, aided no doubt by the prospect of a lucrative trade, caused to be engraved the vast number of 510 dies, for the coinage of 255 different specimens, chiefly antique. These are, without doubt, the best efforts at counterfeiting, and the least dishonest; but a little familiarity is sufficient to detect them. They came to us as part of a large lot, and are retained as showing what the originals are, and as affording facilities for acquiring the art of discrimination, a very important part of the collector's work. It is a satisfaction to know that the utmost skill of man is inadequate to the confounding of truth and error, where diligence and experience are set in opposition.* It should be added, that these pieces are mostly of the usurpers and "emperors for a day," and therefore of little historical interest. These copies or counterfeits are designated by *cb*, in the description.

We deem it an act of justice to remark, in this connection, that the following catalogue of ancient coins (both Grecian and Roman) is taken entire from a small work entitled "PLEDGES OF HISTORY," published by MR. DUBOIS, Assistant Assayer of the Mint, in 1846.

DIVISION I.

GREEK REPUBLICS.

1. S. ABYDOS......2. S. ACHAIA......3. S. ÆGEA.

4, 5, 6. S. ÆGINA. Three sizes; the largest weighs 170 grains, and is worn; the smallest, 13 grains. Ægina had a different standard from most other parts of Greece. The device—a *tortoise*—is emblematic of the island, lying securely in the water. The large and small pieces, having no reverse except the marks of the stake on which they were laid in coining, are believed to date near the origin of the art, and may be twenty-five hundred years old. The middle piece seems of a later era.

---

* A full account of "Die Becker'schen falschen Münz Stämpel" is contained in a pamphlet by Prof. von Steinbüchel, Vienna, 1836. The general price of his silver coin is 1½ florins of Austria, or 73 cents; gold pieces are from 7½ to 12 florins.

7. B. ÆZANIS...... 8. S. AGRIGENTUM...... 9. B. do...... 10. B. ALEXANDRIA, of the Troad......12. B. AMASIA......14. S. AMISUS.

15. S. AMPHIPOLIS. This specimen weighs but seven grains; value less than two cents. A small morsel to be handed down so many centuries.

16 to 19. S. APOLLONIA......20. S. ARADUS......25. S. ARGOS, Acamania......26. S. do. Peloponesus.

28. S. ATHENS. Tetradrachm; weighs 266 grains; value about 70.7 cents. Obv. A head of Minerva, of very ancient style. Rev. A large owl, with the letters *AΘE*, initials of Athens. The devices are in the boldest relief, and the general style of the coin, coupled with historical facts, indicate an age of twenty-one to twenty-three centuries. The piece to the right is an electrotype copy to show the reverse.

29. S. ATHENS. Stater, or piece of four drachms. Obv. A head of Minerva, with the Greek helmet. Rev. The sacred owl.* About 2100 years old. Value 70 cents. From Captain Gardner, U. S. N. (See *Division XV.*, "*Selections.*")

30, 31. B. ATHENS......33. B. BEREA......34. B. BLAUNDOS...... 35. S. BŒOTIA......36. B. BRUTII......37. B. CAMPANIA, Syria...... 38. S. CATANA. *cb*......39. S. CHALCIS, of Eubœa......40. B. do. of Macedonia...... 42. S. CHERSONESUS TAURICA...... 43. B. CLAZOMENE.

44. B. CNOSUS, of Crete. The reverse shows a ground plan of the famous *labyrinth.*

46. S. CORCYRA, magna......49 to 54. B. CORCYRA, nigra.

57 to 61. S. CORINTH. No. 57, tetradrachm, is of beautiful workmanship. Obv. Head of Minerva. Rev. Pegassus, or the winged horse.

62. B. CORINTH......63. B. COTIACUM......64. B. CYRENE......65. B. CYZICUS......66 to 68. S. DYRRACHIUM......69. B. do......70. S. EPHESUS, Ionia......71. S. EPIRUS......73. S EUBŒA......74. S. GELAS......75. B. do......76. S. HERACLEA, of Lucania......78. S. do.

---

* The proverbial saying of the Greeks, "taking owls to Athens," was of the same import as the modern one of "carrying coals to Newcastle."

of Macedonia......80. S. HISTRŒA......81. S. ILISTŒA......82. S. ISTRUS......83. S. LARISSA......84. B. LAMPSACUS......85. S. LESBOS......86. S. LETE......87. S. LOCRI......88. B. do......89. B. LEUCADIA......91, 92. S. MACEDONIA......93. B. MAMERTINI......94. S. MARONEA......95. B. do.

97, 98, 99. S. MASSILIA. These are interesting, as belonging to a colony of Greeks who, to escape the oppressions of a Persian governor, emigrated to the coast of Gaul, (about six hundred years before Christ,) and settled upon the spot now known as *Marseilles.* The finished workmanship attests their civilization, in which respect they are said to have exerted great influence upon the surrounding Gauls.

100. B. MILETUS, Ionia......101. B. MYCONUS......102. B. MYSIA. ......103, 104. S. NEAPOLIS, of Campania (Naples)......105 to 107. B. do......108. S. NEAPOLIS, Macedonia.

110. B. NEMAUSUS. Greek colony in France, now *Nismes.* Obv. Heads of Augustus and Agrippa, in whose day this was struck.

111. B. ŒNIADÆ......113 B. PÆSTUM......115. B. PANORMUS...... 116. S. PARIUM......117. B. PELLE......118. S. PERGAMUS...... 119. S. PHARSALIA......120. B. PHARUS......121. S. PHOCIDIS...... 122. B. PHŒNIA......123. S. PYTOPOLIS......124. S. RHEGIUM...... 126, 127. S. RHODES......128. B. do......129. B. SARDIS......130. S. SICYON, island......131. S. do. Achaia......133. S. SIDE......134, 135. S. SIPHNUS......136. B. do......138. B. SMYRNA......139. S. SYRACUSE......140. B. SYRACUSE......141. S. TARENTUM......142, 143. B. TAUROMENIUM......146. B. TEANUM......147. B. TENEDOS, of the Troad......148. S. THASUS......149. S. THESSALY......150. S. THESSALONICA......153, 154. S. THRACE......157, 158. S. VELIA. ......159. B. VALENTIA, Italy.

DIVISION II.

GREEK MONARCHIES.

MACEDON.

This kingdom was founded about eight hundred years before Christ; four hundred and fifty years later it was enlarged by the conquests of Philip; and became still more conspicuous from the military career of his son, Alexander the Great. But the kingdom began to decline at his death, and at length, B.C. 148, became a province of the Roman empire.

9. Small silver coin, of one of the early kings, uncertain which, but evidently earlier than Alexander I., who flourished about B.C. 500. It bears the Macedonian horse on the obverse, and there is no reverse except the punch-marks.

10, 11. Bronze coins of AMYNTAS II. B.C. 398–371.

12. Gold stater of PHILIP II. B.C. 371–336.

13. Silver tetradrachm, of the same.

14. Hemidrachm, of the same.

15. Bronze coin, of the same.

17. Gold stater of ALEXANDER III. (THE GREAT.) B.C. 336–323. Obv. Head of Minerva. Rev. A female figure, with wings, representing Victory, and bearing a trident.

18, 19. Tetradrachms of the same. The head represents Hercules, clothed with the lion's skin; but it is believed that a likeness of Alexander is also intended. Rev. Figure of Jupiter seated, holding an eagle. Legend, *ΑΛΕΞΑΝΔΡΟΥ.* "(Money) of Alexander."

Alexander was so jealous of his personal appearance as to allow the imitation of it, in painting, sculpture, or engraving, by only three of his best artists; all *mediocre* hands were strictly forbidden to attempt it.

The lion's skin is said to have been displayed, as showing the descent of the Macedonian royal line, by Caraunus, from Hercules. It is curiously alluded to by the Emperior Constantine VI., Porphyrogenitus, writing in the tenth Christian century. "The kings of Macedonia, instead of the crown, the diadem, and the purple, bear [upon their effigy] the skin of a lion's head. More honorable to them is this than to be decked with pearls and precious stones."

20, 21, 22. Drachms, of the same. (No. 22 has a ring, and appears to have been worn as a pendant ornament; but how long ago, is uncertain. Its being a fashion among the oriental ladies of the present day, is some proof that it was also the custom a thousand years ago, as the fashions there are said to undergo but little change.)

23. Drachm, of PHILIP III., brother of Alexander. B.C. 323–316.

25, 26. Bronze coins, of CASSANDER. B.C. 316–299.

27. Bronze, of PHILIP IV. B.C. 298.

28. Silver, of ALEXANDER IV. B.C. 298–294.

29, 30. Bronze, of the same.

31 to 36. Bronze, of ANTIGONUS I. B.C. 279–243.

37. Tetradrachm, of PHILIP V. Died B.C. 179.

This piece is so remarkably brittle, that a slight fall broke it; yet upon assay of a fragment, it was found to be 97 per cent. fine.

38. Bronze coin, of PERSEUS. B.C. 179–168. He was taken by the Romans, and was the last king of Macedon.

39. Small bronze; uncertain whose.

PERSIA.

The ancient coins of the Persian empire are divisible into three classes. 1. The earliest is that of the dynasty of Cyrus, which began B.C. 560, and ended with Darius III., B.C. 331, by the conquests of Alexander of Macedon. The first coinage is attributed to Darius I., who ascended the throne B.C. 521; from whose name the coins, whether of gold or silver, are usually called *darics;* but they cannot now be assigned to any particular monarch. 2. The second series commences with the Greek domination. In the partition of the vast conquests of Alexander, Syria, Persia, and Bactria constituted one empire, under Seleucus, a Greek general. But at the end of half a century, Persia was erected into a separate monarchy by Arsaces, founder of the dynasty of Arsacidæ, which lasted from B.C. 256 to A.D. 223. The coins of this class bear inscriptions in Greek. 3. The rule of the Greeks was overthrown by Ardeshir, or Artaxerxes, a Persian, A.D. 223–226, the first of a new line of monarchs, (called *Sassanides*, from Sassan, the father of Ardeshir,) who maintained the throne until A.D. 637, when Persia became a part of the empire of the Caliphs. The coins of this third division are in the ancient Persian or Pehlevi character and language, which, along with the worship of fire, were diligently restored by this native dynasty.

40. Silver daric. Obv. The figure of an archer. Rev. The marks of the stake on which the piece lay in coining. The weight is $83\frac{1}{2}$ grains; the fineness (by specific gravity of two specimens) varies from 60 to 80 per cent. There is no legend. The style of the coin indicates a high antiquity. (See *Division XV.*, "*Selections.*")

41, 42, 43. S. Drachms, of PHRAATES I. B.C. 180–170. Different types.

44 to 47. S. Drachms, of MITHRIDATES I., of the Arsacian line. B.C. 156–134. The reverses of the Greek series are very similar, and generally to this effect: "THE GREAT AND ILLUSTRIOUS ARSACES, KING OF KINGS, AND FRIEND OF THE GREEKS." (*Arsaces* was the official name of every monarch of that line.)

48 to 52. S. Drachms of PHRAATES II. B.C. 134–129. Different types.

53 to 55. S. Drachms, of PHRAATES III. B.C. 70–61.

56. S. Potin, of PHRAATES IV. B.C. 30–A.D. 13. (*Base.*)

57. S. Drachm, of GOTZARES. A.D. 45–48.

The foregoing are in a fair style of work, though inferior to the coins of the other Greek dynasties, especially of Syria and Egypt. The later specimens of the Arsacian line (of which we have a few, for temporary examination only,) are very barbarous, indicating more attention to arms than to arts. Such is a specimen of VOLOGESES III., *alias* ARSACES XXVIII., about A.D. 190.

58 to 67. Silver coins of the Sassanian kings. A.D. 223–637.

The legends, although they have engaged the attention of the best numismatists, and that for a long period, cannot be satisfactorily made out; only the name of *Shahpur* (Sapor) can sometimes be discerned. The reverse bears an altar, on which a fire is burning, attended by two magi or priests. The earliest specimens are of good workmanship, in a bold style; but the devices of later times present little else than a confused jumble of lines. The silver appears to be of good quality; the coins are remarkably *thin*, as compared with the Greek.

EGYPT.

This ancient realm had no coined money anterior to the Greek kings, a dynasty which resulted from the conquest by Alexander of Macedon, and began at his death. From the accession of Ptolemy I. to the death of the last Cleopatra (B.C. 323 to B.C. 30) is a period of two hundred and ninety-three years, interesting to the numismatist as well as to the historian.

72. G. Maneh, of Ptolemy II., Philadelphus, King of Egypt. B.C. 284–246. Obv. Head of Arsinoe, his wife and sister, niece of Alexander the Great. Found in Assyria in 1856. Weight nearly the same as our avoirdupois ounce, 950 fine. Value $17.70. (See *Division XV.*, "*Selections.*")

73. Silver tetradrachm of Ptolemy II., Philadelphus. B.C. 284–246.

74 to 78. Bronze coins of the Ptolemies, uncertain which. No. 74 is an enormous coin, weighing over three ounces.

79. Bronze, of Cleopatra, mother of Ptolemy VIII.

80. Bronze, of Ptolemy VIII. B.C. 116–106.

81. Bronze, of Cleopatra, wife of Mark Antony; killed herself B.C. 30. Egypt then became a province of the Roman empire. (See *Division XV.*, "*Selections.*")

SYRIA.

Seleucus, surnamed Nicator, (conqueror,) was the founder of the Grecian dynasty, called after his name the *Seleucidæ*, which ruled in Syria, B.C. 312–B.C. 65. (See under *Persia.*) The coins of this series are, for the most part, in the best style of Greek workmanship; the legends are simple and easily read.

81. S. Tetradrachm, of SELEUCUS I. B.C. 312–281. (See *Division XV.*, "*Selections.*")

82. S. Tetradrachm, of ANTIOCHUS I., SOTER, son of Seleucus. B.C. 280–261.

83. S. Tetradrachm, of ANTIOCHUS the Great. B.C. 223–187.

84. S. Tetradrachm, of SELEUCUS II., son of Antiochus the Great. B.C. 187–175.

85. S. Tetradrachm, of ANTIOCHUS IV., EPIPHANES, also a son of Antiochus the Great, and famous for his wars with the Jews. B.C. 175–164.

86. Bronze, of the same. The face bearded.

Bis. 86. S. Tetradrachm, of ALEXANDER BALAS. B.C. 150–146. (See *Division XV.*, "*Selections.*")

87. S. Drachm, of the same.

88. S. Tetradrachm, of DEMETRIUS I., SOTER. B.C. 162–150.

89. S. Tetradrachm, of DEMETRIUS II., NICATOR. B.C. 146–144.

90. S. Tetradrachm, of ANTIOCHUS EUPATOR.

Bis. 90. S. Tetradrachm, of ANTIOCHUS VI. B.C. 146–143. Contemporary with the Maccabees. (See *Division XV.*, "*Selections.*")

91. S. Tetradrachm, of DEMETRIUS II. or III.

92. S. Tetradrachm, of ANTIOCHUS EUERGETES.

93. Same; another type.

94. S. Tetradrachm, of ANTIOCHUS EPIPHANES, (GRYPUS). B.C. 124–97.

95. Same; another type.

96. S. Tetradrachm, of SELEUCUS VI., NICATOR.

97. S. Drachm, of ANTIOCHUS DIONYSIUS. B.C. 143.

98. S. Tetradrachm, of PHILIP. B.C. 93–86; twenty-first king of the dynasty, and the last but two. Syria was subdued by Pompey, and made a Roman province, B.C. 65.

101. Jewish shekel, of SIMON MACCABEUS, who flourished about 145 B.C. The legends are in the Samaritan character; on one side is the budding rod of Aaron, with "*Jerusalem the Holy;*" on the other, a cup of incense, or pot of manna, and the legend "*Shekel of Israel.*" The weight is 217 grains; the fineness (by sp. gr.)

about 95 per cent.; consequent value, $55\frac{1}{2}$ cents. This specimen is one of the rarest, and most remarkable, in the collection. It is in fine preservation. 102. A copy of the foregoing (made here) to show the reverse side. (See *Division XV.*, "*Selections.*")

103. A shekel with similar devices, the legends being in the Hebrew character. It is well-known to be an invention, and is but a few centuries old. It weighs 197 grains.

This specimen was presented to the collection by the Bank of Pennsylvania. It had lain in the Branch Bank at Lancaster, sewed up in a buckskin cover, for many years; but no one knew how long, nor by whom it was deposited there. It is curious, even as a fabrication. It is engraved in the old standard European books on ancient coins.

104. Copy of the preceding (made here) showing the reverse.

LESSER MONARCHIES OF GREECE, ASIA MINOR, ETC.

105. Gold stater, of LYSIMACHUS, King of Thrace. B.C. 320.

106. Silver tetradrachm, of the same.

107. S. Drachm, of the same.

108. Brass, of RHŒMETALCES, King of Thrace; Augustus Cæsar on the reverse.

109. Brass, of PATRÆUS, King of Pronia.

110, 111. Brass, of ALEXANDER II., of Epirus.

112. do. of ABGARUS, King of Edessa.

113. do. of AGATHOCLES, of Sicily.

114. Drachm, of PHILISTIS. *cb.*

115. Brass, of HIERO II.

116. do. of PHINTIAS.

117. Denarius of JUBA I., King of Numidia.

118. Brass, of COTYS II., Bosphorus.

119. do. of PRUSIAS I., King of Bithynia.

121, 122. Brass of PRUSIAS II.

124. Drachm of ARIARATHES VII., King of Cappadocia.

125. do. of ARIOBARZANES III.

126. Small brass, of AGRIPPA II., of Judea. A.D. 48.

BACTRIA.

(NOW BOKHARA AND CABUL.)

This remote Greek monarchy was founded about B.C. 250, by a secession from the great Syro-Persian empire.

A large number of the coins of Bactria and adjacent regions were lately discovered by British officers in the service of the East India Company. The details of the manner and the localities in which they were found may be seen in the recent work of Prof. Wilson, on the "Antiquities and Coins of Affghanistan," where they are also fully and admirably illustrated.

137,* 138. Large and small brass, (or copper,) of EUKRATIDES, about B.C. 180.

139. Silver, of ANTIMACHUS. B.C. 140.

140† to 143. Silver, of MENANDER. B.C. 126.

144. Brass, of the same.

145. Brass, of AGATHOCLES, who attempted to form a new monarchy. B.C. 135.

146. Silver, of APOLLODOTUS. B.C. 110.

147, 148. Brass, of the same.

149. Silver, of HERMÆUS. B.C. 98.

150, 151. Brass, of the same. After this dynasty came a succession of Barbarian and Indo-Scythian princes, whose history is still more scanty and obscure.

153. Brass, of AZES. B.C. 50.

154, 155, 156. Brass, of SOTER MEGAS, "the Great Deliverer,"—name unknown. B.C. ——.

157 to 160. Brass, of KADPHISES, supposed about A.D. 100.

161 to 165. Brass, of KANERKES, date unknown, but supposed not later than A.D. 300.

169, 170. Silver coins of Rajpoot princes, not later than A.D. 1200.

171 to 174. Silver Hindoo coins, of the middle ages.

---

* For No. 137, see Division XV., "Selections."

† For No. 140, see Division XV., "Selections."

ROMAN.

REMARKS ON THE COINS OF THE ROMAN EMPIRE.

The coins, of which these are specimens, were the current money of ancient Rome—an empire founded (by the usual reckoning) seven hundred and fifty-three years before Christ, and finally extinguished A.D. 1453. According to their respective places in this vast tract of time, they exemplify the rudeness and poverty of a petty colony, the grandeur of an immense dominion, and the decay and barbarism of its feeble remnants.

When we come to display these relics in their historical order, only one considerable difficulty is presented. We know indeed that the rough pieces of base metal were the earliest currency of Rome, sufficient for a poor and warlike horde. The pieces of silver, bearing only the insignia and name of growing Roma, must also be referred to an early period. But after that, and until the change from a republic to a despotism, the regulations of the coinage were such as to make it impossible now to arrange the coins in chronological order. The operations of the mint were under the control of the senate, and by that body intrusted to an official board, who seem to have had the power to enstamp such devices as they chose, but not to place the head or effigy of any individual on the coin, as was then the practice in neighboring monarchies. This distinction, it may be observed, has prevailed down to this day; and it is to the precedent set by the republics of Greece and Rome, as well as to an obvious propriety, that we owe the rule which excludes from our coins the heads of the Presidents. But while this honor was denied, even to a consul or a conqueror, the senate permitted or overlooked the insertion in the legend of the *name* of an officer of the mint, or of a consul, prætor, or provincial governor, for whose disbursements any specific grant of bullion was wrought into coin; or if not an individual name, a general family surname; to which was frequently added some device to illustrate a famous action of the man, or of his ancestor. This evasion of the strict republican rule does not, however, give much aid to the numismatist, especially where the name and exploit were those of an ancestor, or where the same name belongs to persons of different eras. The whole difficulty in the case has, by common consent, long since been resolved into a classification of such pieces as FAMILY COINS, in opposition to Imperial; and they are anomalously arranged in the *alphabetical order* of family names. The limit of this arrangement is not exactly defined, but it may be said to extend from almost the commencement of the use of silver, down to the days of Augustus, although the rule in regard to portraits was broken through by his predecessors. The *family coins* may therefore represent a period of two hundred and fifty years, terminating about the birth of Christ.

Augustus took charge of the gold and silver coinage as an imperial prerogative, leaving the brass still under the care of the senate; a most striking exemplification of the change of affairs, and of the relative power of prince and people. This accounts for the S. C. (Senatus Consulto) on the inferior moneys. After the time of Gallienus, about the middle of the third Christian century, even this remnant of senatorial authority disappears.

In respect to the date of Roman coins, it is to be noticed, generally, that although the art of coining probably originated in Greece, or Asia Minor, (as some contend,) about the time of the foundation of the Roman colony, it appears not to have reached that obscure and rude people until the reign of Servius Tullius, near the close of the second century of Rome. Reckoning from that term as far downward as we can verify the coinage of the Lower Empire, which is not nearer to its overthrow than a century and a half, the range of date is more than eighteen hundred years. It may be added, that there is no single series to be compared with it in extent, variety, and completeness. There was scarcely an emperor or usurper, though hurled from his seat in a fortnight or a month, who did not leave a diversity of monetary monuments for coming ages.

But more particularly, as to the date of any individual piece; it is ascertained, in many cases, by the year of the "tribunitian power" of the emperor; thus, TR. P. VI. of Claudius, is equivalent to A.D. 46.

It is solved also by the year of his consulship; thus, Vespasian Cos. III. answers to A.D. 71: but as that title was not annually resumed like the preceding, this is a less direct means of information. The renewal of the inaugural vow every five or ten years, (VOT. V., VOT. X.) likewise determines the date; and when a victory or other great event is symbolized on the coin, its age is determined by the aid of history. But often we can only approach the date within a few years, that is, within the limits of a reign; and the brevity of many of them gives even more precision than an annual mark.

Notwithstanding the large use made of emblems in allusion to Christianity, from and after the time of Constantine there is no instance of a Christian date on a Roman coin; nor, indeed, is it to be found on the coinage of any country, until a period subsequent to the fall of the Lower Empire.

For about three centuries Roman money consisted solely of bronze, a mixture of copper and tin; at first cast in moulds, but afterward stamped, when other metals came into use. In the year of Rome 487, (B.C. 286,) silver was introduced into the coinage, and gold, sixty years later; though it is believed that this last was of trifling amount prior to the conquests of Julius Cæsar. In his time, bronze coins began to be displaced by copper and brass; the latter, a composition of copper and calamine, (ore of zinc,) being wrought with some trouble, and much admired, is said to have been accounted worth twice as much as copper. This mixture disappeared about the close of the third Christian century, and thereafter copper alone was used for the inferior coinage.

The gold coin was maintained at almost absolute purity (990 to 995 thousandths) from first to last. The exceptions in our collection are in the instance of Michael I. Rhangabe, (A.D. 811–813,) who, besides a bezant of good weight and fineness, issued one very inferior in both respects, the fineness being not above 600; and again, in the reigns of Michael VII., Ducas, Romanus IV., and Nicephorus III., extending from 1067 to 1081, we have gold coins of the same inferior quality. They were restored by the next prince, Alexius I.

The silver coin, down to the reign of Augustus inclusive, was also intended and considered as pure, and is found to be 950 to 985 thousandths fine. But in the ensuing reigns, there was a constant downward tendency, ending in an absurd and extravagant debasement. In the coinage of Nero, we find the quality of 82 per cent.; from Vespasian to Hadrian, it ranges from 78 to 85. The *very* base silver begins with Septimius Severus, about A.D. 200; and in the times of Elagabalus and Philip, (say half a century further on,) the coins contained not more than 40 to 45 per cent. of silver, the alloy being copper, with a portion of tin to preserve the color. In some cases it would seem as if the emperors of those troubled times resorted to the expedient of issuing copper with a mere plating of silver. But a salutary and permanent reform is to be dated from the reign of Diocletian, in the early part of the fourth century. Silver of a good quality, say 91 to 96 per cent. fine, was used from that time, down through all the decline of the empire.* The silver coin appears, however, not to have been abundant in the later times, the currency chiefly consisting of gold for large payments, and copper for petty dealings. This is fairly inferred from the proportions in which the three kinds are now extant, or are from time to time recovered.

As it regards the denominations of Roman coins, the modifications and changes, in a range of eighteen centuries, have occasioned so much perplexity, that the professed collectors pay but little attention to the subject, finding it more convenient to use their own technical terms; such as, *gold* (or *silver*) *of the usual size;* gold or silver *quinarius,* half size; *large medallions, small medallions; first, second,* and *third brass;* or *large, middle,* and *small brass.* The

---

* The degrees of fineness above stated are from our own trials; by assay, in the case of silver coins not valuable; by specific gravity, where the pieces were too scarce to be cut—a very good approximation for gold coins, and sufficient for rare silver. Whatever difference there is between our rates and those to be found in the Preface of Akerman on Roman Coins, (and it is not important,) is chargeable to the very unsteady character of the coins, even of the same reign—possibly of the same year. The weights (hereafter given) are also our own, and show about the same correspondence with those given by Akerman.

We have found also, in the silver coins, a larger quantity of gold than would be suffered to remain in the present state of the *parting* art. It is small enough, however, to show that the ancients took some pains in that business.

expressions are not very definite, but sufficiently so for their purposes. So as to intrinsic value; whether a gold piece is 12 or 24 carats, whether a silver one is pure or base, is a circumstance which they hardly deign to inquire into; the degree of rarity is everything.

But every intelligent reader of Roman history desires some idea of the meaning of the money-terms which he meets on every page; the coins to which they apply, together with the intrinsic values. We have space for a few details only.

As, sestertius, denarius, aureus, were the principal money-terms of the Romans.

The *as*, or *æs libralis*, "pound of brass," and its divisions, were the earliest Roman coins. Originally the *as* weighed a Roman pound of 12 ozs., (equal to 12 oz. avoird.,) but by successive reductions in a long course of years it was brought down to half an ounce before the Christian era. In this form it was often called by the diminutive term *assarium*. In the time of Constantine it had declined to 20 grains.

The *sestertius*, called also *nummus*, "the coin," by eminence, was a brass coin, of about one ounce in the time of Augustus, and so continued for two centuries, when it began to lose weight, and is not easily to be traced. The Romans were used to reckon by the sestertius for small sums, and by the *sestertium* or great sesterce, (equal to 1000 sestertii,) for large amounts. This last was only a money of account.

The *denarius* was the principal silver coin, weighing at first about 60 grains, and though somewhat lighter than the Greek drachm, passed as its equivalent. In the second Christian century it weighed 50 to 55 grains; in the third, 48 to 50. The fineness being also in a course of depreciation, the value of the piece, at first near 16 cents, fell, under the first emperors, to 14 or 15 cents; 11 or 12 in the times of Vespasian, Trajan, and the Antonines; and about 6 cents under Elagabalus. Its character was somewhat restored by Diocletian; but it seems impossible, from the great fluctuation in weight, to put a value upon the denarius of the empire after its partition.*

---

* It seems to be taken for granted, while it is by no means certain, that the English penny was based upon the later Roman denarius. The early pennies

From this coin we ascertain the value of inferior ones already named. It was at first worth ten times the *as;* but afterwards, and before the Christian era, was equal to 16 *ases.* It was also equal to four *sestertii,* or two *quinarii.* The quinarius was a silver coin, not very common.

The *aureus,* or gold coin, was double the weight of the denarius, under the first emperors, and intrinsically worth about five dollars; sometimes a quarter dollar more, but oftener less by that much. So it continued down to Pertinax, A.D. 192, as we find from our own specimens, and, as we learn from other sources, until Severus Alexander, thirty years later. During that century the gold coinage partook somewhat of the confusion, and especially the depreciation, of the other moneys. The aurei in our cabinet, from Decius to Numerian, vary 20 grains (85 cents) one from another, and on the average are worth about $3.25. From Diocletian to Constantine the Great, the aureus, now assuming the name of *solidus,* is about $3.50. But it was again reduced, by the sons of Constantine, to 70 grains, or three dollars value; and, singularly enough, maintained that weight, within a grain or two, during eight or nine centuries thereafter. The gold solidus, or *bezant* of the Byzantine empire, was the currency of all Europe in the middle ages, and is often met with in the histories of those eventful times; and (except in one or two cases of gross deterioration of fineness) may be understood as a piece of nearly fine gold, about three dollars in value, or, more exactly, $2.90.

The encomiums of amateurs prepare us for a severe disappointment, when we come for the first time to inspect the coins of Rome. Their appearance is much below what would be expected, from the reputation of Roman arts and civilization. There is, it is true, a wide diversity of skill exhibited in the die-sinking branch. Many of

---

weigh nearly a pennyweight, and are worth six cents. The coin has since passed from silver to copper, and is worth only two cents. And (to trace the lineage down to our own day and country) by the debasement of moneys of account, the *penny* in the United States, though differing in different States, is so little above a cent, that it is common to use the two terms interchangeably. We may remark here, that the translation of the word *denarion* (denarius) into *penny,* in the New Testament, although in one sense legitimate, gives a very incorrect idea.

the heads are admirable, to a cultivated taste and eye of modern times; and, in general, as far down as to Constantine, there is a good deal of character, and evident approach to a real portrait, even where the finish is rather barbarous. But the reverse side of the coin was evidently handed over to the apprentices, and, with occasional exceptions, is beneath criticism.

That Rome certainly had artists capable of exquisite engraving, we know from the long and large series of gems still extant. The inquiry, why there should be such a difference between the gems and the coins, is most probably to be solved by such an answer as this, that the *masters* of the art, imported from Greece, were but few in number, and the public taste did not exact much skill for the coinage, the principal office of which was to pass from hand to hand in barter, and not to be kept for show. It has been so, almost down to our own day. The English guineas and shillings of the last, and the Spanish dollars and fractions of this century, are not worthy to stand as specimens of the general state of arts.

From and after the sons of Constantine, the style of execution continually deteriorates; and we are left to wonder that a people not destitute of letters could tolerate such a burlesque of coinage. Though there were but few of the emperors who were so fortunate as to transmit their throne, with their face, to a son or near relation, the portraits present a long gallery of striking similitudes. On taking up a large brass coin of the great Justinian, the oracle of lawyers, we seem to behold the visage and the workmanship of an untutored Indian.

The other, and more mechanical parts of the mintage, (and this will apply to Grecian as well as Roman,) allow of no higher praise. Unless coins are so shaped as to lie flat, and admit of being piled one upon another, and render apparent any diminution by filing or clipping, they are not well fitted for their proper uses. These objections apply very generally to ancient coins. Other faults, chargeable to the want of machinery and metallurgic skill, need not be dwelt upon.*

---

* Manual of Coins, page 12.

DIVISION I.

ERA OF THE REPUBLIC.*

All the coins of this era, except the earliest bronze and the earliest silver, (which last are known by the simple inscription ROMA,) are arranged under family names. As far as known, there are about one hundred and seventy-five families represented in coins still extant, of which one hundred and twenty-six are in this collection. As an example of the mode of arrangement, the pieces which bear the names A. POST. (Aulus Postumius) and C. POST. (Caius Postumius) are placed together, under the title POSTUMIA. If the cognomen only is given, as in the case of BRVTVS, on various types of Marcus Junius Brutus, it is nevertheless referred to the well-known family name, JUNIA; and, by the same rule, certain coins of Julius Cæsar are retained in the family JULIA.

The types in this series are not generally of the most common kind, and would repay the inspection of a practiced numismatist. For the more general reader, we have occasionally interrupted the roll, to call attention to a specimen of historical interest.

3. TRIENS, or piece of four ounces, indicated by the four dots, under the rude figure of a ship. Very early coinage.

4, 5. B. SEXTANS, of two ounces.

6. B. UNCIA, ounce. Small size.

7, 8. B. TRIENS. Small.

9. B. SEXTANS, of Campania.

10, 11. ROMA, silver denarii.

12. ROMA, silver quinarius.

13. ABURIA. This, and the following specimens in this division, are all silver denarii, except where otherwise mentioned.

---

* This word is used in opposition to the *imperial* era, and in the modern sense. Even under the most grinding despotism, Rome always flattered herself with the title of "Republic." The coins of Julian celebrate the *Securitas Reipublicæ*.

14. ACCOLEIA......15, 16. ACILIA......17. ÆLIA......18, 19, 20. ÆMILIA......21. AFRANIA......22. ALLIA......23, 24. ANNIA. (The latter is brass.)......25. ANTESTIA......26. ANTIA. ......27. ANTONIA.

(The legionary coins of Mark Antony, usually placed here, have been transferred to the next division.)

28. B. APRONIA......29, 30. AQUILLIA. The reverse of No. 30 shows a woman kneeling before a soldier; underneath, SICIL. This commemorates the suppression of a noted revolt of the slaves in Sicily, by Manlius Aquillus.

31. B. ASINIA......32. ATTILIA......33. AURELIA......34. BŒBIA...... 35, 36, 37. CÆCILIA...... 38. B. CÆCINIA...... 39. CÆSIA......40. CALIDIA.

41. CALPURNIA. Rev. A horseman riding at full speed; an ear of wheat above; legend L. PISO FRUGI. In the year of Rome 507 there was a great scarcity of food in the city, and Calpurnius Piso was dispatched to Africa to purchase corn. This trivial honor is magnified by no less than one hundred and thirty varieties of denarii.

42, 43. CARISIA...... 44, 45, 46. CASSIA...... 47. CESTIA. *cb*......48. CIPIA......49, 50, 51. CLAUDIA......52. CLAUDIA. *cb*......53. B. CLOVIA......54, 55. CLOULIA. The latter a quinarius...... 56. CŒLIA...... 57. CONSIDIA...... 58. COPONIA. ......59, 60, 61. CORDIA......62 to 65. CORNELIA......66. CREPERIA......67, 68. CREPUSIA......69. CUPIENA......70. CURIATIA...... 71. CURTIA...... 72. DIDIA...... 73. DOMITIA. ......74, 75. EGNATIA......76. EGNATULEIA......77. EPPIA. ......78. FABIA......79. FANNIA......80. FARSOLEIA......81. FLAMINIA......82. FLAVIA......83, 84. FONTEIA......85. FUFIA......86. FULVIA......87. FUNDANIA......88, 89, 90. FURIA......91. GELLIA......92. HERENNIA......93. HORATIA. *cb*......94. HOSIDIA.

95, 96. HOSTILLIA. In a battle with the Vientes, (in the early days of the republic,) the Roman troops were seized with a panic, and, in his extremity, Tullus Hostilius, their leader, offered his vows to Pallor and Pavor, the gods of *fear* and *trembling*. Two terrified heads display these attributes. On the reverse is the name of L. Hostilius Saserna, a descendant of Tullus, and an officer of Julius Cæsar; for this person they were evidently coined.

97. JULIA......98 to 101. JUNIA. No. 98, a remarkable type, is a coin of Marcus Brutus, and commemorates the fact that his ancestor, L. Junius Brutus, was the first consul of Rome. He is seen guarded by lictors, and preceded by a herald.

102 to 105. LICINIA......106. LIVINEIA......107. LUCILIA. ......108, 109. LUCRETIA......110. B. LURIA......111. LUTATIA...... 112. B. MÆCILIA...... 113. MÆNIA......114. MAIANIA...... 115. MAMILIA......116. MANLIA......117 to 119. MARCIA......120. MARIA......121, 122. MEMMIA......123, 124. MINUTIA......125. MUSSIDIA......126. NÆVIA......127. NONIA......128. NORBANUS......129. NORBANUS. *cb*......130. NUMONIA. *cb*...... 131. OPEIMIA...... 132–134. PAPIA...... 135. PAPIRIA......136. PEDANIA......137, 138. PETILLIA. 139. PETRONIA......140. PINARIA......141. PLÆTORIA...... 142. PLANCIA......143–145. PLAUTIA......146. POBLICIA. 147, 148. POMPEIA......149, 150. POMPONIA.

151, 152. PORCIA. The Porcian law, declared in the year of Rome 453, exempted Roman citizens from the indignity of scourging. Rev. of No. 152 represents a citizen protected by a magistrate from the lictor, and underneath, the word PROVOCO, "I appeal." (See in the New Testament, Acts, xxii. 24–27, where the Apostle Paul availed himself of this immunity.)

153–155. POSTUMIA......156, 157. PROCILIA......158, 159. QUINCTIA......160. RENIA......161. ROSCIA......162. RUBRIA......163, 164. RUSTIA......165. RUTILIA......166. SATRIENUS......167. SCRIBONIA......168. SEMPRONIA...... 169. SENTIA......170. SERGIA......171–173. SERVILIA...... 174. SICINIA......175. SILIA......176. SPURILIA......177. SULPICIA......178. TERENTIA......179. THORIA......180. TITIA.

181, 182. TITURIA. Reverse of the first represents two soldiers throwing their shields upon a prostrate female. The city of Rome was betrayed to the Sabines by Tarpeia, on condition of receiving "what they wore on their left arms," intending their gold bracelets. As soon as the city was taken, the solders, to fulfill their vow, and punish her perfidy, threw upon her their bracelets *and shields*, and she was crushed to death. The place was afterward famous as the "Tarpeian Rock." Reverse of the second represents the Romans carrying off the Sabine women. The family Titurla traced their descent from the Sabines.

183. TREBANIA......184. TALLIA......185–188. VALERIA. (The last is brass.)......189. VARGUNTEIA.......190. VETTIA. ......191. VETTURIA......192–194. VIBIA......195. VIBIA. *cb.* ...... 196–198. VOLTEIA ...... 199–202. Uncertain. Two are of base metal.

DIVISION II.

JULIUS CÆSAR TO TRAJAN (INCLUSIVE,)

B.C. 49 TO A.D. 117.

I. CAIUS JULIUS CÆSAR was born in the year of Rome 654 (B.C. 100.) Created Triumvir, with Pompey and Crassus, at the age of forty, and Dictator at fifty-two. He was made Perpetual Dictator B.C. 44, and assassinated in the same year, aged fifty-six.

1. G. Head of Julius. DICT(ator) PERP(etuo). PON(tifex) MAX (imus). Rev. Head of Caius (Octavius).
2. S. Æneas carrying Anchises.
3. Dictator the second time.
4. Head of Julius vailed. Perp. Dictator.
5. Julius crowned. Perp Dictator.
6. Pontifical instruments. Rev. Elephant.
7. B. JULIUS DIVOS.
8. Silver, of Marcus Brutus the conspirator. Head of the elder Brutus.
9. Brass, of Pompey the Great. Rev. PIUS. IMP(erator). Prow of a vessel.

II. CAIUS OCTAVIUS, afterward AUGUSTUS, grand-nephew of Julius Cæsar, was born B.C. 63. He was joined with Mark Antony and Lepidus in the government, at the death of Julius; became sole master of the empire, B.C. 31; received the title of Emperor two years after; and died A.D. 14, aged seventy-six.

11. G. AUGUSTUS DIVI F. IMP. X. Rev. ACT(ium). Commemorates that decisive battle.

12. Gold, of Sextus Pompey, naval commander, reduced by Augustus B.C. 36. MAG(nus) PIUS IMP(erator) ITER(um). Rev. Heads of Pompey the Great and Cneius. PRÆF(ectus) CLASS(is) ET ORÆ MARIT (imæ), "Commander of the fleet and sea-coast." Ex. S.C. *cb.*

13. Silver, same as the preceding. *cb.*

14. Silver of the same, different type. *cb.*

15. Mark Antony; Cæsar on the reverse.

16. Antony; legends on both sides made up of his titles.

17. Lepidus; Cæsar on the reverse.

18. Augustus. DIVUS JULIUS.

19. The same. Rev. SIGNIS RECEPTIS.

20. Aqueduct on the reverse.

21. Rev. Horses on a triumphal arch. IMP. CÆSAR.

22. Rev. Pontifical instruments. COS. ITER. "Consul a second time."

23. S. P. Q. R. OB CIVES SERVATOS.

24. Fine head of Augustus, without legend. Rev. DIVI F(ilius), "the son of God," probably in reference to the deified Julius. (See *Division XV.*, "*Selections.*")

Bis. 24. A counterfeit. Copper plated, with silver. Obv. Head of Augustus.

25. Rev. Horseman at full speed. AUGUST.

26. A Bull. IMP. X., *i.e.* the title of Imperator, Emperor, conferred the tenth time. It was then merely a military distinction.

27. A quinarius. Rev. ASIA RECEPTA.

28. B. Rev. Within a wreath, AUGUSTUS TRIBUNIC(ia) POTEST (ate).

29. DIVUS AUGUSTUS PATER. The deceased Augustus sainted, or deified. Rev. S. C. (Senatus Consulto).

30. Silver, of Agrippa, son-in-law of Augustus. *cb.*

31. Brass, of Agrippa. Consul third time. Struck on the occa-

sion of his marriage with Marcella, the emperor's niece. He was born B.C. 69; died A.D. 12. A great general, and an upright man.

32. S. Caius and Lucius, grandsons of Augustus.

35 to 54. Twenty silver coins of Mark Antony, the series struck for the respective legions under his command. The reverse shows a ship or military ensigns, with the number of the legion, as LEG. VI., etc. They were probably used in payment of the troops, and otherwise served to display the power of the general. Four of the series are wanting.

III. TIBERIUS CÆSAR, son of the Empress Livia, was adopted by Augustus, A.D. 4, and succeeded to the empire A.D. 14, at the age of fifty-six. While on a sick bed, he was smothered at the instigation of Caligula, which finished a cruel reign of nearly twenty-three years. (A.D. 37.)

55. G. TI. CÆSAR DIVI. AUG. F(ilius) AUGUSTUS. Rev. PONTIFEX MAXIMUS. 56. The same type in silver.

57. Base silver or *potin* struck at Alexandria in Egypt; legends in Greek.

58. Large brass. An altar, with figures of Victory.

59, 60. Brass, with the usual legends, and Rev. S. C.

61. Silver, of Drusus, son of the emperor. (Poisoned by his wife A.D. 23.) Rev. Head of Tiberius. *cb.*

62. Brass, of Drusus. Rev. S. C.

63. Livia, mother of Tiberius. SALUS AUGUSTA. (Died A.D. 29, aged eighty-six.)

64. S. Antonia, daughter of Mark Antony, and mother of the Emperor Claudius. ANTONIA AUGUSTA. (Poisoned A.D. 38, aged seventy-six.) *cb.* 65. Brass, of the same.

66. S. Germanicus, son of Antonia, and nephew of Tiberius, who adopted him. (Poisoned A.D. 19, by the Gov. of Syria.) *cb.* 67, 68. Brass, of the same.

69. Large brass. Agrippa, Sen., wife of Germanicus, and grand-daughter of Augustus. (Exiled and starved to death by Tiberius, A.D. 33, aged forty-eight.)

70. B. NERO ET DRUSUS, CÆSARES. Sons of Germanicus, and

brothers of Caligula. (Nero died in exile, A.D. 30; Drusus was starved by order of Tiberius, A.D. 33.)

IV. Caius Cæsar, called CALIGULA, (from his military dress,) was adopted by his grand-uncle Tiberius, whom he succeeded, A.D. 37, at the age of twenty-five. His oppressive reign was cut short by an assassin, A.D. 41.

72. S. C. CÆSAR AUG. Rev. S. P. Q. R. P. P. OB C. S., *i.e.* "the Senate and People of Rome, to the Father of his Country, for preserving the citizens."

73. B. Usual legend. Rev. Vesta seated.

V. Tiberius CLAUDIUS, nephew of Tiberius, was born at Lyons, B.C. 10, and succeeded to the empire A.D. 41. He married his niece, Agrippina the younger, A.D. 49, by whom he was poisoned, A.D. 54.

79. G. TI. CLAUD. CÆSAR. AUG. P. M. TR. P. VIIII. IMP. VI. Rev. S. P. Q., etc.

80. S. Same legend; with GERM(anicus.) *cb.*

81. B. Rev. LIBERTAS AUGUSTA.

82. S. Agrippina, wife of the emperor, and mother of Nero. AGRIPPINÆ AUGUSTÆ. Head of Claudius on the reverse. (She was killed by order of Nero, A.D. 59, aged forty-three.)

83. Agrippina and Nero, face to face. *cb.*

VI. NERO, stepson of Claudius, was declared *Cæsar*, A.D. 50, at the age of thirteen years, and succeeded to the empire at seventeen. Having become odious through his excesses, and hearing that a successor was elected, he slew himself, A.D. 68.

87. G. NERO CÆSAR AUGUSTUS. Rev. JUPPITER (so spelt) CUSTOS —"Jupiter the Keeper."

88. S. NERO CÆSAR. Youthful profile.

90. Large brass. NERO CLAUD. CÆSAR, etc. ROMA on the reverse. Supposed to have been struck on the rebuilding of Rome after the fire.

91. The temple of Janus closed. PACE P(opulo) R(omano) TERRA MARI(que) PARTA JANUM CLUSIT.

92. Coined at Alexandria, in Egypt. Greek.

93. Coined at Alexandria, in Cilicia. Greek.

VII. GALBA, born B.C. 3, was governor of Spain under Nero; created emperor by the army and senate, A.D. 68; murdered by the guards, after a reign of seven months, A.D. 69.

95. G. IMP. SERV(ius) GALBA AUG. Rev. S. P. Q R., etc.

96. S. Rev. LIBERTAS PUBLICA.

97. B. Same reverse.

98. S. CLODIUS MACER. PROPRAE(tor) AFRICÆ. This provincial governor declared independence upon the death of Nero, but was reduced, and put to death by order of Galba. *cb.*

VIII. OTHO, governor of Lusitania, (now Portugal,) took part in the revolt against Nero. After following in the train of Galba for a short time, he procured his death, and was proclaimed as his successor. But the empire had to be disputed with Vitellius; and having suffered a defeat, Otho killed himself, A.D. 69, after a reign of only three months, and in his thirty-seventh year.

103. S. IMP(erator) OTHO CÆSAR AUG(ustus) TR(ibun.) P(otestate). Rev. SECURITAS P(opuli) R(omani). By the looks of the head, the artist seems to have aimed to confirm the historical fact that the emperor wore a wig.

104. Rev. PONT(ifex) MAX(imus). "Sovereign pontiff."

105. Rev. VICTORIA OTHONIS. Otho was thrice victorious before his overthrow at Brixellum.

No brass coins of this emperor have come to light.

IX. VITELLIUS proclaimed emperor by the legions in Germany, was successful against Otho, and acknowledged by the senate, A.D. 69. After eight months of gluttony, he fell by the hands of the soldiers, aged fifty-six.

111. G. A(ulus) VITELLIUS GERM(anicus), IMP(erator), AUG(ustus), TR(ib.) P(ot.) Rev. A tripod, with a globe and dolphin on the top, and an eagle beneath; XV VIR SACR(is) FAC(iendis.) Commemorates his offering sacrifice to the shade of Nero, his patron.

112. S. Same as the preceding.

113. Rev. FIDES EXERCITUM. Two hands joined, in token of the *faith of the army.*

114. Heads of the two children of Vitellius. LIBERI IMP., etc. *cb.*

X. VESPASIAN was created governor of Judea by Nero, A.D.

66, and became emperor on the death of Vitellius; died A.D. 79, in his seventieth year, having reigned ten years.

119. G. IMP. CÆSAR VESPASIANUS AUG. Rev. CONS(ul) ITER(um) TR(ib.) POT(estate).

120. S. Rev. Pontifical instruments. AUGUR. PONT. MAX.

121. JOVIS CUSTOS.

122. VICTORIA AUGUSTI.

123. A *congius* (a dry measure of about a half peck) with ears of wheat standing out of it. Expresses his distribution of congiaries, or gifts of corn, to the Roman populace.

124. A vailed female beside a palm-tree. JUDÆA DEVICTA. Commemorates the destruction of Jerusalem, A.D. 70, by Titus.

125. Consul the seventh time.

126. Figure of Capricorn, under which sign Vespasian was born. DIVUS AUGUSTUS VESPASIANUS. Apotheosis of the deceased emperor.

127. DIVA DOMITILLA AUGUSTA. Domitilla was married to Vespasian, A.D. 40, and died before his accession. She was afterward deified. *cb.*

XI. TITUS succeeded his father, A.D. 79, at twenty-eight years. A change of character made him a good prince; but the Romans enjoyed the benefit of it only two years. His death was not without suspicion of poisoning, by Domitian.

135. G. T. CÆSAR IMP. VESPASIAN. Rev. COS. IIII. (Fourth year of his consulate.)

136. S. CERES AUGUST.

137. A soldier standing on the head of a captive.

138. A statue on a pillar; usual legends.

139. Capricorn.

140. Curule chair.

141. B. ÆQUITAS AUGUSTI.

142. B. CERES AUGUST.

143. S. Julia, daughter of Titus, and after his death a concubine of her uncle Domitian. On the reverse is a peacock, the emblem of female deification, which honor was conferred on her by Domitian. *cb.* 144. Brass, of Julia.

XII. DOMITIAN, brother of Titus, succeeded to the empire at the age of thirty, A.D. 81, and reigned fifteen years. He fell by a conspiracy of his household; and though universally detested, received the usual honor of deification. He was the last of "the twelve Cæsars," a classification more popular than proper.

151. G. CÆS. AUG. DOMIT. COS. III. Rev. PRINCEPS JUVENTUTIS. The title "Prince of Youth" was given by his father, A.D. 69.

152. S. Rev. A dolphin and anchor; usual titles.

153. Copy of an equestrian statue.

154. Victory holding a buckler.

155. COS. XIIII. LUD(os) SÆC(ulares) FEC(it). Alludes to his celebration of the secular games.

156. B. The same subject. Priest and musicians.

157. S. Domitia, wife of the emperor.

XIII. NERVA was called to the empire by the senate, in his sixty-fourth-year, A.D. 96. His virtuous but feeble administration was strengthened by the association of Trajan. After a reign of two years only, he was allowed the distinction of dying a natural death, and was voted a deity. A.D. 98.

159. G. IMP. NERVA CÆS. AUG. P(ontifex) M(ax.) TR(ib.) POT(estate). Rev. Pontifical instruments. COS. III. PATER PATRIÆ.

160. S. The same type.

161. AEQUITAS AUGUST(i).

162. FORTUNA AUGUST(i).

163. Two hands joined. CONCORDIA EXERCITUUM. Expresses the ratification by the army of his election; now more important than the voice of the senate. 164. B. The same type.

XIV. TRAJAN, born in Spain, A.D. 53, succeeded Nerva, A.D. 98, and reigned nineteen and a half years. His military exploits, his energy and leniency, (except toward the Christians,) endeared him to the Romans as the best of all their emperors, and they early conferred on him the title of OPTIMUS PRINCEPS, which appears on most of his coins. Died in Cilicia, A.D. 117.

167. G. IMP. TRAIANO OPTIMO AUG. GER(manicus), DAC(icus), P(ont.) M(ax.) TR. P(otest.) Rev. COS. VI. P(ater) P(atriæ) S. P. Q. R. Germany and Dacia were among his conquests.

168. S. Three military ensigns. "The senate and people of Rome, to the best prince."

169. Rev. Ceres, with legend as above.

170. Equestrian statue.

171. Victory, writing on a shield.

172. PARTHICO, P. M., etc. Expresses his victories in Persia.

173. Front of the Forum, a superb building erected by Trajan. *cb.*

174. The emperor on a throne, with attendants, assigning kingdoms to three persons below and before him. REGNA ADSIGNATA. *cb.*

175. PARTHICO DIVI TRAIAN, etc.

176. Victory. (A quinarius.)

177. Large brass. A crowd of titles in the legends.

178. G. Plotina, wife of Trajan. (Died A.D. 129, and was one of the few empresses sans reproche.) Rev. Vesta seated. *cb.*

179. S. Marciana, sister of Trajan. Rev. CONSECRATIO. *cb.*

180. G. Matidia, daughter of Marciana, and mother-in-law of the Emperor Hadrian. Plotina on the reverse. *cb.*

181. B. Greek coin of Trajan and Plotina (Perinthus in Thrace.)

DIVISION III.

HADRIAN TO ELAGABALUS*—A.D. 117–222.

XV. HADRIAN, through the management of the Empress Plotain, succeeded upon the death of Trajan, A.D. 117. He is noted as the traveling emperor; his long and prosperous reign being spent in marches and journeys to all parts of the empire. His coins, which are numerous, afford a medallic history of his life. Died in his seventy-second year, and twenty-second of his reign, A.D. 138.

1. G. HADRIANUS AUG. COS. III. Pater Patriæ. Rev. LIBERALITAS AUG(usti). The emperor was liberal in largesses to the people.

2. S. Rev. AFRICA. A female figure, representing Africa, recumbent. Commemorates his visit there.

3. HISPANIA. Figure of Spain, recumbent.

---

* Spelt thus upon the coins.

4. Restitutori Hispaniæ. The emperor raising a female (Spain) from the ground.

5. Aegyptos. Emblems of Egypt.

6. Nilus. The god of the Nile, recumbent.

7. Restitutori Galliæ. The emperor raising prostrate Gaul.

8. Ceres.

9. Cos. III. Moon and star.

10. The emperor marching before three soldiers. Disciplina Aug(usti). The army in Germany becoming relaxed in discipline, the emperor visited them, and inured them to hardships by his own example. *cb.*

11. B. Rev. Hilaritas P(opuli) R(omani). A female, holding a stalk of wheat; citizens at her feet. The "hilarity" of the ancient lazzaroni depended very much on the supplies of corn drawn from the industrious provinces.

12. Salus Augusta. A female making offerings to a serpent, in behalf of the emperor's health.

13. Silver, of Sabina, wife of Hadrian. Rev. Veneri Genetrici.

14. Sabina Augusta, Hadriani Aug. Rev. Concordia Aug. Commemorates the making up of a quarrel between the emperor and his wife. They lived so unhappily, that she destroyed herself, after a union of thirty-seven years, A.D. 137.

15. Silver, of Aelius Cæsar. He was adopted as Hadrian's successor, but died before him, A.D. 138.

16. B. S. HAΔPIANOC CEB. Hadrianus Augustus. Coined at Cesarea in Cappadocia.

XVI. ANTONINUS PIUS succeeded Hadrian, by whom he had been adopted, A D. 138; and reigned twenty-three years. In contrast to the policy of his predecessor, he never traveled farther from Rome than to his villa; but the vast empire was governed with unexampled wisdom and mildness, and it was an age of peace and plenty. His devotion to the gods, and to the memory of his patron, early procured him the surname of Pius; which became a standing title to all succeeding emperors. The *Christian* religion was openly tolerated. He died A.D. 161, in his seventy-fifth year, universally lamented.

22. G. ANTONINUS AUG. PIUS. P. P. Rev. TR. POT. COS. II.

23. S. Rev. ITALIA. A woman sitting on a globe.

24. Rev. The youthful head of Aurelius, who was adopted at the age of seventeen, A.D. 138.

25. Rev. Aurelius more advanced.

26. Rev. A Female at an altar. PIETAS.

27. DIVUS ANTONINUS. Rev. CONSECRATIO.

28. Rev. A funeral pile. CONSECRATIO.

29. Rev. An altar. DIVO PIO. The honor of deification was eagerly conferred by the senate.

30. Large brass. Reverse same as No. 12.

31. B. Rev. Romulus and Remus sucking the wolf.

32. G. DIVA FAUSTINA. Deification of the elder Faustina, wife of Antoninus; born A.D. 105, died 141.

33. S. Faustina vailed; DIVA FAUSTINA. Rev. AETERNITAS.

34. Rev. JUNONI REGINÆ.

35. Rev. AUGUSTA.

36. DIVA FAUSTINA PIA. Rev. A peacock; CONSECRATIO.

37. B. Rev. CONSECRATIO. These and other types show the honors paid by the good emperor to her memory, though while living she occasioned him no little grief and scandal.

38. B. Greek coin of Antoninus; Laodicea.

XVII. MARCUS AURELIUS Antoninus, and LUCIUS VERUS, brothers-in-law, who had been of the rank of *Cæsars* for twenty-three years, succeeded A.D. 161, as *Augusti*, colleague emperors. Though the former was a Stoic philosopher, and the latter a debauchee, they lived without discord, and (as their coins show) were much engaged with the barbarians. The immense empire was now beginning to tremble with its own weight. Verus died 169, in his fortieth year. Marcus ruled alone for eleven years more, and died at the age of fifty-nine. He was greatly esteemed for his virtues; and "the age of the Antonines" is justly esteemed as a bright one in Roman history.

43. G. AURELIUS CÆSAR AUG. PII. F. Rev. TR. POT. III. COS. II.

44. S. The same legends.

45. ANTONINUS AUG. ARMENIACUS. Rev. A female on the ground, personifying captive Armenia.

46. Rev. Victory holding a shield, with the motto VIC. PAR. Records the success of the Romans in Parthia.

47. B. Rev. A trophy, and two captives seated; DE SARM. The victory over the Sarmatians.

48. PROFECTIO AUG. Emperor on horseback.

49. S. FAUSTINA AUGUSTA. Rev. A female with an infant in her arms, and two other children at her feet; FECUND(itas) AUGUSTÆ. She was the daughter of Antoninus Pius, and wife of Marcus; died A.D. 175. Her dissolute life could not exempt her from deification.

50. Rev. SÆCULI FELICIT(as). "The happiness of the age."

51. A fine head of this handsome woman. Rev. CONCORDIA.

52. B. Rev. LÆTITIA.

53. S. L. VERUS AUG. ARMENIACUS. Rev. Sundry usual titles.

54. L. VERUS ARM. PARTH. MAX. (The two emperors were somewhat disposed to conquer per alium, and triumph in persona.)

55. DIVUS VERUS. Rev. CONSECRATIO.

56. Silver, of Lucilla, daughter of Marcus, and wife of Verus. Rev. VOTA PUBLICA.

57. Rev. DIANA LUCIFERA.

XVIII. COMMODUS, son of Marcus Aurelius, was admitted to the rank of Cæsar at five years of age, and of Augustus at sixteen; and succeeded to the empire in 180, at nineteen years. He gloried chiefly in fighting as a gladiator in the public games, and assumed the name of Hercules. An end was put to his cruelties by assassination, A.D. 192.

64. G. M. COMMODUS ANTON(inus) AUG. PIUS. Rev. The customary titles.

65. S. Rev. HILARITAS.

66. The usual titles.

67. L. ÆL(ius) AUREL(ius) COMM(odus). Rev. The club of Hercules; HERCULO ROMANO AUGU(sto).

68. B. Rev. Sacrificial instruments; PIETAS AUG. Records the piety of Commodus.

69. G. CRISPINA AUGUSTA. Rev. VENUS FELIX. This empress

was banished for gross misconduct, and afterward put to death, 183; and was even refused an apotheosis. *cb.*

70. Rev. An altar; Dis Genitalibus.

XIX. PERTINAX, the son of a wood-chopper, rose to the highest posts in the army and state, and was declared emperor upon the death of Commodus, A.D. 192. His virtues were conspicuous; but the iron age of Rome had commenced, and a good ruler could scarcely keep his place. He was murdered by a few soldiers, after a reign of three months, and in his sixty-sixth year.

78. G. Imp. Cæs. P. Helv(ius) Pertin(ax) Aug. Rev. Provid (entia) Deor(um). Cos. II.

79. Same legends as the gold. *cb.*

80. B. Same legends.

XX. DIDIUS JULIANUS, a wealthy citizen of Rome, hearing that the army had offered the empire at public sale, ran to the camp, and outbid a competitor. He was acknowledged by the senate; and, on the approach of Severus, was deposed and beheaded by the same authority, after a reign of two months, and at sixty years of age, A.D. 193.

85. G. Imp. Cæs. M. Did. Julian. Aug. Rev. P. M. Tr. P. Cos.

86. S. Rev. Rector Orbis. The emperor holding a globe. *cb.*

87. Manlia Scantilla, empress. Rev. Juno Regina. "Juno, the queen."

88, 89. Didia Clara, daughter of Julian. Rev. Hilar(itas) Temp (orum). The "hilarity of the times" was precarious and intermittent. (89. *cb.*)

90. The same type in brass.

XXI. SEPTIMIUS SEVERUS, a native of Africa, and commander in Germany, was proclaimed emperor by his legions, on hearing of the death of Pertinax; and marching to Rome, received the homage of the senate. He was successful against two powerful competitors, and reigned eighteen years, dying at York, in Britain, A.D. 211, at the age of sixty-five. His surname expressed his character—severe, and caring little for the opinion of others; yet, on the whole, such a ruler as the times required.

93. S. Severus Pius Aug. Rev. A female seated on a lion; In-

DULGENTIA AUG(usti) IN CARTH(aginem). The occasion was his investing Carthage with peculiar privileges.

94. Rev. RESTITUTOR URBIS. "Restorer of the city." Severus built temples, and restored the secular games in Rome.

95. Rev. Trophy and captives. Legend imperfect.

96. B. Usual titles in the legend.

97. Silver, of Julia Domna, wife of Severus. Rev. VENUS GENETRIX.

98. Rev. MATER DEUM.

99. Rev. JUNO.

100. VESTA.

101. Brass, of Julia. MATER DEUM.

102. Greek coin, (brass,) of Severus; Corcyra, now Corfu.

103. The same; coined at Cesarea, in Cappadocia.

PESCENNIUS NIGER, and CLODIUS ALBINUS, the former governor in Syria, the latter in Britain, started with Severus in the race for the empire, with powerful armies to back them. Niger was subdued in one year, and Clodius in four, after an obstinate conflict.

104. G. IMP. CÆS. C. PESC(ennius) NIGER JUSTUS AUG. Rev. CONCORDIA, P. P. *cb.* (The original of this was unique, and was stolen from the cabinet of the King of France, with other pieces; and has no doubt been melted down. It is proper to add, that on account of the P. P., to which Niger was not entitled, the original itself was suspected.)

105. S. Rev. FORTUNA REDUCI.

106. Moon and stars. SÆCULI FELICIT(as). *cb.*

107. Greek coin of Niger. *cb.*

108. Same, in brass. *cb.*

109. S. D. CLOD. SEPT. ALBIN(us) CÆS.

110. Rev. MINER(va) PACIF(era). COS. II.

111. Brass, of Clodius. Reverse illegible.

XXII. CARACALLA and GETA, sons of Severus, succeeded as joint emperors, A.D. 211. Their mutual hatred ceased only upon the murder of Geta, in the next year; and Caracalla acted the tyrant alone, for five years longer. He died by the hand of one of his soldiers, at the instigation of Macrinus, while on the march into Persia,

A.D. 217, aged thirty years. (*Caracalla,* being a nickname only, never appears on the coins; the true name of this emperor was Marcus Aurelius Antoninus.)

113. S. IMP. ANTONINUS AUG. Rev. JOVI CONSERVATORI. "To Jupiter, the Preserver."

114. ANTONINUS PIUS AUG. BRIT(annicus). Rev. PROFECTIO AUG(usti). Caracalla was with the army in North Britain; and figures in Ossian as "Caracul."

115. ANTONINUS PIUS AUG. GERM(anicus). A quiet retreat through Germany brought him this victorious surname.

116. Rev. LÆTITIA PUBL(ica). "The public joy."

117. Rev. VICTOR(ia) ANTONINI AUG. (These four are large denarii, which began to be coined in this reign.)

118. B. Usual titles in the legend.

119. S. PLAUTILLA AUGUSTA. (Plautilla was married to Caracalla, A.D. 202; afterward exiled, and put to death, A.D. 212.)

120. Rev. VENUS VICTRIX.

121. Rev. The emperor and empress joining hands; PROPAGO IMPERI.

122. Brass, of Plautilla. PIETAS AUG.

123. S. GETA CÆS(ar) PONT. COS. Rev. VOTA PUBLICA. Rev. PRINC(eps) JUVENTUTIS. (These two were coined before Geta became emperor.)

124. SEPT. GETA PIUS AUG. BRIT(annicus). Rev. Usual titles.

125. Brass, of Geta. PONTIF. COS. II.

126. Greek coin (brass) of Caracalla, struck at Byzantium.

XXIII. MACRINUS having, for his own safety, procured the murder of Caracalla, was deliberately elected emperor by the army in Syria, A.D. 217. He was killed the next year, after suffering a defeat by Elagabalus.

127. S. IMP. C(æsar) M(arcus) OPEL(ius) SEV(erus) MACRINUS AUG. Rev. FIDES MILITUM. "Faith of the soldiers."

128. AEQUITAS AUG(usti). "Equity of the emperor."

129. B. Rev. The emperor in a quadriga, or car with four horses.

130. Silver, of DIADUMENIANUS, son of Macrinus; created Cæsar,

and afterward Augustus, at nine years; shared the fate of his father. *cb.*

131. B. Rev. PRINC. JUVENTUTIS.

XXIV. ELAGABALUS, or Heliogabalus, a boy-priest in the Temple of the Sun, in Syria, and of distant relation to Caracalla, was commended by his mother to the Roman soldiery there, as a son of that emperor, and by them proclaimed, in opposition to Macrinus. His faction having succeeded, the youth was acknowledged by the senate, and reigned about four years. He was killed A.D. 222, at the age of about eighteen years, after a course of debauchery and cruelty that is scarcely credible. His real name was Avitus Bassianus, and his imperial name Marcus Antoninus; but he is only known by the designation above, which was the Syrian title of the sun, as a deity.

135. S. IMP. ANTONINUS PIUS AUG. Rev. The emperor sacrificing; INVICTUS SACERDOS AUG. "The unconquered priest, emperor."

136. Rev. The emperor on horseback. PROF(ectio). Probably his "march" to Rome.

137. Rev. SACERDOS SOLIS ELAGAB(ali) D(ei). He gloried in this character, and introduced the worship of the sun at Rome.

138. Large silver. Rev. SALUS ANTONINI AUG.

139. B. The emperor in a car. P. M. TR. P. V. COS. IIII. P. P.

141. Large silver. JULIA MÆSA AUG. The grandmother of Elagabalus, and by him created a member of the senate. Rev. PIETAS AUG.

142. Silver, of Julia Mæsa. Rev. PUDICITIA.

143. The same. Rev. FECUNDITAS.

144. JULIA SOÆMIAS AUG. Rev. VENUS CELESTIS. Julia Soæmias was the mother of the emperor, and was killed at the same time with him.

145. JULIA PAULA AUG. Rev. The emperor and empress joining hands. CONCORDIA. She was the first wife of Elagabalus, and repudiated in about a year, notwithstanding this "concord."

146. Paula, with Elagabalus on the reverse. *cb.*

147. JULIA AQUILIA SEVERA. Rev. CONCORDIA. A vestal virgin

taken by Elagabalus as his second wife; repudiated to make room for a third, but afterward recalled.

148. Greek coin, brass, of Elagabalus; struck at Marcianopolis, in Mæsia.

149. Same; struck at Nice, in Bithynia.

DIVISION IV.

SEVERUS ALEXANDER TO CLAUDIUS GOTHICUS, A.D. 222–270.

XXV. SEVERUS ALEXANDER, the cousin of Elagabalus, and adopted by him, succeeded A.D. 222, at the age of seventeen, and reigned thirteen years. The downward course of things was somewhat retarded by this wise and virtuous administration; but was renewed by the barbarous murder of the emperor, and the elevation of the chief conspirator.

1. S. IMP. ALEXANDER PIUS AUG. Rev. SPES PUBLICA.

2. Rev. MARS ULTOR. "Mars, the Revenger."

3. IMP. C. M. AUR. SEV. ALEXANDER. AUG. Rev. Usual titles.

4. B. Rev. The emperor in a car. Usual titles.

5. S. SALL(ustia) BARBIA ORBIANA AUG. The emperor on the reverse. She was the wife of Alexander. *cb.*

6. Rev. CONCORDIA AUGG.

7. Brass, of the same. CONCORDIA AUGUSTORUM.

8. S. JULIA MAMÆA. AUG. Rev. FELICITAS PUBLICA. She was the emperor's mother, and influential in the government. Killed with him.

9. Rev. VENUS VICTRIX.

10. Rev. A female holding an infant. VENERI FELICI.

11. Rev. VESTA.

12. B. FELICITAS PUBLICA.

13. Brass, Greek, of Alexander. Byzantium.

XXVI. MAXIMIN I., the Thracian giant, succeeded the prince whose murder he had procured. His successes against the Germans could not atone for his cruel temper, and the Romans declared for Gordian and his son, who had assumed the purple in Africa. They were quickly subdued by the forces of Maximin; but in marching for Rome, to encounter a new pair of emperors, he was murdered by his own soldiers, A.D. 238. He had reigned three years, and was aged sixty-five.

15. S. Imp. Maximinus Pius Aug. Rev. Pax Augusti.

16. Rev. Victoria Germ(anica).

17. Rev. Fidus Militum. Perhaps alludes to his rescue by the soldiers, when he was sticking fast in a marsh, in Germany.

18. B. Rev. Salus Augusti.

19. Rev. Military standards.

20. Same reverse as No. 17.

21. S. Diva Paulina. Rev. A peacock carrying the deceased empress to heaven. Consecratio. There was some ground for this compliment.

22. Jul(ius) Verus Maximus Cæs(ar). Rev. Pietas Aug. This prince was of an opposite disposition to his father, but shared his fate, A.D. 238.

23. Brass, of the same. Rev. Principi Juventutis.

XXVII. BALBINUS, a senator, and PUPIENUS, a soldier, both advanced in years, were chosen in Rome to succeed the two Gordians, while Maximin was still living. His defeat confirmed them in the empire, which they governed wisely; but a mutiny of the soldiers brought them to a violent end, after reigning only about a year, A.D. 239.

29. Large silver. Imp Cæs. D(ecimus) Cæl(ius) Balbinus Aug. Rev. Two hands joined; Pietas Mutua Augg. "The devotion of the emperors to each other."

30. Rev. Providentia Deorum. *cb.*

31. Imp. Cæs. M(arcus) Clod(ius) Pupienus Aug. Rev. Two hands joined; Patres Senatus—(which may mean the emperors, as "fathers of the senate," or the senate, as "the conscript fathers.")

32. Small silver, of Pupienus. Victoria Augg. *cb.*

33. Brass, of Pupienus. Legend imperfect.

XXVIII. GORDIAN III., a youth of only fifteen years, succeeded to the empire by common consent, and his reign displayed courage and moderation. He was undermined, however, by the arts of Philip, the pretorian prefect; and the support of the army being withdrawn, he was easily cut off, A.D. 244, having reigned six years.

36. Small silver. Youthful head. IMP. GORDIANUS PIUS FEL(ix) AUG. Rev. Usual titles.

37. Large silver. Rev. LÆTITIA AUG. N.

38, 39. Rev. JOVI STATORI. Figure of Jupiter Stator.

40. Rev. SAECULI FELICITAS.

41. ORIENS AUG. The emperor flattered as the "rising sun."

42. JOVI CONSERVATORI. "To Jupiter, the Preserver."

43. MARS PROPUG(nator). "Mars, the Champion."

44. Usual official titles.

45. L. Brass. SECURITAS PERPET(ua).

46. As No. 38.

47, 48. Silver, of Sabina Tranquillina, empress; married to Gordian in 241. (No. 48, *cb.;* No. 47 doubtful.)

XXIX. PHILIP, an Arab chief, afterward a Roman general, proved an excellent ruler, notwithstanding the base means of his promotion; and was in high esteem with the senate and people. His son, Philip II., though but a child, was associated in the empire. Their reign, with their lives, was cut short by the successful revolt of the army in Pannonia (Austria) under Decius. Philip was killed, A.D. 249, in his forty-sixth year, and sixth of his reign. The younger Philip was aged thirteen.

50. Small silver. IMP. M(arcus) JUL(ius) PHILIPPUS AUG. Rev. The emperor on horseback; ADVENTUS AUGG. "Arrival of the emperors."

51. Large silver. Rev. SECURIT(as) ORBIS. "The safety of the world."

52, 53, 54, 55. Rev. SECULARES AUGG. These coins severally bear on the reverse a lion, a stag, a goat, and a column with Cos. III.; and another, of the empress, bears a hippopotamus. The secular games were celebrated with magnificence, A.D. 247, and third year of Philip, as being the 1000th year of Rome, by the computation of

Varro. Other coins of the same date (not in this collection) bear the legend MILLIARIUM SÆCULUM, the "millennium" of Rome.

56. Rev. ÆQUITAS AUGG.

57. VIRTUS AUG.

58. An elephant and his rider; ÆTERNITAS AUGG.

59. Base silver. Greek coin of Philip; Antioch in Syria.

60. B. Rev. A stag; SÆCULARES AUGG.

61. FELICITAS TEMP(orum). "The happiness of the times."

62. Large silver. OTACIL(ia) SEVERA AUG. Rev. PIETAS AUGUSTÆ. She was married to Philip some years before he became emperor, and survived him a very short time. She was of pure character, and is said to have professed the new religion, and to have caused her son, the younger Philip, to be baptized. The emperor was not (as some have affirmed) the first Christian emperor, but he suppressed the persecutions.

63. Otacilia. Rev. SÆCULARES AUGG. A hippopotamus, with open mouth. The display of wild animals formed a part of these games.

64. B. MARCIA OTACIL(ia) SEVERA. Rev. PIETAS AUGUSTÆ.

65. Large silver. M. JUL. PHILIPPUS CÆS. Rev. The younger Philip holding a globe and spear; PRINCIPI JUVENT(utis).

66. Base silver. Greek coin of the younger Philip; Antioch in Syria.

67. Brass, of the same. Reverse imperfect.

68. The same. SÆCULARES AUGG. COS. II.

69. Large silver. IMP. TI(berius) CL(audius) MAR(ius) PACATIANUS AUG. Rev. SALUS AUGG. The name of this usurper is not found in history, but he is referred to this date by another legend (not in this collection), ROMÆ ÆTER. AN. MILL. ET PRIMO. "Year 1001 of eternal Rome." His coins are found only in France. This is one of several instances in which Roman coins discover the omissions of historians. *cb.*

70. Pacatianus. Rev. Hercules in conflict with the lion; VIRTUS AUG. "Courage of the emperor." *cb.*

XXX. TRAJAN DECIUS, sent to suppress a mutiny in Pannonia, placed himself at the head of it; and having vanquished his master, was acknowledged as emperor. His reign of two years was spent in warring against the Goths, and destroying the Christians; the former of whom had become formidable to the state, as the latter had to the state religion. He fell in battle, A.D. 251, aged sixty years.

71. G. IMP. C. M. Q. TRAIANUS DECIUS AUG. Rev. A figure holding an ensign; GENIUS EXERC. ILLYRICIANI. The Illyrian army promoted him.

72. S. ADVENTUS AUG. His arrival at Rome.

73. DACIA. The battle-ground.

74. GEN. ILLYRICI.

75. B. PANNONIA.

76. Reverse as No. 71.

77. G. HER(ennia) ETRUSCILLA AUG. Rev. PUDICITIA AUG. This empress is known only by her coins, and by an inscription.

78. S. Same reverse.

79. B. Same reverse.

80. Greek coin of Etruscilla. Rev. SAMION. Island of Samos.

81. S. Q. HER(ennius) ETR(uscus) MES(sius) DECIUS NOB(ilis) C(æsar). This prince perished in battle with his father.

82. Brass, of the same.

83. S. CN. VALENS HOSTILIANUS QUINTUS AUG. This prince survived his father, was made colleague to Gallus, and died in a few months, either of plague or poison.

84. Rev. SECURITAS AUGG. (This legend seems a sarcasm upon the times, and especially upon this prince.)

XXXI. GALLUS, commanding on the Danube, was proclaimed by his army, and elected by the senate successor to Decius. A precarious peace was purchased of the Goths; but the empire was afflicted with plague and famine. Gallus was killed by his own soldiers, when about to march against Æmilian, A.D. 254; having reigned less than three years, and aged forty-seven.

85. S. IMP. C. C. VIB. TREB(onianus) GALLUS AUG. Rev. LIBERTAS PUBLICA.

86. Rev. APOLL(ini) SALUTARI. (An appeal to Apollo, the god of physic, to stay the plague.)

87. Rev. VICTORIA AUGG.

88. B. Rev. VIRTUS AUGG.

89. Greek coin of Gallus. Antioch in Syria.

90. S. IMP. CÆS. VIB. VOLUSIANUS AUG. Rev. CONCORDIA AUGG. Volusian was associated with his father in the empire, and perished with him.

91. Reverse as No. 88.

92. B. Reverse same as preceding.

93. S. IMP. ÆMILIANUS PIUS FELIX AUG. Rev. SPES PUBLICA. Æmilian, a Moor by birth, and governor of Mæsia, having successfully resisted a Persian invasion, was proclaimed emperor by his troops, and was acknowledged after the death of Gallus, but survived his elevation only three months.

94. S. C. CORNELIA SUPERA AUG. Rev. JUNO REGINA. This lady, wife of Æmilian, is known only by her coins. *cb.*

95. Rev. VESTA. *cb.*

XXXII. VALERIAN, of illustrious family, and pure character, was promoted to the empire upon the fall of Gallus and Æmilian, A.D. 254, being then sixty years of age. His troubled reign was terminated in 260, by his being taken prisoner by the King of Persia, in whose hands, after much cruel treatment, he died.

99. S. IMP. C. P. LIC(inius) VALERIANUS AUG. Rev. VICTORIA AUGG.

100. ORIENS AUG.

101. DIVA MARINIANA. Wife of Valerian. Rev. A peacock, bearing the departed spirit. CONSECRATIO.

102. Rev. Peacock, with wings outspread. CONSECRATIO.

103. B. Same as the preceding.

104. Greek coin, brass, of Valerian; Tarsus, in Cilicia.

XXXIII. GALLIENUS was adopted into the empire, A.D. 254, at the age of thirty-six, and became sole emperor upon the captivity of his father, an event which gave him no concern. In this reign, "heaven and earth seemed to concur in heaping afflictions upon the empire." Usurpers seized upon the fairest provinces, and maintained their ground; the barbarians grew bolder in their irruptions; and the plague, raging everywhere and lingering for years, cut off a vast proportion of the people. Gallienus allowed nothing to interfere with his ease and pleasures, except a campaign against the Germans, and another against a rebel general, in which he perished, A.D. 268.

107. S. GALLIENUS P. F. AUG. Rev. VICT(oria) GERMANICA.

108. Rev. GERMANICUS MAX(imus).

409. A quinarius. VICTORIA AUG. *cb.*

110. DIVO PIO. Head of Antoninus Pius. (Gallienus caused the issue of a series of coins in billon, bearing the heads of his most eminent predecessors. There is a vast variety of dies in this reign, without any improvement in the art.)

111. Small brass. Rev. JOVI CONSERVATORI.

112. Billon, of Salonina, empress.

113. Rev. VENUS FILIA.

114. B. VESTA.

115. Billon, of Saloninus Valerian, son of Gallienus. Rev. PRINC. JUVENT.

116. Rev. PIETAS AUG.

117. Quinarius. Same reverse. *cb.*

118. A boy riding a goat. JOVI CRESCENTI.

119. Brass, of the same. Rev. A funeral pile.

USURPERS. During the feeble reign of Gallienus, the purple was assumed by about twenty generals, in different parts of the empire. Most of these were soon overthrown; but there were two extensive monarchies, which stood out against Gallienus and his immediate successor. The first, created by the famous Zenobia, Queen of Palmyra, included Syria and Egypt, and lasted six years, 267–73. The other, originated by Postumus, was composed of Gaul, Spain, and Britain, and continued fifteen years, 258–73. All these provinces were eventually restored to Rome, by the bravery and address of Aurelian.

POSTUMUS, governor of Gaul, assumed the title of emperor, 258; was killed by his troops, 267.

VICTORINUS, a general of Postumus, was associated with him, 265; and was also killed by his soldiers, 267.

LÆLIANUS, competitor of Postumus, was also killed by his own troops.

MARIUS, successor to Victorinus, was killed almost as soon as crowned.

TETRICUS, a senator, and governor of Aquitaine, succeeded to this monarchy, and reigned undisturbed six years. In 273, he abdicated with his son; and both retired to Rome for the remainder of their lives. A vast variety of coins were issued by these emperors, or usurpers.

120. Plated brass, or copper. IMP. C. POSTUMUS P. F. AUG. Rev. Hercules and Postumus, face to face. FELICITAS AUG.

121. Base silver. Front face of Postumus. Rev. INDULG(entia) PIA POSTUMI AUG. *cb.* It is uncertain what this "pious indulgence" was.

122. Profile; same reverse. *cb.*

123. Billon. SÆCULI FELICITAS.

124. A quinarius. VICTORIA AUG. *cb.*

125. Billon or copper; same reverse.

126. PAX AUG.

127. Plated brass. Rev. VIRTUS AUG.

128. Rev. JOVI PROPUGNATORI.

129. Large brass. Heads of Postumus and Hercules side by side, and on the reverse, face to face. *cb.*

130. Plated brass. A woman recumbent, personifying the Rhine; SALUS PROVINCIARUM. "Safety of the provinces."

131. S. IMP. C. VICTORINUS P. F. AUG. Rev. VIRTUS AUG. *cb.*

132. Brass, or copper. Rev. PROVIDENTIA AUG.

133. Rev. PAX AUG.

134. Silver, of Marius. Rev. CONCORDIA MILITUM. *cb.*

135. Rev. SÆ(culi) FELICITAS. *cb.*

136. Silver, of Lælianus. Rev. TEMPORUM FELICITAS. *cb.*

137. Gold, of Tetricus the elder. Usual titles. *cb.*

138. S. Rev. PAX ÆTERNA. *cb.*

139. Heads of Tetricus senior and junior. Rev. ÆTERNITAS AUGG. *cb.*

140. Copper, of Tetricus senior. PIETAS AUG.

141. SALUS AUG.

142. G. C. PES(uvius) TETRICUS CÆSAR. Rev. SPES AUGG. *cb.*

143. S. Same reverse. *cb.*

144. C. Rev. PIETAS AUGUST(orum). Sacrificial utensils.

145. Rev. SPES PUBLICA.

146. Rev. PRIN. JUVENTUTIS.

XXXIV. CLAUDIUS II., surnamed GOTHICUS, succeeded Gallienus, as the dying choice of that prince, and with the consent of the army and senate. By a brave onset he repulsed the daring Goths, which gained him the above surname. Two years after his accession, and at the age of fifty-five, he was carried off by the plague, A.D. 270.

148. G. IMP. CLAUDIUS PIUS FELIX AUG. Rev. VICTORIA AUG.

149. S. Rev. PAX EXERC(ituum). *cb.*

150. Small brass. FIDES EXERCIT.

151. Rev. LÆTITIA.

152. Silver, of QUINTILLUS, brother of Claudius, who assumed the empire upon his death, but retained it only a few days.

153. Small brass, of the same.

DIVISION V.

AURELIAN TO THE END OF THE WESTERN EMPIRE, A.D. 270–475.

XXXV. AURELIAN, general of cavalry, succeeded, A.D. 270. His reign of five years was employed in clearing the empire of the numerous foes, foreign and domestic, who had for years been threatening its existence. He was entirely successful, and the Roman rule was everywhere re-established. He was a severe disciplinarian, such as the times required; but his severity gave ground for a conspiracy, which cost him his life, A.D. 275. He was over sixty years of age at his death.

3. Middle brass. IMP. AURELIANUS AUG. Rev. CONCORDIA AUG.

4. Small brass. Rev. VIRTUS AUG.

5. Small brass, of Severina, empress. Rev. CONCORDIA MILITUM.

XXXVI. On the death of Aurelian, a singular contest arose between the army and senate, each requesting the other to nominate a successor. Six months elapsed in this generous strife; at length, the senate chose TACITUS, one of their own body, seventy-five years old, and of exemplary character. He lived only six months after his elevation. The historian Tacitus was claimed by the emperor as his ancestor.

10. B. IMP. C. M. CL(audius) TACITUS AUG. Rev. FELICIT(as) TEMP(orum).

11. Rev. A woman holding a purse; UBERITAS. "Plenty."

12. Rev. CONCORDIA MILITUM.

13. Silver, of Florianus, brother of Tacitus, who assumed the purple as successor, but was murdered by his troops, A.D. 276. *cb.*

14. Brass, of the same. VIRTUS AUG.

XXXVII. PROBUS, during a reign of six years, was warring from the Rhine to the Nile, and always with success. In a recess of peace, having set the soldiers to draining a marsh, a mutiny was raised, and he fell, A.D. 282, aged fifty. "In civil and military virtue, he was equal to any predecessor."

17. G. IMP. C. M. AUR(elius) PROBUS AUG. Rev. SECURITAS SÆCULI. In the exergue, SIS, for Siscia, either his birthplace or the place of coinage.

18. Plated brass. Rev. ROMÆ AETERNÆ. (He repaired the city.)

19. Small brass. SOLI INVICTO.

20. Rev. VICTORIA GERM. The Germans were driven from Gaul with immense loss; nine kings submitted, and sixteen thousand German youth were taken into the Roman army.

XXXVIII. CARUS, pretorian prefect under Probus, succeeded that prince by election of the army, A.D. 282, at the age of fifty-two. He was killed in his tent by lightning, in a campaign against Persia, about one year after.

26. B. IMP. CARUS P. F. AUG. Rev. SPES PUBLICA. P. XXI.

27. Rev. PAX EXERCIT. P. XXI.

XXXIX. CARINUS and NUMERIAN, sons of Carus, succeeded their father, A.D. 283. The former was plunged in debauchery; the latter, a virtuous youth, contracted a disease of the eyes in grief for his parent, which obliged him to travel in a close litter. In this hidden place he was murdered by his ambitious father-in-law, Aper, A.D. 284. Carinus also died by violence, a year after.

29. Small brass. M. Aur(elius) Carinus Nob(ilis) C(æsar). Rev. Principi Juvent.

30. Pietas Augg. (These two were struck before the death of Carus.)

31. Washed brass, of Magnia Urbica, a lady known only by her coins, but supposed to be the wife of Carinus. Rev. Venus Genetrix. *cb.*

32. Brass, of the same. Rev. Venus Victrix.

33. B. S. Divo Nigriniano. This deified youth is supposed to have been a son of Carinus. *cb.*

34. Base silver, of Julianus, usurper. *cb.*

35. G. Rev. Aur(elius) Numerianus Nob. C. Rev. Principi Juvent.

36. S. Rev. Pietas Augg. *cb.*

37. B. Imp. Numerianus Aug. Rev. Pietas Augg.

38. Rev. Providentia Augg. xxi.

39. Brass, same legends as the gold coin. (No. 35.)

XL. DIOCLETIAN, a master-spirit, though born a slave, received the empire from the army, A.D. 285, at the age of forty. The next year he associated MAXIMIAN HERCULES; and in 292, the two called to their aid Galerius and Constantinus Chlorus, as Cæsars, and the empire was divided into four jurisdictions: Diocletian in the East, Maximian over Italy and Africa, Galerius in the region between the Adriatic and Euxine, and Constantius in the West. The two emperors abdicated in 305. This long reign was signalized by the increase of despotism, by incessant wars, and by a systematic effort to root out Christianity.

41. G. Diocletianus P. F. Aug. Rev. Jovi Conser. Augg.

42. S. Rev. XCVI. Aq. (Struck at Aquileia in Italy.)

43. Rev. The emperor and officers sacrificing before a camp. Virtus Militum.

44. B. Rev. Jovi Tutatori Augg "To Jupiter, Defender of the Emperors."

45. Rev. Genio Populi Romani. Aq. P. "To the Genius of the Roman People."

46. Rev. Vot. XX., within a wreath.

47. Concordia Militum.

49. G. Imp. C. M. A. Maximianus Aug. Rev. Virtuti Herculis.

50. S. Reverse same as No. 44.

51. Reverse as on No. 41. *cb.*

52. B. D(omino) N(ostro) Maximiano Beatissimo Sen. Aug. "To our most blessed lord, Maximian the elder."

53. Rev. Genio Augg. et Cæsarum N. N. Ka. (Carthage mint.)

54. As No. 47.

55. Imp. Carausius P. F. Aug. Rev. Pax Aug. This remarkable man was a Roman admiral on the coast of Britain. In 287 he seized upon that island, made it an empire for himself, and forced an acknowledgment of his claim by the Roman emperors. He reigned with éclat for six years, when he fell by the hand of his minister Allectus; who was subdued by the forces of Constantius, two years after, 295. (The coins extant of these two usurpers or emperors are comparatively few, although they are of considerable variety in device. This specimen was lately dug up in England.)

XLI. The administration now presents a confused multitude of Augusti and Cæsars. GALERIUS and CONSTANTIUS CHLORUS succeeding their patrons in 305, Severus and Maximin Daza were called to take part in the government. In 306, the restless Max. Hercules returned to the empire, with his son MAXENTIUS; Severus was made emperor; Constantius died (in Britain), and his son Constantine took the rank of Cæsar. In 307, Severus died, and LICINIUS became an emperor. 308, Maximin Daza assumed the purple in the East, and Constantine in the West, so that the Romans now supported the burden of *six* emperors, each with his court and camp. Four of these died or were killed nearly at the same time: Maximian in 310; Galerius, 311; Maxentius, 312; and Maximin Daza, 313. History hesitates to decide which was the greatest tyrant.

58. S. Constantius Cæs. Reverse as No. 43.

59. Small brass. Rev. Concordia Militum.

60. Small brass, of Theodora, second wife of Constantius.

62. Silver, of Galerius. Maximianus Nob. C. Rev. A camp; Virtus Militum.

63. B. Imp. C. Gal(erius) Val(erius) Maximianus P. F. Aug. Rev. Genio Imperatoris.

64. Reverse as No. 45.

65. Brass, of Valeria, wife of Galerius.

66. Brass, of Severus. Rev. Salvis Augg. et Cæss. Fel. Kart.

67. Do., of Maximin Daza. Reverse as No. 63.

68. Small brass, of the same.

69. Brass, of Maxentius. Rev. Conserv. Urb. Suæ. "Preserver of his own city."

70. Small brass, of Romulus, infant son of Maxentius.

XLII. CONSTANTINE the Great, succeeding his father in the West, in 306, had but one colleague or competitor remaining in 313. LICINIUS, his brother-in-law, reigned in the East; and after various collisions and compacts, the latter was forced to yield his throne in 323, and his life the year after. Constantine remaining sole emperor, restored peace and solidity to the empire, built a new capital (Constantinople), and established Christianity as the state religion. He died in 337, at the age of sixty-three.

73. G. Constatinus Magnus. Rev. Jupiter, standing; Jovi Conservatori Augg. TS. B. This must have been struck before his conversion to Christianity (in 311), or before his open avowal of it.

75. Small brass. Rev. Soli Invicto Comiti. (The sense is obscure.)

76. Rev. A camp; Providentia Augg.

77. Rev. Mars, standing; Marti Conservatori.

[There is a rare type extant, not in this collection, bearing the monogram of Christ, and the legend, In hoc Signo Vinc(es), the Latin version of *Touto Nika*, (Gr.,) "by this (sign) conquer." This sign was the appearance of a splendid cross in the heavens, which, as he affirmed some years afterward, was presented to his view, near Milan, on his march against Maxentius; and to which he attributed both his victory and his conversion. It is remarkable as the introduction of the Christian emblems, which become more and more common, until scarce anything else appears on the coins. See the series of the Lower Empire.]

78. S. FLAV(ia) MAX(ima) FAUSTA AUG. Rev. The empress suckling two infants; SPES REIPUBLICÆ. SIRMIUM. (She was the daughter of Maximian, sister of Maxentius, and wife of Constantine. Having caused the death of Crispus by a false charge, she was condemned by the emperor to the same fate, 326, after a union of nineteen years.) *cb.*

79. Small brass, same type.

80. Same figure, with SALUS REIPUBLICÆ.

81. JUL(ius) CRISPUS NOB(ilis) CÆS. Rev. VIRTUS EXERCIT. Crispus was the son of Constantine, and a favorite of the army; but was put to death on an accusation of the empress, his stepmother, 326.

82. Rev. VICT(oriæ) LÆTÆ PRINC. PERP. SIS(cia.)

83. S. FL(avius) DELMATIUS NOB. CÆS. He was a nephew of Constantine, and governed Greece; killed by the soldiers, 337. *cb.*

84. Small brass, of the same. Rev. GLORIA EXERCITUS.

85. B. IMP. LIC(inianus) LICINIUS P. F. AUG. Reverse as No. 73.

86. Small brass; same reverse.

87. Reverse as No. 75.

88. Small brass, of the younger Licinius. (Put to death, 326, at the age of eleven years.)

XLIII. The empire now underwent another division and reunion. CONSTANTINE II. had the West; CONSTANS, the middle provinces, with Italy; and CONSTANTIUS II., the East. The first fell in a war with his next brother, A.D. 340; the second was overcome by Magnentius, 350; and from the overthrow of that usurper, in 353, Constantius II. remained sole emperor, finishing a long and inglorious reign in 361, aged forty-four.

89. G. No legend around the head. Rev. CONSTATINUS CÆSAR.

90. S. Rev. VOTIS XXX. MULTIS XXXX. ANT. (for the mint at Antioch.)

91. Small brass. CONSTATINUS JUNIOR NOB. C. Rev. GLORIA EXERCITUS.

92. Rev. CÆSARUM NOSTRORUM. VOT. V.

93. Reverse same, with VOT. X.

94. Rev. A camp; PROVIDENTIA CÆSS.

95. G. CONSTANS AUGUSTUS. Rev. VICTORIA DD. NN. AUGG. TR. On a shield held by two genii or angels, VOT. X. MULT. XX. (See No. 101.)

96. B. Rev. A soldier holding the military ensign or labarum, on which is the monogram of Christ. FEL(icium) TEMP(orum) REPARATIO. "The restoration of happy times."

97. Small brass. Reverse as No. 95, except the shield.

98. CONSTANTINOPOLIS. Helmeted head, personifying the new city.

99. G. FL. JUL. CONSTANTIUS PERP. AUG. Rev. A shield, with VOT. XX. MULT. XXX. Legend. GLORIA REIPUBLICÆ. SMNT.

100. Gold quinarius. Rev. VICTORIA AUGUSTI. VOT. XXX.

101. S. Rev. VOTIS XXV. MULTIS XXX. ANT. (This inscription, the style of which now becomes common, is a brief way of saying that the emperor has renewed or accomplished his inaugural vow twenty-five times, *i.e.* has enjoyed the title of Augustus, or Cæsar, for twenty-five years, and it is hoped that he will complete at least as many as thirty. This is the only plausible interpretation of MULT. XXX. It seems but a feeble compliment to a monarch; however, as will be seen by the next coin, as soon as he had accomplished VOTIS XXX., the wish was ready for MULT. XXXX.)

102. VOTIS XXX. MULTIS XXXX. It must be counted from the time he was created Cæsar by his father in 323.

103. B. A soldier leading a child; FEL. TEMP. REPARATIO. The favorite legend of Constantine's family.

104. Rev. GLORIA ROMANORUM.

105. Small brass. CONSTANTIUS JUN. NOB. C. Rev. A globe on a pedestal.

106. Rev. GLORIA EXERCITUS.

107. Rev. VOT. XX. MULT. XXX.

108. Silver, of Vetrania, a Roman general and usurper, in Pannonia; reigned ten months. *cb.*

109. Brass, of Magnentius, a more formidable usurper, in Gaul; reigned three years, and was subdued, after refusing a share of the empire offered by Constantius, 353.

110. Small brass, of the same.

111. Silver, of Decentius, brother and coadjutor of Magnentius.

112. Large silver, of the same. The Christian symbol behind the head. *cb.*

XLIV. JULIAN, nephew of Const. the Great, was famous for his efforts to bring back the empire to paganism, chiefly by his pen. Some real reforms were also brought about in the government, and the manners at court. But the desire of figuring as a conqueror led him into Persia, from whence he with difficulty effected a retreat, and on the way lost his life, 363, at the age of thirty-two, and after a reign of two years, counting from the death of Constantius II., or about three from his elevation by the army at Paris.

113. G. Fl(avius) Cl(audius) Julianus P. P. Aug. Rev. Virtus Exercitus Romanorum. Sirm.

114. S. D(ominus) N(oster) Fl., etc. Rev. Vot. X., Mult. XX. Counting from his *Cæsarship.* The long beard recalls the derision of the citizens of Antioch, where he wintered, and the consequent production of the *Misopogon,* one of the emperor's literary efforts.

115. Large brass. Rev. The sacred bull Apis; Securitas Reipub(licæ.) Const. Julian was partial to the Egyptian deities.

116. Small brass, of the same.

117. Small brass of Helena, wife of Julian, and sister of Constantius II. Securitas Reipublicæ.

XLV. While the generals were in conclave, the soldiers proceeded to elect JOVIAN, a subordinate officer, and a man of no pretensions. He survived his elevation only seven months, A.D. 364. Christianity was restored to imperial favor.

123. B. D. N. Jovianus P. P. Aug. Rev. Vot. V. Mult. X. Sirm.

124. Reverse the same, except the mint-mark, which is Sis. (When these pieces were struck, the imperial vow for five years was evidently just assumed, not completed; showing that these dates are to be variously understood.

XLVI. VALENTINIAN I., son of Count Gratian, received the empire from the army, and at their instance placed his brother VALENS over the Eastern provinces. The tendency toward a division of Rome was thus accelerated. The former died 375, having reigned eleven years; the latter survived him three years, and was burnt to death in a cottage, where he had taken shelter in battle.

129. G. Head and titles of Valentinian. Rev. VICTORIA AUGG. TR. OB.

130. S. Rev. VOT. X. MULT. XX. ANT.

131. Small brass. Rev. The Christian cipher on a military standard; GLORIA ROMANORUM. SISC.

132. Rev. SECURITAS REIPUBLICÆ.

133. S. URBS ROMA. TRPS.

134. Small brass. RESTITUTOR REIPUBLICÆ. SIS.

135. SECURITAS REIPUBLICÆ.

136. Silver, of Procopius, a usurper at Constantinople. *cb.*

XLVII. GRATIAN, a youth, and VALENTINIAN II., a child, succeeded to the throne of their father in the West, 375. On the death of Valens, they associated the famous Theodosius, of Spain, who was stationed in the East. Gratian fell in 383, at the age of twenty-four, while on the march against a usurper in Gaul; his brother perished by the hand of an assassin, in 392, aged twenty-one; and the whole empire remained to Theodosius.

137. G. Head and titles of Gratian. Reverse as No. 129.

138. S. Rev. URBS ROMA. TR. PS.

139. B. Rev. REPARATIO REIPUBLICÆ. P. CON.

140. Small brass. Rev. SECURITAS REIPUBLICÆ. SIS.

141. B. D. N. MAGNUS MAXIMUS P. F. AUG. Reverse as on No. 139. A usurper in Gaul, who maintained his power four years, 383–87.

142. G. Head and titles of Valentinian, jun. Reverse as No. 129.

143. B. Reverse as No. 139.

144. Smallest brass. Rev. SALUS REIPUBLICÆ.

XLVIII. THEODOSIUS I. was called to a participation of the empire in 379, at the age of thirty-three. He became sole emperor in 392, and was the last to enjoy that distinction. In 395 he expired, after an illustrious reign, and left the realm to be divided between his two sons.

145. G. Head and titles of Theodosius. Reverse as No. 129.

146. Small silver. VOT. MULT. XXXX.

147. B. Rev. REPARATIO REIPUB. SIS.

148. Reverse as No. 131.

149. Small brass. CONCORDIA AUGGG. SIS.

150. Brass, of Flacilla, empress. Rev. A female figure, and the Christian monogram. SALUS REIPUBLICÆ. CONS.

XLIX. From the accession of Honorius, in 395, about eighty years elapsed to the extinction of the Western empire. The period was marked by a succession of feeble or nominal princes; by the daring inroads of barbarians; the loss, one by one, of the provinces of Britain, Gaul, Spain, and Africa; and finally, the establishment of a Gothic monarchy in Italy itself.

153. Gold, of HONORIUS. Reverse as No. 129. (Died in 423.)

154. S. Rev. VIRTUS ROMANORUM. (A remarkable legend for the times.)

155. B. Reverse imperfect.

156. Silver, of CONSTANTIUS III., associate of Honorius, for seven months only. *cb.*

158. S. JOHN, secretary to Honorius, afterward a usurper of the throne, 425. *cb.*

159. Gold, of VALENTINIAN III. Placidius. Reverse as No. 129. (425–55.)

160. Silver, of Justa Grata Honoria, sister of the preceding. Rev. A figure holding a large cross upright; BONO REIPUBLICÆ. CONOB. *cb.*

163. Gold, of SEVERUS III. An emperor created by Ricimer, a barbarian general in the Roman service, and really at the head of affairs. Reverse as No. 129. (461–65.)

166. Silver, of Ælia Euphemia, wife of Anthemius. *cb.*

168. Silver, of OLYBRIUS, emperor for three months. 472. *cb.*

169. Small gold, of JULIUS NEPOS. Rev. A cross; CONOB. 474. Romulus Augustus, commonly styled AUGUSTULUS, the last, and merely nominal emperor, was deposed by Odoacer, 475. The Roman empire in the West is usually considered as ended at this date.

DIVISION VI.

BYZANTINE EMPIRE.

At the death of Theodosius I., A.D. 395, the empire was divided between his two sons, Arcadius and Honorius, the former ruling at Constantinople, the latter at Rome. Although no formal or absolute separation between the East and West was intended by this arrangement (for it had often been practiced before), yet such was the ultimate effect. It is not easy to mark the extent of the later Roman empire, either as to time or territory. Even after the imperial line in the West had ceased (A.D. 475), there was more or less recognition of the sovereign authority of the emperor at Constantinople, by the barbaric kings, and the popes, in Italy; and Justinian (A.D. 534–553), by his renowned generals, Belisarius and Narses, vindicated his title to that region, and to Africa. The crowning of Charlemagne at Rome, A.D. 800, and his proclamation as Emperor of the West* by Pope Leo III., seems to be the most decided limitation of the power of the Eastern emperor, and a proper commencement for the distinctive name of "*Byzantine*," "*Eastern*," or "*Lower*" Empire. But as the authority of the monarch at Constantinople was, on the whole, but feebly acknowledged, and more feebly felt, west of the Adriatic Sea, from the time of the division as above stated (395), there is a propriety in dating the Byzantine empire from that event; and a mixture of unfitness in still designating it, as all historians and numismatists do, as the Roman empire. This is especially realized as we descend to the last days of the Greek dynasty, and find scarce any part of the immense dominion left, except its trembling capital. But the conquest of Constantinople by the Turks, in 1453, affords an undisputed resting-point.

---

* This title has precariously descended almost to our own day. When the Emperor of Germany changed his title to Emperor of Austria (A.D. 1804), he dropped the old honorary suffix, *Romanus Imperator*. But historians scarcely speak of the Roman empire as properly continued under the successors of Charlemagne.

The coins of this division, if of no interest as works of art further than to prove the extreme degeneracy of taste and skill, are equal to any, as curiosities, and as illustrations of history.

Although the series takes in eight centuries of time, there is a general similarity of tone, especially if we start with the second Theodosius; so that one may be sure, by a casual glance at any of them, that it is Byzantine, and not Roman proper. However, they fairly admit of subdivision, and it is not a forced coincidence, which places the line at A.D. 811, about midway in the whole series.*

Previous to Michael I. (811–813), we have these peculiarities. On the gold and silver (there is but little of the latter) we have the emperor, head and bust, and always front face; on the reverse, the monotonous and unjustifiable VICTORIA AUG., at least not justifiable in any other sense than that the Augustus had triumphed over his predecessor. Within this legend, on a high throne, the cross stands conspicuous and erect. As for the copper coins, there is not much variation from the colossal and unintelligible M, K, or I, occupying the field of the reverse. Occasionally, when the imperial power was divided, a number of heads or figures were crowded upon the coin, on both sides.

But from the accession of Michael Rhangabe, we observe a new phase in the coinage, and a more decided display of religious sentiment. The bust or full length of Christ, signalized by the nimbus, and legend, IHSЧS XPISTЧS, NICA(tor), or REX REGNANTIЧM, or bASILEЧS bASILE(on), expressive of his pre-eminence as Conqueror, and King of kings, generally occupies one side of the gold and silver coins; on the reverse, the emperor is sometimes alone, and sometimes shares the space with the Virgin, MHP ΘΨ, (Mater Theou,

* That is, by leaving off at about A.D. 1300; there are no coins certainly known later than Andronicus II., who reigned 1282–1328.

The coincidence is more remarkable in another respect. The war against the use of images, which agitated both church and state from the time of the edict of Leo the Isaurian, 726, was brought to an end about 800, by the defeat of the Iconoclasts. The renewed worship or veneration of images was, no doubt, one cause of the marked change in the devices of the coinage, as stated farther on.

"Mother of God,") the two holding aloft, and between them, the standard of the cross. The imperial heads or faces, which in the former series seemed to follow the usual human outline, are here fantastically compressed into triangles or trapeziums. As we near the crusading era, the figures are nearly all at full length, standing or sitting. The legends also have completed the transition from the Latin language to the Greek. On the copper, the vast letters M, K, etc., are nearly superseded by inscriptions, to the same effect as above cited, occupying the field. It is remarkable, however, that while the reading on the copper is quite conspicuous and distinct, that of the gold and silver is so affectedly minute, that a modern eye can scarcely make it out without a magnifier.

(It should be here explained, that we continue the use of the numismatic term *brass*, in the lower coinage, although *copper* seems to be more proper, in every case.)

8. Gold, of ARCADIUS, Emperor. 395–408. VICTORIA AUGGG.

9. S. Rev. VIRTUS ROMANORUM.

10, 11. Middle brass. GLORIA ROMANORUM.

12. Small brass. VIRTUS EXERCITI.

13. Very small brass. SALUS REIPUB.

15. Gold, of THEODOSIUS II., son of Arcadius, and Emperor. 408–450. IMP. XXXXII. COS. XVII. P. P.

16. Small brass. CONCORDIA AUGG. Expresses a season of harmony between the Eastern and Western emperors.

17. Gold, of MARCIAN. 450–457. Reverse as No. 8.

18. G. LEO I. 457–474. The usual reverse. VICTORIA AUGG.

19. G. ZENO. 474–491.

20. G. ANASTASIUS. 491–518.

22. Large brass. M.

23. Middle brass. K. E.

24. Small brass. K.

25. Very small brass. I. By this series, the mysterious initials, already mentioned, would seem to stand for denominations of coin; but some subsequent instances rather oppose this inference.

26. Gold, of JUSTIN I. 518–527.

27, 28, 29. Large and middle brasses, of the same.

30. Gold, of JUSTINIAN I. 527–565. (Died at the age of 82.)

31, 32, 33. Large and middle brasses of the same; ANNO XIIII–XVI–XVIIII. They do not answer to our preconceptions of the era of the Civil Code and Pandects.

34. Small silver coin, of GELIMAR, king of the Vandals in Africa. (His kingdom was overthrown, and himself captured, by Belisarius, A.D. 534. He was honorably treated, and provided for, by Justinian.) D. N. RX. GELIMA. Head of the prince.

36. Gold, of JUSTIN II. 565–578.

37, 38. Large brass, of Justin, with Sophia, empress.

39. Large brass, of TIBERIUS II. ANNO VI. 578–582.

40. Gold, of MAURICE. 582–602.

41, 42. Large and small brass, of the same. ANNO X.–IIII.

43. Gold, of FOCAS (as it is on the coins), usually spelt Phocas. 602–610.

44. Large brass, of the same.

45. Middle brass, Phocas, and Leontia, empress.

46. Gold, of HERACLIUS I. 610–640. Heads of the emperor and son.

47. Large silver, of the same. (Weighs 100 grs.)

48, 49, 50. Large and middle brasses, of the same.

51. Silver, of CONSTANS II. 641–668.

52. Gold, of CONSTANTINE IV., surnamed POGONATUS, on account of his beard, which is conspicuous. 668–685.

53. Small brass, of the same.

54. Gold, of JUSTINIAN II. 685–711. The loss of his nose, with his throne, occasioned the surname of RHINOTMETUS.

57. Gold, of ANASTASIUS II. 713–716.

58, 59, 60. Small brasses, of LEO III., the Isaurian. 717–741.

61. Gold, of MICHAEL I. Rhangabe. 811–813. Rev. Head of Christ; IHSYS XRISTOS.

62. Pale gold; the same head, with IC. XC.

63. Large brass, of MICHAEL II., with Theophilus. 820–829.

64. Gold, of THEOPHILUS. 829–842. Rev. Heads of his sons.

65, 66. Large brass, of the same.

67. Gold, of BASIL I. 866–886. Rev. Figure of Christ, sitting; IHS XRS REX REGNATIHM. (The spelling of those times was not critically exact.)

68. Middle brass, of Basil and his sons.

69, 70. Middle brass, of LEO VI., surnamed the Wise. 886–911. Rev. LEOh Eh θEO BASILEυS ROMEOh. "Leo, in (or under) God, King of the Romans." *Basileus* was then considered an equivalent to *Imperator* or *Autocrator*.

71. Middle brass, of Leo and his brother Alexander. LEOh s. ALEXAhGROS (so spelt) BASIL. ROMEOh. This, as in the previous coin, is an inscription, spread over the whole reverse of the piece.

72. Gold. of ROMANUS I., with his son Christophorus. 919–944.

73. Gold, of CONSTANTINE X., with his son Romanus II. 911–959. A part of the time he was colleague with Romanus I.

74. Middle brass, of Constantine alone.

75. Same, of Constantine, and his mother Zoë.

76. Same, of ROMANUS II. 959–963. Reverse as No. 69.

78. Gold, of NICEPHORUS II. PHOCAS. 963–969.

79, 80, 81. Large brasses, of JOHN ZIMISCES. 969–975. Large inscriptions on the reverse, of "Jesus Christ, King of kings," with slight variety.

82. Same. IC. XC. NI KA., arranged in the four angles of a cross. "Jesus Christ, the Conqueror."

85. Large thin silver, of CONSTANTINE XII., Monomachus. 1042–1054. Rev. The Virgin standing, with uplifted hands.

86. Gold, of ROMANUS IV. 1068–1071. The emperor and Virgin standing side by side; the latter with her hand on the emperor's head. Rev. Christ, seated.

87. Gold, of the same, and nearly the same devices.

88. Pale gold, concave. Michael VII. 1071–1078.

89. Pale gold. NICEPHORUS III. Botoniates. 1078–1081 The emperor at full length, holding the globe and labarum.

90. Same, in gold, except the emperor in *half* length.

92. Gold, of ALEXIUS I. Comnenus. 1081–1118. AΛEXIω ΔECπOT. Tω. KOMNHMO. "Alexius Comnenus, despot."

93. Gold, of the same. Rev. Figure of Christ, seated, as if in the act of teaching; holding in one hand the Sacred Scriptures, the other hand uplifted. IC. XC.

95. Gold, of JOHN II. Comnenus, surnamed the Handsome. 1118–1143.

96. Gold, of MANUEL I. Comnenus, surnamed Porphyrogenitus, "born to the purple." 1143–1180. (It was somewhat a rare honor to be born to a reigning emperor, and actually to succeed him, the two conditions requisite to this title, which occurs in several instances.)

97, 98. Silver, of the same.

99, 100. Small brass, of the same.

101. Middle brass, ANDRONICUS I. 1183–1185.

102. Small brass, ISAAC II., Angelus. 1185–1203.

103, 104. Coins in middle brass, bearing the head of Christ, with IC. XC. on one side, and an ornamented cross on the other; they are believed to be of the brief dynasty of Latin princes, or Crusaders, who turned aside from their way to Jerusalem, A.D. 1203, to capture Constantinople. They retained the Byzantine empire, or a large part of it, near sixty years. The throne was restored to the Greek dynasty, by the victories of Michael VIII. Paleologus, A.D. 1261.

106. Pale gold, of ANDRONICUS II. Paleologus. 1282–1328. Rev. The Virgin, with uplifted hands, surrounded by the walls of Constantinople.

107, 108, 109. Small silver, doubtfully ascribed to John V. and John VIII., the latter of whom died A.D. 1448, five years before the final triumph of the Turks.

113. A leaden seal of the Byzantine empire.

MODERN COINS.

UNITED STATES.

THE second general division of this work, and, in fact, the main portion thereof, will embrace the "modern coins of the world." And first, we propose to give a chapter upon the coins of the United States. In so doing we shall not confine ourselves to a mere catalogue, as is the case in other portions of this work, but shall endeavor to present a brief history of the coinage, together with other matters of interest pertaining thereto.

In order to accomplish this object in a satisfactory manner, it will be necessary to give, by way of preface, a short history of the currency and coins of the American Colonies. In the latter part of the subject we shall confine our remarks to the coins contained in the cabinet, except in so far as is necessary to elucidate the subject under consideration.

During the infancy of the American Colonies, their currency was as multifarious in its character as in the ancient time of which we have made mention in the introduction. There was, however, this difference between the ancients and the colonists: while the former made use of cattle and commodities as currency, from the fact that they were too barbarous to appreciate a more refined mode of conducting their mercantile transactions, our ancestors of the "New World" were driven to that resort because they were *unable* to obtain a currency of a more convenient character. From the time that our Pilgrim fathers landed upon this continent, they were treated by the home government more as enemies and exiles than as loyal subjects. So far from throwing about them its protecting influence, and thereby building up the commerce of the Colonies, the home government began and continued the policy of throwing all the obstacles in its power in the way of their commercial prosperity. No coinage for circulation in the Colonies was provided for, and the exercise of the right of coinage by the colonists themselves was treated as a treasonable usurpation of the royal prerogative.

For these reasons, our ancestors were driven to the necessity of using the produce of the soil and the stock from their pastures as their media of exchange. Peltry also was one of the first, and for many years the principal article of currency. It was offered in great abundance by the Indians, who were very ready to barter it for "beads, knives, hatchets, and blankets, and especially for powder, shot, guns, and strong water."*

In most of the Colonies *wampum* was extensively used; and was frequently paid into the treasury in payment of taxes. In the Colony of Massachusetts, the cattle and products of the land were received at the treasury for a like purpose, as appears from various enactments of the Colonial Assembly. Thus in 1636, an act was passed relative to a tax assessed upon the several towns: "It is agreed that good merchantable corne shall passe for payment in this rate at 5*s*. the bushell, to bee so delivered at Boston at the appointment of the Treasurer to bee called for when the Treasurer please." And again, in May, 1645, in regard to another tax, the following record occurs: "This levy of £616 15*s*, each towne's proportion is, as above expressed. It is determined yt (that) each towne shall pay ye one halfe of their rate to ye treasurer within three months, in cattle, to be valued by three men, indifferently chosen by ye treasurer and owner thereof, in beaver, money, wheate at 4*s*, barley at 4*s*, rye at 3*s*. 6*d*, pease 3*s*. 6*d*, corne 2*s*. 8*d*, and ye other halfe at or before ye last of ye first month next."† Musket balls were also current; and were made so, in Massachusetts, by an order of the court, as follows: "It is likewise ordered, that muskett bulletts of a full boare shall passe currantly for a farthing a peece, provided that noe man be compelled to take above 12*d* att a tyme of them."

* Felt, Massachusetts currency.

† Felt, from Massachusetts Colonial records.

In some of the other Colonies, especially Virginia and Maryland, tobacco was used as a medium of exchange, as well as the articles above enumerated; and "in the first days of the 'Old Dominion,' tobacco would purchase the *most valuable commodity.* From 100 to 150 lbs. of it bought many a good wife."*

The earliest coinage for America is said to have been executed in 1612,† when the Virginia Company was endeavoring to establish a Colony on the *Summer Islands* (the Bermudas.) This coin was of the denomination of a shilling, and was struck in brass. On the obverse was a Boar, and the legend, "SOMMER ISLAND," with the value "XII." The reverse presented a ship, under sail, firing a gun.

MASSACHUSETTS.

In considering the coins contained in the cabinet collection, our attention is first arrested by the "pine-tree" money of Massachusetts. This coinage was instituted by the Colonial Assembly in 1652, after the fall of Charles I. and the consequent establishment of the Commonwealth, with Cromwell at its head. The mint building was ordered to be erected upon the land of John Hull, in the City of Boston, by an act passed on the 27th day of May, 1652; and was to be sixteen feet square by ten feet high. The before-mentioned John Hull, who appears to have been the *spirit* of the enterprise, was appointed by the same act to be the mint master; and it was "enacted by the authoritie of this Court, that all psons whatsoeuer haue libertie to bring in vnto the Mint howse, at Boston, all bullion, plate, or Spanish coyne, there to be melted, and brought to the alloy of sterling siluer by John Hull, master of the sd Mint‡ & his sworne officers & by him to be coyned into twelue pence, six pence & three pence peeces, which shalbe for forme flatt, & square on the sides & stamped on the one side, with NE, and on the other side with XII*d*, VI*d*, & III*d*, according to the value of each peece, together with

* Felt, from Massachusetts Colonial records. † Hickcox.

‡ John Hull was not alone in this enterprise, but had associated with him Robert Saunders, to which the court assented, and the oath of office was administered to them jointly.

a priuie marke, which shalbe appoynted euery three monethes by the Gouernor, & Knowne only to him & the sworne officers of the Mint." * * * * * * "And the Mint Master for himselfe & officers, for theire paynes and labour in meltinge, refineinge, and coyninge, is allowed by this Court to take one shillinge out of euery twenty shilling wch he shall stamp as aforesd." These pieces, as a reference to the annexed engraving will show, were mere *planchets* stamped with the letters, etc. provided for in the above act; leaving a fine margin for the practice of clipping, which the colonists were not long in taking advantage of. Consequently it became necessary, on the nineteenth October following, to pass a second act for the remedy of this evil, by virtue of which shillings, sixpences, and threepences were coined of the following type. On the obverse a pine-tree, inclosed by a double ring, containing the legend, "MASATHUSETS IN;" and, on the reverse, a double ring as on the obverse, containing the legend, "NEW ENGLAND, AN. DOM.," with the date in figures, and the denomination occupying the field within the minor circle. (See Plate I. No. 1.) Ten years subsequent, in May, 1662, a twopenny piece was added to the coinage by an order of the court, which was of the same type as the larger coins. (See Plate I. No. 2.)

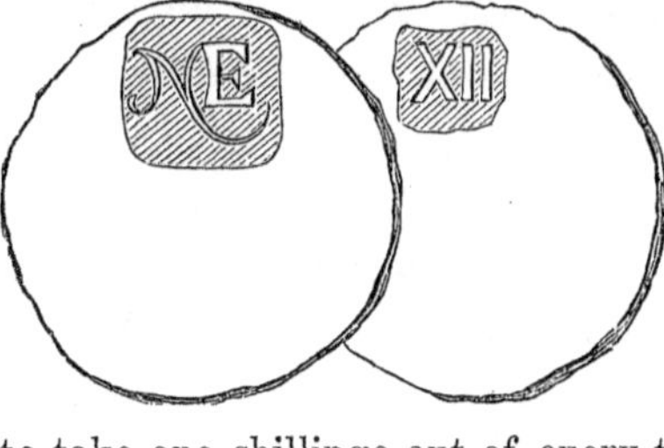

This coinage was not discontinued until 1686; yet they appear to have continued the use of the same date, the shillings, sixpences, and threepences, all bearing the date 1652, while the twopenny pieces are all dated 1662. This fact is mentioned in a report made by the officers of the London Mint to the Commissioners of the Royal Exchequer, relative to the moneys of Massachusetts, in the following words: "Though they have continued this unwarrantable way of coyning moneys ever since ye year 1652, yet there is no alteration of date appears upon the coyne, but the same date, viz: 1652, as at the first coyning of them."*

After the suppression of their mint, the Colony of Massachusetts

* Felt.

issued no more coins until after the establishment of the Confederacy, which will be noticed presently.

MARYLAND.

The silver coins of Lord Baltimore, Lord Proprietor of Maryland, were the shilling, sixpence, and fourpence, or groat. The dies for this coinage were prepared in London, and specimens of the coins which he proposed to put in circulation were sent over by Lord Baltimore to his brother, Philip Calvert, and to the governor and council. These specimens, together with his lordship's letter, were laid before the council on the "3d of March, 1659–60," but were not adopted until the following year, on account of the troubles occasioned by the attempt of Governor Fendall to revolutionize the Colony.

The coins are all of the same type. On the obverse they present a profile bust of Lord Baltimore, with the legend, "CÆCILIUS DNS: TERRÆ: MARIÆ & CT." (Cecilius, Lord of Maryland, etc.) On the reverse are the family arms of Lord Baltimore, the value, and the legend, "CRESCITE ET MULTIPLICAMINI." (Increase and multiply.) (See Plate I. No. 3.) These coins are all exceedingly rare. There was also a copper coin struck at the same time, (not in the collection,) the obverse of which was the same as the silver; but on the reverse it had a crown beneath two flags, and the legend, "DENARIUM TERRÆ MARIÆ."

VIRGINIA.

In the time of George III. a copper coinage was executed, which was intended for circulation in Virginia. Of this there were two sizes: one about the diameter of the English half penny, and another somewhat smaller. The obverse presented a head of the king *laureated*, with the legend, "GEORGIUS III. REX." On the reverse, the arms of Great Britain, and the Electoral Dominions, with "VIRGINIA," and the date "1773." These coins were finely executed. The head is evidently copied from the pattern guinea of 1772, which was the finest specimen of engraving exhibited upon any coin of that reign. (See Plate I. Nos. 8 and 9.)

ROSA AMERICANA.

In the reign of George I. coins were issued by order of the British government, which are believed to be the only coins ever struck by that authority for general circulation in the American Colonies. These coins, popularly known as the "Rosa Americanas," were made of a mixed metal, resembling brass. They were first issued in 1722, and are of three sizes, the largest being about the size of a half crown; the second rather smaller than the English half penny; and the third about the size of the farthing.

Those struck with the date 1722 have on the obverse a bust of the king *laureated,* and on the larger pieces the legend stands, "GEORGIUS D. G. MAG. BRI. FRA. ET HIB. REX.;" while on the smaller pieces it is "GEORGIUS DEI GRATIA REX." On the reverse is a double rose: legend, "ROSA AMERICANA, 1722;" and on a scroll, the inscription, "UTILE DULCI." On the smaller pieces the latter inscription forms part of the legend. Those bearing the date 1723 have the rose crowned. (See Plate II. Nos. 5 and 6.)

COINS OF THE PERIOD OF THE CONFEDERATION.

During the period of the Confederacy, which preceded the adoption of the Constitution, extending from 1778 to 1787, the right of coining money was vested not only in the Federal Congress, but in the different States. Many of them took advantage of their right by issuing copper coins—cents and half cents.

VERMONT issued a grant in June, 1785, to Reuben Harmon, Jr., giving him the exclusive right to coin copper money within that State, for the space of two years, from the first of July following. Under this grant, Harmon established a mint at Rupert, and issued cents of the following description: The obverse bore a device representing the sun rising from behind a range of hills, with a plow beneath. Legend. "VERMONTENSIUM RESPUBLICA, 1786;" and on the reverse an eye, surrounded by diverging rays and thirteen stars. Legend. "QUARTA DECIMA STELLA."* (See Plate I. No. 6.)

---

* Harmon afterward changed the type of his coins, as follows: Obv. A laureated bust, facing to the right. Legend. "AUCTORI(tate) VERMON(tensium).'

CONNECTICUT issued a grant, on the 20th October, 1785, to Samuel Bishop, Joseph Hopkins, James Hillhouse, and John Goodrich, authorizing them to coin coppers to an amount not exceeding ten thousand pounds. This grant was limited to the term of five years. The mint, however, only continued in operation three years. These have, on the obverse, a *laureated* bust adorned with drapery, and the legend, "AUCTORI CONNEC." On the reverse is a female figure seated, holding in the right hand an olive branch, and in the left a staff. Legend. "INDE ET LIB." The date occupies the *exergue*. (See Plate I. No. 5.)

NEW JERSEY, following the example of the two preceding States, issued a grant in June, 1786, to Walter Mould, Thomas Goodsby, and Albion Cox, authorizing them to coin copper cents to the amount of £10,000. There appears to have been some disagreement between the parties, which resulted in a dissolution of the partnership; for we find that, on the twenty-second of October of the same year, a second act was passed by the Assembly, authorizing Thomas Goodsby and Albion Cox to coin *two-thirds* of the amount contemplated in the preceding act. Thus two mints were established. These establishments appear to have continued in operation during the years 1786, 1787, and 1788. There was a large emission of cents of these dates, and they are now quite common. The type was as follows: Obv. A horse's head and a plow, with the legend, "NOVA CÆSAREA," and the date. Rev. A heart-shaped shield, and the legend, "E PLURIBUS UNUM." (See Plate I. No. 7.) There are almost countless varieties of this coinage, but the types are not materially different.

MASSACHUSETTS passed an act on the 17th October, 1786, providing for the establishment of a mint within the Commonwealth of Massachusetts, for the coinage of gold, silver, and copper; and in the spring of 1787 Joshua Witheral was authorized to provide for the necessary buildings and machinery. The first regular issue of copper coins did not take place until 1788,* but specimens are frequently found bearing the date 1787. The latter were, probably, trial pieces, struck during the time that the machinery and dies were being pre-

---

Rev. A female seated, holding an olive branch in the right, and supporting a staff with the left hand. Beneath is the date, "1788." Legend. "INDE ET LIB."

* Hickcox and Felt.

pared. There were no gold or silver coins issued, although the act contemplated the coinage of such pieces. The copper coins issued were the cent and half cent, of the same type. The cent has upon its obverse the American eagle, grasping in the right talon a bundle of arrows, and in its left an olive branch; upon its breast is a shield, inscribed with the word "CENT." Legend. "MASSACHUSETTS," and the date. On the reverse is an Indian of full length, with his bow and arrow; near his forehead appears a single star. Legend. "COMMONWEALTH." The half cents are the same, except that the shield has the inscription, "HALF CENT." (See Plate II. Nos. 1 and 2.) This coinage ceased upon the adoption of the Constitution, or at least very soon after.*

Before leaving the subject of the colonial coins, it will be necessary to notice several specimens of private coinage. These were issued by various individuals, both in this country and abroad, during the war of the Revolution, and after. As they are of a general character, we shall notice them in the order of date.

1781. North American Token. Obv. A female seated, with her left hand resting upon a harp. "NORTH AMERICAN TOKEN."...... "1781." Rev. A ship under canvas, "COMMERCE." (See No. 33, *Division V.*)

1783. In 1783, a silversmith, named J. Chalmers, of Annapolis, Maryland, commenced the coinage of shillings, sixpences, and threepences. The shilling has, on the obverse, two hands clasped in friendship, and inclosed in a wreath, with the legend, "I. CHALMERS, ANNAPOLIS." The field, on the reverse, is divided into two sections, in one of which is a serpent, and in the other, two birds holding a branch in their beaks. The legend is "ONE SHILLING."......"1783." (See Plate I. No. 4.)

The sixpence has, on the obverse, a star within a wreath of laurel, and the legend, "I. CHALMERS, ANNAPOLIS;" and on the reverse, two hands clasped in friendship, upon a cross *potent*, and the legend, "I. C. SIXPENCE. 1783." (See No. 17, *Division V.*)

---

* It is said that coinage was continued, until the copper on hand at the time the Constitution was ratified was disposed of.

The threepence has, on the obverse, two hands clasped in friendship, and the legend, "I. CHALMERS, ANNAP^{S} *;". and on the reverse, an olive branch inclosed in a wreath of laurel, and the legend, "THREE-PENCE. 1783." (See No. 18, *Division V.*)

1783. A cent. Obv. An eye, surrounded by diverging rays and a circle of thirteen stars. Legend. "NOVA CONSTELLATIO." Rev. The initials "U. S." inclosed in a wreath of laurel. Legend. "LIBERTAS JUSTITIA."......"1783." (See Plate II. No. 3.) Felt speaks of this piece as having been current in Massachusetts, as though it were coined in that Colony, but does not say so distinctly, merely conveying that idea by implication. Its origin is unknown.

1785. Apparently a guinea, restruck. Obv. A female seated upon a box of merchandise; in her left hand she extends a pair of scales, and supports with her right a staff, with a flag partially unfurled, and surmounted by a liberty-cap. Legend. "IMMUNE COLUMBIA." The date, "1785," beneath. Rev. An eye, surrounded by diverging rays and a circle of thirteen stars, "NOVA CONSTELLATIO." (See No. 36, *Division V.*)

1787. New York doubloon. Obv. "The arms of the State of New York, as found on the great seal of 1777, viz.: The sun rising from behind the hills, with a representation of the sea in front;"* beneath is the name "BRASHER." Legend. "NOVA EBORACA COLUMBIA EXCELSIOR." Rev. A spread-eagle grasping a bundle of thirteen arrows in the left talon, and an olive branch in the right; upon its breast is the United States shield. Legend. "UNUM E PLURIBUS."......"1787." This is said to have been "struck in New York by EPHRAIM BRASHER, a goldsmith, whose place of business was No. 1 Cherry Street."† (See No. 37, *Division V.*)

1791. Kentucky cent. Obv. A hand holding a scroll, upon which is inscribed, "OUR CAUSE IS JUST." Legend. "UNANIMITY IS THE STRENGTH OF SOCIETY." Rev. A triangle of fifteen stars, connected together with small rings or links, and surrounded by diverging rays. On the stars are engraved the initials of fifteen States. Legend. "E PLURIBUS UNUM." Mr. Hickcox states that this piece was struck

* Hickcox. † Ibid.

in Lancaster, England, in 1791, and is called "the Kentucky cent," from the fact that the star designated K., for Kentucky, is placed at the top of the triangle. (See Plate II. No. 4.)

FEDERAL COINAGE.

During the interval which elapsed from the establishment of the Confederacy in 1778 to the adoption of the Constitution in 1788, coins were issued not only by the several States, but a large amount of base coppers were emitted by private persons, while others were foisted upon the community by speculators from abroad. These issues had a deleterious effect upon the condition of our currency; and the attention of Congress was early called to the subject of a national coinage, as a remedy for the existing evils. Another, and probably a greater difficulty, existed, in the fact that the *pound* of account, which was at first the same as the pound sterling of England, had become much depreciated in value, by reason of the excessive issues of *paper;* and, as these issues were much larger in some Colonies than in others, the pound was differently rated in the different localities.

NOTE:—In expressing sums of money, in writing or print, the people of this country have adopted a mark called the "*dollar sign*" ($). The origin of this mark is enveloped in considerable obscurity. We have little doubt, however, that it was intended to mean "pieces of eight." The Spanish dollar, from which our unit was more immediately derived, consists of eight reals (the real being the unit of Spanish moneys); and the common name of the Spanish dollar (at home) is "piece of eight," or still more commonly, "*eights;*" the mark being merely a figure 8 crossed by the plural sign.

This sign ($) is also used in Portugal for expressing *millreis;* and, from this fact, some may doubt the correctness of the foregoing explication; but as the *millreis* is nearly equivalent to the old Spanish dollar, and as the Portuguese have always been very intimately connected, through their commerce, with the Western world, and especially with the West India Islands, it is easy to see how a sign, which has long been so familiar to the trading community throughout the Western hemisphere, could have been adopted by that country.

As early as 1782 the preliminary steps were taken toward the introduction of a national coinage. "Congress* directed the Financier of the Confederation, Robert Morris, to lay before them his views upon the subject of coins and currency. The report was presented in January, 1782, and is stated by Mr. Jefferson to have been the work of the Assistant Financier, Gouverneur Morris. The three grand benefits which have been secured to the people of this country—the establishment of a uniform national currency; the rejection of mere moneys of account, or rather making them the same with real moneys; and the adoption of a decimal notation—all seem to have occupied the mind of the Assistant Financier. He first labored to harmonize the moneys of the States, and found that the $\frac{1}{1440}$th part of a dollar (Spanish) was a common divisor for the various currencies. Starting with this fraction as his unit, he proposed the following table of moneys:—

"Ten units to be equal to one penny.

"Ten pence one bill.

"Ten bills one dollar, (about two-thirds of the Spanish dollar.)

"Ten dollars one *crown*.†

"The report contains this observation: 'Although it is not absolutely necessary, yet it is very desirable, that money should be increased in a decimal ratio; because by that means, all calculations of interest, exchange, insurance and the like, are rendered much more simple and accurate, and of course more within the power of the great mass of the people.'"

A large amount of copper, belonging to the Federal Government, was then lying at Philadelphia, and Mr. Morris assured Congress that if this plan was adopted, a mint could immediately be estab-

---

* The portions of this article embraced in quotation marks are compiled from the revised edition of the "Manual of Coins and Bullion," issued in 1842 by Messrs. Eckfeldt & Dubois.

† "This last coin was to be of gold. He apologized for introducing the name of *crown*, in a country where that emblem had lost favor, by stating that his project was to have on the coin the representation of an Indian, with a bow in his left hand, and thirteen arrows in the right, with his right foot on a crown." (*Sparks's Life of Gouverneur Morris*, i. 273.)

lished, as the necessary machinery could easily be constructed, and persons found who could carry on the operations.

"The subject was discussed repeatedly in Congress, but no further step was taken until 1784, when Mr. Jefferson, on behalf of a committee appointed for the purpose, brought in a report, disagreeing with that of the Financier, except as to the decimal system. The following remarks occur in this document: 'The most easy ratio of multiplication and division, is that of ten. Every one knows the facility of decimal arithmetic. Every one remembers, that when learning money arithmetic, he used to be puzzled with adding the farthings, taking out the fours, and carrying them on; adding the pence, taking out the twelves, and carrying them on; adding the shillings, taking out the twenties, and carrying them on; but when he came to the pounds, where he had only tens to carry forward, it was easy and free from error. The bulk of mankind are schoolboys through life. Certainly, in all cases, where we are free to choose between easy and difficult modes of operation, it is most rational to choose the easy The Financier, therefore, in his report, well proposes that our coins should be in decimal proportions to one another.'

"He found fault with the *unit* of Mr. Morris, first, on account of its diminutive size: 'A horse or bullock of eighty dollars value would require a notation of six figures, to wit, 115,200 units;' secondly, because of its want of correspondence in value with any known coins. In lieu of this the Spanish dollar was proposed, as being of convenient size, capable of easy actual division, and familiar to the minds of the people. It was added, that the course of our commerce would bring us more of this than of any other foreign coin; and besides, the dollar was already as much referred to, as a measure of value, as the respective provincial pounds. Upon this basis, it was proposed to strike four coins, viz. :—

"A golden piece, of the value of ten dollars.

"A dollar in silver.

"A tenth of a dollar, also in silver.

"A hundredth of a dollar, in copper.

"The Assistant Financier conceded something to Mr. Jefferson's views, but adherred to the main principles of his own scheme. It would be out of place to enter into the arguments offered on behalf of each proposition; it is sufficient to say, that Congress, in 1785, adopted Mr. Jefferson's report, and in the following year made legal provision for a coinage upon that basis."

Notwithstanding the fact that Congress had proceeded thus far in the establishment of a national mint, there appears to have been some difficulty in bringing the project to a practical issue; and in 1787, we find the Board of Treasury reporting several propositions from private coiners for the coinage of copper. These proposals were referred to an appropriate committee, who reported in favor of the proposal of Mr. James Jarvis; whereupon Congress instructed the Board to contract with Mr. Jarvis for 300 tons of copper coin, which were to conform to the standard adopted in the report of Mr. Jefferson. The devices and inscriptions for this coinage were also regulated by an act of Congress, as follows:—

1787, July 6. "*Resolved*, That the Board of Treasury direct the contractor for the copper coinage to stamp on one side of each piece the following device, viz.: Thirteen circles linked together, a small circle in the middle, with the motto, 'UNITED STATES,' round it; and in the center, the words, 'WE ARE ONE;' on the other side of the same piece the following devices, viz.: A dial with the hours expressed on the face of it; a meridian sun above, on one side of which is to be the word 'FUGIO,' and on the other the year in figures, '1787.'" The words, "MIND YOUR BUSINESS," inscribed beneath the dial, which have gained for this piece the name of "Franklin Cent," appear to have been added without the authority of Congress; and, indeed, some pretend to say that it was done at the suggestion of "Poor Richard" himself, and hence they derive its popular name. The principal foundation, however, for this opinion, as well as the name applied to the coin, appears to be that "it sounds like him." (See Plate II. No. 7.) A portion of these coppers is said to have been coined at the mint in New Haven, of which Mr. Jarvis was a partner; and the remainder at the mint of Mr. Harmon, at Rupert, in Vermont, whither the dies were transported by one Abel Buel, who was also a partner in the New Haven mint.

NATIONAL COINAGE.

The Constitution of the United States was received by Congress in September, 1787, and was soon after submitted to the several States, who were represented in the Convention in which that instrument was framed, for their ratification. In this instrument it is expressly provided that Congress shall have power "To coin money, regulate the value thereof, and of foreign coin," (Sec. VIII.;) and a subsequent paragraph (Sec. X.) prohibited the exercise of a like power by any State.

The attention of the first Congress, which commenced its session on the 4th March, 1789, was so much engrossed in carrying out the designs of the Constitution in the formation of a Federal Government, that little attention was paid to the subject of a national mint. A proposition, however, was made by a foreigner, Mr. John Mitchell, for the coinage of coppers, for circulation in this country. This proposal was referred by Congress to Mr. Jefferson, who reported in the following year against it. Immediately after the report of Mr. Jefferson, Congress, on the 15th of April, 1790, instructed the Secretary of the Treasury, Alexander Hamilton, to prepare a plan for the establishment of a mint. Mr. Hamilton made a very elaborate and careful report, in which, accepting of the dollar as a unit, he proposed the following coins: A *gold* piece, equal in weight and value to ten units or dollars; a *gold* piece, equal to a tenth part of the former, and which shall be a unit or dollar; a *silver* piece, which shall also be a unit or dollar; a *silver* piece, which shall be in weight and value a tenth part of the silver unit or dollar; a *copper* piece, which shall be of the value of the hundredth part of the dollar; a *copper* piece, which shall be half the value of the former.

This report was transmitted to Congress on the 28th of January, 1791, and on the third day of March of the same year the following resolution of the Senate and House of Representatives was passed. We give a *fac-simile* of the resolution, bearing the original signature of Jefferson, which is now in the possession of the Mint.

Congreſs of the United States:

AT THE THIRD SESSION,

Begun and held at the City of Philadelphia, on Monday the ſixth of December, one thouſand ſeven hundred and ninety.

RESOLVED *by the* SENATE *and* HOUSE *of* REPRESENTATIVES *of the United States of America in Congreſs aſſembled*, That a mint ſhall be eſtabliſhed under ſuch regulations as ſhall be directed by law.

Reſolved, That the Preſident of the United States be, and he is hereby authorized to cauſe to be engaged, ſuch principal artiſts as ſhall be neceſſary to carry the preceeding reſolution into effect, and to ſtipulate the terms and conditions of their ſervice, and alſo to cauſe to be procured ſuch apparatus as ſhall be requiſite for the ſame purpoſe.

FREDERICK AUGUSTUS MUHLENBERG,
Speaker of the Houſe of Repreſentatives.

JOHN ADAMS, *Vice-Preſident of the United States, and Preſident of the Senate.*

APPROVED, March the third, 1791.

GEORGE WASHINGTON, *Preſident of the United States.*

DEPOSITED among the ROLLS in the OFFICE of the SECRETARY of STATE.

TH: JEFFERSON, *Secretary of State.*

On the second of April of the following year (1792) the law "Establishing a Mint and Regulating the Coins of the United States" was approved by the President. This act provided first, that the officers to be employed at the Mint should be a Director, an Assayer, a Chief Coiner, an Engraver, and a Treasurer,* and that the coins to be struck should be as follows:—

"GOLD—The EAGLE, of ten dollars, to weigh 270 grains; the HALF and QUARTER in proportion; all of the fineness of 22 carats, or 917 thousandths.

"SILVER—The DOLLAR, of 100 cents, to weigh 416 grains; the HALF, QUARTER, TENTH or DIME, and TWENTIETH or HALF DIME, in proportion; the fineness to be 1485 parts in 1664, or 892.4 thousandths.

"COPPER—The CENT to weigh 264 grains; the HALF CENT in proportion."

Washington immediately proceeded to carry out the intention of this act, and as Philadelphia was then the seat of government, he provided for the erection of suitable buildings, by purchasing a lot of ground on Seventh Street, between Market and Arch Streets. At this time the lot in question was occupied by an old still-house and a frame tenement building. Having proceeded thus far, Washington, on the first of July following, appointed DAVID RITTENHOUSE to be "Director of the Mint." Rittenhouse very soon thereafter entered upon the duties of his office. The necessary men were employed, and on the nineteenth of July they commenced the work of removing the buildings which then occupied the lot, as appears by the following extract from the first record ever kept of the "*Mint operations*."†

"1792, July 19.—The following men began to work at taking down the still-house. To Saturday the 21:—

John Maul - - - - - - - - 3 days.
Jn°. Christian Glouse - - - - - - 3 dito.

---

* The office of "Melter and Refiner" was created by the act of March 3, 1795. (Secs. 1, 2, and 4, Stat. at Large, vol. i. p. 439, chap. 47.)

† This "book," which is a small memorandum, the cover of which (if it ever had one) has been removed by the "hand of time," is now among the archives of the Mint.

John Keyser - - - - - - - - 2 dito.
Nicolas Sinderling - - - - - 2 days.
John Biting - - - - - - - 1½ dito.
Mathias Sumer - - - - - - 1 dito.

"21.—8 carpenters at work this day taking down the still-house frame."

The foundation stone of the Mint was laid on the 31st of July, as appears from the following memorandum in the same book: "1792, July 31.—This day, about 10 o'clock in the forenoon, the foundation stone was laid for the Mint by David Rittenhouse, Esq[r]." As soon as the ceremony of laying the corner-stone was accomplished, the work upon the foundation commenced, as appears from the subjoined memorandum: "Four masons at work since 10 o'clock A.M.," which appears under the same date.

The foundation was completed and ready for the superstructure on Saturday the 25th of August following, and the framework was raised in the afternoon of that day. The work was rapidly pushed forward after this date; and the building was so far completed that the workmen commenced operations "in the shop," preparing the internal arrangements, such as bellows, furnaces, etc., on Friday, the seventh of September. On the Tuesday following, *six pounds of old copper* were purchased for the Mint, at "1s. 3*d*." per pound—this being the first "purchase of copper for coinage."

The coining presses, (three in number,) which they were obliged to import from abroad, arrived at the Mint on Friday, the twenty-first of September; and under date of twenty-fifth of September, the same book from which we have before quoted, states that "Flute began, after breakfast, triming the heavy press." These presses were put in operation in the beginning of October, and were used for striking the half dimes, of which Washington makes mention in his Annual Address to Congress, of the 6th November, 1792, as follows: "There has also been a small beginning in the coinage of half dimes; the want of small coins in circulation calling the first attention to them." Between this time and the close of the year 1792, several other pieces made their appearance from the Mint, all which will be noticed under the head of "*pattern pieces*," at the close of this article. The first *regular* return of coins from the Chief Coiner to the Treasurer of the Mint took place on the 1st of March, 1793, and consisted of eleven thousand one hundred and seventy-eight cents.

Before proceeding to give a history of the national coins, we will state the different changes in standard which have taken place since the act of 1792, as it will be much more satisfactory to the reader if that portion of the subject is presented to him at a glance.

GOLD.—The first change in the standard of the gold coinage took place in June, 1834. The original estimate by which the relative values of gold and silver coins were determined was based upon the supposition that gold was worth fifteen times as much as silver. This was found to be too low, at the market value, which, though always fluctuating, was nearer sixteen to one, upon a general average; consequently an act was passed on the 28th of June, 1834, reducing the standard of the gold coins. This act regulated the fineness of the gold to $899\frac{225}{1000}$ thousandths; the eagle to weigh 258 grains, the other pieces in proportion.

This standard of fineness was of short duration, the government having decided in January, 1837, to place the fineness of the coins, both gold and silver, upon the French basis—nine-tenths; consequently since that date the fineness of our gold coins has been 900 thousandths, the weight being the same as before.

SILVER.—The silver remained unchanged up to 1837, since which time the fineness is 900 thousandths, (except for the three-cent piece; from its first issue in 1851 to March, 1853, the fineness was 750 thousandths; weight $12\frac{3}{8}$ grains,) and the dollar of the weight $412\frac{1}{2}$ grains. The smaller pieces were in proportion of weight until March 3d, 1853, when the half dollar was reduced to 192 grains, (which is sixteen pennyweights, or eight-tenths of an ounce,) the smaller pieces in proportion, including the three-cent piece, which is on the same footing with the other silver pieces, both in weight and fineness.

COPPER.—The weight of the copper coins was reduced before any actual coinage had commenced. On the 14th of January, 1793, the weight of the cent was reduced to 208 grains, the half cent in proportion. A second reduction took place in 1795, and on the 26th of January, 1796, President Washington issued a proclamation, as he had been instructed to do by law, that "on account of the increased price of copper, and the expense of coinage," the cent had been reduced to 7 dwts., or 168 grains, the half cent in proportion.

By the act of February 21st, 1857, the composition of the cent was changed to an alloy of 88 parts copper and 12 parts nickel; and the standard of weight was reduced to 72 grains. The half cent was discontinued.

In giving a history of the coins of the United States we shall not go so far into the details of the subject as to take notice of the different "varieties" caused by cracked dies, the addition or omission of a leaf in the laurel, a larger or smaller letter in the legend or inscription, and the countless other minute and scarcely definable differences which are found, upon close inspection, to exist in the coins of nearly every year in which they have been issued. These little technicalities may be important to those collectors of coins who pay more regard to the selfish desire of *having something which no one else possesses*, than to the historic or artistic interest which attaches to a coin. We therefore confine ourselves to an illustration of those changes in the types of the coins which are of a material and definite character, and which are produced by design and not by accident, introducing, as we proceed, other facts in regard to the coinage which are more purely historic than the description, and which may be of interest, or tend to throw some light upon controverted points. And we may here remark that in the preparation of this article we have obtained (with some measure of labor) a large portion of our information from the private records of the Mint. We have had access to the "Bullion Journals," which exhibit every return of coins, from the Chief Coiner to the Treasurer of the Mint, which has taken place from the establishment thereof to the present time. We have also the annual reports of the Directors of the Mint, as inscribed upon the copy books, from the year 1795 down. So that, whenever we have departed from the popular belief, we have done so on what we are bound to consider the very best authority, placing no more reliance than is necessary in the surmises or generally accepted rumors of the day, as they are doubtful authority, and only to be accepted where it is impossible to obtain more reliable information.

8

In regard to the years in which the coinage of certain denominations have been omitted, we have prepared a table showing these omissions, and also exhibiting the number of pieces, in the several denominations of coin, which have been struck in every year since the establishment of the Mint in 1793, as far as practicable. There are several years in which dies were prepared and specimen coins struck, but not generally circulated, which do not appear upon the records. These pieces, as far as we have been able to ascertain them, have been set down in the table as "patterns," it being impossible to state the number coined.* The amounts set down are compiled from the Bullion Journal, and are consequently as correct as it is possible to make them.

Gold Coinage. The first deposit of gold bullion, for coinage, at the United States Mint, took place on the 12th day of February, 1795. The deposit was made by MOSES BROWN, merchant, of Boston, Mass., and consisted of gold ingots, amounting to two thousand two hundred and seventy-six dollars and twenty-two cents. ($2276.22.) Subsequently, before any coinage took place, several deposits were made.†

The first return of gold coins, from the Chief Coiner, was on the 31st day of July, 1795, and consisted of 744 half eagles. Eight deliveries of half eagles took place after this time and prior to the 17th of September, after which no more gold of this denomination was coined during the year. The first delivery of eagles was on the 22d of September, and consisted of 400 pieces, after which there were four other deliveries of various amounts. The entire amount of the coinage of both denominations will be seen by a reference to the table.

The eagle and its half of this emission were of the same type, as follows: Obv. A female bust, emblematic of Liberty, facing to the right, wearing a liberty-cap, with the hair flowing loosely about it. Above is inscribed the word "LIBERTY," and beneath the date

---

* As we have had only personal experience as our guide, there may be *patterns* in existence which do not appear in the table.

† The first deposit was paid in silver coins.

"1795." To the left of the effigy are ten stars in a line, and to the right five, fifteen in all. Rev. An eagle, with expanded wings, holding a laurel crown in its beak, and grasping a palm branch with both talons. Legend. "UNITED STATES OF AMERICA." (See Plate III. Nos. 1 and 2.)

1796. The gold coins of this year have sixteen stars upon the obverse, eight upon each side of the effigy.* The first coinage of quarter eagles took place in this year. The first issue, which was made on the twenty first of September, was of the same type as the eagle. The amount, however, was very small, being only 66 pieces. Subsequently the die was altered, and on the eighth of November there was a coinage of 897 pieces of the following type: Obverse same as the eagle. (A portion, and probably a small one, had no stars upon the obverse.) Rev. An eagle with raised wings, holding in its beak a scroll, incribed "E PLURIBUS UNUM," and grasping in the right talon a bundle of arrows, and in the left an olive branch. Upon its breast is the United States shield. Above the eagle are clouds, and sixteen stars. Legend. "UNITED STATES OF AMERICA." (See Plate III. Nos. 5 and 6.) The other pieces, the eagle and its half, were not altered until the following year (1797), when the reverse above described was adopted for those pieces likewise. (See Plate III. Nos. 3 and 4.)

No further changes were made in the devices on the gold coins until the year 1807. In this year it became apparent to the Director of the Mint (Robert Patterson) that the gentleman who was then engraver, Mr. Robert Scott,† "though indeed a meritorious and faithful officer, was yet so far advanced in life that he could not very long be expected to continue his labors;"‡ and, in anticipation of such a contingency, he employed Mr. John Reich, with the approbation of the President, to act as assistant engraver, and under date of April 2d, 1807, wrote to the President as follows: "Mr. Reich is now preparing a set of new dies, in which some improvements in the

---

* It was the original intention to add an additional star for every new State, but it was concluded to abandon the practice for fear that the stars would become too numerous.

† Mr. Scott was appointed in November, 1793.

‡ The Director's letter to the President, under date of March 25, 1807.

devices will be introduced, (adhering, however, to the strict letter of the law,) which, it is hoped, will meet with public approbation." Half and quarter eagles had already been issued of the old type. At precisely what time the new dies were put in use we cannot ascertain, but judge that it could not have been before the latter part of summer, consequently there was issued from the Mint about 33,496 half eagles, and 6812 quarter eagles, bearing the old devices. If our conclusions be correct, the first issue of coins of the new type took place on the 30th of September,* and consisted of 15,967 half eagles, after which there were five other deliveries of the same denomination. The new coinage was of the following description: Obv. A bust of Liberty, facing to the left, wearing a liberty-cap, upon the band of which is inscribed "LIBERTY." Beneath is the date "1807." To the left of the effigy are seven stars, and to the right six, thirteen in all. Rev. An eagle, with its wings expanded in flight, the United States shield upon its breast. In the left talon it grasps three arrows, and in the right an olive branch. Above floats a scroll, inscribed "E PLURIBUS UNUM." Beneath is the value, "5 D." Legend. "UNITED STATES OF AMERICA." There were no quarter eagles issued of the new pattern, as there was only one delivery of this denomination (on the fifteenth of February, as above,) during the year. The new quarter eagle appeared in the year 1808. (See Plate III. Nos. 7 and 8.)

In 1813, the appearance of the obverse of the half eagle, which was the only gold coin struck for a number of years, was slightly changed, the head of Liberty appearing in rather better flesh, and the thirteen stars arranged in a circle around the edge, instead of being at the sides of the effigy, as before; otherwise it continued the same.† (See Plate IV. No. 1.)

Upon the change of standard in 1834, another alteration took place in the type of the gold coinage. Up to June of that year they continued the same as before, but the change of standard having taken place in that month the type was changed, in order to distinguish

* There was no gold of any kind coined at the Mint after the middle of June, until this time.

† The quarter eagle of this type did not appear till 1821. (See Plate IV. No. 2.)

the new standard from the old merely by sight. The obverses of the new coins were very similar to the old, except that the liberty-cap is removed from the head of the goddess, and instead the hair is confined by a band inscribed with the word "LIBERTY." There was a peculiar heaviness also in the old style which does not appear in the new. The scroll, bearing the motto "E PLURIBUS UNUM," is omitted from the reverse. (See Plate IV. Nos. 3 and 4.)

The act reducing the standard was passed on the 28th of June. Up to this time there had already been coined 74,709 half eagles, and 4000 quarter eagles; 50,141 of the half eagles had been issued from the Mint on the thirty-first of March, the remainder, including the quarter eagles, were in the hands of the Chief Coiner at the time the act passed, and were returned by him to the Treasurer two days after, on the thirtieth. This fact makes it extremely doubtful whether there was any issue of quarter eagles of the old standard; as it is probable that the last return would be immediately re-coined at the reduced standard, as they would yield a considerable profit.

Some time elapsed after the passage of the act providing for the issue of the "Benton Mint Drops," as they were popularly called,* before the necessary dies could be prepared. The dies for the half eagle were ready for use toward the latter part of August, and on the twenty-fifth a coinage of 98,075 pieces took place. The dies for the quarter eagle were not prepared until the latter part of September, and on the thirtieth 18,400 pieces were delivered. The entire coinage of the new standard consisted of 658,028 half eagles, and 112,234 quarter eagles—there being no eagles.

The next change of type took place very near the end of the year 1838. The pattern then adopted for the gold coins has been continued down to the present time. It is as follows: Obv. A bust of Liberty; the shoulders undraped. The hair is looped up in a roll behind, and intwined with beads; a couple of stray curls hang loosely upon the neck. The front of the head is embellished with a tiara, inscribed with the word "LIBERTY." Around the edge are thirteen

---

* Thomas H. Benton, who was the principal advocate of this measure, obtained the cognomen of "Old Bullion," from his connection therewith.

stars, and beneath, the date "1838." There was no noticeable change in the type of the reverse. (See Plate IV. No. 5.)

This pattern first made its appearance on the twenty-sixth of December, and consisted of 6700 eagles,* and on the thirty-first of December the Chief Coiner returned to the Treasurer 500 eagles, making 7200 eagles of the new type issued in this year. This pattern was adopted on the half eagle of 1839, and on the quarter eagle of 1840. (See Plate IV. Nos. 6 and 7.)

In 1849, two new pieces were added to the gold coinage, viz., the double eagle, or twenty-dollar piece, and the gold dollar. The obverse of the double eagle is the same as the new coinage of 1838. The reverse has a very small eagle, its body hidden by the United States shield. From its beak depends a highly ornamented scroll, inscribed "E PLURIBUS UNUM." In the left talon are three arrows, and in the right an olive branch. Above is a circle of thirteen stars bathed in the diverging rays of the sun. Legend. "UNITED STATES OF AMERICA."......"TWENTY D." The dies for this coin were prepared in the year 1849, and one piece was struck therefrom and placed in the Mint Cabinet. (See Plate V. No. 1.) The first issue took place in the following year.

The head on the obverse of the dollar of this year (1849) is the same as the other gold coins, and is encircled by thirteen stars. On the reverse the value and date, "1 DOLLAR 1849," are inscribed between two branches of laurel, crossed. Legend. "UNITED STATES OF AMERICA." Of this denomination there was a large issue. (See Plate V. No. 2.)

This dollar, after a few years trial, was found to be rather small in diameter, and many complaints were made against it on that account. Consequently, in 1854 an alteration in the size was determined upon. The enlarged dollar of this year (1854) has, as its emblem of Liberty, a beautiful Indian head crowned with feathers. The band in which the feathers are confined is inscribed with the word "LIBERTY." Legend. "UNITED STATES OF AMERICA." On the reverse is inscribed "1 DOLLAR 1854" within a wreath of cereals. This dollar being

---

* This was the first coinage of this denomination since the year 1804.

considerably larger in diameter than the old piece, has a proportionate decrease in thickness. (See Plate V. No. 3.)

This year also witnessed the advent of another new coin—the three-dollar piece. This coin has upon its obverse an Indian head much more graceful in appearance than any effigy which ever before graced an American coin. Like the dollar, it has a feathered crown inscribed with the word "LIBERTY;" but this crown is quite an improvement upon the former. Otherwise it is merely an enlargement of the dollar. (See Plate V. No. 5.) This is the last change in the gold coinage of the United States which we have to notice, with the exception of a slight alteration in the dollar of 1856, to make it correspond with the type of the three-dollar piece. (See Plate V. No. 4.)

Silver Coinage. The first deposit of silver bullion for coinage took place on the 18th day of July, 1794. The deposit was made by the Bank of Maryland, and consisted of "coins of France," amounting to eighty thousand seven hundred and fifteen dollars seventy-three cents and five-tenths ($80,715.73.5.)

The first return of silver coins from the Chief Coiner to the Treasurer was made on the fifteenth day of October, and comprised 1758 dollars. The second delivery was on the first day of December, and consisted of 5300 half dollars. This embraced the entire silver coinage of the year. There was a small coinage of half dimes, but they were only struck as pattern pieces, for the purpose of trying the dies, and were not regularly issued. The types were as follows: Obv. A head of Liberty, facing to the right, with flowing hair. Above was the word "LIBERTY," and beneath the date "1794." To the left of the effigy were eight stars, and to the right seven, fifteen in all. On the reverse was an eagle with raised wings, encircled by branches of laurel, crossed. Legend. "UNITED STATES OF AMERICA." On the edge of the dollar was inscribed "HUNDRED ⊟ ⊙ ⊟ ⊙ ⊟ * * CENTS * * ⊟ ⊙ ⊟ * * ONE * * DOLLAR * * OR * * UNIT ⊟ ⊟ * * *." (See Plate V. No. 8.) The half dollar, of the same type, has on the edge "FIFTY * * ⊟ ⊙ ⊟ CENTS * * * * OR * ⊟ HALF * * A * * DOLLAR * * ⊟ ⊙ ⊟ ⊙ * ⊙ * *." (See Plate VI. No. 1.)

In the following year (1795) a change took place in the type of the dollar. Henry Wm. De Sausure was appointed to the Directorship of the Mint on the eleventh of July; and it is probable that the alteration was made soon after. Mr. De Sausure resigned his office on the twenty-eighth of October following, after which date there was no further coinage of dollars during the year; and, as there is no very great difference in the degrees of rarity of the two varieties of this year, we are forced to believe that there was a large emission of the new type, which would place the date of its first coinage early in August. The obverse has a full bust of Liberty, adorned with drapery; from beneath the hair appears a ribbon, which is tied in a bow behind. The reverse has an eagle with expanded wings, standing upon clouds, between branches of laurel and lily, crossed. Otherwise it is the same as before. (See Plate VI. No. 2.) The first return of half dimes took place on the thirtieth of March, amounting to 7756 pieces. They are of the same type as the dollars of 1794, but have a grained edge. (See Plate VII. No. 2.)

In the year 1796, the quarter dollar and dime were added to the coinage. The first delivery of the former occurred on the ninth of April, amounting to 1800 pieces, while the first coinage of the dime took place on the eighteenth of January, amounting to 14,520 pieces. They are the same pattern as the new dollar of 1795, but have grained edges. (See Plate VI. Nos. 4 and 6.)

The silver coins of 1797 have *sixteen* stars—one star for each State. Tennessee, the sixteenth State, was admitted into the Union in the latter part of the preceding year. (See Plate VI. No. 3.)

In 1798, however, for the reason stated in another place, the number of stars was reduced to thirteen, being emblematic of the original thirteen States. The reverses of the dollar and dime, which were the only silver pieces coined in this year, underwent an entire change, as follows: An eagle with raised wings, bearing the United States shield upon its breast. From its beak floats a scroll, inscribed "E PLURIBUS UNUM." In the right talon it grasps a bundle of thirteen arrows, and in the left, an olive branch. Above are clouds and thirteen stars. Legend. "UNITED STATES OF AMERICA."* (See Plate VI. No. 7, and Plate VII. No. 1.)

* For a half dollar of this type, see Plate VII. No. 3.

There is much dispute among numismatists in regard to the coinage of dollars in the year 1805. It is often contended that 321 pieces were struck; and, in fact, the Director's Report of that year is the authority for the statement. In "*Bullion Journal A*," we find the following entry on page 363, under date of June 28, 1805. We give the entry as it stands upon the Journal:—

"*Silver Coinage......Dr. to Chief Coiner his account of silver received from him in pursuance of a warrant of the Director No.* 349.

"34,000 *Quarter dollars.*

"321 *Dollars, being found amongst Spanish dollars brought to the Mint.*"

This entry settles the question, that the *issue* of that number of pieces took place; and also, that they were *not* dollars of 1805, *but of previous dates.*

No further change of importance took place until the employment of Mr. Reich, as Assistant Engraver, in 1807, who, as before stated, immediately commenced the preparation of new dies. Up to the time the new die made its appearance there had been issued from the Mint about 301,076 half dollars, 220,643 quarter dollars, and 165,000 dimes of the old type. The attention of the Assistant Engraver, which appears to have been first directed to the silver coins, seems to have been confined to the preparation of dies for the half dollar only, as we find that there was no coinage of the smaller denominations after the time above alluded to. The emission of half dollars of the new type was very large, as a reference to the table will show. The new die is described as follows: Obv. A bust of Liberty, with the Roman mantle, facing to the left. Upon the head is a liberty-cap, inscribed with the word "LIBERTY." The hair falls gracefully over the shoulders. Upon the left of the effigy are seven stars, and to the right six, thirteen in all. Beneath is the date "1807." Rev. An eagle, with its wings expanded in flight, grasping three arrows in the left, and an olive branch in the right talon. Upon its breast is suspended the United States shield. The motto, "E PLURIBUS UNUM," floats upon a scroll above. Legend. "UNITED STATES OF AMERICA."......"50 C." On the edge is inscribed "FIFTY CENTS OR

HALF A DOLLAR;" the ornaments being omitted.* (See Plate VII. No. 4.)

In 1831, a very marked change occurred in the quarter dollar, the diameter having been considerably reduced, with a consequent increase in thickness. The change of type, however, only affected the size of the devices, which were reduced to correspond with the size of the coin, and the omission from the reverse of the scroll bearing the motto "E PLURIBUS UNUM." (See Plate VIII. No. 3.)

The other silver coins remained unchanged until the year 1836. In this year, the dollar, which had not been coined since the year 1804, again made its appearance, but this time in an entire new costume. On the obverse it presents the goddess of Liberty seated upon a rock, supporting with her right hand the United States shield, across which floats a scroll, inscribed "LIBERTY;" and with her left, the staff and liberty-cap.† Beneath is the date "1836." On the reverse is an eagle in flight, facing to the left, surrounded by twenty-six stars, of different magnitudes, according to the size of the States which they represent.‡ Legend. "UNITED STATES OF AMERICA."...... "⊙ONE DOLLAR⊙." The dies for this coinage were designed and engraved by Mr. Christian Gobrecht, whose name appears upon the base which supports the effigy of Liberty. The edge is perfectly plain. There was a coinage of 1000 pieces, which were returned to the Treasurer on the thirty-first day of December. It is probable, however, that they were intended merely as specimen pieces, being issued for the purpose of courting public approbation. (See Plate VIII. No. 1.) A change also occurs in the half dollar of this year, similar to that made in the quarter dollar of 1831. The value, on the reverse, is in full, "50 CENTS," instead of "50 C.," as before. The new half dollar has a grained edge also. This change took place near the end of the year, so that there are specimens of both

---

* The quarter dollar was not issued for a number of years, but appeared in the new dress, for the first time, in 1815. The half dime did not appear until 1829. (See Plate VII. No. 7.)

† This effigy has graced our coinage ever since, to the present day.

‡ The twenty-sixth star was intended for Michigan, which was then an applicant for admission into the Union, but was not admitted until the beginning of the following year.

the old and new type. (See Plate VIII. No. 2.) The dime and half dime were unchanged.

The two latter pieces were altered in the following year (1837), but not until a large issue of the old pattern had been accomplished. The obverse has the same device as the pattern dollar of 1836, there being no stars. The reverse has "ONE DIME," or "HALF DIME," inscribed within a wreath of laurel. Legend. "UNITED STATES OF AMERICA." (See Plate VIII. Nos. 4 and 5.)

In 1838, a pattern dollar was struck, which we shall notice under the head of "experimental pieces." The first half dollars and quarter dollars of this year were of the same type as the new half dollars of 1836, with the exception that the value stands "HALF DOL." upon the former. But during the year new dies were prepared, upon the obverse of which is an effigy of Liberty, copied from the pattern dollar of 1836. Around the edge are thirteen stars, and beneath, the date "1838." The reverse of the half dollar was unchanged. (See Plate IX. No. 2.) The quarter dollar has "QUAR. DOL.," instead of "25 C.," as before. (See Plate IX. No. 3.) The dime and half dime are the same type as the new die of 1837, with the addition of thirteen stars to the obverse. (See Plate IX. Nos. 4 and 5.)

In the following year (1839) another pattern dollar was issued, for which see "experimental pieces."

On the 21st of July, 1840, the new dollar made its appearance. The obverse is the same as the dollar of 1836, with the addition of thirteen stars. The reverse has the eagle, with expanded wings, bearing the United States shield upon its breast, and grasping an olive branch in the right, and three arrows in the left talon. Legend. "UNITED STATES OF AMERICA."......"ONE DOL." The edge is grained, being the first authorized dollar bearing such an edge. (See Plate IX. No. 1.)

In 1851, the three-cent piece was added to the coinage. On the obverse it has a star, bearing the arms of the United States. Legend. "UNITED STATES OF AMERICA."......"1851." Rev. An ornamental "C," within which is the number "III," (3 cents). Around the edge are thirteen stars. (See Plate IX. No. 6.)

In 1853, the weight of the half dollar and the smaller pieces was reduced by the law of March third, as before noticed. The only alteration made in the types of the reduced pieces was the addition of two arrow-heads, one at each side of the date; and, on the reverse of the half and quarter dollar, the eagle appears surrounded by diverging rays. These serve to distinguish the old from the new standard. Of the old standard, there were issued in this year 44,200 quarter dollars, 95,000 dimes, 135,000 half dimes, and 11,400,000 three-cent pieces, or *trimes*, as they were then called. Of the new standard full sets were issued. (See Plate IX. No. 7.)

In the following year (1854) the diverging rays were removed from the reverses; and in 1856 the arrow-heads also disappear. (See Plate X. No. 1.)

The standard of the silver dollar having remained undisturbed, no alteration was made in its appearance; but the pattern adopted in 1840 is still continued in favor.

In the present year (1860) a change has been effected in the types of the dime and half dime, the old laurel wreath being displaced by a wreath of *cereals*, and the legend, "UNITED STATES OF AMERICA," is removed from the reverse, and substituted for the thirteen stars upon the obverse." (See Plate X. Nos. 2 and 3.)

Copper Coinage.—The first year of active operations at the Mint (1793) was devoted exclusively to the coinage of cents and half cents. During the year three different patterns of the former made their appearance. The first is described as follows: Obv. A head of Liberty, facing to the right, with the hair flowing backward, as if blown by the wind. Above, is inscribed the word "LIBERTY," and beneath, the date "1793." Rev. An endless chain, within which is inscribed "ONE CENT," and the fraction "$\frac{1}{100}$." Legend. "UNITED STATES OF AMERICA." The reverse of this cent met with much opposition from the people, who little relished the idea which the chain seemed to embody. They had too recently experienced the effects of the "chains and slavery" which follow so closely upon the skirts of royalty, to look upon such an emblem with favor; and we find many sarcastic remarks upon the chain cent in the current newspapers of the day. Whether this fact induced a change in the type, we are not prepared to say. The original intention may have been to add a link for each new State; and the anticipated growth of our young Republic induced its abandonment. At all events, a new die for the reverse was speedily prepared. This *second* pattern has a wreath, composed of two laurel branches, as a substitute for the chain; the fraction $\frac{1}{100}$ appears beneath the wreath; otherwise the *second* issue was the same as the first. The *third* variety has a bust of Liberty, with flowing hair, facing in the same direction as before, and the pole and liberty-cap are added; the reverse being the same as the *second* issue. The edges of all these are grained. The half cent made its first appearance on the twentieth of July. These were of the same style as the third variety of the cent, but the bust is turned in the opposite direction—to the left. (See Plate X. Nos. 1, 2, and 4.*)

In 1794, the diameter of the cent was slightly increased, and the inscription, "ONE HUNDRED FOR A DOLLAR," appears upon the edge. The entire coinage of cents in this year amounted to 918,521, according to the record, instead of "12,513,300," as we have seen it confidently stated. The half cent has the bust somewhat enlarged, and facing to the right; and upon the edge is inscribed, "TWO HUNDRED FOR A DOLLAR." (See Plate X. Nos. 3 and 5.)

In the latter part of the year 1795, a still further increase in diameter was effected, and the inscriptions upon the edge were omitted, never to be resumed; the copper coins from that day to this having always presented a plain edge. Both the obverse and reverse of this coinage have deeply-indented borders. The head upon the half cent is reduced in size from that of the previous year, but still faces in the same direction. (See Plate XI. Nos. 1 and 3.)

The following year (1796) the diameter of the cent was again changed to correspond with that of 1794; and during the year a change in the type of the obverse was also effected, as follows: A bust of Liberty, facing to the right, and adorned with drapery. A portion of the hair is confined by a band, which is tied in a bow behind; the remainder falls loosely over the shoulders. (See Plate XI. No. 2.) The half cent was not altered until the year 1799 or

* The *third* variety being similar to the cent of 1794, we illustrate one of that year instead. (See Plate X. No. 3.)

1800, when it was made to correspond with the new cent of 1796, the bust facing in the same direction. (See Plate XI. No. 4.)

The copper coins experienced no other change until the introduction of the new die for the cent, engraved by Mr. Reich, in 1808. This cent has, on the obverse, a bust of Liberty, facing to the left; the hair is confined by a band inscribed with the word "LIBERTY." To the left of the effigy are seven stars, and to the right six; beneath is the date "1808." On the reverse, the value, "ONE CENT," is inscribed within a wreath, composed of a single branch of laurel. Legend. "UNITED STATES OF AMERICA." The fraction $\frac{1}{100}$ is omitted. The half cent was not altered until the following year (1809), when it was made to correspond to the above description. (See Plate XI. Nos. 5 and 6.)

The coinage of the cent, which had been suspended during the year 1815, was resumed in January, 1816, and a new pattern adopted for the obverse, as follows: A head of Liberty, facing to the left. The hair is confined in a roll behind, while the front of the head is bedecked with a tiara, inscribed with the word "LIBERTY." Around the edge are thirteen stars, and beneath, the date "1816." The reverse was unaltered. (See Plate XI. No. 7.) In the following year (1817) a cent of this pattern made its appearance, bearing *fifteen* stars, but was soon discontinued, the type adopted in 1816 having been continued as long as the copper cent was issued.* (See Plate XII. No. 1.)

The type of the half cent was not changed until the year 1840, when new dies, of the same style as the cent, were prepared. (See Plate XII. No. 4.) These dies were only used to strike patterns, no issues of half cents having been made in this, or the eight years following, to 1848. In each of these years dies were prepared for the half cent, but none were issued for general circulation. Fine proof specimens were placed in the Mint Cabinet, where they now remain.

In the year 1857, the old familiar coppers disappear from among our authorized coins. They continued to be coined during the month

* The cent of 1839, however, was slightly altered in the effigy, the head being higher and more arched on the top, above the tiara; from which it has acquired the cognomen of "booby-head." (See Plate XII. No. 2.)

of January, in which time 333,456 cents and 35,180 half cents were struck. The latter were nearly all retained in the Mint, and subsequently melted up, this denomination having been abolished by the same law that authorized the substitution of the nickel for the copper cent.

The new cent was issued for general circulation in May following. The obverse has a flying eagle, like that upon the pattern dollar of 1836, without the stars. Above is the legend, "UNITED STATES OF AMERICA," and beneath, the date "1857." On the reverse, the value, "ONE CENT," is inscribed within a wreath of *cereals.* (See Plate XII. No. 5.)

This pattern was short-lived, as in the year 1859 it was supplanted by the following: Obv. An Indian head, facing to the left, and bedecked with a falling crown of feathers, upon the band of which is inscribed "LIBERTY." Legend. "UNITED STATES OF AMERICA." ......"1859." Rev. "ONE CENT," inscribed within a wreath of laurel. (See Plate XII. No. 6.)

In the present year (1860) a new device for the reverse has been adopted; being a wreath of oak, within which is inscribed "ONE CENT." Above is suspended a small shield, bearing the arms of the United States. (See Plate XII. No. 7.)

Besides the National Mint at Philadelphia, there are four Branch Mints. Three of these were created by Act of Congress, of March 3d, 1835, viz.: branches at NEW ORLEANS, La., DAHLONEGA, Ga., and CHARLOTTE, North Carolina. The fourth is located at SAN FRANCISCO, Cal., and was established by Act of Congress, of July 3d, 1852. The three former branches did not go into operation until the year 1838; the latter in 1854. The coins of the Branch Mints are distinguished from those of the National Mint by the initial letters which will be found upon them. These are as follows: Branch at New Orleans, which coins gold and silver, the letter O. (see Plate V. No. 6;) Dahlonega, which coins gold only, the initial D. (see Plate IV. No. 10;) Charlotte, which also coins nothing but gold, the initial C. (See Plate IV. No. 9.) San Francisco, which coins gold and silver, the letter S. (See Plate V. No. 7.) The coins of the National Mint bear no distinguishing marks or initials.

EXPERIMENTAL PIECES.

(UNAUTHORIZED COINS OF THE UNITED STATES.)

Since the establishment of the United States Mint many coins have made their appearance therefrom, which do not belong to the national authorized series, being of an experimental character, and not intended for general circulation. Among these we include the "Washington half dime," which we have before mentioned. We consider, however, that the piece in question *was* intended "for general circulation," from the fact that Washington makes mention of it, *in that light*, in his annual address to Congress, (before quoted.) But as it partakes of the experimental character, we exclude it from the regular series. These pieces will be noticed in the order of time as far as possible.

1792. Half dime. Obv. A female head, emblematic of Liberty, facing to the left. This is popularly supposed to represent the features of Martha Washington, who is said to have sat to the artist while he was designing it. The hair is short and unconfined. Immediately beneath is the date, the whole being encompassed by the legend, "LIB(erty) PAR(ent) OF SCIENCE AND INDUSTRY." On the reverse is a small eagle volant, beneath which is inscribed the value, "HALF DISME." Legend. "UNI. STATES OF AMERICA." (See Plate XIII. No. 1.) This piece is said to have been struck from the private plate of Washington, which is not unlikely, considering the great interest which he took in the operations of the infant mint, visiting it frequently, and personally superintending many of its affairs. This coin, as before shown, made its appearance in the month of October, 1792. Subsequently several other pieces were struck, before the close of the year, as follows:—

CENT. Obv. A bust of Liberty, with flowing hair, facing to the right. Beneath is the date "1792." Legend. "LIBERTY PARENT OF SCIENCE AND INDUSTRY." Rev. "ONE CENT," inscribed within a wreath of laurel. Beneath is the fraction "$\frac{1}{100}$." Legend. "UNITED STATES OF AMERICA." This cent conforms, in size and weight, to the standard adopted in the law of 1792, which underwent a reduction before any regular issue of cents took place. It is also very similar in appearance to the "Washington half dime," which fact seems to indicate it as the first trial cent of the United States Mint. It was the work of an artist named BIRCH, which name appears upon the lower portion of the effigy. (See Plate XIV. No. 1.)

DIME. Obv. A bust of Liberty, with flowing hair, facing to the left. Beneath is the date "1792." Legend. "LIBERTY PARENT OF SCIENCE AND INDUSTRY." Rev. A small eagle volant. Beneath is inscribed the value, "DISME." Legend. "UNITED STATES OF AMERICA." This piece, of which we have duplicates, was struck in copper, being merely a trial of dies for the dime. Only a few specimens were struck, and it is nearly *unique*. (See Plate XIII. No. 2.)

CENT. Obv. An undraped bust of Liberty, with flowing hair, facing to the right. Beneath is inscribed the date "1792." Legend. "LIBERTY PARENT OF SCIENCE AND INDUST." Rev. "ONE CENT," inscribed within a wreath of laurel, beneath which is the fraction "$\frac{1}{100}$." Legend. "UNITED STATES OF AMERICA." (See Plate XIV. No. 3.) This cent is of the same diameter as the trial dime described above, and is said to have been made small with a view to the insertion of a plug of silver in the center, to bring the value up to the standard required by law.

CENT. Obv. A bust of Liberty, facing to the right, the hair confined by a fillet. Above is inscribed the word "LIBERTY," and beneath, the date "1792." Rev. A portion of a globe, on which stands an eagle, with raised wings. Legend. "UNITED STATES OF AMERICA." This cent has a grained edge, like the cents of 1793. Some numismatists give it the preference as the first trial cent of the Mint. (See Plate XIV. No. 2.)

1794. The first year in which the legal half dime was coined, a trial piece was struck in copper, during the preparation of the dies. It is of the same type as the legal half dime, except that the reverse is without the wreath, which was added when the regular coins were struck. (See Plate XIII. No. 3.)

1815. A *platina* piece struck from the dies for the legal half dollar of that year. It was an experiment, *platina* being then a new metal. Its intrinsic value is $5.50. *Unique.* (See No. 100, *Division V.*)

1836. A gold dollar made its appearance, bearing on the obverse a liberty-cap inscribed with the word "LIBERTY," and surrounded by diverging rays. Rev. The value "1 D." encircled by a single branch of palm. Legend. "UNITED STATES OF AMERICA."......"1836." (See Plate XV. No. 1.)

In the same year a composition two-cent piece was struck, upon the obverse of which is an eagle with expanded wings, floating upon clouds. Legend. "UNITED STATES OF AMERICA."......"1836." Rev. The value, "TWO CENTS," inscribed within a wreath of laurel. *One-tenth silver.* (See Plate XIV. No. 8.)

1838. "Flying eagle dollar." Obverse same type as the legal dollar of 1840, (the present pattern). Rev. A flying eagle, facing to the left. Legend. "UNITED STATES OF AMERICA."......"ONE DOLLAR." This was the first dollar ever struck at the United States Mint with a grained edge. (See Plate VIII. No. 6.)

A half dollar, of the same pattern as the dollar just noticed, was struck at the Mint at the same time. (See Plate XIII. No. 4.)

Two other half dollars were produced in this year. The *first* has the same obverse as the authorized coinage. On the reverse is an eagle, engraved by Mr. Gobrecht. In the right talon it grasps an olive branch, and in the left four arrows. Legend. "UNITED STATES OF AMERICA."......"HALF DOLLAR." This piece is said to be *unique.* (See No. 105, *Division V.*) The *second* has a bust of Liberty, by Mr. Kneass. It faces to the left, is adorned with drapery, and has a tiara upon the forehead. A band, inscribed with the word "LIBERTY," is cast over the hair, and partially confines it. To the left of the effigy are *seven,* and to the right *six* stars. Beneath is the date "1838." The reverse is the same as the legal half dollar. (See Plate XIII. No. 5.)

1839. A dollar, of the same type as the pattern dollar of the previous year, was struck. The Director's Report of that time states that 300 of these were coined, but we have been unable to find any memorandum to that effect on any of the Mint Records, where it should properly appear, if such were the case. They are not as rare as the dollars of 1838, and the coinage was probably more extensive. (See No. 107, *Division V.*)

Same year, a half dollar, bearing a bust of Liberty, by Mr. Gobrecht. This bust is undraped, and faces to the right. The hair is confined in a roll behind, and the front of the head is adorned with a tiara, inscribed with the word "LIBERTY." In other respects it conformed to the type of the authorized coinage. (See Plate XIII. No. 6.) Both this head and that of Mr. Kneass, of the previous year, are finely executed, and, being exceedingly rare, command high prices in the market.

1849. Two pattern three-cent pieces were struck in this year. For the obverse the die of the legal half dime was used, while the reverse of the first presents the number "III," and the other the figure "3." These were one-half silver. They are exceedingly rare. (See Plate XIII. Nos. 7 and 8.)

1850. A third pattern for the three-cent piece then in contemplation was produced. On the obverse is a liberty-cap inscribed with the word "LIBERTY," and surrounded by diverging rays. Beneath is the date "1850." Rev. The denomination "III" encircled by a single branch of palm. Legend. "UNITED STATES OF AMERICA." (See Plate XIII. No. 9.)

In the same year the "ring cent" was produced. This piece is about the size of a dime, and has a small hole in the center, around which is inscribed, on one side, "U. S. A."......"ONE-TENTH SILVER;" and on the other, "CENT."......"1850." (See Plate XIV. No. 6.)

A dollar and half dollar, in gold, embodying the same idea, were also struck. These had only the legend "UNITED STATES OF AMERICA" upon one side, the other being plain. (See Plate XV. No. 2.)

1852. Another "ring dollar." This was struck in silver, and had upon one side the legend "UNITED STATES OF AMERICA," and the date "1852," and upon the other, the denomination "DOLLAR," and a *demi-wreath* of laurel. (See No. 116, *Division V.*)

1853. The first "nickel cent" was produced in this year. The obverse is an imitation of the legal copper cent. The reverse has the value, "ONE CENT," inscribed within a wreath of laurel, there being no legend. Sixty per cent. nickel, remainder copper. Nearly as large as the present nickel cent. (See Plate XIV. No. 7.)

1854. A copper cent appeared of the same pattern as the legal cent, but smaller in size, and the stars were omitted; weight, 96 grains. (See Plate XIV. No. 4.)

Same year. A cent of the same size as the preceding, but of a different type. Obv. A flying eagle, thirteen stars, and the date. Reverse same as the legal cent. This cent was composed of 95 per cent. copper, 4 tin, and 1 zinc, and is the rarest of the pattern cents of this period, being almost *unique*. (See Plate XIV. No. 5.)

1855. Three cents, of the same type as the piece just mentioned, were coined. The *first* was of the same composition also; but the *second* contained one-tenth nickel to nine-tenths copper; weight, 96 grains. The *third* was two-tenths nickel, remainder copper. They are all very rare. (See Nos. 120, 121, 122, *Division V.*)

1856. The nickel cent, which was adopted in the following year, (1857,) was first coined in this year. Its type and composition have been already stated. (See No. 123, *Division V.*)

In 1858, a new device was contemplated for the nickel cent, and several varieties of that cent were coined. Of these there were three different obverses. 1st. The obverse of the legal cent of 1857–8. 2d. A small eagle *volant*, presented in a different position from that on the legal cent. 3d. An Indian head, with a falling crown of feathers, (afterward adopted.)

These obverses were combined with four different reverses in such a manner as to produce *eleven* different varieties. These were as follows: 1st. A wreath of *cereals*, within which is inscribed "ONE CENT." This was the same as the legal cent of 1858. 2d. An oak wreath, inclosing the inscription, "ONE CENT," above which is a small shield, bearing the arms of the United States. The objection to this was that the shield had the appearance of a harp. 3d. Same as the preceding, with the shield omitted. 4th. A wreath of laurel, within which is inscribed "ONE CENT, (afterward adopted, in combination with the Indian head above.)

The large, or authorized eagle, was combined with the three last-named reverses; while the other two obverses were combined with the four reverses, making eleven in all. (See Plate XV. Nos. 5, 6, and 7.)

1859. A new half dollar was proposed in this year, and several varieties were coined. First, we have a beautiful bust of Liberty, facing to the right, the hair being done up in a braid behind, and crowned with a chaplet of oak. Around the shoulders of the effigy floats a scroll, inscribed "LIBERTY." Legend. "UNITED STATES OF AMERICA."......"1859." This fine head was the work of Mr. Longacre, the present engraver of the Mint. This was combined with three different reverses, differing, however, only in the inscription. One has "½ DOLLAR" inscribed within a wreath of *cereals;* another, "50 CENTS," within a similar wreath; and a *third,* "HALF DOLLAR," with the same wreath. These reverses, which are very graceful, were engraved by Mr. Paquet, one of the engravers of the Mint. (See Plate XV. No. 3.)

Mr. Paquet also produced a half dollar of the following description: Obv. The goddess of Liberty in a sitting posture, facing to the left, her left hand resting upon the United States shield, while with the right she supports the *fasces.* Beneath is the date "1859," and around the edge thirteen stars. On the reverse is the American eagle, with its wings expanded in flight, grasping an olive branch in the right and three arrows in the left talon, while from its beak floats a scroll, inscribed "E PLURIBUS UNUM." Upon its breast is suspended the United States shield. Legend. "UNITED STATES OF AMERICA."......"HALF DOLLAR." (See Plate XV. No. 4.)

Near the close of the year another pattern cent was struck. This is the same as the cent of the year 1860. (See Plate XV. No. 8.)

PRIVATE ISSUES.

NORTH CAROLINA.

Mr. C. BECHTLER established a mint at Rutherfordton, North Carolina, and commenced the coinage of gold half and quarter eagles and one dollar pieces. These coins circulated freely at the South and West.

"To obtain a proper understanding of them will require some attention. There are two series, the first bearing no date, but issued earlier than 1834, of the three denominations of five, two and a half, and one dollar, professedly 20 carats fine, and 150 grains to the piece of five dollars. These are now scarce. The second series is that which bears the date of 1834. In that year there was an important reduction of standards in the national gold coins, to which Mr. Bechtler conformed, and, by way of distinction, afterward used the uniform date of that year. The denominations are as before, but there are three grades of fineness and weight; thus, at 20 carats, the five-dollar piece is to weigh 140 grains; the same at 21 carats, to weigh 134 grains; and at 22 carats, to weigh 128 grains. The pieces of 20 carats are stamped 'NORTH CAROLINA GOLD;' those of 21, 'CAROLINA GOLD;' and those of 22, 'GEORGIA GOLD.' It is probable that all of the gold was raised in North Carolina, and that these stamps are only to assist in indicating the different qualities, as they are generally understood in that region, Georgia gold being usually the best, and North Carolina the poorest.

"This coinage has no emblematical device, but simply the name and residence of the manufacturer, the weight and fineness, and the designation just stated. (See Nos. 43 to 51, *Division V.*)

"The following is the result of numerous trials of these coins at the Mint:—

DENOMINATION.	Professed weight.	Professed fineness.		Average weight.	Variations in fineness.	Variations in value.	Average value.
	Grains.	*Carats.*	*Thous.*	*Grains.*	*Thous.*		D. C. M.
Five-dollar piece before 1834	150	20	833	148.0	829 to 846	$5.28 to $5.39	5 34*
Five-dollar piece, since 1834, "N. C. gold"	140	20	833	139.8	813 to 819	4.89 to 4.93	4 90 7
Five-dollar piece, "Carolina gold"	134	21	875	134.4	833 to 852	4.82 to 4.93	4 89 0
Five-dollar piece, "Geo. gold"	128	22	917	127.6	856 to 899	4.70 to 4.94	4 84 6
Two-and-a-half-dollar piece, "N. C. gold"	70	20	833	70.0	....	....	2 47 0
Two-and-a-half-dollar piece, "Georgia gold"	64	22	917	63.6	....	....	2 39 0
One dollar, "N. C. gold"	28	20	833	27.6	804 to 816	95½ to 97 cts.	0 96 2

"There is not much variation in weight, but the fineness (as shown above) is exceedingly irregular and inferior, causing an average loss of $2\frac{1}{2}$ per cent. on the nominal value."

* The half eagle of the National coinage of that date would be worth $5.36.

Some time subsequent to the year 1842, the mint passed from the hands of C. Bechtler into the possession of A. Bechtler, whose name was substituted upon the coins for that of the former. The only marked effect which this change produced upon the coins was a considerable deficiency in value, as compared with the former emissions. (See No. 52, *Division V.*) Since the year 1849 this establishment has been abolished.

COINS OF TEMPLETON REID.

In 1830, when the first extensive produce of Georgia gold commenced, a mint was established at the mines, and the coinage of three denominations of gold—the ten, five, and two-and-a-half dollar pieces —was commenced. These coins have upon one side the name of "TEMPLETON REID, ASSAYER," and the denomination. The ten-dollar piece has, upon the reverse, merely the inscription, "GEORGIA GOLD," surrounded with a circle of stars, and is not dated. The other pieces have the date added upon the reverse; and, in the case of the five-dollar piece, the denomination also. Like the Bechtler coins, they have no devices other than the stars upon the ten-dollar piece. (See Nos. 55, 56, 57, *Division V.*) By assays made at the Mint, the ten-dollar piece is found to be 942 thousandths fine, and weighs 248 grains; consequent value, $10.06. (Our eagle of the same date would be worth $10.66.) The two-and-a-half-dollar piece is 932 thousandths fine; weighs 60.5 grains; consequent value, $2.43. The five-dollar piece was not tested. This coinage was not long continued, and is seldom found in circulation, even at home.

Afterward, when the California gold-fields began to attract attention, Templeton Reid removed his establishment to that region, and in 1849 commenced the coinage of twenty-five* and ten dollar pieces. These were similar in type to the Georgia pieces. The ten-dollar piece (now in the Cabinet) has, upon the obverse, "TEMPLETON REID, ASSAYER," and the date "1849;" and on the reverse, "CALIFORNIA GOLD."......"TEN DOLLARS." (See No. 58, *Division V.*) This piece weighs 260 grains, and appears to be composed of California gold,

---

* This piece was formerly in the Cabinet, but was abstracted therefrom.

without artificial alloy, which (if true) would place the value at about $9.75.

CALIFORNIA COINS.

Previous to the establishment of the Branch Mint at San Francisco, in 1854, many private Refineries, Assay Offices, and Companies struck gold coins of various denominations. This, although an apparent usurpation of governmental power, seems to have been excusable in the Californians, from the very great expense attending the transportation of bullion from the gold region to the Atlantic States for coinage, and its return in the form of currency. But this fact does not excuse the apparent discrepancy between the nominal and intrinsic values of many of the pieces, which usually exhibits a depreciation of the latter. We have only space for a brief description of these issues.

J. S. O.—A ten-dollar piece, not dated, of the following description: Obv. "10 DOLLARS" surrounded by a circle of thirty-one stars. Rev. "J. S. O." (said to be the initials of Dr. J. S. Ormsby, of Pennsylvania, to whom this coinage is attributed.) Legend. "UNITED STATES OF AMERICA."......"CAL.": 842 thousandths fine; weighs 258½ grains; value $9.37. (See No. 59, *Division V.*)

MINER'S BANK.—A ten-dollar piece, not dated. Obv. "TEN D.' Legend. "MINER'S BANK."......"SAN FRANCISCO." Rev. An eagle, in imitation of the National coinage. Above is inscribed "CALIFORNIA." Beneath are thirteen stars, arranged around the edge. (See No. 60, *Division V.*) The average weight is 263½ grains; the fineness about 865 thousandths (part of the alloy being copper); and the average value $9.87, with a risk of having it as low as $9.75.

N. G. & N.—1849. A five-dollar piece. Obv. An eagle, with expanded wings, grasping an olive branch in the right, and three arrows in the left talon. Upon its breast is suspended a shield, inscribed with the figure "5." Legend. "CALIFORNIA GOLD"...... "WITHOUT ALLOY." Rev. "N. G. & N."......"1849."......"SAN FRANCISCO," inclosed in a circle of twenty-two stars. Legend. "FULL WEIGHT OF"......"HALF EAGLE." (See Nos. 61, 62, *Division V.*) The claim put forth upon the reverse of this piece is verified by trials at the Mint, the variation not exceeding one grain in any case. But its claim to be "*California gold, without alloy*," allows of a pretty wide margin. As far as the investigations of the Mint have extended, they are found to contain no alloy, except that introduced by nature, which is usually more than enough. Three specimens gave severally 870, 880, and 892 thousandths, with the consequent values of $4.83, $4.89, and $4.95½, without the silver, and, including that, 2½ cents more.

PACIFIC COMPANY.—1849. Ten and five dollar pieces. Obv. An eagle *volant*, grasping an olive branch in the right, and a hammer in the left talon. Legend. "PACIFIC COMPANY CALIFORNIA."......"1849." Rev. A liberty-cap and staff, surrounded by diverging rays and stars. Beneath is inscribed the value in dollars. (See Nos. 63, 64, *Division V.*) These pieces are very much debased in fineness, and irregular in weight. A ten-dollar piece weighed 229 grains; a five-dollar piece, 130 grains; assay of a third, 797 thousandths fine. At these rates, the larger piece would be worth $7.86, the smaller $4.48; but the value is very uncertain.

OREGON EXCHANGE CO.—1849. Pieces of ten and five dollars. Obv. A beaver, beneath which is inscribed "O. T." (Oregon Territory,) and the date "1849." Legend. "K. M. T. R. C. S." (said to be the initials of the persons composing the company.) Rev. "10 D(ineros) 20 G(ranos) NATIVE GOLD. TEN D"(ollars.) Legend. "OREGON EXCHANGE COMPANY." (See Nos. 65, 66, *Division V.*) A five-dollar piece, tried at the Mint, was found to weigh 127½ grains, was 878 thousandths fine, and contained only the native alloy; the consequent value being $4.82, excluding the silver, which, in sufficient quantities, would produce 2½ cents more.

CINCINNATI MINING & TRADING CO.—1849. Ten and five dollar pieces. Obv. An Indian head, crowned with feathers. Legend. "CINCINNATI MINING & TRADING COMPANY." Rev. An eagle, in flight, facing to the left, grasping the United States shield in the right, and three arrows and an olive branch in the left talon. Legend. "CALIFORNIA. TEN (or *five*) DOLLARS."......"1849." (See Nos. 67, 68, *Division V.*) These pieces are too rare to admit of their being cut for assay; but appear to be of native gold, and weigh respectively 258 and 132 grains. They may be rated at $9.70 and $4.95.

MASSACHUSETTS & CALIFORNIA CO.—1849. Five-dollar piece. Obv. The value "FIVE D." inscribed within a wreath of laurel. Legend. "MASSACHUSETTS & CALIFORNIA CO."......"1849." Rev. The crest and arms of Upper California. Around the edge are arranged thirteen stars. (See No. 69, *Division V.*) This piece is apparently debased with copper, but is too rare to be devoted to the test of an assay; consequently we are unable to state its value. It weighs 115½ grains.

BALDWIN & CO.—1850. Ten and five dollar pieces. The first has upon the obverse a mounted horseman, throwing a lasso. Beneath is the date "1850." Legend. "CALIFORNIA GOLD."......"TEN DOLLARS." Rev. An eagle, in imitation of the National coinage. Above is inscribed "BALDWIN & CO.," and beneath, "***** SAN FRANCISCO *****." (See No. 70, *Division V.*) This piece weighs 263 grains; is 880 thousandths fine; value $9.96. The five-dollar piece is in imitation of the National coinage. The name "BALDWIN & CO." is inscribed upon the tiara of the Liberty head. The legend on the reverse stands "S. M. V. (Standard Mint Value) CALIFORNIA GOLD." (See No. 71, *Division V.*) Average value, $4.92. These coins contain some copper—about 20 thousandths.

MOFFAT & CO.—This company coined money for a number of years; from 1849 to the time the Mint was established at San Francisco, in 1854. The Cabinet contains the following specimens:—

1849.—Ten-dollar piece. An imitation of the National coinage. Upon the *tiara* of the Liberty head is inscribed "MOFFAT & CO." The reverse has the legend "S. M. V. CALIFORNIA GOLD." (See No. 72, *Division V.*) This piece is about 897 thousandths fine, weighs 258¼ grains; making an average value of $9.97.7.

1850.—Five-dollar piece, of the same type and relative value of the piece just mentioned. (See No. 73, *Division V.*)

1853.—Twenty-dollar piece, in imitation of the National coinage. Like the two preceding pieces, the *tiara* is inscribed "MOFFAT & CO." The legend, on the reverse, is "SAN FRANCISCO CALIFORNIA." (See

Nos. 74, 75, *Division V.*) This conforms very nearly to the National standard.

Moffat & Co. also issued gold ingots or stamped bars. These had "MOFFAT & CO.," the fineness *in carats*, and the value stamped upon them. The specimens contained in the Cabinet (see Nos. 76, 77, *Division V.*) are respectively $16.00 and $9.43; the first professing to be $20\frac{3}{4}$ carats, and the other $21\frac{7}{16}$ carats.

UNITED STATES ASSAY OFFICE.—This office was established by an act of Congress, in 1850, and several denominations of coin were issued soon after, among which are the following:—

1851.—Fifty-dollar piece. This coin, of which there are two varieties, is of an octagon shape, and is popularly known as the "*California slug.*" The first variety has an eagle, with raised wings, grasping the United States shield, and three arrows in the right and an olive branch in the left talon. From its beak floats a scroll, inscribed with the word "LIBERTY." Above the eagle is another scroll, inscribed "880 THOUS." Legend. "UNITED STATES OF AMERICA." Beneath is "50 D. C." (California.) These are inclosed in a beaded circle, and (though in relief) are sunk into the piece in such a manner as to leave a raised rim around the outside. Upon the edge is inscribed "AUGUSTUS HUMBERT UNITED STATES ASSAYER CALIFORNIA OF GOLD. 1851." The transposition of the three last words being evidently an error. (See No. 81, *Division V.*) The *second* variety is similar in type, but is much more finished. Upon the scroll, above the eagle, is inscribed "887 THOUS.," and the legend stands "UNITED STATES OF AMERICA."......"FIFTY DOLLARS." The raised rim does not appear upon this piece; but outside of the circular line, inclosing the field, is inscribed "AUGUSTUS HUMBERT UNITED STATES ASSAYER OF GOLD CALIFORNIA," and the date "1851." The edge is *grained.* Both of these pieces have a peculiar *lining* upon the reverse; but no devices or letters. (See No. 82, *Division V.*) They come up to their professed standards (*i.e.* 880 and 887 thousandths) in fineness. And, if not much worn, will yield their full value.

1853.—Twenty dollars. Obverse same type as the fifty-dollar piece, the scroll above the eagle being inscribed "900 THOUS.," which appears to be its true standard. The reverse is lined in a similar manner to the fifty-dollar pieces; but across the center it has an open space, on which is inscribed "UNITED STATES ASSAY OFFICE OF GOLD SAN FRANCISCO, CALIFORNIA. 1853." The edge is grained. (See No. 83, *Division V.*) These coins are found to be equal to the legal standards.

CALIFORNIA HALF AND QUARTER DOLLAR PIECES.—For several years gold half and quarter dollars were issued. The half dollars contained in the Cabinet (two specimens) are round, and have upon the obverse a head of Liberty, in imitation of the National coinage, surrounded by a circle of thirteen stars. One has upon the reverse the date "1852" inscribed within a wreath of laurel. Legend. "HALF DOL. CALIFORNIA GOLD." On the other is the date "1853" inscribed within a wreath of laurel, and the legend "CALIFORNIA GOLD. HALF D." (See No. 84, *Division V.*)

The quarter dollar is of an octagon shape, and is one of a series of the same form, consisting of the dollar, and its half and quarter. On the obverse is a head of Liberty, in imitation of the National coinage, and four stars; and on the reverse, "$\frac{1}{4}$ DOLLAR. 1854," inscribed within a circle of pellets. (See No. 85, *Division V.*)

COINS OF UTAH.

The Mormons, at Great Salt Lake, have issued a series of coins, consisting of the twenty, ten, and five, and two-and-a-half dollar pieces. Of these we have a set of the date 1849. Upon the obverse they have an eye, surmounted by a device having the appearance of a *mitre.* Legend. "HOLINESS TO THE LORD." On the reverse they have two hands clasped in friendship, and the date "1849." The legend on the ten-dollar piece stands "PURE GOLD."......"TEN DOLLARS." But on the other pieces it is "G. S. L. C. P. G." (meaning "Great Salt Lake City, Pure Gold,") and the value in dollars, as upon the ten-dollar piece. (See Nos. 87 to 90, *Division V.*) These coins are about 899 thousandths fine, with considerable variation, and they contain only the native silver alloy. The weight is also variable, and the values very deficient; the ten-dollar piece ranging from $8.50 to $8.70. The relation of the pieces to one another seems to be well maintained, notwithstanding the irregularity in weight and fineness.

DIVISION VI.

SPAIN.

The first emperor of Spain was SANCHO III. (the Great), King of Navarre, who ascended the throne in the year 1000, assuming the title of emperor. In the year 1034 SANCHO made a division of his dominions among his four sons, giving *Navarre* to GARCIAS, *Castile* to FERDINAND, *Aragon* to RAMIREZ, and *Sobrarva* to GONZALES. The latter division, however, only lasted three years. The three former remained distinct until the sixteenth century. Spain came into the house of Austria by the accession of CHARLES I. in 1516, who was afterward, in 1519, elected Emperor of Germany, with the title of CHARLES V. The family of Bourbon first acquired the throne by the person of PHILIP V., grandson to LOUIS XIV. of France. He ascended the Spanish throne, for the first time, in the year 1700.

In the following collection a distinction has been made between the coins of Spain *proper*, and the American colonies, Mexico, Peru, etc. These, having been detached from the mother country by the revolution of 1820–21, now exist as independent kingdoms or republics. The coins of each will, therefore, be found under its own proper title.

The unit of Spanish money is the *real;* of this there are three kinds. First, the Mexican, or Spanish American, of which eight make a silver dollar; second, the real of new plate (*de plata nueva*), of which ten are equal to a dollar; and third, the *real vellon*, of twenty to the dollar. The latter is the one in use in Spain *proper*. It was formerly divided into thirty-four maravedis, or eight and a half cuartos (copper coin), one cuarto consisting of four maravedis. Recently, however, the real has been made to consist of one hundred centimos.*

Before 1853 the GOLD coinage consisted of the *doblon* or doubloon, with its half, quarter or *pistole*, eighth or *escudo*, and the

---

* Letter of JOHN SOMERS SMITH, U. S. Consul at Malaga, to the Treasury Department, June 20, 1859.

sixteenth, called a *veinten*, coronilla, or gold dollar. The doubloon was valued at sixteen dollars. The fineness of this piece and its subdivisions underwent several depreciating changes. Before 1772 the doubloon was coined at the fineness of 917 thousandths, and at the weight of 418 Troy grains, the smaller pieces in proportion. From 1772 to 1785 it was 896 thousandths fine; and after 1785 it was only 875 thousandths fine. The old weight (418 grains), however, has always been retained. Since 1853 the only gold coin has been the doblon of 100 reals,* coined at nine-tenths fine, and at the weight of 129 Troy grains.

The SILVER coins, before 1853, were the dollar, of twenty reals *vellon*, and its half, quarter, eighth, and sixteenth. But the present coinage of silver consists of the dollar and its half; the *peseta*, or piece of four reals; the half peseta, or piece of two reals; and the *one real*. The old silver coins are now becoming scarce, the eighth and sixteenth of a dollar being seldom seen.†

The COPPER coinage has heretofore consisted of the *two-cuarto* piece, of eight maravedis; the *onė-cuarto* piece, of four maravedis; and the *ochavos*, of two maravedis. But this coinage has now been superseded by the new system which has recently been adopted, and which consists of the quarter real of twenty-five centimos; the tenth of a real, of ten centimos; and the twentieth of a real, of five centimos.‡

The coinage of Spain is executed at three different mints, one of which is at Madrid, another at Seville, and one at Barcelona. There was formerly a mint at Segovia, which at one time executed the entire coinage of Spain, but in 1730 the gold and silver coinage was transferred to Madrid; after which the mint at Segovia coined nothing but copper, until it was finally abolished. Segovia is famous for its Roman aqueduct, which is indeed the most remarkable remnant of Roman architecture in Spain, being 2961 feet in length, and in some places rising 102 feet above the valley; built of granite, without cement of any kind. It is from this structure that the coins struck at Segovia derived their mint mark, which was a small aqueduct,

---

* Letter of MR. SMITH, before quoted. † Ibid. ‡ Ibid.

generally placed at one side of the shield. The mint mark of Madrid is an M. surmounted by a crown, that of Seville an S., and that of Barcelona the initial B. These are sometimes placed beneath the device on the reverse, sometimes at the side, and not unfrequently at the end of the legend, and are usually accompanied by the private marks or initials of the Mint Master.

1. S. 1749. Pistareen, of FERDINAND AND ISABELLA. Obv. The Royal arms "FERDINANDUS ET ISABEL. D. G."

2. S. Pistareen, of CHARLES* AND JOANNA. Obv. A crowned shield bearing the arms of Spain (a lion and a castle) "CAROLUS ET JOHANA REGS." Rev. "HISPANIARUM† ET INDIARUM;" two upright pillars, surmounted by crowns. "PLUS UL"(tra). Not dated.

3. S. 1598. Eight reals, of PHILIP II. Obv. Shield, surmounted by a crown; the denomination "VIII." at one side, and the mint mark at the other. "PHILIPPUS. D. G. OMNIUM." Rev. "HISPAN. REGNORUM. REX. 1598," and the arms of Spain.

4 and 5. C. 1636. Maravedi, of PHILIP IV. Obverse of No. 5, two upright pillars in the water, beside a projecting rock. Rev. Crowned shield bearing the arms of the royal house.

6. S. 1672. Crown dollar, of CHARLES II. (Succeeded in 1665, at the age of four years.) Obv. Bust, "CAROL. II. D. G. HISP. ET INDIAR. REX. 1672." Rev. Crowned shield supported by two lions. "ARCHID. AUST. DUX BURG. CO. FLAN.," (Archduke of Austria, Duke of Burgundy, and Count (Comes) of Flanders.) Struck for Belgium.

7. S. 1682. Pistareen, of same. Obv. Arms of Spain. "CAROLUS II. D. G. 1682." Rev. "CHARLES (in monogram) II." surmounted by a crown. "HISPANIARUM REX."

8. S. 1707. One real, of PHILIP V. Obv. Crowned shield, bearing the arms of Spain "1......R." "PHILIP. V. D. G. HISPANIAR. REX." Rev. Royal cipher, crowned, "DEXTERA D(ominus) EXALTAVIT ME. 1707."

9 and 10. S. 1708. Five reals, of same. Similar to preceding.

---

* Afterward CHARLES V., Emperor of Germany.

† The ancient name of Spain was "*Hesperia*," or Western; Spain having been the most western portion of the world known to the ancients. It was also called "*Iberia*," from the River *Iber*, now *Ebro*.

11, 12, and 13. S. 1708–1714. Double reals, of CHARLES III., (the Pretender.) Similar to No. 7, (the arms of the royal house of CHARLES, instead of the Spanish.)

These were struck during the famous "*war of the Spanish succession.*" There appears to have been contemporary sets of the small coins, struck by the several claimants. CHARLES III. was at this time Emperor of Austria, and afterward CHARLES VI. Emperor of Germany.

14 and 15. S. 1716 and 1721. Pieces of two and one real, of PHILIP V. Obv. Crowned shield, bearing the royal arms; arms of Anjou (three *fleurs de lis*) on a shield of pretence. "PHILIPPUS V. D. G." Rev. "HISPANIARUM REX. 1716," and the arms of Spain.

16. S. 1724. Two reals, of LOUIS I. Same type as preceding.

17. S. 1726. One real, of PHILIP V. Same type.

Philip abdicated in 1724 in favor of his son LOUIS I.; but Louis dying the same year Philip again assumed the reigns of government.

18 to 22. S. 1731–1738. Pieces of eight, four, two, one, and one-half reals. All same type as No. 14.

23. S. 1740. Double pistareen, (much worn,) R. R. R.

24. G. 1740. Half pistole. Obv. Bust, "PHILIP V. D. G. HISPAN. ET IND. REX. 1740." Rev. Crowned shield, bearing the royal arms, "INITIUM SAPIENTIÆ TIMOR DOM." Value $2.01.6.

25. G. 1750. Quarter pistole, of FERDINAND VI. Obv. Bust, "FERDINAND VI. D. G.......1750." Rev. Crowned shield, bearing the arms of Spain, "HISPANIARUM REX." Value $1.00.8.

26. S. 1751. One real, of same. Obv. Crowned shield, bearing the royal arms, with the arms of Anjou on a shield of pretence. Rev. Arms of Spain. Value about 11.5 cts.

27. S. 1754. Two reals. Same type.

28. G. 1756. Quarter pistole. Same as No. 25.

29. S. 1758. Two reals. Same as No. 26.

30. S. 1762. Eight reals, of CHARLES III. Obv. Crowned shield, bearing the royal arms, a shield of pretence bearing the arms of Spain and Anjou, "CAROLUS III. D. G." Rev. "HISPANIARUM REX. 1762," and the arms of Spain. Value 1.03.8.

31. C. 1770. Maravedis. Obv. Bust, "CAROLUS III. D. G. HISP.

REX.......1770." Rev. A cross, *fleury*, with the arms of Anjou in the center; arms of Spain in the angles, inclosed in a wreath.

32. S. 1771. Two reals, same as No. 30. Value about 20 cts.

33. S. 1773. Same. Obv. Bust, "CAROLUS III DEI G.......1773." Rev. Crowned shield, bearing the arms of Spain and Anjou.* "HISPANIARUM REX."

34. S. 1774. Eight reals. Same type. Value \$1.03.8.

35. S. 1774. One real. Same.

36. S. 1774. Half real. Same.

37. S. 1779. Four reals. Same.

38. G. 1781. Escudo. Obv. Bust, "CAROL. III. D. G. HISP. ET IND. R.......1781." Rev. Crowned shield hung with the order chain and badge of the order of the *golden fleece*, bearing the royal arms, with the arms of Spain on a shield of pretence, and Anjou on a heart-shield. "IN UTROQ(ue) FELIX A(uspice) D"(eo). Value about \$1.95.

39. G. 1783. Half escudo. Obverse same as preceding. Rev. Crowned shield, bearing the arms of Spain and Anjou, ornamented with the order chain, etc., as above. No legend.

40. G. 1788. Half doubloon, same as No. 30, with the legend in full, as "IN UTROQ. FELIX AUSPICE DEO." Value \$7.79.3.

41. G. 1788. Half escudo. Same as No. 39.

42. C. 1788. Eight maravedis. Obv. Bust, "CAROLUS III. D. G. HISP. REX." Reverse same as No. 31.

43. G. 1792. Half doubloon, of CHARLES IV. Same as No. 40.

44. S. 1792. Eight reals. Obv. Bust, "CAROLUS IIII. DEI G...... 1792." Rev. "HISPANIARUM REX," with a crowned shield, bearing the arms of Spain and Anjou. Value about \$1.03.

45. G. 1793. Pistole, of same. Same type as No. 40. Value about \$3.91.

46. S. 1793. Half real. Same as No. 44.

---

* The reader will understand that where a shield is said to bear the "arms of Spain and Anjou," the latter is always on a shield of pretence. This mode of expression is not in strict accordance with the rules of heraldry, but is adopted in order to save repetition as much as possible.

47. S. 1797. Four reals. Same.

48. S. 1808. Two reals. Same.

49. S. 1808. Dollar. "Siege piece," of FERDINAND VII. Obv. "GNA 1808 UN DURO." Rev. "FER. VII." No device.

50. S. 1809. Five pesetas. "Siege piece," of same. Obv. "5 PS. ......FER......VII......1809," borne at opposite points. Rev. A small shield, bearing five stripes, surmounted by a crown. *R. R.*

The two preceding "siege pieces," or *necessity money*, as sometimes called, were struck by Ferdinand, during the incursion of Napoleon into Spain, during these years. They are merely silver "planchets," cut into the proper form and size, and then stamped with hand-punches. All other means of coining money were suspended, on account of the military operations.

51. S. 1809. Twenty reals, of JOSEPH NAPOLEON. Obv. Undraped bust, "JOSEPH NAP. DEI GRATIA......1809." Rev. "HISPANIARUM ET IND. REX," and the arms, borne on a crowned shield. Value $1.04.6.

52. S. 1810. Five pesetas, of BARCELONA. Obv. "5 PESETAS," beneath which are two palm branches, crossed, inclosed in a wreath. "EN BARCELONA......1810." Rev. A diamond-shaped shield, inclosed in a wreath.

53. S. 1810. Reverse of same. Value $1.01.4.

54. S. 1811. One peseta, of BARCELONA.

Pieces of one and five pesetas, or pistareens, of this type, were struck at BARCELONA during the Peninsular troubles, and bear date from 1809 to 1812. They acknowledge no monarch, and would appear to have been coined by private parties, without authority from any government.

55. G. 1811. Eighty reals, of JOSEPH NAPOLEON. Obv. Bust, "JOSEPH NAP. D. G. HISP. ET IND. R......1811." Rev. Crowned shield, hung with the order chain and badge of the golden fleece. "IN UTROQ. FELIX. AUSPICE DEO." Value $3.90.

56. S. 1812. Twenty reals, of JOSEPH NAPOLEON. Same type as No. 51.

57. S. 1812. Ten reals. Same.

58. S. 1812. Four reals. Same.

59. S. 1813. Eight reals, of FERDINAND VII. Obv. Bust, "FERDI-

NANDUS VII. DEI GRATIA......1813." Reverse same as No. 44. Value $1.04.5.

61. S. 1815. Eight reals. Obv. Bust, *laureated*, "FERDINAND VII DEI GRATIA......1815." Reverse same as preceding.

63. G. 1817. Pistole. Obv. Bust, *laureated*. Rev. The arms of Spain and Anjou, on a shield of pretence; otherwise similar to No. 55. Value $3.90.5.

64. G. 1820. Double pistole, or half doubloon. Same as preceding. Value $7.74.8.

65. S. 1821. Thirty sous. "Siege piece." Obv. "1821......FR.º ......VII......30 SOUS," at opposite points. Rev. A diamond-shaped shield hung with laurel. "SALUS POPULI." Struck during the revolution of 1820–21. Value about $1.04.5.

66 and 67. S. 1821. Ten reals. Obv. Undraped bust inclosed in a double circle. "FERN. 7.º POR LA G. DE DIOS Y. LA CONST......1821." Rev. "RESELLADO (recoined) 10 R.s," inclosed in a wreath composed of two laurel branches, crossed. "REY. DE LAS ESPANAS." Value about 55.3 cts.

68. G. 1822. Eighty reals. Obv. Bust. Rev. Device same as No. 63. Legend same as preceding.

69 and 70. S. 1823. Twenty reals. Obv. Bust, "FERDINANDO 7.º POR LA GRACIA DE DIOS Y. LA CONSTITUTION......1822." Rev. "REY DE LAS ESPANAS......20 R.s," a crowned shield, bearing the arms of Spain and Anjou between two upright pillars, around which is a scroll with "PLUS ULTRA." Value about $1.04.6.

71. S. 1823. Four reals. Same type as preceding, with the pillars and scroll omitted from the reverse.

72 to 75. C. 1824 to 1831. Pieces of eight, four, and two maravedis; all of the same type as No. 31.

76. S. 1830. Two reals. Obv. Bust, enveloped in a Roman mantle, *laureated*. "FERDIN VII DEI GRATIA," and the date. Rev. Crowned shield, bearing the arms of Spain and Anjou. "HISPANIARUM REX."

77 and 78. S. 1833. Pieces of twenty, and two reals. Same type. Obv. Bust, *laureated*. "FERNANDO 7.º POR LA G. DE DIOS," and the date. Rev. "REY DE ESPANA Y DE LAS INDIAS." A crowned shield, bearing the arms, encircled by the order chain and badge of the

golden fleece. On the edge is inscribed "DIOS ES EL REY DE LAS REYES." Value of the dollar $1.05.

79 to 81. S. 1835 to 1848. Pieces of twenty, four, and one real, of ISABELLA II. Obv. Head, "ISABEL 2ª POR LA GRACIA DE DIOS." Rev. Same device as the dollar of Ferdinand, (No. 67). "REYNA DE ESPANA Y DE LAS INDIAS." Value of the dollar $1.05.

82 and 83. 1850 and 1853. Pieces of twenty,* and ten reals. Obv. Bust, "ISABEL 2ª POR LA GRACIA DE DIOS Y LA CONSTITUTION." Reverse same as the dollar of Ferdinand, (No. 69). On the edge is inscribed "LEY PATRIA REY."

84 to 86. S. 1852–53. Pieces of four, two, and one real, all of the same type as the dollar, (No. 72), with the pillars and scroll on the reverse omitted, and the edge grained. (See Plate XVI. No. 5.)

87. G. 1857. Piece of 100 reals. Obv. Bust, *laureated.* "ISABEL 2ª POR LA G. DE DIOS Y LA CONST." and the date "1857." Rev. An oval shield, bearing the royal arms, surmounted by a crown; arms of Spain on a shield of pretence, and the arms of Anjou on a heart-shield. Beneath are two palm branches, crossed; the denomination "100 Rs." Value $4.96.3. (See Plate XVI. No. 1.)

88 and 89. S. 1858. Twenty reals. The head of her majesty, as depicted on these pieces, is quite an improvement in symmetry of outline, if not in likeness, upon the head found upon the coins of the previous issue. Values $1.00.3. (See Plate XVI. No. 4.)

---

* This piece consists of two plates of silver, with a planchet of brass between. It may be interesting to the uninitiated to learn how this was accomplished. When the piece was first issued from the Royal Mint it was a good dollar, of solid proportions; but, unfortunately, it "fell among thieves," who succeeded in extracting about one-third of the silver composing the interior of the coin, and supplying its place with a plate of brass, in this wise: The coin is first fastened into a lathe, and made to revolve; a very thin chisel, in the hands of the operator, is then applied to its circumference, and held on until it has penetrated to the center. In this manner a portion of the interior is cut from the coin, leaving the two outside plates, bearing the impressions, as perfect as ever. A planchet of brass, or other base metal, is then prepared, of the proper thickness, to which the two outside pieces are soldered, and the opening around the edge nicely concealed. This makes a very ingenious imposition, but one which is easily detected, as the sound or ring which it produces, when thrown upon a hard surface, as well as the weight, is very deficient.

PORTUGAL.

The Peninsula of Portugal, originally a part of Spain, was established as an independent monarchy in the year 1092. HENRY of Burgundy, grandson to ROBERT I. of France, enlisted in the cause of ALPHONSO, Emperor of Spain, against the Moors, and distinguished himself by such great bravery, that ALPHONSO rewarded his services (an unusual thing) by creating him count of that part of Portugal now called *Entre Douro e Minho*, where the City of *Oporto*, formerly called *Portus Calle*, is situated, from which the whole country derives its name. He also bestowed upon him his natural daughter THERESA in marriage. HENRY made war upon the *Saracens*, who still possessed a portion of the Portuguese territory, and succeeded in dispossessing them of *Viseu*, *Lamego*, *Braga*, and *Coimbra*. He died in 1112, while on an expedition to assist his sister-in-law, URACA, Queen of Castile, against ALPHONSO, King of Aragon.

There is, probably, no coinage in the world that has enjoyed a wider reputation than the gold coins of Portugal. The "*joe*" and the "*half joe*" are familiar names the world over. The Portuguese have been proverbially great traders. Their vessels have plowed the waters of every sea, and their "*land ho!*" has found an echo upon every coast The consequence has been that their gold currency has sought and found a market in every quarter of the globe. The discovery of Brazil, by CABRAL, in the year 1500,* with her rich deposits of gold, and, at a later period, the consequent influx of the precious metal, served to swell the gold currency of Portugal to gigantic dimensions. But since the *loss* of her "golden possessions," her gold coinage has dwindled into comparatively insignificant proportions. Her silver coins were never very abundant beyond her own limits.

The unit of Portuguese money was formerly the *rei*, of which one thousand was nearly equivalent to the Spanish dollar. But this has

---

* Brazil was first visited in 1499 by Vincent Yañez Pincon, a companion of Columbus; but he appears not to have taken any formal possession of the country, having merely touched upon its coast by accident. Pincon was a Spaniard.

been displaced by the *millrei* of one thousand reis, which is represented by a silver coin.

Since the middle of the seventeenth century Portugal has had three different systems of gold coinage. The *first* was the one known as the *moidore* series, consisting of the *dobrao* of 20,000 reis, and its half; the *moeda d'ouro* (moidore) of 4000 reis, and its half, quarter, and tenth; the latter was also known as the *cruzado*, of 400 reis. These were all 917 thousandths fine; and the dobra was equivalent to 830 Troy grains, the *moidore* to 166 grains, the others in proportion.

In 1722 the *joannese* series made its appearance. This series comprised seven denominations: the *joannese* or *dobra*, of 12,800 reis; the half, of 6400 reis; the quarter, of 3200 reis; the *escudo*, of sixteen *tostoes*, or 1600 reis; the *quartinho*, or quarter moidore, of 1200 reis; the half escudo, of 800, and the *cruzado*, of 400 reis. These were coined at the old standard of fineness (917 thousandths), and the weight of the largest piece was placed at 442.8 grains, the others in proportion. Notwithstanding the fact that this coinage was introduced in 1722, the old moidore series seems to have been continued until 1732.

The "*joe*" series was continued until 1835, when it was abolished by MARIA II., and a third series instituted, consisting of two pieces only, the *coroa d'ouro*, or gold crown of 5000 reis, and its half; the crown to weigh 147.6 grains, the half in proportion; the fineness was the same as before.

Before 1835 the silver coins were the *cruzado*, of 400 reis,* the half, of twelve *vintens*, the piece of six *vintens*, the *testoon*, of 100 reis, and its half. These were originally 917 thousandths fine, but for many years were coined at 899 thousandths. The *cruzado* weighed 226.6 grains, the other pieces in proportion.

The decree of 1835, establishing the *millrei* as the unit, provided for a new system of silver coins in conformity thereto. This system consists of the *coroa* (crown), or millrei of 1000 reis, its half of 500 reis, and the pieces of 200 and 100 reis. The legal fineness is 917

* Current at 480 reis.

thousandths, and the *millrei* should weigh about 148 grains, the others in proportion.

The gold coinage of Portugal is little better than bullion, being always at a premium. Several laws have been enacted to remedy this defect, but, as it appears, without success.

The currency was formerly purely metallic, but, in 1797, the Government issued a large amount of paper in the form of notes, at the rate of 1200 to 20,000 reis each, bearing interest; making it a legal tender in all transactions to pay half in paper and half in specie. The interest was promptly paid for a few years, but was afterward neglected, and the paper was soon reduced to 35 per cent. below par.*

Copper forms a large portion of the currency, as is evinced by the fact that in 1834 any debt could be discharged by paying one-half in Government paper, one-third in silver, and one-sixth in copper.†

95. G. 1557. Cruzado of 400 reis, of SEBASTIAN I. Obv. Crowned shield, bearing the arms of Portugal (five small shields *in cross* on a field *argent*, with a border *gules*, red, bearing seven castles; the *color*, however, is not always represented.) "SEBASTIANUS I. REX POR. ——." Rev. A cross-potent, "IN HOC SIGNO VINCES."

96. S. 1580. 200 reis, of PHILIP II. Obv. Crowned shield similar to preceding, between "L." and "B." "PHILIPPUS D. G. REX PORTUGALIÆ." Reverse same as preceding.

97. G. 1704. Moidore, of 4000 reis, of PETER II. Obv. Crowned shield and the denomination "4.000" "PETRUS II. D. G. PORT. ET ALG. REX." Reverse same as No. 95, with "R's" in the angles of the cross, and the date "1704" in the legend. Value $6.59.5.

98. S. 1704. Eighty reis. Obv. "LXXX" (the denomination) beneath a crown. Legend same as preceding. Rev. A cross, with roses in the angles. Same legend as preceding.

99. S. 1704. Forty reis. Obverse same as preceding. Reverse same as No. 95, with "P's" in the angles of the cross.

100. S. 1714. Eighty reis, of JOHN V. Same type as No. 98.

101. S. 1714. Forty reis. Same.

---

* Manual of Coins and Bullion. † Ibid.

102. G. 1720. Moidore, of same. Same type as No. 97. Value $6.49.

103. G. 1722. 1000 reis. Same as preceding, with roses in the angles of the cross.

104. G. 1723. Escudo, of 1600 reis. Obv. Head, *laureated.* "JOHANNES V. D. G. PORT. ET ALG. REX.......1723." Rev. Crowned shield. No legend.

105. G. 1724. Half escudo. Same type.

106. G. 1725. Five-moidore piece. Same type as No. 102, with "M's" in the angles of the cross. Value $30.70.

107. G. 1729. Joannes, or *dobra,* of 12,800 reis. Same type as No. 104. Value $17.24.2.

This is the famous "joe" coinage, mentioned in the introduction. This series was first introduced in the year 1722, and consisted of this piece and its subdivisions, down to the *cruzado* of 400 reis. But although this series began to be coined in 1722, the old *moidore* series, it appears, was not displaced until about 1732.

108. G. 1730. Quartinho, or quarter moidore, of 1200 reis. Same as preceding.

109. C. 1732. Five reis. Obv. Crowned shield. "JOANNES V DEI GRATIA." Rev. "PORTUGALLÆ ET ALGARBIORUM REX." The denomination "V" and the date "1732" inclosed in a wreath of laurel.

110. G. 1736. Half joe, of 6400 reis. Same as No. 104.

111. G. 1739. 1000 reis. Same as No. 103.

112. G. 1758. Half joe, of JOSEPH I. Obv. Bust, *laureated.* "JOSEPHUS I D. G. PORT ET ALG. REX......1758." Reverse same as No. 104. Value $8.62.

113. G. 1762. Half joe. Same. This piece is spurious. It is not much inferior in fineness to the preceding piece, which is genuine, but is very deficient in weight.

114. S. 1762. Eighty reis. Same type as No. 98.

115. C. 1763. Ten reis. Same type as No. 109.

116. S. 1781. 200 reis, of MARIA I. and PETER III. Obv. Crowned shield; the denomination "200" at the left, and the date "1781" at the right side. "MARIA I ET PETRUS III D. G. PORT. E ALG. REGES." Reverse same as No. 103. Value about 28 cts.

117. G. 1785. Half joe. Obv. Busts of MARIA and PETER in profile. Reverse same as No. 104. Value $8.65.

118. G. 1785. Same, reverse. This piece has been "*clipped*" to the edge of the letters, and remilled.

119. S. 1785. 100 reis. Obv. Crowned shield. Same legend as No. 116. Reverse same as No. 95, with roses in the angles of the cross.

120. G. 1787. Half joe, of MARIA I. Obv. Bust, "MARIA I D. G. PORT. ET ALG. REGINA......1787." Reverse same as No. 104. Value $8.70.

121. S. 1788. 400 reis. Obv. Crowned shield. Same legend as No. 120. Reverse same as No. 119. Value about 56 cts.

122. S. 1788. Forty reis. Same type as No. 98.

123. C. 1795. Twenty reis. Same type as No. 109, with the exception that the wreath on the reverse is composed of two olive branches, crossed.

124. C. 1795. Ten reis. Same.

125. C. 1804. Three reis, of JOHN MARIA, *Regent.* Same type as preceding.

In 1797, the Queen (*Maria I.*) became mentally imbecile, and her son, JOHN MARIA, began to administer the government, as regent. In 1804, the name of MARIA was removed from the coin, and that of the *regent* substituted. In 1816 he became king, with the title of JOHN VI.

126. G. 1807. Half joe. Obv. Bust, *laureated.* "JOANNES D. G. PORT. ET ALG. P. REGENS......1807." Rev. An oval shield, surmounted by a crown. No legend. Value $8.70.

127 and 128. S. 1816. 400 reis, *of the Regency.* Obv. Crowned shield. "JOANNES D. G. PORT." etc. Reverse same as No. 119. Value about 56 cts.

129. S. 1820. 400 reis, of JOHN VI. Obv. A shield, behind which is a globe, surmounted by a crown. "JOANNES VI D. G. PORTUG. BRASIL ET ALGARB. REX." Reverse same as No. 119. Value 56 cts.

130. G. 1823. Half joe. Obv. Bust, *laureated.* Same legend as preceding. Rev. Same device as the obverse of preceding, between branches of olive and laurel, crossed. Value $8.65.

131. C. 1830. Five reis, of MARIA II. Obv. Crowned shield. "MARIA II DEI GRATIA." Rev. The denomination "V" between two roses, and the date "1830" inclosed in a wreath, composed of two laurel branches, crossed. "PORTUGALIÆ ET ALGARBIORUM REGINA."

132. C. 1831. Ten reis, of DON MIGUEL. Obv. Crowned shield. "MICHAEL I DEI GRATIA." Rev. "PORTUGALIÆ ET ALGARBIORUM REX ......1831." The denomination "X" inclosed in a wreath, composed of two oak branches, crossed.

In 1826, DONA MARIA, though only seven years of age, was proclaimed regent in behalf of her father, DON PEDRO, of Brazil, but her right was disputed by her uncle, DON MIGUEL. A vigorous contest ensued, and it was not until 1833 that the queen was firmly seated upon the throne.

133. C. 1832. Forty reis, of same. Obv. "MICHAEL I. D. G. PORTUG. ET ALGARB. REX." Rev. The denomination "40" inclosed in a wreath, composed of two oak branches, crossed. "PUBLICÆ UTILITATI......1832."

134. G. 1834. Half joe, of MARIA II. Obv. Bust, "MARIA II D. G. PORTUG. ET ALGARB. REGINA......1834." Rev. Crowned shield, between oak branches, crossed. Value about $8.65. (See Plate XVI. No. 2.)

135. G. 1838. *Coroa d'ouro*, or gold crown, of 5000 reis. Obv. Bust, "MARIA II PORTUG. ET ALGARB. REGINA ...... 1838." Rev. Drapery suspended from a crown, and forming a canopy over the shield. "5000 REIS." Value $5.81. (See Plate XVI. No. 3.)

In 1835 *Maria* abolished the old system of coinage, and issued an entire new one, consisting of this piece and its parts, as follows :—

136. G. 1838. Half crown. Same type.

137. S. 1838. Silver crown, or *millrei*, of 1000 reis. Same type. Value $1.16.4.

138. S. 1838. Half crown. Same type. (See Plate XVI. No. 6.)

139. S 1838. Piece of 200 reis. Obverse same as preceding. Rev. "200 REIS" inclosed in a wreath, composed of two laurel branches, crossed.

140. S. 1838. Piece of 100 reis. Same type. (See Plate XVI. No. 7.)

AFRICAN COLONIES.

The Portuguese have settlements and claim dominion in various parts of Africa. On the Eastern coast they exert a limited authority over *Mozambique*, and on the opposite shore over the kingdoms of *Congo*, *Angola*, and *Benguela*, in *Lower Guinea*. The following pieces having been struck for these colonies, are not included in the regular series.

143. S. 1762. Four macutas, of JOSEPH I. Obv. Crowned shield, bearing the arms of Portugal. "JOSEPHUS I D. G. REX. P. ET D. GUINEÆ." Rev. "MACUTAS 4" inclosed in a wreath. "AFRICA PORTUGUEGA, 1762."

144. S. 1763. Twelve macutas. Same as preceding. Value 67.9 cts.

145. S. 1770. Six macutas. Same.

146. S. 1783. Twelve macutas, of MARIA I. and PETER III. Obv. Crowned shield. "MARIA I. E PETRUS III D. G. REGES P. E. D. GUINEÆ." Reverse same as preceding. Value 67.9 cts.

147. S. 1783. Ten macutas. Same.

148. S. 1796. Ten macutas, of MARIA I. Obv. "MARIA I D. G. REGINA P. ET D. GUINEÆ;" otherwise same as before.

149. S. 1796. Eight macutas. Same.

150. S. Two macutas. Same.

DIVISION VII.

GERMAN EMPIRE.

The first Emperor of Germany was CHARLEMAGNE, *King of France*, who was crowned at Rome, as Emperor of the West, by POPE LEO III., on Christmas-day, in the year 800. His dominions consisted of all Germany, extending to the Baltic Sea and the mouth of the Vistula; of Gaul and the North of Spain as far as the Ebro; of Italy to Mount Vesuvius, extending eastward over Panonia,

Sclavonia, Bosnia, and Dalmatia. He died A.D. 814, having, the year previous, caused LOUIS, his only surviving son, to be crowned emperor, in a solemn assembly held at Aix-la-Chapelle. The house of CHARLEMAGNE continued to possess the throne of the German Empire until the death of the youthful Emperor, LOUIS III., who died of grief, caused by the dissensions between the Lords and the Bishops, in the year 912. From this time the throne was filled by election, the princes of the different German States being the persons in whom the right of voting for an emperor was vested. The imperial crown was possessed by various houses up to the time of RODOLPH I. (1273), since which time, with the singular exception of ADOLPHUS of Nassau (1291), the scepter of the empire continued in the house of *Hapsburg*, up to the time of the dissolution in 1806, when FRANCIS II. renounced the imperial purple and assumed the title of FRANCIS I., *Emperor of Austria.*

In this division several coins of Hungary, of the earlier dates, will be found. The coins of that kingdom are not properly classed among those of this division, Hungary never having formed a part of the empire; and it is proper here to explain that these exceptions to the general rule have been made in order to save confusion. These pieces were struck by the kings of Hungary *after their elevation to the imperial throne;* at which time another person occupied he throne of Hungary as the *representative* of the Emperor; it never having been usual·for the emperors of Germany to *annex* their own possessions to the empire upon their accession to the throne, for the reason that they might thereby *disinherit* their own house.

One of the most widely known coins in the world is the ducat.* This, for several centuries, was the principal gold coin of the German Empire, and was coined by all the German states and cities. It appears to have been derived from the *bezant* of the Greek-Roman Empire, and first made its appearance in Venice, about the middle of the thirteenth century. OGILVIE derives its name from the legend which it bore at that time, viz., "SIT TIBI, CHRISTE, DATUS, QUEM TU REGIS, ISTE DUCATUS." It was originally made of very pure gold,

* Or *sequin*, as sometimes called.

but soon fell a little below absolute purity, to about 97 per cent. fine. In some portions of the German Empire, it was subsequently much depreciated, so that it is often found to be less than nine-tenths fine. The weight of the German ducat, since the diet of Augsburg, in 1559, should be 53.87 Troy grains.

In some of the German states and other countries (as Denmark), two kinds of ducats were formerly coined, the *specie* and the *current* ducat. The former was usually of the ancient standard, while the latter was more or less alloyed, sometimes approaching *baseness*. Both are now nearly obsolete in every part of the world.

The German coins are noticed more at large in the introduction to German States.

1. G. Ducat, of FREDERICK I., Barbarossa. (1152 to 1190.) Obv. The imperial globe. "FRIDRICUS ROMAN IMPERATOR." Rev. A full-length figure of the patron saint. "MONETA NOVA NORDLINGES."

2. G. Ducat, of SIGISMUND I. (1410 to 1437.) Obv. Full-length figure, crowned, and carrying a scepter, (probably intended for Sigismund.) "SIGISM. ARCHI. DUX AUSTRIE." Rev. An ornamented cross, with shields in the angles. "MONETA AUREA COMITIS TIROL."

3. S. 1541. Thaler, of the Emperor CHARLES V. Obv. Double-headed eagle, surmounted by a crown. "KAROLUS V. ROMANORUM IMPR. SEMPE. A." (Roman Emperor ever august.) Rev. A shield, surmounted by a helmet and a lion's head, *erased*. "KARLWOLF : LUDWIG : & : MARTIN : CO : IN : OTING."

4. G. Ducat, of MAXIMILIAN II. (1564 to 1576.) Obv. The imperial globe or *mound*, and a small shield bearing an eagle. "MAXIMIL II. ROMANO. IMPER." Rev. Five shields, forming a cross, the central one bearing a donkey. "LUDOVI. CO. IN. STOL. RON. RUT. WER."

5. G. 1599. Ducat, of RODOLPH II. Obv. Virgin and child. "RUDOL II D. G. RO(manus) I(mperator) S(emper) A(ugustus) GE (rmaniæ). HU(ngariæ) B(ohemiæ) R"(ex). Rev. A full-length figure dressed in armor, and carrying a spear; between the letters "K." and "B." "S. LADISLAUS REX. 1599." Struck for Hungary.

6. G. Ducat, of MATTHIAS. (1612 to 1619.) Obv. Double eagle, with the imperial globe upon its breast. "MATTH(ias) D. G. R. IMP. S.

AU. G. B(ohemiæ) H(ungariæ) R"(ex). Rev. Bust at full face, grasping a scepter. "MON. NO. AU. EPISCO. CURIEN."

7. G. 1612. Ducat, of MATTHIAS. Obv. Busts of Matthias and his consort, (Annie of Austria,) both crowned. "D. MATHIÆ RO. IMP. ET ANNÆ CONJUG AUGUSS." Rev. Three shields, "1612." "NORIBERGA OVANS FOELICEM GRATULATUR INGRESSUM."

8. G. 1814. Ducat. Obv. Figure of the emperor, crowned; a scepter in one hand and the imperial globe in the other. "MATT. D. G. R. I. S. A. GE. HU. B. REX." Rev. Virgin and child. "AR(chidux) AU(striæ) DU(x.) BU(rgundiæ) MA(rchio) MO(raviæ) CO(mes) TY(rolis) 1614." Struck for Hungary.

9. G. 1646. Ducat, of FERDINAND III. Obv. Figure of Ferdinand, as in No. 7. "FER. III. D. G. R. I. S. A. GE. HU. B. REX." Rev. Virgin and child. "AR. AU. DU. BU. MA. MO. CO. TY. 1646." Struck for Hungary.

12. S. Crown, of same, not dated. (Reigned from 1637 to 1657.) Obv. Bust, *laureated,* and dressed in armor. "FERDINAND III. D. G. ROM IM. S. A. G. H. E(t) B. REX." Rev. A shield, with the imperial crown suspended above by two cherubims, one carrying a sword and the other a scepter, hung with the order chain and badge of the golden fleece. "ARCHIDUX AUS. E(t) CARINTHIÆ. D. B(urgundiæ) EC."

13 and 14. S. Thalers, of same. Obv. Bust, dressed in armor and crowned, a scepter in one hand and a sword in the other. "FERDINAND D. G. ARCHI. AUSTRIAE." Rev. Crowned shield, hung with the order chain and badge, as above. "DUX BURGUN CO. TYROLIS."

23. S. 1646. Crown, of same. Obv. Bust, *laureated,* ornamented with the badge of the golden fleece. "FERDINAND III D. G. RO. I. S. AUG. GER. (a small shield crowned) HU. BOH. REX." Rev. Double-headed eagle surmounted by the imperial crown, a small shield upon its breast, a sword in the dexter, and a scepter in the sinister talon. "ARCHIDUX AUS. DUX BUR. MAR. MO. CO. TY. 1646."

25. G. 1655. Ducat. Same as No. 7. Struck for Hungary.

26. S. 1657. Crown. Same as No. 23.

27. G. 1675. Quarter ducat, of LEOPOLD I. Obv. Bust, *laureated.* "LEOPOLDUS D. G. R. I. S. A. G. H. B. REX." Rev. Eagle, as in No. 23. "ARCHID. AUS. DUX B. E(t) CO. TYR. 1675."

28. S. 1691. Crown, of same. Obv. Bust, as in No. 23. "LEOPOLDUS (Virgin and child) D. G. RO. I. S. AUG. GER. (small shield crowned) HU. BO. REX." Reverse like No. 23.

29. S. 1693. Florin. Same as preceding.

30. S. 1693. Florin. Similar type, with the Virgin and child, and the shield omitted in the legend.

31. G. 1710. Half ducat, of JOSEPH I. Obv. Bust, as in No. 23. "JOSEPHUS D. G. R. I. S. A. G. H. B. REX." Reverse same as above.

32. G. 1714. Ducat, of CHARLES VI. Obv. Figure of the emperor in armor, crowned, the imperial globe in the sinister hand and a scepter in the other; the latter rests upon a shield bearing an eagle, like that in No. 23. "CAROLUS VI D. G. R. I. S. A. G. H(ispaniæ H(ungariæ) B(ohemiæ) R(ex) A(rchidux) A"(ustriæ). Rev. The earth surrounded by clouds and surmounted by a helmet, the whole surmounted by the sun. "CONSTANTIA ET FORTITUDINE," inclosed in a beaded circle. "CONTINUATUR MDCCXIV HIS. AUSPICYS."

33 and 34. G. 1724. Ducats. Obv. Figure of the emperor, as in No. 7. "CAROLUS VI D. G. R. I. S. A. G. H. H. B. R." Rev. Virgin and child. "PATRONA REGNI HUNGARIÆ. 1724." Struck for Hungary.

35. G. 1738. Ducat. Obv. Bust, *laureated.* "CAR. VI. D. G. R. I. S. A. GE. HI. H. BO. REX." Rev. Eagle, like No. 23. "ARCHID. AUST. DUX BURG. ET STYRIÆ. 1738.

36. G. 1738. Ducat. Obv. Figure of the emperor, as in No. 7. Same legend as preceding. Reverse same as No. 33.

37. G. 1742. Ducat, of CHARLES VII. Obv. Bust, *laureated.* "CAR. VII R. IMP. S. A. EL(ectus) FRANCO(furt) F. D. 24 M. JAN. 1742." Rev. A tomb, bearing an open volume, with the words "DEGA LOCUS;" the sun appears at the left of the field. "UNIONE ET OBSERVANTIA LEGUM."

38. S. 1760. Thaler, of FRANCIS I. Obv. Bust, as in No. 23. "FRANC. D. G. R. I. S. A. GE. JER(osolymæ) R. LO(tharingiæ) B(urgundiæ) M(agnus) H(etruriæ) D(ux)." Rev. Double-headed, or Austrian eagle. "10 EINE FEINE MARCKT. 1760." "LEGE VINDICE."

39. S. 1763. Thaler. Obv. Austrian eagle. "FRANCISCUS D. G. ROM. IMP. SEMP. AUG." Rev. Peace, crowned; an olive branch in her left hand. To the left is a pedestal, supporting a smoking urn;

an oval shield leaning against the pedestal. "BENEDICTUS DOMINUS QUI DOBIT FACEM INFINIBUS NOSTRIS;" "X ST. E. F. MARK," and the date beneath.

40. G. 1787. Ducat, of JOSEPH II. Obv. Head, *laureated.* "JOS. II. D. G. R. I. S. A. GE. HU. BO. REX." Rev. Austrian eagle. "ARCHI. A. D. BURG. LOTH. M(agnus) D(ux) H(etruriæ) 1787."

41. G. 1792. Ducat, of FRANCIS II. Obv. Head, *laureated.* "FRANCISCUS II. ROMANORUM IMPERATOR." Rev. An altar, surrounded by diverging rays, supporting a crown, the imperial globe, and a sword and scepter. "PACIS ET DECUS." In the *exergue* is the date of his election.

42. C. 1800. Six kreuzers. Obv. Bust, *laureated.* "FRANZ. II. ROM(er) KAI(ser) KON(ig) Z(u) HU(ngarn) U(nd) BO. ERZH(erzog) Z(u) OEST(erreich). Rev. Austrian eagle. "SECHS KREUZER ERBLAENDISCH 1800."

43. C. 1800. One kreuzer. Obv. Bust, "FRANCIS II. D. G. R. I. S. A. GE. HU. BO. REX. A. A." Rev. Austrian eagle, and the date. No legend.

AUSTRIA.

When the Empire of Germany was established under CHARLEMAGNE, that district which afterward obtained the appellation of Lower Austria was declared a military frontier for repelling the incursions of the Huns, and other barbarous tribes to the eastward. It was called *Ost-reich*, the "*East country*," from its relative position to the rest of Germany. Its governor received, from CHARLEMAGNE, the title of *Margrave*, in German *markgraf*, or "Lord of the Marches." Toward the middle of the twelfth century Lower Austria received the addition of that territory called Upper Austria, and at the same time the Margrave received the title of Duke. In the year 1247 the male line, originally from Bamberg, now in Bavaria, became extinct by the death of RODOLPH, and a long interregnum ensued. The reigning emperor of Germany declared both that duchy and Styria to have lapsed to the imperial crown, and appointed a lieutenant to govern it on the part of the Empire. But afterward

PREMISLAUS OTTOACRE II., *King of Bohemia,* succeeded in substantiating his claim to the succession, and was invested with the government of Austria and Styria; and soon after the territories of Carinthia, Istria, and part of Friuli, devolved upon him by succession. But PREMISLAUS cast a blight upon all his bright prospects by his imprudence in refusing to acknowledge RODOLPH of Hapsburg as Emperor of Germany. An appeal to arms was the result, and in the year 1278 PREMISLAUS was defeated and slain in a battle fought at Marckfeld. By this victory RODOLPH acquired Austria, gave it to his son ALBERT, and, having obtained the sanction of the Electors of the Empire, the reign of the house of Hapsburg over Austria commenced A.D. 1282.

ALBERT afterward, in 1298, succeeded ADOLPHUS of Nassau, as Emperor of Germany, from which time until 1806 the house of Hapsburg, as stated in another place, continued to occupy the imperial throne—thus rendering the history of Austria and the Empire nearly synonymous. Austria became a member of the Germanic body in the year 1500, which position she still continues to occupy.

Prior to the year 1800 there were four distinct series of coins minted within the Austrian dominions, consisting of the Austrian *proper,* the Hungarian, the Lombard, and the Brabantine or Belgian. The former, or Austrian, was to be known by its double-headed eagle; the Hungarian, by its images of the Virgin and child; the Lombard, by its shield, quartered with eagles and serpents; and the Belgian, by its X shaped cross,* profusely ornamented. About the end of the last century the latter series ceased, the province of Belgium having been detached from the Austrian rule in 1795 and annexed to the French Republic.† About the same time *Lombardy* also passed from the Austrian rule; but at the pacification of Europe in 1815, *Lombardy,* with *Venice* annexed, reverted to Austria, and an Austrian monetary system was decreed for that country. Since this time there have been the three series of Austrian, Hun-

---

* St Andrew's Cross.

† The coins of Belgium will be found under the head "*Netherlands and Belgium,*" *Division viii.*

11

garian, and Lombard coins, but they appear to have differed only in the *type*, being otherwise in such harmony with each other as to be, in some respects, interchangeable.

The recent treaty of peace, however, which has been concluded between the Emperor Napoleon, the King of Sardinia, and the Emperor of Austria, will render still another change necessary in the Lombard coins. The latter province having, by the terms of this treaty, been cut off from Venice, withdrawn from the Austrian rule, and annexed to the Kingdom of Sardinia, the coinage will have to undergo still another transition, from an Austrian to a Sardinian character.*

Prior to the Convention of 1857, the gold coins proper to Austria were the single, double, and quadruple ducat. The ducat was coined at the Augsburg standard, viz., 986 thousandths fine, and to weigh 53.87 grains, the larger pieces in proportion. The quadruple ducat was a fine broad piece, but very thin, and easily bent, being no thicker than the single ducat.†

The silver coinage embraced six denominations: the *reichthaler*, or rixdollar; the *gulden*, or florin, which was half of the former;‡ the piece of twenty kreutzers, which was one-third of the florin; and the pieces of ten, five, and three kreutzers. These were all coined according to the standard adopted in 1753, known as the *Convention* rate. (See Introduction to German States.)

On the 24th of January, 1857, Austria became a party to a convention of the German States, by which the old system was to be abolished, and a new one, based upon the decimal system, introduced. Decrees were issued in Austria, in April, 1858, and April, 1859, to carry out the provisions of this agreement, but the war which ensued produced so great a turmöil in financial, as well as political circles, as to defeat the purposes of the Convention. In fact, about the only currency now known in Austria consists of paper and copper; the

---

* How long this state of affairs will be maintained, the present condition of politics in Europe furnishes no very reliable guarantee.

† The gold coins of Austria have always been at a premium against silver, and consequently used only as bullion.

‡ This was the unit of their moneys of account, and consisted of sixty kreutzers.

former being received as a legal tender at the Government offices.* The new system is treated of at length in the Introduction to German States.

47. S. 1618. Crown, of MAXIMILIAN, *Archduke* (son of MAXIMILIAN II.) Obv. Bust, ornamented with the order chain and badge of the order of St. Michael. "MAXIMILE. D. G. ARC. AU. DUX BUR. STIR. COM." Rev. "ET CAM. MAG. PRUSS. AD. CO(mes) H(etruriæ) ET TIROL." A shield, surmounted by a crown, and bearing four scepters *in cross*, with a shield of pretence in the center; the arms quartered in the angles of the cross.

48. S. 1743. Florin, of MARIA THERESIA. Obv. Bust, "M. THERESIA D. G. REG(ina) HUN. BOH." Rev. "ARCHID. AUST. DUX BURG. COM. TYR. 1743." A crowned shield, bearing the arms, quartered; a shield of pretence, surmounted by a crown, and bearing a lion *rampant*. Value 50.3 cts.

49. S. 1755. Thaler. Obv. Bust, "M. THERESIA D. G. R. IMP. GE. HU. BO. REG." Rev. "ARCHID AUST. DUX BUR. COM. TYR. 1755," and the Austrian eagle. Value $1.00.5.

A 50. G. 1759. Half ducat. Obv. Bust, "M. THERESIA D. G. RO. I. GE. H. BO. REG." Rev. Austrian eagle. "AR. AU. DUX. B(urgundiæ) M(oraviæ) P(rinceps) TRAN(sylvaniæ) CO. TY. 1759." Value $1.13.4.

B 50. C. 1762. One kreutzer. Obv. Bust, "M. THERES. D. G. R. I. G. H. B. R. A. AUST." Rev. "EIN KREUTZER 1762" on a shield. No legend.

51 and 52. S. 1766. Thalers. Obv. A crowned shield supported by two *griffins;* beneath is a palm and olive branch, crossed. "M. THERESIA D. G. R. IMP. HU. BO. REG." Rev. "AD NORMAM CONVENT. 1766," inclosed in a wreath composed of palm and laurel branches, crossed. Legend. ARCHID. AUST. D. BURG(undiae) MARGGR. BURGOVIAE." "JUSTITIA ET CLEMENTIA," on the *edge*. Value $1.00.5.

53. S. 1779. Florin. Similar to No. 49. Value 50.2 cts.

54 and 55. S. 1780. Thalers. Obverse same as No. 51. Rev.

---

* Letter of S. S. REMAK, U. S. Consul at Trieste, to the Treasury Department, May 9, 1859.

Legend. "ARCHID. AUST. DUX BURG. CO. TYR. 1780." Austrian eagle. Edge same as No. 51.

56. S. 1805. Thaler, of FRANCIS II. Obv. Head, *laureated.* "FRANCISCUS II. D. G. ROM. ET HAER. AUST. IMP." Rev. Austrian eagle, a sword in the dexter, and the imperial globe in the sinister talon. "GERM. HUN. BOH. REX. A. A. D. LOTH. VEN. SAL. 1805." "LEGE ET FIDE," on the edge. Value $1.01.

57. C. 1807. Thirty bank or paper kreutzers, of FRANCIS I.* Obv. Bust, in a square compartment. "FRANZ. KAIS. V OEST. KOEN. Z. HUNG. BOEH. GALIZ. U. LOD." Rev. Austrian eagle in a similar compartment; a scepter in the sinister talon. "DREYSSIG. KREUTZER. ERBLAENDISCH. 1807." "WIENERST BANCO ZETT THEILUNGS MÜNZ. Z. 30. K."

58. C. 1812. Three kreutzers. Obv. Bust. Legend same as preceding. Rev. "3 KREUTZERS. 1812," occupying the field. Legend. "SCHEIDMUNZE DER WIENER WAEHRUNG."

59 and 60. C. 1816. One kreutzer. Obv. "K(aiserliche) K(önigliche) OESTERREICHISCHE SCHEIDMÜNZE." Shield, surmounted by the imperial crown, and bearing the Austrian eagle. Rev. "EIN KREUTZER. 1816." Branches of palm and laurel, crossed, beneath.

61. C. 1816. Half kreutzer. Same type as preceding.

62 and 63. C. 1816. Quarter kreutzer. Same.

64. S. 1821. Thaler. Obv. Bust, *laureated,* "FRANCISCUS I D. G AUSTRIAE IMPERATOR." Rev. The Austrian eagle, "HUN. BOH. LOMG. ET VEN. GAL. LOD. IL(lyriae) REX. A. A. 1821."

65 and 66. B.S. 1826. Twenty kreutzers. Obv. Bust, *laureated,* inclosed in a wreath of two laurel branches, crossed. "FRANCISCUS I D. G. AUST. IMPERATOR." Rev. Austrian eagle; beneath is a small compartment, containing the denomination "20," at either side of which is a palm and a laurel branch. "HUN. BOH. LOMB. ET VEN. GAL. LOD. IL. REX. A. A. 1826." About one-half silver. Value 16.7 cts.

67. B.S. 1828. Three kreutzers. Similar to preceding, the denomination on the eagle's breast.

---

* The titles Francis I. and II., above used, apply to the same individual. He was Francis II. as Emperor of Germany; but, the Empire having been dissolved in 1806, he became Francis I. of Austria.

68. G. 1830. Quadruple or piece of four ducats. Obv. Bust, *laureated.* "FRANCISCUS I D. G. AUSTRIAE IMPERATOR." Rev. Austrian eagle, beneath which is "(4)." Legend same as No. 64. Nearly pure gold (986 thousandths fine.) Value $9.12.2.

69. B.S. 1833. Five kreutzers. Obverse, wreath omitted; otherwise similar to No. 65. Value 4.2 cts.

70. B.S. 1833. Three kreutzers. Similar to preceding.

71. G. 1834. Ducat. Similar to No. 68. Value $2.27.4.

72. B.S. 1834. Twenty kreutzers. Same as No. 69.

73. S. 1834. Thaler. Similar to No. 68. "JUSTITIA REGNORUM FUNDAMENTUM," on the *edge.* Value $1.00.8.

74. S. 1835. Same.

75. G. 1840. Quadruple, of FERDINAND I. Obv. Bust, *laureated,* dressed in ermine, and bedecked with four order chains. "FERD. I. D. G. AUSTR. IMP. HUN. BOH. R. H. N. V." Rev. "REX LOMB. ET VEN. DALM(atiæ) GAL. LOD. ILL. A. A. 1840." Austrian eagle, ornamented with four order chains. Value $9.14. (See Plate XVII. No. 1.)

76. G. 1840. Ducat. Obv. Head, *laureated;* otherwise same as preceding. Value $2.28.5.

77. S. 1840. Thaler. Same type. "TUERI RECTA," on the *edge.* Value $1.01. (See Plate XVII. No. 4.)

78. S. 1840. Florin. Same.

79. B.S. 1840. Twenty kreutzers. Same, with all the order chains omitted, except the *golden fleece.* Edge *grained.* Value 16.8 cts.

80. B.S. 1840. Ten kreutzers. Same as preceding.

81. B.S. 1840. Five kreutzers. Same.

82. B.S. 1840. Three kreutzers. Same, with the denomination "3" on the eagle's breast.

83. S. 1848. Two gulden, of the ARCHDUKE JOHN, *of Austria, (Administrator of the German Confederation.)* Obv. "ERZHERZOG JOHANN VON OESTERREICH," inscribed in four lines. Beneath is a palm and laurel branch, crossed. Legend. "ERWÄHLT ZUM REICHSVERWESER UBER DEUTSCHLAND D. 29. JUNI, 1848." Rev. Double-headed eagle. Legend. "CONTUIRENDE VERSAMMLUNG J. D. F. STADT FRANKFURT 18 MAI 1848." "ZWEY GULDEN," on the edge.

The National Assembly met at Frankfort, in May, 1848, and determined upon the reorganization of Germany into one integral empire, excluding the German possessions of Austria, and offering the imperial crown to the King of Prussia. This movement was headed by the Archduke JOHN, who was, in consequence, made Administrator by the Assembly.

84. B.S. 1849. Six kreutzers. Obv. Crowned shield. "6" at one side, and "K." at the other. Legend. "MAGYAR KIRALYI VALTO. PEUZ." Rev. "HAT. KRAJCZAR. 1849."

85 and 86. C. 1851. One kreutzer. Obv. Austrian eagle. "K. K. OESTERREICHISCHE SCHEIDEMÜNZE." Rev. "1 KREUZER —— 1851."

HUNGARY.

93. G. 1549. Ducat, of FERDINAND. Obv. Virgin and child. "FERDINAND D. G. R. UNGARIE." Rev. A figure in armor carrying a spear, the letter "K." at one side, and "B." at the other. "S. LADISLAUS REX 1549." Ferdinand succeeded CHARLES V. as Emperor of Germany in 1558.

94. G. 1558. Ducat, of JOHN SIGISMUND. Obv. Same device as preceding. "JOAN SIGISM. R. UNG. 1558." Rev. Crowned shield, "YSABE D. G. REG. UNGA. S. F. V."

95. S. 1609. Crown, of MATTHIAS. Obv. Bust, in armor, crowned, ornamented with the order chain and badge of the *golden fleece.* "MATTHI. II D. G. REX HUN. DESIG. IN REGEM BO.," Virgin and child. Rev. Crowned shield hung with the order chain, etc., as above, "ARCHID. AUS. DUX. BUR. MAR(chio) MO(raviæ) CO. TY. 1609."

96. G. Ducat, of MATTHIAS. Obv. Shield. "MATHIAS D. G. R. UNGARIE." Rev. Figure (probably of the saint,) crowned, with a scepter in one hand and the imperial globe in the other. "S. LADISLAUS REX."

97. G. Ducat, same as preceding, with a battle-ax substituted for the scepter.

98. G. 1650. Ducat. Obv. Bust, in armor, carrying a scepter. "GEO. RA. D. G. P. TRA." Rev. Virgin and child. "PAR. REG. HUN. DO. ET SI. CO. 1650."

99. G. 1688. Ducat. Obv. Bust, as in preceding. "MIC. APOFI. D.

G. P. TRAN." Rev. A cap pierced with a sword, and hung upon a branch; a crown suspended above; eagles' heads protuding from the edge of the field, at either side; at one side is a crescent and seven castles, at the other a small eagle; beneath are the initials "A. F." Legend. "PAR. REG. HUNGA. DO. & SICU. CO. 1688."

100. G. 1698. Quarter ducat, of LEOPOLD I. Obv. Bust, *laureated.* "LEOPOLD D. G. R. I. S. A. G. H. B. RE." Rev. Virgin and child. "S. IMACUL VIR. MA. MAT. D. P. H. 1698."

101. G. 1742. Ducat, of MARIA THERESIA. Obv. Full-length figure of MARIA, crowned. The imperial globe extended in the left hand; the initial "K." at one side, and "B." at the other. "MA. THERESIA D. G. REG. HU. BO." Rev. Virgin and child; beneath is a small shield crowned. "PATRONA REGNI HUNGARIÆ, 1742." Value $2.26.9.

All the succeeding coins in this division bear, on one side, the images of the Virgin and child.

102. S. 1757. Thaler. Obv. Bust, "M. THER. D. G. R. IM. GE. HU. BO. R. A. A. D. B(urgundiæ) C. T." Rev. "S. MARIA MATER DEI PATRONA HUNG. 1757." "JUSTITIA ET CLEMENTIA," on the edge. Value $1.00.5.

103. S. 1761. Same.

104. S. 1780. Florin. Obv. A crown, suspended by two angels, above a shield, bearing the Hungarian arms, and hung with the order chain of *St. Stephen;* beneath is a palm and laurel branch, crossed. "M. THER. D. G. R. IMP. HU. BO. R. A. A. D. B. C. T." Reverse same as preceding, with the letter "B." inclosed in an oval compartment, substituted for the shield. Value 50.2 cts.

105 and 106. S. 1782. Thaler, of JOSEPH II. Obverse same device as preceding. "JOS. II D. G. R. IMP. S. A. G. H. B. REX. A. A. D. B. & S." Reverse same as preceding. "VIRTUTE ET EXEMPLO," on the edge. Value $1.00.8.

107. G. 1835. Ducat, of FERDINAND I. Obv. The king, crowned; the imperial globe extended in the left hand, and a scepter in the right. "FERD. I D. G. AUST. IMP. HUNG. B. REX. H. N. V. R. L. V. D. G(aliciæ) L. I. A. A." Rev. Small shield beneath the Virgin. Same legend as before. Value $2.28.1.

108. S. 1839. Thaler. Obv. Head, *laureated.* Same legend as

preceding. Reverse same as preceding, with the shield omitted. "TUERI RECTA" on the edge. Value $1.01.

109. S. 1839. Florin. Same type. Value 49.6 cts.

110. B.S. 1839. Twenty kreutzers. Same, with "20" beneath the Virgin; edge grained. Value 16.8 cts.

111. B.S. 1839. Ten kreutzers. Same type.

112. G. 1848. Ducat. Obv. Same device as No. 107. "V. FERD. MAGY H. T. ORSZ. KIRALYA ERD N. FEJED." Rev. Device same as No. 107. "SZ. MARIA IST ANNYA MAGY. OR. VEDOJE, 1848." Value $2.28.1. (See Plate XVII. No. 2.)

113. B.S. 1848. Twenty kreutzers. Obv. Head, *laureated.* Same legend as preceding. Reverse same as preceding with "20" substituted for the shield. Value 16.8 cts.

114. C. 1848. One kreutzer, *struck during the Revolution.* Obv. A crowned shield, bearing the arms of Hungary. "MAGYAR KIRALYI VALTO PENZ." Rev. "EGY KRAJCZÁR. 1848," inscribed in three lines.

115. C. 1849. Three kreutzers, *struck during the Revolution.* Obv. A crowned shield, bearing the arms of Hungary. At one side is the figure "3," and at the other the letter "K." Legend. "MAGYAR KIRALYI VALTO PENZ." Rev. "HÁROM KRAJCZÁR 1849," in three lines.

RAGUSA.

Ragusa is an Austrian dependency, situated on the eastern shore of the Adriatic.

117. S. 1793. Thaler. Obv. Bust, "RHACUS RESPUBL." Rev. Shield, bearing the word "LIBERTAS," surmounted by a crown, and nclosed between two branches, crossed. "DUCE DEO. FIDE ET JUST."

DIVISION VIII.

NETHERLANDS.

Soon after their incorporation into the empire founded by CHARLEMAGNE, in the ninth century, the territories comprised in the present kingdoms of the Netherlands and Belgium were divided, in accordance with the *feudal* principle, which was then prevailing throughout the whole of Europe, into several small principalities consisting of the Duchies of Gueldres, Brabant, Luxemburg, and Limburg, the Marquisate of Anvers (Antwerp), the Counties of Holland, Zealand, Zutphen, Flanders, Artois, Hainaut, and Namur, with the Lordships of Utrecht, Groningen, Overyssel, Friesland, and Mechlin. These were afterward grouped together, and formed the seventeen provinces of the Netherlands. Among these petty provinces thus united Flanders was the most important, and upon the matrimonial alliance contracted between the Count of Flanders and the house of Burgundy about the year 1443, when his estates passed into the house of Burgundy, the principal authority over the other provinces passed with them. And, in like manner, upon the marriage of Maximillian with Mary of Burgundy, in 1477, the seventeen provinces passed into the house of Austria. But afterward, by reason of the injustice and cruelty practiced upon them by PHILIP II. of Spain, son of the Emperor Charles V., seven of the provinces, namely, Holland, Zealand, Utrecht, Guelderland, Overyssel, Groningen, and Friesland, organized a rebellion, under the leadership of the Prince of Orange, and finally succeeded, after a sanguinary war, in compelling the Spanish monarch to acknowledge their independence, and they were afterward acknowledged by all Europe as an independent State, under the title of the UNITED PROVINCES. These provinces were governed by a stadtholder; and in 1667 the celebrated "Perpetual Edict," for abolishing the office of stadtholder, was passed, through the influence of DE WITT, the Pensionary, or Prime Minister, who was intent upon placing the liberties of the Republic on a firm foundation. But in 1672 he and his brother were butchered by the mob, and WILLIAM III. was elected stadtholder. On the death of William, in 1702, the stadtholderate was again abolished, but was revived in 1747, and declared hereditary in the house of Orange. In 1795, however, it was conquered by the French, and erected into the BATAVIAN REPUBLIC. In 1806 it was metamorphosed by Napoleon into the Kingdom of Holland, and in 1810 was incorporated into the French Empire. After the fall of Napoleon it was, in 1815, erected into a kingdom with Belgium. This union, however, did not prove very harmonious, and in 1830 the Belgians took advantage of the revolution in France to cast off the yoke of their Dutch neighbors, in which they were successful. The Netherlands, consequently, now exist as a distinct kingdom, comprising the seven principalities above mentioned, the boundary line between them and the Kingdom of Belgium being fixed by treaty.

The intricacy of its political history is tolerably portrayed in the coinage of the Netherlands. For many years prior to the revolution, there were several series of coins minted at the same time; and, it is said, that there are some twenty different denominations of silver coins circulating there to this day. Each of the seven provinces had its own mint. Their coins, however, seem to have differed but little except in the device. They are generally quite readily distinguished by the name of the Province, which appears in an abbreviated form at the end of the legend. Thus the coins of Holland *proper*, are known by *Holl.* or *Holland;* those of Utrecht, by *Tra.* or *Traject;* those of Zealand, by *Zel.* or *Zeelandia*—sometimes merely the initial *z.;* of West Friesland, by *Westf.;* of Overyssel, by *Tran.*, *Transisal.*, or *Transisalania;* of Gueldre, by *Geldria;* and of Groningen, by *Gron.* These distinctions have disappeared since the close of the last century. Many of these coins have stamped upon them, evidently with a hand-punch, the abbreviations "*Hol. Utr.*" etc., (meaning *Holland, Utrecht*, etc.) This was done by the authorities of these provinces, in order to render the coinage of another province current within their own jurisdiction; or, more concisely speaking, to *legalize* them.

A 1. G. Ducat, of UTRECHT. Obv. Image of a saint. A small shield beneath. "SANCTUS MARTINENS." Rev. Shield. "MONETA NOVA AUREA TRAJECTEN." No date.

B 1. G. Ducat, of the City of ZUTPHEN, in GUELDRE. Obv. A mounted horseman, dressed in armor, and crowned, wielding a sword. "KAROLUS DUX GELRIUL C. ZUT." Rev. An ornamented cross; a shield in the center. "MON. NOVA. AUREA. DUCIS. GELN."

2. S. Florin, of the imperial City of ZWOLLEH, country of Zallant, in Overyssel. Obv. Crowned shield. "FLOR. ARG. CIVITA IMP. ZWOLLAE." Rev. Double-headed eagle.

3. S. 1585. Crown, of Holland. Obv. A knight, both legs hidden by a shield. "MO. NO. ARG. ORDIN. HOL." Rev. Lion *rampant*. "CONFIDENS. DNO. NON. MOVETUR."

4. S. 1623. Crown, of WEST FRIESLAND. Obv. Bust, in armor, carrying a sword. "MO. ARG. PRO(vinciae) CONFOE(derati) BELG(ii) WESTFRI." Rev. Crowned shield, bearing a lion *rampant*, carrying a sword and a bundle of arrows. "CONCORDIA RES PARVAE CRESCUNT."

5 and 6. S. 1624 and 1643. Crowns, of UTRECHT. Same as No. 3.

7. S. 1678. Thirty stivers, of ZEALAND. Obv. A knight, carrying a sword; behind, a crowned shield, bearing three bars, "*wavy, azure*" (blue) with a lion *issuant*. "LUCTOR ET EMERGO." Rev. Shield bearing the arms of the different provinces of the Netherlands; above is "30 ST." (30 stivers.) "MO. NO. ARG. ORIDIN. ZELANDIA 1678."

8. S. 1678. Six stivers, of WEST FRIESLAND. Obv. Crowned shield, bearing two lions *current*. "MO. NO. ORDIN. WEST. FRISIÆ 1678." Rev. A vessel under sail. "DEUS. FORTITUDO ET SPES NOSTRA."

9. S. 1682. Three guilder, of UTRECHT. Obv. Crowned shield, with a cross, and a lion *rampant*, borne double. "MO. NO. ARGENT ORDIN TRAJ 1682." Rev. A full-length figure of *Pallas*, holding in her dexter hand a lance, with the point resting upon the ground; a liberty-cap hung upon the other end; her left arm resting upon a clasped book, which stands upon its end, and is supported by a pedestal. "HAC NITIMUR. ...... HANC TUEMUR."

10. S. 1684. Twenty-eight stivers, of the City of DAVENTER or DEVENTER. Obv. Double-headed eagle. "LEOP. JON. D. G. ELEC. ROM. IMP. SEM. AUG." Rev. Crowned shield, bearing an eagle. "FLOR. ARG. CIV. DAVENTRIAE."

11 and 12. S. 1685. Twenty-eight stivers, of the City of DAVENTER. Obv. Same device as preceding. "FERDINAND II D. G. ROM. IMP. SEM. AU." Rev. Crowned shield. Same legend as preceding.

13. S. 1685. Twenty-eight stivers, of OVERYSSEL. Obv. Crowned shield. "MO. NO. ARGENT. ORD. TRANSIS. 1685." Rev. Double-headed eagle. "DA. PAC. DOM. IN DIEBUS NOSTRIS."

14. S. 1686. Thirty stivers, of WEST FRIESLAND. Obv. A knight, wielding a sword, one leg hidden by a crowned shield, bearing two lions *current*. "DEUS FORTI ET SPES NOST." Rev. Three shields. "MO. NO. ARG. ORDIN. W. FRISIAE."

15. S. 1686. Thirty stivers, of UTRECHT. Obv. Seven shields, bearing the arms of the seven provinces composing the "*Union.*" "MO. NO. ORD. TRAJECT." Rev. Crowned shield, supported by two lions. "CONCORDIA RES PARVAE CRESCUNT."

16. S. 1686. Thirty stivers, of the City of DAVENTER. Obv. Crowned shield, supported by two lions. "MO. NO. ARG. CIV. DAVENTRIÆ." Rev. Device similar to No. 14. "AUXILIANTE DEO. 1686."

17. S. 1686. Six stivers, of the City of MAGENSIS. Obv. Shield, bearing a double-headed eagle, surmounted by the imperial crown. "MO. NO. ARG. CIVI NOVI MAGENSIS." Rev. A mounted horseman wielding a sword. "CONCORDIA RES PARVAE CRESCUNT."

18. S. 1687. Ten-schilling piece, of ZEALAND. Obv. Seven shields. "MO. NO. ARG. ORDIN ZEELANDIAE 1687." Rev. Device similar to No. 14, with a shield like No. 7. "LUCTOR ET EMERGO."

19. S. 1689. Same.

20. S. 1689. Rix dollar, of the City of DAVENTER. Obv. A crowned shield, bearing an eagle, supported by two lions. "MO. NO. ARG. CIV. DAVENTRIAE." Rev. Device similar to No. 7, with an eagle upon the shield. "AUXILIANTE DEO. 1683." Value $1.20.

21. S. 1689. Six stivers, of the City of ZUTPHEN. Obv. Crowned shield. "MO. NO. ARG. CIV. ZUTPHANIAE." Reverse same as No. 17.

22. S. 1690. Twenty-eight stivers, of the City of ZUTPHEN. Obv. Crowned shield. "FLOR. ARG. CIV. ZUTPHANIAE 1690." Rev. Double-headed eagle. "IN DEO SPES NOSTRA."

23 and 24. S. 1690. Twenty-eight stivers, of WEST FRIESLAND. Obv. Bust, carrying a sword, "NIS DOMINUS NOBISCUM 1690." Rev Crowned shield. "FLORENUS. ARGENT. ORDI. FRISLAN."

25 S. 1691. Six stivers, (restruck) of GRONINGEN. Similar type to No. 21.

26. S. 1696. Ten schillings, of ZEALAND. Obv. Similar to No. 14, with a shield like No. 7. "MO. NO. ARG. PRO CONFÆ BELG. COUR. ZEL." Reverse same as No. 4.

27. S. 1703. One guilder, of WEST FRIESLAND. Obv. Same device as the reverse of preceding. "MO. ARG. ORD. FÆD. BELG. WESTF." Reverse same as No. 9.

28. S. 1709. One guilder, of ZEALAND. Same type as preceding.

29. S. 1713. Same.

30. S. 1718. One guilder, of OVERYSSEL. Same type as preceding.

31. B.S. 1738. One stiver, of HOLLAND. Obv. A bundle of arrows. Rev. "HOLLANDIA 1738." No device.

32. S. 1748. Ten stivers, of HOLLAND. Same type as No. 27.

33. S. 1753. Six stivers, of ZEALAND. Obv. Crowned shield like that in No. 7. Legend same as No. 8. Rev. Same device as No. 8. "ITA RELINQUENDA UT ACCEPTA."

34. B.S. 1759. Two stivers, of HOLLAND. Obv. Crowned shield, bearing a lion *rampant*. Rev. "HOLLANDIA 1759."

35. G. 1761. Ducat, of UTRECHT. Obv. A knight, dressed in armor, carrying a sword in the right hand, and a bundle of arrows in the left. "CONCORDIA RES. PAR. CRES. TRA." Rev. "MO. ORD. PROVIN. FOEDER BELG. AD LEG. IMP." No device. Value $2.25.8.

36. S. 1761. One guilder, of ZEALAND. Same type as No. 26. Value 41 cts.

37. S. 1762. Ten schillings, of ZEALAND. Same as preceding. Value $1.21.6.

38. G. 1763. Fourteen guilders, of UTRECHT. Obv. Same device as No. 17. "MO. AUR. PRO. CONFÆD. BELG. TRAJECT." Reverse same as No. 4. Value $5.61.

39. G. 1763. Ducat, of HOLLAND. Same as No. 35.

40. S. 1763. One guilder, of ZEALAND. Same as No. 27.

41. S. 1764. Three guilders, of ZEALAND. Same as No. 27. Value $1.21.6.

42. C. 1767. One centime, of OVERYSSEL. Obv. Crowned shield,

bearing a lion *rampant.* "VIGILATE ET ORATE." Rev. "OVERYSSEL, 1767."

43. S. 1768. Ten schillings, of ZEALAND. Same as No. 26. Value $1.21.6.

44. S. 1774. Three guilders, of WEST FRIESLAND. Obv. Device similar to the reverse of No. 17. "MO. NO. ARG. CONFÆ. BELG. PRO. WESTF." Rev. Crowned shield, like No. 4, supported by two lions. "CONCORDIA," etc. Value $1.21.6.

45. S. 1776. Ten stivers, of ZEALAND. Same as No. 26.

46. S. 1780. Six stivers, of ZEALAND. Same as No. 33.

47. C. 1781. One centime, of ZEALAND. Obv. Shield, bearing the same device as that in No. 7. "LUCTOR ET EMERGO." Rev. A shield, with "ZELANDIA 1781."

48. S. 1785. Half ducatoon,* of UTRECHT. Same type as No. 44. Value 65.6 cts.

49. B.S. 1786. Four stivers, of ZEALAND. Same as No. 26.

50. B.S. 1787. Ten stivers, of WEST FRIESLAND. Same type as No. 27, with a small oval beneath the shield containing the letters "O. V. C." interlaced.

51. B.S. 1791, Two stivers, of HOLLAND. Same as No. 34.

52. C. 1791. One centime, of UTRECHT. Obv. Crowned shield, supported by two lions. Rev. "STAD. UTRECHT, 1791."

53. C. 1793. One centime, of GUELDRE. Obv. Crowned shield, bearing two lions *rampant, combatant.* "IN DEO EST SPES NOSTRA." Rev. "D. GELRIÆ, 1793."

54. S. 1794. One guilder, of HOLLAND. Same as No. 27. Value 41 cts.

55. B.S. 1794. Quarter guilder, of UTRECHT. Same as preceding.

56 and 57. S. 1802–1804. Rix dollar, of UTRECHT. Similar to No. 26. Value $1.04.5.

58 and 59. S. 1808. Fifty stivers, or rix dollar, of LOUIS NAPOLEON. Obv. Head, "NAP. LODEW. I. KON VON HOLL." Rev. Crowned shield; the date "1808" beneath. "HOLLAND KONINGRIJK." Value $1.04.2.

---

* The ducatoon series was coined for the foreign trade in the East Indies.

60. G. 1809. Ducat, of Napoleon. Obv. "LODEW. NAP. KON.," etc.; otherwise same as preceding. Value $2.25.8.

61. G. 1837. Ten Guilders, of William I. Obv. Head, "WILLEM KONING. DER. NED. G. H. V. S." Rev. Crowned shield, bearing a lion *rampant*, with a sword and a bundle of arrows. "10——G." (Ten guilders.) "MUNT. VAN HET. KONINGRYK DER NEDERLANDEN. 1837." "GOD. ZY. MET UNS.," on the edge. Value $4.01.

62. G. 1827. Five guilders. Same as preceding; edge grained.

63 and 64. S. 1824–32. Three guilders. Same type; edge like No. 61. Value $1.25.

65. S. 1832. One guilder. Same type as preceding.

66. B.S. 1832. Half guilder. Same.

67 and 68. B. S. 1825–30. Twenty-five centimes. Obv. "W." surmounted by a crown. "18——25." Rev. Device same as No. 61. No legend; edge plain. Value 10.4 cts.

69. B.S. 1827. Ten centimes. Same type.

70. B.S. 1827. Five centimes. Same.

71. S. 1846. One gulden, of William II. Obv. Head, "WILLEM II. KONING. DER NED. G. H. V. S." Reverse and edge same as No. 61. Value 41 cts. (See Plate XVII. No. 5.)

72. S. 1852. $2\frac{1}{2}$ gulden, of William III. Same type as preceding. Value $1.04.2.

BELGIUM.

Belgium came under the dominion of the German emperors upon the accession of Maximilian I., in 1493, who, as before stated, had previously contracted a matrimonial alliance with the house of Burgundy, who at that time possessed the government of Belgium. Upon the abdication of Charles V. it passed, by the person of his son, Philip II., to the monarchy of Spain, where it remained until the peace of *Utrecht* in 1713, which terminated the *war of the Spanish succession,* upon which occassion it was ceded to Austria who continued to retain possession until 1791, when the armies of the French Republic overran the country, and in 1795 it was incorporated as part and parcel of France.

After this date (1795) no coins of Belgium *proper* appear until 1829–30. After its incorporation with France, its own coinage was abolished and the French coins introduced; and upon the acquisi tion of its independence in 1830 and the establishment of Belgium into a kingdom, under LEOPOLD I., the monetary system of France was continued, instead of the old Dutch system of *florins* and *crowns*, which had been previously used.

84. S. 1612. Six stivers, of the imperial City of CAMPEN. Obv. Double-headed eagle. "MATTH(ias) I D. G. RO. IMP. SEM. AUGU." Rev. Crowned shield. "FLOR. ARG. CIVI. IMP. CAMPEN."

85. S. 1616. Quarter crown, of ALBERT and ELIZABETH. Obv. St. Andrew's cross, with the badge of the *golden fleece* suspended from the center; a crown suspended above; the royal cipher in the second and third angles. "ALBERTUS ET ELISABET DEI GRATIA." Rev. "ARCHID. AUST. DUCES BURG. BRAB." Crowned shield, surrounded by the order chain of the *golden fleece*.

86 and 87. S. 1619. Crown, of same. Obv. Busts, in profile. Rev. Two lions supporting a shield, the crown resting upon their bowed heads; badge of the *golden fleece* beneath. Same legends as preceding.

88. S. 1626. Crown of the City of CONSTANTINE; FERDINAND II. Obv. Double-headed eagle, surmounted by the imperial crown. "FERD. II D. G. ROM. IMPER. SEMPER. AUG." Rev. Shield, with the date; "16" at one side and "26" at the other. "MON. NO. CIVITAT. CONSTANTIENSI."

89. S. 1631. Crown, of PHILIP IV. (Spain.) Obv. Cross, arranged as in No. 85, with "16" and "31" in the second and third angles. "PHIL. IIII D. G. HISP. ET INDIAR. REX." Rev. Device similar to No. 85. "ARCHID AUST. DUX BURG. BRAB."

90. S. 1636. Crown, of same. Obv. Bust. Rev. Crowned shield, supported by two lions. Legend same as preceding.

91. G. 1655. Double ducat, of the City of CAMPEN; FERDINAND II. (Austria.) Obv. Image of Ferdinand, with the imperial globe and scepter. "FERD. II D. G. RO. I. UNGA. BO. REX." Rev. "MO. NO. AUREA CIVITA. IMPERI. CAMPEN." No device.

92. S. 1705. Crown, of PHILIP V. (Spain.) Obv. Device simi-

lar to No. 85. "PHILIPPUS V. D. G. HISPANIARUM ET INDIARUM REX." Rev. Crowned shield, surrounded by two order chains; the arms of *Anjou* on a shield of pretence. "BURGUND. DUX. BRABANT. 1705."

93. S. 1758. Florin, of FRANCIS I. (Austria.) Obv. Austrian eagle, surrounded by the order chain of the *golden fleece.* "FRANCIS D. GRATIA ROMAN IMPERAT. S. A." Rev. "GERM. JERO. REX. LOTH. BAR. MAG. HET. DUX. 1758." Device, similar to No. 85, with crowns in the second and third angles of the cross.

94. S. 1759. Florin, of MARIA THERESIA, (Queen of Hungary, and wife of Francis I.) Obv. St. Andrew's cross, with crowns in the angles. "MAR. THERESIA D. G. R. IMP. GERM. HUNG. BOH. REG." Rev. "ARCH. AUST. DUX BURG. BRAB. COM. FLAND. 1759." Austrian eagle.

95. S. 1764. Crown, of same. Same type as preceding, with "JUSTITIA ET CLEMENTIA," on the edge.

96 and 97. S. 1764. Crown, of FRANCIS I. Same type as No. 93, with "IN TE DOMINE SPERAVI," on the edge.

98. S. 1780. Crown, of MARIA THERESIA. Same type as No. 95.

99. C. 1787. One kreutzer, of JOSEPH II. Obv. Bust, *laureated.* "JOS. II. D. G. R. IMP. D. B." Rev. "AD USUM BELGII AUSTR. 1787," inclosed in a wreath composed of two laurel branches, crossed.

100. S. 1788. Quarter crown, of same. Obv. Bust, *laureated.* "JOSEPH II D. G. R. I. S. A. GER. HIE(rosolymæ) HUN. BOH. REX." Rev. Device same as No. 93. "ARCH. AUST. DUX. BURG(undiæ) LOTH(aringiæ) BRAB(antiæ) COM(es) FLAN(driæ) 1788."

101. S. 1789. Florin. Same as preceding.

102. S. 1790. Crown, of LEOPOLD II. Same type as preceding, with "PIETATE ET CONCORDIA," on the edge.

103. S. 1790. "Lion d'argent." Obv. A lion *rampant,* carrying a sword, and supporting an oval shield, bearing the word "LIBERTAS;" the date, 1790," beneath. "DOMINI EST REGNUM." Rev. Eleven shields, bearing the arms of the different Belgian provinces, arranged in a circle around a sun. Legend. "ET IPSE DOMINABITUR GENITUM." "LEONE QUID FORTIUS," on the edge.

104. S. 1790. Quarter florin. Obv. Lion *rampant.* "MON. NOV. ARG. PROV. FOED. BELG.......1790." Rev. Hands, clasped, with a bundle of arrows. "IN UNIONE SALVUS." "X SOLS."

The two preceding pieces belong to the "lion series," a set of coins projected by the Belgian Provinces, in 1790. The project was never fairly carried into effect, only a few pieces appearing of the above date. It consisted of the *gold lion*, or piece of *fourteen florins*, the *silver lion, florin, half florin* and *quarter florin*.

105. G. 1793. Sovereign, of FRANCIS II. Obv. Head, *laureated*. "FRANC. II D. G. R. IMP. S. A. GE. HIE HU. BO. REX." Rev. Shield, surmounted by the imperial crown; St. Andrew's cross appearing from behind, with the order chain and badge of the *golden fleece* suspended from the two upper limbs, and inclosing the shield. "ARCH. AUST. DUX BURG. LOTH. BRAB. COM. FLAN. 1793."

106. S. 1793. Crown, of same, similar to No. 100.

107. S. 1795. Quarter crown. Same.

108. G. 1829. Ducat. Obv. A knight, in armor, carrying a sword in the dexter, and a bundle of arrows in the sinister hand. "CONCORDIA RES PARVAE CRESCUNT." Rev. "MO AUR. REG. BELGII AD LEGERN IMPERII." No device.

New System of Francs.—110. G. 1835. Forty francs, of LEOPOLD I. Obv. Head, *laureated*. "LEOPOLD PREMIER ROI DES BELGES." Rev. "40 FRANCS, 1835," inclosed in a wreath of oak. "DIEU PROTEGE LA BELGIQUE," on the edge.

111. G. 1835. Twenty francs. Same.

112. S. 1835. Five francs. Same.

113. S. 1835. Two francs. Same. (See Plate XVII. No. 6.)

114. S. 1838. One franc. Same, with the edge grained.

115. S. 1835. Half franc. Same as preceding.

116. S. 1835. Quarter franc. Same.

117. C. 1835. Ten centimes. Obv. An "L." in ornamented text, surmounted by a crown. Same legend as preceding. Rev. A lion *sejant*, supporting a tablet, bearing the inscription, "CONSTITUTION BELGE, 1831." Legend. "L'UNION FAIT LA FORCE."

118. C. 1835. Five centimes. Same type.

119. C. 1835. Two centimes. Same.

120. C. 1835. One centime. Same.

121. G. 1839. Ducat. Same as No. 108.

FRANCE.

The Franks, from whom ancient Gaul obtained the name of *France*, were of German origin, and inhabited the country between the Weser and the Rhine. They originally consisted of several tribes, who, upon the invasion of Germany by the Romans, united together for the common defense, and assumed the name of Franks, or "*free men.*" Their first irruption into Gaul took place in the middle of the third century of the present era, or between the years 234 and 254. They experienced many repulses, however, from the arms of the Romans, and were not finally established until the beginning of the fifth century.

The first king, of whom any authentic history remains, was *Pharamond,* who reigned from 417 to 428, when he is supposed to have been killed in the war with *Ætius.* He was succeeded by his son CLODIO. *Clodio,* after extending his conquests as far as the River *Somme,* died in the year 448, and was succeeded by *Merovæus,* from whom the first race of French kings received the appellation of *Merovingians.*

The earliest coins of France represented in this collection are the *deniers* of the Carlovingian kings, commencing with *Charlemagne.* The coinage of money seems, however, to have had a much earlier origin, and began under the Merovingian dynasty, at which time it consisted almost wholly of gold pieces, which were imitations of the Roman and Byzantine coins, the principal denomination being the *tremises,* or third part of the *sol d'or,* or *gold sou.* The *denier,* which was the principal coin issued by the Carlovingian kings, was, as its name indicates, derived from the Roman *Denarius,* and was equal to the *twelfth* part of a *sou.*

Upon the establishment of a regular system of moneys, the *livre tournois* was taken as the integral money of account, and was equivalent to twenty *sous,* or *sols.* This system was continued until the introduction of the present admirable system, in 1795, which takes the *franc* as its integer, and which is based upon no less a foundation than the dimensions of the earth. "First, the distance from the equator to the pole, which was ascertained by certain computations, being divided into ten million parts, gave the *metre* or standard of long measure, equal to 39.371 inches. Next, a cube of pure water, at the temperature of melting ice, measuring each way the hundredth part of this metre (called a *centimetre*) gave a certain weight, which was called the *gramme*. This was the standard of weight, and is equivalent to 15.435 Troy grains." This was subdivided into *decigrammes*, or tenths; *centigrammes*, or hundredths; and *milligrammes*, or thousandths; and the weight of the *franc* was placed at 5000 milligrammes, or 5 grammes, equivalent to 77.175 Troy grains. This system was first introduced in the third year of the "French Republic" (1795), but was not fully established until eight years after.

Previous to 1772, there were no less than *thirty-one* mints in France; but at that time the number was reduced to eighteen, and at the present time there are *six*. The coinage of each may be known by its mint-mark; that of *Paris* being the letter A; *Bordeaux*, K; *Lille*, W; *Lyons*, D; *Rouen*, B; and *Strasbourg*, B B. Each coin also bears another small mark, or figure, such as an anchor, lion, caduceus, etc., being the mark of the Superintendent or Director.

—. S. Denier, of CHARLEMAGNE (A.D. 767–814.) Obv. A cross *potent*. Legend. "CARLUS REX. FR." (Charles, King of France.) Rev. An ornamented cross. Legend. "VILO MET(Z)." (City of Metz.) (See *Division XV.*, "*Selections.*") The value of the denier is about 7 cts.

18. B.S. Denier, of LOUIS I., *the Meek*. (814–40.)

19. B.S. Denier, of CHARLES III., *the Simple*. (898–923.) Obv. A cross. "CARLUS REX. F." Rev. "HET * ALO."

20. B.S. Denier, of LOUIS IV. (936–54.) Obv. A cross, with pellets in the angles. "H. LUDOVICUS IIII." Rev. A church. "XPISTIANA (Christian) RELIGIO" (Religion.) In fine preservation.

21. B.S. Denier, of LOUIS V., *the Slothful*. (986–87.) Obv. A cross. "LUDOVICUS REX." LOUIS reigned only one year, and is supposed to have been poisoned by QUEEN BLANCHE.

22. B.S. Denier, of JOHN II., *the Good*. (1350–64.) Obv. Two

lahels reversed, and inclosed in a circle composed of a series of pellets. "COMES GENOHANIS." Rev. A cross, with pellets in the angles, inclosed as above. "SIGNUM DEI VIVI."

23. B.S. Denier, of CHARLES VII. (1422–61.) Obv. Crowned shield, bearing the arms of *Anjou* (three *fleurs de lis*). "KAROLUS FRANCORUM REX." Rev. Cross, the limbs extending to the edge; *fleur de lis* and crowns in the angles.

24. B.S. Denier, of CHARLES VIII. (1483–98.) Obv. Shield bearing the arms of *Anjou*. "KAROLUS FRANCOR. REX." Rev. Cross *potent*, with crowns and *fleur de lis* in the angles. "SIT NOMEN D(omi)NE, BENEDICTUM."

25. B.S. Denier, of same. Obv. The initial "K." crowned between two *fleurs de lis*. Rev. Cross, with each limb terminating in a crown, *fleur de lis* in the angles. Same legend as preceding.

26. B.S. Same. Obv. Shield, bearing the arms of *Anjou*, inclosed in a *trefoil* compartment. Rev. Cross *potent*, in a *quarterfoil* compartment, with *fleur de lis* and crowns in the angles. Same legends as preceding.

27. B.S. Denier, of LOUIS XII. (1498–1515.) Obv. Device same as preceding. "LUDOVICUS FRANCOR. REX." Reverse same as preceding.

28. B S. Same. Obv. "LUDOVI D. G. FRAN.," etc. Device and reverse same as preceding.

29. G. Crown, of FRANCIS I., *Count of Angoulême*. (1515–47.) Obv. Arms of *Anjou*, and a *dolphin*, quartered, (borne double.) "FRANCISCUS DEI GRACIA FRANCOR. REX." Rev. A cross of *fleur de lis*. "XPS(Christus): VINCIT: XPS: RENAT: XPS: IMPERAT."

30. B.S. Denier, of same. Similar to No. 27.

31. S. 1550. Denier, of HENRY II. Obv. Crowned shield, bearing the arms of *Anjou;* a crescent, surmounted by a crown at each side, the initial "H." beneath. "HENRICUS 2. D. G FRANCORUM REX." Rev. Cross of *fleurs de lis*, with "H's" and crowns in the angles. Legend same as No. 24. The first piece bearing a date. HENRY ascended the throne, at the death of his father, in 1547, and died of a wound received at a tournament, in 1559.

32. S. Denier, of CHARLES IX. (1560–74.) Same type as No.

24. CHARLES commenced to reign under the regency of his mother, CATHERINE DE MEDICIS.

33. S. 1563. Quarter crown, of same. Obv. Bust, "CAROLUS IX DEI G. FRA. REX." Rev. Crowned shield, with the initial C. surmounted by a crown at each side. Same legend as No. 24.

34. S. 1578. Half crown, of HENRY III. Obv. Bust, *laureated.* "HENRICUS III D. G. FRANC. ET POL(oniarum) REX. Rev. Cross *flory*, with "H." in the center. Same legend as No. 24.

35. S. 1580. Quarter crown, of same. Obv. Cross *flory*. Rev. Crowned shield. Same legends as preceding.

36. S. 1581. Two livres, of same. Obv. "H." surmounted by a crown; three *fleurs de lis*, one beneath, and one at each side. Reverse same as the obverse of preceding. Same legends as preceding.

37. G. 1592. Crown, of CHARLES X., *Pretender*. Obv. Crowned shield. "CAROLUS X D. G. FRANCOR. REX 1592." Rev. Cross *flory*. "CHRISTUS REGNAT. VINCIT ET IMPERAT."

CHARLES, *Cardinal of Bourbon*, and presumptive heir to the throne, was supported by the *Catholic League*, a sect formed and headed by the *Duke of Guise*, to oppose HENRY III. HENRY was assassinated in 1588; and HENRY III. *of Navarre* succeeded him as HENRY IV., and experienced the same opposition from the *League*. The dominion of Charles, however, never extended farther than his empty title. Coins were struck by the *League*, in his name, *six years after his death.*

38. G. 1641. Half louis d'or, of LOUIS XIII. Obv. Head, *laureated.* "LUD. XIII D. G. FR. ET NAV. REX." Rev. Eight L's arranged as a cross, with a crown surmounting the termination of each limb, the mint-mark in the center, and *fleurs de lis* in the angles. "CHRS. REGN. VINC. IMP."

39. S. Half crown, of LOUIS XIV. (restruck.) Obv. Bust, "LUD. XIIII D. G. FR. ET NAV. REX." Rev. Circular shield, surmounted by a crown between sprigs of palm, crossed. Same legend as No. 24.

40. S. 1644. Livre, of same. Obverse same as preceding. Rev. Crowned shield, with same legend as preceding.

41. G. 1648. Louis d'or, of same. Similar type to No. 38.

42. C. 1656. Liard. Obv. Bust, crowned. "L. XIIII ROY DE FR.

ET DE NA." Rev. "LIARD DE FRANCE," and three *fleurs de lis*. Half a farthing of English money.

43. G. 1668. Louis d'or. Same as No. 41.

44. S. 1680. Crown (louis d'argent). Obv. Bust, "LUD. XIIII D. G. FR. ET NAV. REX." Rev. Crowned shield. Same legend as No. 24.

45. S. 1680. Half crown. Same as preceding.

46. S. 1690. Crown, of eight livres. Obverse same as preceding. Reverse similar to No. 38.

47. S. 1692. Half crown. Same type.

48. S. 1693. Same. Reverse like No. 39.

49. G. 1694. Louis d'or. Obverse same as No. 44. Rev. Four *fleurs de lis* and crowns, in cross, with L's in the angles. Legend same as No. 38.

50. G. 1703. Louis d'or (restruck). Reverse like No. 38, with scepters in the angles.

51. S. 1709. Crown. Obverse same as No. 44. Rev. Three crowns and three *fleurs de lis*, with the mint-mark in the center. Legend same as No. 24. "DOMINE SALVUM FAC REGEM.," on the edge.

52. S. 1709. Half crown. Same as preceding.

53. G. 1710. Double louis d'or. Obverse same as No. 44. Reverse same as No. 38.

54. S. 1710. Livre. Same as No. 51.

55. S. 1713. Quarter crown. Same as No. 51.

56. S. 1713. Counter, or "Play-money," of the Province of *Bretagne*, used by gamblers. The "*banker*" or *dealer* issuing them at an arbitrary valuation, and redeeming them at the end of the game, in the same manner as gamblers of this country use *ivory* and *composition* counters. Obv. "LUDOVICUS MAGNUS REX," bust. Rev. Shield, surmounted by a crown, and draped with ermine. "JETTON DES ESTATS DE BRETAGNE."

57 and 58. C. 1715. One sou, of LOUIS XV. Obv. Head, "LUDOV. XV. D. GRATIA." Rev. "FRANCIÆ ET NAVARRÆ REX." Crowned shield. Value 9.4 mills.

59. S. 1718. Crown, familiarly known as the "*Petit Écu*," or

little crown, a title which it derives from the device. Obv. Youthful bust of Louis, *laureated.* "LUD. XV D. G. FR. ET NAV. REX." Rev. Crowned shield. Same legend as No. 24. "DOMINE SALVUM FAC REGEM," on the *edge.*

60. S. 1720. Quarter crown. Obverse same as preceding. Reverse same as No. 38.

61. S. 1728. Crown. Obverse same as preceding. Reverse same as No. 39. Value $1.12.4.

62. G. 1728. Louis d'or. Obverse same as preceding. Rev. Two oval shields, surmounted by a crown. Same legend as No. 38. Value $4.80.

63. S. 1729. Half crown. Same as No. 61. Value 54.1 cts.

64. S. 1744. Six sols, or sous. Same as preceding. Value 5 cts.

65. S. 1756. Counter, of *Bretagne,* (see No. 56.) Obv. Bust, *laureated.* "LUD XV REX CHRISTIANISS." Rev. Crowned shield, draped with *ermine.* "JETTON DES ESTATS DE BRETAGNE. 1756."

66. S. 1766. Same. Obv. Bust, *laureated.* "LUDOVICUS XV. REX CHRISTIANISSIMUS." Reverse similar to preceding.

67 and 68. S. 1768–74. Crown. Same type as No. 61, with oak branches substituted for the laurel. Value $1.12.4.

69. G. 1777. Louis d'or, of LOUIS XVI. Obv. Bust, "LUD. XVI D. G. FR. ET NAV. REX." Reverse same as No. 62. Value $4.52.

70. S. 1780. Crown, of same. Same type as No. 61. Value $1.13.4.

71 and 72. S. 1782. Counters, of *Bretagne,* (see No. 56.) Similar type to No. 65.

73. S. 1782. Twelve sols. Similar to No. 61. Value 11.3 cts.

74. S. 1786. Crown. Same type. Value $1.13.4.

75. G. 1786. Double louis d'or. Obverse same as No. 69. Rev. Double shield, surmounted by a crown. Same legend as No. 38. Value $9.11.9.

76. G. 1789. Louis d'or. Same as preceding. Value $4.52.

77. S. 1791. Half crown. Same type as No. 61. Value 56.1 cts.

78 and 79. S. 1791. Thirty louis. Obv. Head, "LOUIS XVI ROI DES FRANCAIS......1791." Rev. An angel, writing upon a tablet, upon which is already inscribed the word "CONSTITUTION." Beneath

is "L'AN 3 DE LA LIBERTE." Above "REGNE DE LA LOI." "30" at one side, and "SOLS" at the other. Value 28.6 cts.

The coinage of this epoch, and of this type, is usually called the *Constitutional Currency*, having been issued under the Constitution which was extorted from LOUIS XVI. by the revolutionists, in 1791.

80. S. 1791. Fifteen sous. Same type. Value 14.3 cts.

81 and 82. C. 1791. One sou. Same type as No. 57.

83. S. Medalet, of the unfortunate MARIA ANTONETTE, Queen of LOUIS XVI., and daughter of the famous MARIA THERESIA, of *Austria.* Obv. Bust of Maria. "MARIE ANT. JOS. I. REINE DE FR. ET DE NAV." Rev. Two shields joined, and surmounted by a crown; one bearing the arms of *Hapsburg*, and the other of *Anjou;* beneath is the inscription, "MAISON DE LA REINE."

84. S. 1792. Crown. Same type as No. 78, with a *fasces* surmounted by a liberty-cap to the right, and a *cock* standing upon one leg, to the left of the device on the reverse. "LIBERTE, EGALITE," on the edge.

85. B. 1792. Two sous (*bell metal*). Obv. Bust. Rev. A *fasces*, surmounted by a liberty-cap, and inclosed between two branches of oak, crossed. They were, at this time, engaged in the demolition of the churches, and the bells thus obtained were converted into money.

86. B. 1792. One sou (*bell metal*). Same type.

87. C. 1792. Two sous. Same type.

88 and 89. S. 1793. Six livres, of the Republic. Obv. Same device as the reverse of No. 84. Rev. "SIX LIVRES," and the mint-mark inclosed in a wreath of oak. "REPUBLIQUE FRANCAISE." Beneath is "L'AN II.;" meaning the *second* year of the Republic. Struck at *Paris.* Value $1.13.6.

90. S. 1793. Same. Struck at *Bayonne.*

91. C. 1795. Five centimes. Obv. Bust of Liberty. "REPUBLIQUE FRANCAISE." Rev. "5 CENTIMES —— L'AN 4."

92. C. 1796. Five centimes. Same type. Made large.

93. S. 1797. Five francs. Obv. HERCULES, uniting *Liberty* and *Equality.* "UNION ET FORCE." Rev. "5 FRANCS —— L'AN 6," inclosed in a wreath composed of oak and laurel branches, crossed.

Legend. "REPUBLIQUE FRANCAISE." "NATIONALE GARANTIE," on the edge. Value 96.8 cts.

94. B. 1797. Five centimes (*bell metal*). Obv. A wreath and scales, surmounted by a liberty-cap. "LIBERTE, EGALITE."......"1797." Rev. A tablet. "REPUBLIQUE FRANCAISE."......"L'AN II."*

95 and 96. C. 1798. One centime. Same type as No. 91.

97. C. 1798. Ten centimes. Same type.

98. C. 1799. Same.

99. C. 1799. Five centimes. Same type.

100. S. 1799. Five francs. Same type as No. 93. Value 96.8 cts.

101 and 102. S. 1802–03. Five francs. Obv. Bust of Napoleon. "BONAPARTE PREMIER CONSUL." Rev. "5 FRANCS," inclosed in a wreath composed of two laurel branches, crossed. Legend. "REBUBLIQUE FRANCAISE.......AN XI." "DIEU PROTEGE LA FRANCE," on the *edge*. Value 96.8 cts.

103. G. 1803. Forty francs. Same type as preceding. Value $7.68.5.

104. S. 1803. Half franc. Same type. Value 9.6 cts.

105 and 106. S. 1803. Quarter franc. Same type.

107. G. 1803. Twenty francs, of NAPOLEON EMPEROR. Obv. Head, "NAPOLEON EMPEREUR." Reverse same as No. 101.† Value $3.84.1.

108. S. 1804. One franc. Same type. Value 19.3 cts.

109. G. 1806. Forty francs. Same type. Value $7.68.5.

110 and 111. S. 1806. Five francs. Same type. Value 96.9 cts.

112. S. 1808. One franc. Same type. Value 19.4 cts.

113 and 114. B.S. 1808. Ten centimes. Obv. "N," surmounted by a crown; raised edge bearing a wreath of laurel. Rev. "10 CENT.," and the mint-mark in the field. "NAPOLEON EMPEREUR....... 1808," on the raised *edge*.

---

* This coin bears two dates, *l'an ii* being equivalent to 1794. The only way to account for this is that they may have used an old die for the reverse. This was often done in those times, even at our own Mint—the labor of producing dies being much greater then than now.

† A strange state of affairs. We here find Napoleon claiming to be *Emperor* of a *Republic!*

115. S. 1808. Half franc. Same type as No. 107. Value 9.6 cts.

116. S. 1810. Same, with "EMPIRE FRANCAIS," substituted for "REPUBLIQUE FRANCAISE." Value 9.6 cts.

117. G. 1811. Forty francs. Same type as preceding. Value $7.68.5.

118. G. 1811. Twenty francs. Same type. Value $3.84.1.

119. B. 1814. Ten centimes (*bell metal*). Similar to No. 113.

120 and 121. G. 1814. Twenty francs, of LOUIS XVIII. Obv. Bust, "LOUIS XVIII ROI DE FRANCE." Rev. Shield, bearing the arms of *Anjou*, surmounted by a crown, and inclosed between two branches of laurel, crossed. "PIECE DE 20 FRANCS.......1814." "DOMINE SALVUM FAC REGEM," on the *edge*. Value $3.84.1.

122 and 123. S. 1814–15. Five francs. Same type. Value 97 cts.

124. G. 1817. Forty francs. Same as No. 120, with "40" at the left, and "F." at the right side of the shield, and no legend. Value $7.68.5.

125. G. 118. Twenty francs. Same type. Value $3.84.1.

126. S. 1820. Five francs. Same type. Value 97 cts.

127. S. 1821. Two francs. Same type. Value 38.8 cts.

128. S. 1822. Half franc. Same type. Value 9.7 cts.

129. S. 1823. One franc. Same type. Value 19.4 cts.

130. S. 1824. Five francs. Same type.

131 and 132. S. 1825–28. Five francs, of CHARLES X. Same type as preceding. Value 97 cts.

133. S. 1828. Two francs. Same type. Value 38.8 cts.

134. S. 1828. One franc. Same type. Value 19.4 cts.

135. S. 1827. Half franc. Same type. Value 9.7 cts.

136. S. 1828. Quarter franc. Same, with the wreath on the reverse omitted. Value 4.8 cts.

137. G. 1830. Forty francs. Same type as No. 131. Value $7.69.

138. G. 1830. Twenty francs. Same type. Value $3.84.5.

139. S. 1831. Five francs, of LOUIS PHILIPPE I. Obv. Head, "LOUIS PHILIPPE I ROI DES FRANCAIS." Rev. 5 FRANCS, 1831," inclosed in a wreath, composed of two laurel branches, crossed. "DIEU PROTEGE LA FRANCE," on the edge. Value 96.9 cts.

140. S. 1831. Two francs. Same as preceding, with the head *laureated*, and the edge grained. Value 39 cts.

141. S. 1831. One franc. Same as No. 139, with the edge grained. Value 19.2 cts.

142. G. 1833. Forty francs. Similar to No. 139, with the head *laureated.* Value $7.70.5.

143 and 144. S. 1833. Five francs. Same as No. 139, with the head *laureated.* Value 96.9 cts.

145. S. 1833. Half franc. Same as preceding, with the edge grained. Value 9.5 cts.

146. S. 1833. Quarter franc. Same type. Value 4.7 cts.

147. G. 1834. Twenty francs. Same as No. 142. Value $3.85.2.

148. S. 1841. One franc. Same as No. 145. Value 19.2 cts.

149. S. 1846. Fifty centimes. Same type.

150. S. 1848. Five francs. Same as No. 143.

151. S. 1848. Five francs, of the REPUBLIC. Obv. *Hercules* uniting *Liberty* and *Equality.* Copied from the coins of the Republic of 1793. "LIBERTE EGALITE FRATERNITE." Rev. "5 FRANCS. 1848," inclosed in a wreath of oak and laurel branches, crossed, Legend. "REPUBLIQUE FRANCAISE." "DIEU PROTEGE LA FRANCE," on the edge. Value 97 cts.

152. G. 1848. Twenty francs. Obv. An angel writing upon a tablet, which bears the inscription "24, 25 FEV. 1848," a *fasces* and a cock at either side of the device, "REPUBLIQUE FRANCAISE." Rev. "20 FRANCS. 1848," inclosed in a wreath of oak leaves. "LIBERTE EGALITE FRATERNITE." Edge same as preceding. Value $3.84.5.

153. S. 1849. Five francs. Same type as No. 151. Value 97 cts.

154. S. 1849. Five francs. Obv. Female head, encircled with a heavy chaplet of cereals; the forehead bound with a band bearing the letters "CONCOR;" hair tied in a roll behind; neck encircled by a string of beads. "REPUBLIQUE FRANCAISE." Rev. "5 FRANCS. 1849," inclosed in a wreath composed of oak and laurel, *mixed.* "LIBERTE, EGALITE, FRATERNITE." Edge same as No. 151. Value 97 cts.

155. S. 1850. Fifty centimes. Same as preceding, with the edge grained.

156. G. 1851. Twenty francs. Obv. Female head, bound with a chaplet of cereals; hair tied in a braid behind; a *fasces* at one side and a laurel branch at the other. Same legend as No. 154. Rev. "20 FRANCS," inclosed in a wreath composed of oak and laurel branches, crossed. Legend and edge same as No. 154. Value $3.84.5. (See Plate XVIII. No. 1.)

157. G. 1851. Ten francs. Same type as preceding, with the edge grained. Value $1.92.1.

158. S. 1851. Two francs. Same as No. 154, with the edge grained. Value 28.8 cts.

159. S. 1851. One franc. Same as preceding. Value 19.4 cts. (See Plate XVIII. No. 5.)

160. S. 1851. Twenty centimes. Same type.

161. C. One centime. Obv. Head of Liberty, wearing the cap. "REPUBLIQUE FRANCAISE." Rev. "UN CENTIME. 1851."

162. S. 1852. Five francs. Obv. Head of NAPOLEON. "LOUIS NAPOLEON BONAPARTE." Rev. "5 FRANCS. 1852," inclosed in a wreath of oak and laurel, *mixed*. "REPUBLIQUE FRANCAISE." Edge same as No. 154. Value 97 cts.

163. S. 1852. One franc. Same as preceding, with the edge grained. Value 19.4 cts.

164. C. 1852. Ten centimes, of NAPOLEON III. Obv. Head, inclosed in a beaded circle. "NAPOLEON III EMPEREUR......1852." Rev. An eagle, inclosed as above. "EMPIRE FRANCAIS......DIX CENTIMES."

165. S. 1853. Twenty centimes. Obv. Head, "NAPOLEON III EMPEREUR." Rev. "20 CENT. 1853," inclosed in a wreath composed of two laurel branches, crossed. "EMPIRE FRANCAIS." (See Plate XVIII. No. 8.)

166. S. 1854. One franc. Same type. Value 9.4 cts. (See Plate XVIII. No. 7.)

167. G. 1854. Five francs. Same type. Value 97 cts. (See Plate XVIII. No. 4.)

168. C. 1854. Ten centimes. Same as No. 164.

169. S. 1855. Five francs. Obv. Same as No. 165. Rev. Two scepters, in *saltiere*, through a circular shield, bearing an eagle, and surrounded by an order chain; the drapery suspended from a crown,

and forming a canopy behind the shield and scepters. "5——F." "EMPIRE FRANCAIS......1855." "DIEU PROTEGE LA FRANCE," on the edge. Value 97 cts. (See Plate XVIII. No. 6.)

170. G. 1855. One hundred francs. Same as preceding, with the shield made square. Value $19.40.

171. G. 1857. Fifty francs. Same type. Value $9.70. (See Plate XVIII. No. 2.)

172. G. 1857. Twenty francs. Same as No. 165. Value $3.85. (See Plate XVIII. No. 3.)

GREAT BRITAIN.

The coinage of Britain, prior to the Roman invasion, like its history, presents but a meager aspect. In fact, very little is known in regard to the metallic currency of Britain prior to that epoch, except that the Britons had, at a very early period, used a kind of ring money, which was very similar in its character to the ancient rings of the Greeks, and from whom, it is highly probable, that the use of such rings, as currency, had been borrowed.* The Britons, however, seem to have had some knowledge of the art of coining money, as is evinced by various specimens of *tin* money, which have recently come to light, and which are supposed to have been coined long before the invasion, and also by numerous specimens of the coins of the British sovereigns, who still held sway in the island after the first visits of the Roman legions. Cæsar himself mentions the fact that the Britons had coins of tin and brass rings, adjusted to a certain weight. And even an examination of the *ring money* itself, in its different stages, clearly points to this fact. Thus we find that from being made of mere pieces of wire bent into the form of a ring and *passing by weight*, the practice of cutting them to a certain *weight* and passing them by *tale* followed soon upon their first introduction, and, as a still further advance toward a perfect coin, the *cast brass rings*,

* The *African rings*, especially the larger one, contained in the Cabinet collection, (see medals, "*Miscellaneous*,") are very similar to the *British ring money* here referred to.

which are found in great abundance in Ireland and some parts of Britain, (and which are *solid* rings, instead of being open at one side as before,) appear to have been adjusted to a graduated system, founded upon the *pennyweight* or *half pennyweight* as a unit. Therefore it is easy to conceive that the transition from a system so nearly resembling an actual coinage to the present form of metallic money, must have followed in the natural course of events. But the invasion of the Romans, and the consequent turmoil and continued warfare, which resulted between the would-be conquerors and the native Britons, and which was the cause of the final relinquishment of the island by the former, seems to have swept away not only every vestige of their history and religion, but their arts and sciences likewise. After the departure of the Romans (about A.D. 414) until the commencement of the Saxon heptarchy, some doubt exists as to whether the Britons had any coins at all; but it is quite probable that they continued the coinage of money after the same style of the Roman coinage. But upon the commencement of the Saxon rule in Britain an entire new system was introduced, which was very unlike the coinage of the Romans, and which, it is thought, was brought to the shores of Britain by the Saxons upon their first arrival in the country. The earliest coin of the Saxons was called the "*Skeattæ*,"* and is supposed to have been an imitation of the Byzantine *quinarius;* the latter finding its way through the east and north of Germany from Constantinople. After the *skeattæ* came the *silver penny*, which was the only coin of the country, with the exception of occasional half pennies, up to the reign of EDWARD III., (1327–1377,) when the first regular issue of *groats*, or four-penny pieces took place. This coin, however, was not originated in this reign. In fact, a coin of this denomination was contemplated full a century earlier, as appears from the following extract from *Grafton's Chronicle*, published at London in 1569: "Also about this time (1227, 11*th year of Henry IId.*) a parliament was holden at London, in the which it was

---

* A term which Ruding derives from a Saxon word, meaning "a portion," and supposes that these coins were a portion of some merely nominal sum by which large amounts were calculated.

ordered that the English Grote should be coyned of a certaine weight, and of the one side the king's picture, and one the other side a crosse as large fully as the grote, to advoyd clippyng." And in the time of the *first* Edward it is said a groat was coined, but not generally circulated, being intended as a *pattern.* The latter piece, however, has long been much in dispute among numismatists, from the fact that the coins of the three Edwards, whose reigns came in succession, are so near alike as to require the most minute and ingenious reasoning to make any distinction between them. But the best authorities, including Hawkins, Ruding, and Humphrey, concur in the belief that the *pattern groat* belongs to the reign of Edward I.

The first coinage of gold took place in 1257, the forty-first year of the reign of Henry III.,* and consisted of the *gold penny,* which was ordained to be of the finest gold, to weigh two sterlings, and be current for twenty pence. But this coinage met with so much opposition from the traders and others, as to cause its discontinuance; and we have no further mention of a *gold coinage* until the seventeenth year of the reign of Edward III., 1334, when an extensive issue took place, consisting of three different denominations, viz.: the *florin, half florin,* and *quarter florin.* The *florin,* according to the indenture made between the king and his moneyers, was to be equal in weight to two *petit florins,* of *Florence,* of good weight. Fifty pieces to be coined from the *pound tower* of London, the half and quarter in proportion, and all to be of fine gold, by which was meant twenty-three *carats* three and a half *grains,* fine gold, and *half a grain alloy,*† thus coining fifteen pounds sterling from the pound weight of gold. No regular copper coinage was issued by the government of Great Britain until the reign of Charles II., but copper was previously coined by private individuals, under *patents* from James I., Charles I., and the Commonwealth, but were in small quantities, and circulated principally in Ireland. This deficiency was previously supplied from the small coins of the continent, and from the issue of private "tokens" by individuals and towns.

---

* Ruding's Annals of the Coinage, p. 186, vol. i.

† Ruding, p. 217, vol. i.

In the arrangement of the coins in the latter portion of this division, it will be noticed that the strict chronological rule has been partially laid aside, and the pieces arranged under their respective monarchs, according to their denomination or value, the largest in value taking the precedence. This arrangement commences with the coins of CHARLES II.

SCOTLAND, BEFORE THE ANNEXATION.

The earliest coins attributed to Scotland, with any degree of certainty, are those of ALEXANDER I., who reigned from 1107 to 1124; Humphrey thinks it highly probable that a regular coinage was known in Scotland at least a couple of centuries earlier. This surmise is supported by the fact that the southern portion of Scotland formerly belonged to the Saxon Kingdom of Northumberland, and the coins of that kingdom circulated there, while the major portion of the north was under the dominion of the kings of Norway, who certainly coined money as early as the *tenth century.* Coins have recently, however, been attributed to MALCOLM III., (1055), a contemporary of WILLIAM, *the Conqueror*, and also to DONALD VIII. (1093), but with what degree of certainty it is impossible to state. Scotland was annexed to England upon the demise of ELIZABETH, in 1603, by the accession of JAMES VI. to the English throne.

1. S. Penny, of ALEXANDER I. (1107–1124.) Obv. A crowned head and a scepter. "ALEXANDER REX." Rev. A cross with double limbs, each terminating in a pellet, with stars in the angles.

2. S. Penny, of DAVID I. (1124–1153.) Obv. Crowned head and a cross inclosed in a beaded circle. "DAVID DEI GRACIA I." Rev. "SCOTORUM REX." A cross *potent*, (that is, a cross with *crutch-shaped* limbs.)

3 and 4. S. Pennies, of WILLIAM I. (1165–1214.) Obv. Very rude head and a scepter. Rev. A cross with double limbs, and stars in the angles. In the name "WILIAM" in No. 3, the "*iam*" is in *monogram* or cipher.

5. S. Penny, of ALEXANDER III. (1249–1292.) Obv. Crowned

head and scepter, inclosed in a beaded circle. "ALEXANDER DEI GRA." Rev. "SCOTORUM REX." Cross *potent*, with stars in the angles.

6. S. Penny, of JOHN BALIOL. (1292–1297.) Obv. Head, surmounted by a crown, said to be an attempt at a real portrait of the king. "JOHANNES DEI GRA." Rev. "SCOTORUM REX." Same device as preceding.

—. S. Groat, of ROBERT BRUCE. (1306–1329.) Obv. Crowned bust in profile, and a scepter, in a *tressure* of six arches. "ROBERTUS DEI GRA. REX SCOTORUM." Rev. A cross extending to the edge of the piece, with *mullets* in the angles; these are surrounded by a double circle in which is inscribed "VILLA DE PERTH." Outside of this is still another circle, containing a legend, which is partially defaced. (See *Division XV.*, "*Selections.*")

7. S. Penny, of DAVID II. (1329–1331, and 1342–1370.) Obv. Bust, crowned, and a scepter. "DAVID DEI GRA. REX SCOTORUM." Rev. Cross *potent*, with stars in the angles. "VILLA EDINBURGH." In an outer circle is another inscription, but so nearly effaced from clipping as to be unintelligible.

8. S. Groat, of same. Same type as preceding.

9. S. Groat, of ROBERT II. (1370–1390.) Obv. Bust at full-face, surmounted by a crown. "ROBERTUS DEI GRA. REX. SCOTORUM." Rev. Cross *potent*, with pellets in the angles. "DNS. PTECTOR. MS. Z. LIBATOR. MS.," and in an inner circle "VILLA EDINBURGH." 10. S. Same.

11. S. Groat, of JAMES III. (1460–1488.) Same type as preceding.

12. S. Groat, of JAMES IV. (1488–1513.) Obv. Bust, at three-quarter face, with long, flowing hair, and crowned. Rev. Crowns, and pellets in the angles of the cross. Same inscriptions as before.

13. S. Groat, of JAMES V. (1513–1542.) Obv. Bust, in profile. "JACOBUS 5 DEI GRA. REX. SCOTORUM." Rev. Shield, bearing a lion *rampant*, the cross protruding from behind.

14. S. Half penny, of same. Same type.

15. S. 1555. Shilling, of MARY. Obv. "MARIA DEI GRA. SCOTOR. REGINA. 1555." Rev. Same device as preceding. "DILICTE. DNI. COR. HUMILIE."

16. S. Half penny of same, (not dated.) Obv. Thistle, sur-

mounted by a crown, between "M." and "R." "MARIA D. G. R. SCOTORUM." Rev. St. Andrew's cross and a crown. "OPPIDU EDINBURG."

17. S. 1570. Thirty-shilling piece, of JAMES VI. Obv. Crowned shield, with the initials "J." and "R." crowned, at either side. "JACOBUS 6. DEI GRATIA REX SCOTORUM." Rev. A sword supporting a crown upon its point, a hand pointing toward "XXX.," (the denomination,) and the date "1570." "PRO. ME. SI. MEREOR. IN. ME."

18. S. 1602. One-eighth piece, (one-eighth of the "*thistle* mark,") of same. Obv. Crowned shield. "JACOBUS 6 D. G. R. SCOTORUM." Rev. A thistle, surmounted by a crown.

GREAT BRITAIN.

G. An imitation of the Greek "*Stater.*" Obv. A head of Minerva, with the Greek helmet. Rev. A female figure, *very rude.* This piece has no letters, or figures of any kind by which its exact date can be ascertained. It is probable, however, that it was not coined before the first visit of Cæsar with his Roman legion. (See *Division XV.*, "*Selections.*")

1. G. Two small coins, about as old as the Christian era. They bear no inscriptions. The first has on one side a representation of the *sun*, with three dots, or pellets, beneath. The second, a full-length figure of a man. They are something after the Greek style of coins, being *dished*, or concave at one side.

2. S. Skeattæ, of ETHELBERT I., *King of Kent.* (560–616.)

"A sceattæ, of Ethelbert I., King of Kent, from 561 to 616, is the earliest Saxon coin which has yet been appropriated. It bears on the obverse the name of the monarch, and on the reverse a rude figure, which occurs on many of the sceattæ, and which is supposed to be intended to represent a bird."—*Ruding*, p. 116, vol. i.

3. S. Penny, of BURGRED, *last King of Mercia.* (852–874.) Obv. An extremely rude attempt at a portrait. "BURGRED REX." Rev. Moneyer's name.

—. S. Penny, of ETHELBERT I., *fourth* "*King of England,*" and brother of Alfred the Great. (Reigned from A.D. 858 to 871.) Obv. A rude bust. "AEDELBEARH(t) REX." Rev. A cross, upon which is inscribed "DUDVI." and "NE......MO." In the angles of the cross are the initials "A. N. E. T." (See *Division XV.*, "*Selections.*")

4. S. Penny, of EDRED. (946–955.) Obv. A small cross, *pattée.* "EADRED REX." Rev. "HYNSEDHO." (Moneyer's name.)

5. S. Penny, of EDGAR. (958–975.) Obverse same as preceding, with "EDGAR REX." Rev. "HANAHN." (Moneyer's name.)

6. S. Penny, of WILLIAM, *the Conqueror.* (1066–1088.) Obv. Bust, in full-face, surmounted by a helmet. "PILLEM REX," (the Saxon P. being used for W.) Rev. A cross, with small circles in the angles, containing the letters respectively of "*P. A. X. S.*;" the moneyer's name in the legend. A fine duplicate of this will be found in *Division XV.*, "*Selections.*"

7. S. Same. Coined at a different mint.

8. S. Penny, of HENRY I. (1100–1135.) Obv. Rude face. "HENRICUS REX." Rev. Cross, with double limbs, and *quarterfoils* in the angles. Moneyer's name in the legend.

9. S. Penny, of HENRY II. (1154–1189.) Obv. Head, crowned; a scepter extending into the legend and forming a portion of the "X" in "HENRICUS REX." Reverse same as preceding.

10. S. Same. Coined at a different mint.

11. S. Two coins of JOHN, *as Lord of Ireland.* (1179–1199.) Obv. Head, "JOHANNES DOM." Rev. Cross, with double limbs; rings in the angles.

12. S. Penny, of JOHN, *after his accession.* (1199–1216.) Obv. Head, inclosed in a triangle. "JOHANNES REX," a scepter forming a portion of the "*X.*" Rev. A triangle, inclosing a crescent, stars, etc. Struck in Dublin.*

13. S. Half penny. Same as preceding.

14. S. Penny, of HENRY III. (1216–1272.) Obv. Head, surmounted by a crown and a scepter. "HENRICUS REX III." Rev. Cross, with double limbs; pellets in the angles.

---

* The triangle found on the Irish coins of John, Henry III., and Edward I. are supposed to be a symbol of the Trinity; the ancient arms of Trinity Priory, in Ipswich, being represented in a similar manner. It may have been an allusion to the fact that the first English mint established in Ireland was in the monastery of the Trinity, in Dublin.

15. S. Penny, of EDWARD I. (1272–1307.) Obv. Head, with flowing hair, surmounted by a crown. "EDW. R. ANGL'A H. DNS." Rev. Cross, with pellets in the angles. "CIVITAS LONDON."

16. S. Same, with the head inclosed in a triangle. "EDW. R. ANGL'A. DNS. HYB." Rev. Same as preceding, with "CIVITAS DUBLINIA."

17. S. Penny, of EDWARD II. (1307–1327.) Obv. Head, crowned. "EDWAR. R. ANGL. DNS HYB." Rev. Same as No. 15, with "VILL SCIEDMUNDI."

18. S. Groat, of EDWARD III. (1327–1377.) Obv. Bust, with flowing hair, surmounted by a crown. "EDWAR. DI GRA. REX ANGL. E FRANC." Rev. Cross *potent*, with pellets in the angles. "VILLA CALISIE," (Calais,) and in an outer circle, "POSUI DEUM AJUTOREM MEUM." (I have made God my help.)

19. S. Penny, of same. Same type as No. 17, with "CIVITAS EBORACI." (City of York) on the reverse.

20. S. Penny, of HENRY IV. (1399–1413.) Obv. Head, crowned. "HENRIC. DI GRA. REX. ANGL. D. H." Reverse same as No. 18.

21. S. Groat, of HENRY V. (1413–1422.) Same type as No. 18. *Calais.*

22. G. Noble, of HENRY VI. (1422–1461.) Obv. A vessel sailing upon the water, containing an image of the king, crowned, and carrying a sword and shield, the latter bearing the arms of England and France. Rev. *Fleur de leuced* cross, with an "H." in the center; lions and crowns in the angles. Value $4.34.

23. S. Groat of same. Obv. Head, at full-face, surmounted by a crown. "HENRIC DI. GRA. REX ANGL. Z. FRANC." Reverse same as No. 18, with "CIVITAS EBORACI." (York.)

24. S. Groat, of same. Same as preceding, with "CIVITAS LONDON."

25 and 26. S. Groats, of EDWARD IV. (1461–1483.) Same type as preceding.

27. G. Angel, of HENRY VII. (1485–1509.) Obv. St. George and the Dragon. "HENRIC DI GRA. REX AGLIE (Angliae) Z. FR(anciæ). Rev. A vessel, upon which is suspended a shield bearing the arms of England and France, quartered. Above the shield is a cross,

(the mast,) with the initial "H." at one side, and a rose at the other. "PER CRUCE TUA SALVA. NOS. XPL.," (an abbreviation of the Greek word *XPIΣTE, i.e. Christe.*) RED.

28. S. Groat, of HENRY VII. Same type as No. 24, with the arched or imperial crown substituted for the open crown of *fleur de lis.*

29. S. 1503.* Groat, of same. Obv. Bust, in profile, surmounted by a crown. "HENRIC VII DI GRA. REX ANG. Z. F." Rev. Shield, with the arms of England and France, quartered; a cross extending into the legend. Same legend as No. 18. The bust on this piece is said to be a very fair attempt at a portrait profile of the king.

30. S. Half groat, of HENRY VIII. (1509–1547.) Same type as preceding.

31. S. Half groat, of same. Struck for Ireland. Obv. Same device as the reverse of No. 29. "HENRIC VIII DI GRACIA ANGLIA." Rev. "FRANCIA HIBERNIE REX." A harp, surmounted by a crown, the letters "H." and "R." crowned, at each side.

32. S. Medalet, of same. Obv. Bust, at full-face, with a sword and the imperial globe. "HENRY THE VIII." Rev. Shield, bearing the arms of England and France, surmounted by a crown, and encircled by the *garter.*

33 and 34. S. Shilling, of EDWARD VI. (1547–1553.) Obv. Bust, in full-face, crowned, a rose to the left, and the denomination "XII." to the right of the device. "EDWARD VI D. G. AGL. FRA. Z. HIB. REX." Reverse same as No. 29.

35, 36, and 37. S. Half groats, of MARY. (1553–1558.) Obv. Bust, in profile, crowned. "MARIA. D. G. ANG. FRA. Z. HIB. REGI." Reverse same as No. 29, with the legend "VERITAS TEMPORIS FILIA." (Truth is the daughter of time.)

38. S. Penny, of same. Obv. Bust, crowned. "PHILIP Z. MARIA. D. G. REX Z. REGI." Reverse same as No. 29.

39. S. 1555. Shilling. Obv. Busts of the king and queen facing each other; a crown suspended above, and the date "1555." "PHILIP ET MARIA D. G. REX ET REGINA ANG." Rev. Shield, surmounted by

---

* Said to have been struck in this year. Not dated.

a crown, and the denomination "XII." Same legend as No. 18. The first piece bearing a date. The first English coin bearing a date was a shilling issued in the year preceding the date of the above piece (1554.)

40. S. 1557. Crown. Obv. Bust of PHILIP. "PHS. D. G. HISP. ANG. Z. REX. COMES. FLAN.......1557." Rev. St. Andrew's cross behind a shield, surmounted by a crown; beneath is the badge of the *golden fleece.* "DOMINUS MICHIA ADJUTOR."

—. G. Ryal or Royal, of ELIZABETH. (1558 to 1602.) Obv. The queen enthroned. "ELIZABETH D. G. ANG. FRA. ET HIB. REGINA." Rev. A large rose, in the center of which is a small shield, bearing the Danish arms of Britain, and the arms of Anjou, *quartered.* "A. DNO. FACTU. EST ITUD. ET. EST. MIRAB. IN OCULIS NRS." (*"A Domino factum est istud et est mirabile in oculis nostris."* It is the work of the Lord, and wonderful in our eyes.) *R. R. R.* (See *Division XV., "Selections."*) *A fine proof.*

41. S. Shilling, of ELIZABETH. (1558–1603.) Obv. Bust, crowned. "ELIZAB. D. G. ANG. FR. ET. HIB. REGI." Reverse same as No. 29.

42 and 43. S. 1582. Groats. Same type as preceding, with a rose accompanying the bust.

44. S. 1582. Penny. Same as preceding.

45 and 46. G. Twenty shillings, of JAMES I. (1603–1625.) Obv. Bust, *laureated.* "JACOBUS D. G. MAG. BRI. FR. ET HIB. REX." Rev. Crowned shield, with the arms quartered; cross *fleury,* extending into the legend "FACIAM EAS IN GENTEM UNAM." These pieces were buried about 1630,* at Richmond's Island, Saco River, *Maine,* and dug up in 1856.

47. S. Shilling, of same. Obv. Bust, crowned. Same legend as preceding. Rev. Shield, bearing the arms of England and France, *quartered,* in the first and fourth quarters; Ireland and Scotland in the second and third. "QUE DEUS CONJUNXIT NEMO SEPARET."

48. S. 1604. Sixpence. Same type as preceding, with the legend "EXURGAT DEUS DISSIPENTUR INIMICI," and the date on the reverse.

---

* An interesting history of these pieces appeared in a New England paper some time since, from which this fact is deduced.

49 and 50. S. 1606–11. Same. Rev. Same legend as No. 47.

51 and 52. S. Half crown, of CHARLES I. (1625–1649.) Obv. The king on horseback, dressed in armor, with a sword. "CAROLUS D. G. MA. BR. FR. ET HI. REX." Rev. Circular shield. "CRISTO AUSPICE REGNO."

53. S. Shilling. Obv. Bust, crowned. Otherwise same as preceding. The denomination "XII" accompanying the bust.

54. S. Same. With same legend on the reverse as No. 47.

55. S. Threepence. Obverse same as preceding. Rev. Shield, with same legend as No. 51.

56 and 57. S. Threepence. Same as preceding, with a *demi-fleur de lis*, and the denomination accompanying the bust, and a shield like No. 51.

58. S. Sixpence. Same type as No. 53.

59. S. Same. With a change in the shape of the shield on the reverse.

—. S. 1642. Pound sterling, of CHARLES I. Obv. The king on horseback. "CAROLUS D. G. MAG. BRIT. FRA. ET HIB. REX." Rev. "RELIG. PROT. LEG.—ANGL. LIBERT PAR." (English laws and liberties of Parliament,) inscribed between two parallel lines. Above are three *fleurs de lis*, and "XX" (20 shillings); and beneath, the date "1642." Legend. "EXURGAT DEUS DISSIPENTUR INIMICI." (Let God arise, let his enemies be scattered.) *R. R. R.* (See *Division XV.*, "*Selections.*")

60 and 61. S. 1654. Half crown and shilling, of the COMMONWEALTH. Obv. Shield, bearing the cross of St. George, inclosed in a wreath composed of a *palm* and *olive* branch, crossed. "THE COMMONWEALTH OF ENGLAND." Rev. Two shields, joined, one bearing the cross of St. George, and the other the harp of Ireland. "GOD WITH US. 1654."

—. S. 1658. Half crown, of CROMWELL, *Protector*. Obv. Bust of Cromwell, *laureated*, facing to the left. "OLIVAR D. G. R. P. ANG. SCO ET HIB. &C., PRO." (Protector of the Republic of England, Scotland, and Ireland, etc.) Rev. A crowned shield, bearing the arms of the Commonwealth; a shield of pretence, bearing a lion *rampant*. "PAX

QUÆRITUR BELLO. 1658." *On* the edge are the letters "HAS. NISI. PEBITURUS MIHI A DIMAT. NEMO." *R. R.* (See *Division XV.*, "*Selections.*")

CHARLES II.—1660–1685.

62. G. 1679. Five guineas. Obv. Bust, *laureated.* "CAROLUS II DEI GRATIA." Rev. Four crowned shields in cross, bearing the arms of England, Ireland, Scotland, and France; scepters in the angles. "MAG. BR. FRA. ET HIB. REX. 1679." "DECUS ET TUTAMEN ANNO. REGNI. TRICESIMO PRIMO," on the edge.

63. S. 1672. Crown. Same type as preceding, with the star of the *garter* in the center, and linked C's in the angles of the cross.

64. S. 1669. Half crown. Same as preceding.

65. S. 1677. Same.

66. S. 1668. Shilling. Same type.

67. S. 1671. Scotch shilling. Obverse same as preceding. Rev. Four shields *in cross*, with the denomination "$\frac{\text{XIII}}{4}$." (denoting the value *in Scotch money*) in the center; linked C's, surmounted with crowns, in the angles. Same legend as before.

68. S. 1674. Sixpence. Same type as No. 63.

69. S. 1679. Fourpence. Obverse same as preceding. Rev. Four C's linked together, and forming a cross, a harp, a *fleur de lis*, a rose, and a thistle, in the angles; a crown suspended above. "MAG. BR. FRA. ET HIB. REX. 16–79."

70. S. 1679 and 1681. Twopence (2 *pieces*). Rev. Two C's linked and surmounted by a crown; otherwise same as preceding.

71. C. 1678. Farthing. Obv. Bust and titles (as above). Rev. A thistle, surmounted by a crown.

JAMES II.—1684–1688.

The coins of this reign have the bust of the king turned to the left, the reverse of that of his predecessor, a custom which is hereafter constantly adhered to. They are, in other respects, similar to the last of CHARLES II., having the bust and name on one side, and the arms and titles on the other, with no other motto. The arms are arranged on four shields as a cross, but without linked letters in the angles; the inscriptions on the *edges* are "*Anno regni secundo,*" etc. The lesser pieces, or *Maundy-money*,* are marked "'IIII" to "I," with a crown above.

72. G. 1688. Guinea. Value $4.88.

73. S. 1687. Crown.

74. S. 1685. Half crown.

75. S. 1687. Same. Reverse.

76. S. 1686. Fourpence. (Maundy-money.) Two pieces.

77. S. 1687. Threepence. (Maundy-money.)

78. S. 1686. Twopence. (Maundy-money.)

79. B. 1689. Shilling. The famous "*gun-money.*" Obv. Bust, *laureated.* "JACOBUS II DEI GRATIA." Rev. Two scepters in saltiere, through a crown, between "J" and "R." in decorative italic cipher, with the date "1689," and the value "XII." above. "MAG. BR. FRA. ET HIB. REX." After the revolution in 1688, a proclamation was issued by James, in Ireland, for making shillings and sixpences from mixed metal. They were made from old pieces of ordnance, etc., and have consequently obtained the name of "*gun-money.*"

William and Mary, and William III.—1688–1702.

80. G. 1692. Guinea. Obv. Busts, in profile, one over the other. "GULIELMUS ET MARIA DEI GRATIA." Rev. Crowned shield; arms of Nassau on a shield of pretence. "MAG. BR. FR. ET HIB. REX ET REGINA. 1692." Value $5.00.

81 and 82. S. 1689. Half crown. Same type as preceding. "DECUS ET TUTAMEN ANNO REGNI PRIMO.," on the edge. Value about 57 cts.

83. S. 1693. Half crown. Obverse same as preceding. Rev. Four crowned shields, arranged as a cross, with the arms of Nassau in the center; the initials "W." and "M." interlaced, and the numerals "1. 6. 9 3." (date) in the angles. Same legend as before. "DECUS ET TUTAMEN ANNO REGNI QUINTO." on the edge.

84. S. 1689. Fourpence. (Maundy-money.) Obv. Same as preceding. Rev. Crowned numeral. Same legend as before. Value 7 cts.

85. S. 1689. Threepence. (Maundy-money.) Same type.

* Small pieces distributed by the king to the poor on *Maundy-Thursday* every year. Each person receives a small white bag, containing as many pieces as the king numbers years in age.

86. C. 1691. Farthing. Obv. Busts, as in No. 80. "GULIELMUS ET MARIA." Rev. Figure of Britannia, seated. "BRITANNIA;" beneath is the date "1691."

WILLIAM III.—The queen died in 1795, and William continued to reign as William III.

87. S. 1696. Crown. Obv. Bust, *laureated.* "GULIELMUS III DEI GRA." Reverse same as No. 83, without the initials and numerals in the angles. "DECUS ET TUTAMEN ANNO. REGNI. OCTAVO." on the edge. Value $1.14.

88. S. 1701. Half crown. Same type.

89. S. —. Shilling. Same type.

90. S. 1696. Sixpence. Same type.

ANNE.—1702–1714.

The coins of this reign have the same devices as those of the preceding, with trifling variations. The bust of the queen on the obverse is turned to the *right*, and the hair simply bound by a *fillet;* the legend is "ANNA DEI GRATIA." The reverse has the four shields arranged as a cross, with the star of the *garter* substituted for the arms of Nassau of the last reign.

91. G. 1714. Guinea. Value $5.05.

92. S. 1703. Crown. Value $1.14.

93. S. 1707. Same.

94. S. 1708. Half crown. Value 57 cts.

95. S. 1708. Shilling. Value 23.4 cts.

96. S. 1711. Sixpence.

GEORGE I.—1714–1727.

The coins of this reign have the king's bust turned to the *left*, and his titles as well as his name appear on the obverse, and for the first time (as a permanent addition) "FIDEI DEFENSOR." (Defender of the Faith.) On the reverse are his German titles. His own arms, or the arms of the house of Hanover, occupy the fourth shield. The *maundy-money* has the bust, with "GEORGIUS DEI GRATIA." and on the reverse a crowned numeral, with the king's English titles only.

97. G. 1726. Guinea. Obv. Bust, *laureated.* "GEORGIUS D(ei) G(ratia) M(agnus) BR(itanniæ) FR(ancorum) ET HIB(erniæ) REX F(idei) D"(efensor.) Rev. Four shields arranged as a cross, with the star of

the *garter* in the center, and scepters in the angles. "BRUN(svicensis) ET L(uneburgensis) DUX. S(acri) R(omani I(mperii) A(rchi) TH(esaurius) ET EL"(ector.) Value $5.00.

98. G. 1718. Quarter guinea. The first issue of this denomination. Value $1.25.

99. S. 1723. Shilling. Value 22.6 cts.

100. S. 1723. Sixpence.

101. S. 1723. Twopence. (*Maundy-money.*) Value 3.7 cts.

102. C. 1721. Half penny. Same type as the *farthing* of William and Mary, No. 86.

103. C. 1721. Farthing. Same type.

GEORGE II.—1729–1760.

104. G. 1748. Double guinea. Obv. Bust, *laureated.* "GEORGIUS II DEI GRATIA." Rev. Crowned shield, with the arms of Hanover in the fourth quarter. "M. B. F. ET H. REX. F. D. B. ET L. D. S. R. I. A. T. ET E." and the date. Value $10.16.

105. G. 1751. Guinea. Same type. Value $5.00.5.

106. S. 1753. Crown. Obverse same as preceding. Rev. Four shields arranged as a cross, with the star of the *garter* in the center, and *fleurs de lis* and roses in the angles. Same legend as preceding. "DECUS ET TUTAMEN." etc., on the edge. Value $1.14.

107. S. 1743. Half crown. Same type, with roses substituted for the *fleurs de lis.* Value 56.7 cts.

108. S. 1745. Shilling. Same type. Value 23.4 cts.

109. S. 1733. One penny. (*Maundy-money.*) Obverse same as preceding. Rev. Crowned numeral. "MAG. BRI. FR. ET HIB. REX." and the date.

110. S. 1746. Half crown. Same type as No. 107, with the roses omitted. Value 56.7 cts.

111. S. 1758. Shilling. Same type. Value 23.4 cts.

112. S. 1757. Sixpence. Same type. Value 11.7 cts.

113. C. 1752. Half penny. Obv. Bust, *laureated.* "GEORGIUS II REX." Reverse same as No. 86.

114. C. 1742. Irish half penny. Obverse same as preceding. Rev. Crowned harp, with "HIBERNIA" above, and the date "1742" beneath.

George III.—1760–1820.

115. G. 1774. Guinea, *unworn.* Obv. Bust, *laureated,* facing to the right. "GEORGIUS III DEI GRATIA." Reverse same as No. 104. These pieces were struck merely as pattern, or show pieces. Value $5.05.

116. G. 1787. "Spade guinea." (So called from the shape of the shield on the reverse, which is very simple, and pointed like a spade.) Obverse and legends same as preceding. Value $5.04.6.

117. G. 1801. Half guinea. Obverse same as preceding. Rev. Shield, encircled by the garter, surmounted by a crown; a shield of pretence surmounted by a crown, and bearing the arms of Hanover. "BRITANNIARUM REX FIDEI DEFENSOR." Value $2.52.3.

118. G. 1762. Quarter guinea (2 pieces.) Same type as No. 115. Value $1.26.2 each.

119. G. 1813. Guinea. Same pattern as the half guinea of 1801, (see No. 117,) with the exception of the head on the obverse, which is entirely different, and would scarcely be thought to represent the same individual. Value $5.05.9.

120. G. 1813. Half guinea. Same type.

121. G. 1813. Seven-shilling piece. Rev. A crown, with the date "1813" beneath, otherwise same as preceding. Value $1.65.6.

122. S. 1787. Shilling. Obverse same as No. 116. Rev. Four shields arranged as a cross, with the star of the *garter* in the center, and crowns in the angles. Same legend as No. 116. Value 23.8 cts.

123. S. 1787. Sixpence. Same type. Value 11.9 cts.

124. G. 1817. Sovereign. Obv. Bust, like No. 119. "GEORGIUS III D. G. BRITANNIA REX F. D......1817." Rev. St. George and the dragon, encircled by the *garter.* Edge grained. Value $4.83.

125. G. 1818 Same.

The name *Guinea,* which first came into use in the reign of Charles II., now disappears. It was first applied to the coin because the gold of which it was *first* made came from *Guinea,* in Africa.

126. G. 1817. Half sovereign. Obv. Bust, same style as preceding. "GEORGIUS III DEI GRATIA......1817." Rev. Crowned shield,

with the arms of Hanover on a shield of pretence. "REX FID. DEF BRITANNIARUM." Value $2.41.1.

127. S. 1819. Crown. Same type as No. 124, with "DECUS ET TUTAMEN," etc., on the edge. Value $1.12.

128. S. 1820. Same.

129. S. 1817. Half crown. Obverse same as No. 126. Rev. Shield, encircled by the *garter*, and the order chain and badge of the *order of the garter*, the whole surmounted by a crown; arms of Hanover on a shield of pretence. "REX FID. DEF. BRITANNIARUM."

130. S. 1820. Same, with the order chain and badge omitted. Value 56.2 cts.

131. S. 1816. Shilling. Same type as preceding, with the legend on the obverse standing. "GEOR. III D. G. BRITT. REX F. D.," and the legend on the reverse omitted. Value 22.4 cts.

132. S. 1820. Sixpence. Same type. Value 11.2 cts.

133. S. 1820 Fourpence. (*Maundy-money.*) Obverse same as No. 126. Rev. A crowned numeral. "REX FID. DEF. BRITANNIARUM."

134. S. 1762. Threepence. (*Maundy-money.*) Same as preceding, with the legend "MAG. BRI. FR. ET HIB. REX." on the reverse.

135. S. 1817. Threepence. (*Maundy-money.*) Same as No. 133.

136. S. 1818. Twopence. (*Maundy-money.*) Same type.

137. S. 1820. Penny. (*Maundy-money.*) Same type.

138. C. 1775. Half penny. Obv. Bust, *laureated.* "GEORGIUS III REX." Reverse same as No. 86.

139. C. 1773. Farthing. Same type.

140. C. 1797. Two-penny piece. Obv. Bust, *laureated;* raised edge, bearing the legend "GEORGIUS III D. G. REX." Rev. Britannia, seated, holding a trident in her left, and an olive branch in her right hand; raised edge, corresponding with the obverse, with "BRITANNIA" and the date "1797."

The copper of this date, and since, was coined by a MR. BOULTON, at *Soho*, near Birmingham, who had a contract with the Government for the purpose.

141. C. 1797. Penny. Same type.

142. C. 1799. Half penny. Obv. Bust, *laureated.* "GEORGIUS III

DEI GRATIA REX." Rev. Same device and legend as preceding. The raised edge is omitted from both sides of this piece.

143. C. 1805. Irish penny. Obv. Bust, *laureated.* "GEORGIUS III D. G. REX." Rev. Crowned harp, with "HIBERNIA" above, and the date "1805" beneath.

144. C. 1799. Farthing. Same type as No. 142, with "I FARTHING" beneath the device on the reverse.

145. C. 1806. Penny. Obverse same as No. 143, with the date "1806" beneath the bust. Reverse same as No. 142.

146. C. 1806. Farthing. Same type as preceding.

GEORGE IV.—1820–1830.

147. G. 1821. Half sovereign. Obv. Head, *laureated.* "GEORGIUS IIII. D. G. BRITANNIAR. REX : F. D." Rev. St. George and the dragon, with the date beneath. No legend. Value $2.41.3.

148. G. 1825. Quarter sovereign. Obverse same as preceding. Rev. Crowned shield; arms of Hanover on a shield of pretence; beneath is a rose, with branches of thistle and shamrock crossed behind it. "ANNO 1825." Value $1.21.

149. G. 1823. Sovereign. Obv. Head, *without the* laurel; otherwise same as No. 147. "DECUS ET TUTAMEN," etc., on the *edge.* Value $4.84.

—. G. 1826. Pattern five-sovereign piece. Obv. Head of the king, facing to the left. "GEORGIUS IV. DEI GRATIA"......"1826." Rev. A shield, bearing the arms of Great Britain, with the electoral arms upon a shield of pretence, displayed upon a mantle of ermine, draped from a crown. "BRITANNIARUM REX FID. DEF." Upon the edge is inscribed "DECUS ET TUTAMEN. ANNO REGNI SEPTIMUS." *R. R. R.* (See *Division XV.*, "*Selections.*")

150. G. 1826. Sovereign. Obv. Head. "GEORGIUS IV DEI GRATIA ......1826." Rev. Finely engraved shield, draped with ermine, and surmounted by a crown; arms of Hanover on a shield of pretence. "BRITANNIARUM REX. FID. DEF." Edge same as preceding. Value $4.84.

151. G. 1826. Half sovereign. Same as preceding, with the drapery around the shield omitted, and the edge *grained.* Value $2.41.3.

152. G. 1826. Quarter sovereign. Same type. Value $1.21.

The four preceding pieces are of the new series begun in 1824. In that year the king disapproved of the likeness on the coins, consequently a series of new dies were engraved, bearing a bust copied from that of *Chantrey*,* which was said to be highly flattering to the king.

153 and 154. S. 1822. Crown. Same type as No. 147.

155. S. 1821. Half crown. Obv. Head, *laureated.* "GEORGIUS IIII D. G. BRITANNIAR REX F. D." Rev. Crowned shield, with the arms of Hanover on a shield of pretence, also crowned; a rose beneath; a thistle at one side, and shamrock at the other. "ANNO—1821." Value 56.2 cts.

156. S. 1823. Half crown. Obverse same as preceding. Rev. Device same as No. 129. "ANNO......1823."

157. S. 1824. Shilling. Same type as preceding, with the order chain and badge omitted. Value 22.5 cts.

158. S. 1824. Sixpence. Same type. Value 11 cts.

159. S. 1826. Half crown. Obv. *Chantrey's* head. "GEORGIUS IV DEI GRATIA......1826." Rev. Shield, surmounted by a crowned helmet; arms of Hanover on a shield of pretence; beneath is a scroll, bearing the motto "DIEU ET MON DROIT." Value 56.2 cts.

160. S. 1825. Shillings (*two pieces*). Obverse same as preceding. Rev. A sprig of rose, thistle, and shamrock, united beneath a crown; the latter being surmounted by a crowned lion. "BRITANNIARUM REX : FIDEI DEFENSOR." Value 22.5 cts.

161. S. 1830. Fourpence. (*Maundy-money.*) Obverse same as No. 155. Rev. A crowned numeral, and the date "1830," inclosed between branches of oak, crossed. Value 7.5 cts.

162. S. 1830. Threepence. (*Maundy-money.*) Same type as preceding.

163. S. 1828. Twopence. (*Maundy-money.*) Same type.

164. C. 1827. Half penny. Obverse same as No. 159. Rev. Britannia, wearing a Greek helmet; beneath are sprigs of rose, thistle, and shamrock, united. "BRITANNIAR REX FID. DEF."

165. C. 1826. Farthing. Same type.

---

* Humphrey.

166. C. 1827. Half farthing. Same type.

167. C. 1822. Irish penny. Obv. Head, (same as No. 155.) "GEORGIUS IV D. G. REX." Rev. Crowned harp, with "HIBERNIA" above, and the date beneath.

168. C. 1822. Irish half penny. Same type.

WILLIAM IV.—1830–1837.

169. G. 1831. Sovereign. Obv. Undraped bust, "GULIELMUS IIII D. G. BRITANNIARUM REX. F. D." Rev. Shield, with the arms of Hanover on a shield of pretence, and the order chain and badge of the order of the *garter*, displayed upon a mantle of ermine, suspended from a crown. "ANNO—1831." Value $4.85.

170. G. 1831. Half sovereign. Similar to preceding, with the mantle of ermine omitted. Value $2.42.

171. G. 1831. Quarter sovereign. Same type. Value $1.21.

172. S. 1831. Crown. Same type as No. 169. Value $1.12.4

173. S. 1831. Half crown. Same type. Value 56.2 cts.

174. S. 1831. Shilling. Obverse same as preceding. Rev. "ONE SHILLING" beneath a crown, inclosed between branches of oak and laurel, crossed; the date beneath. Value 22.6 cts.

175. S. 1831. Sixpence. Same type.

176. S. 1831. Fourpence. (*Maundy-money.*) Obverse same as preceding. Rev. A crowned numeral and the date inclosed between branches of oak, crossed.

177. S. 1831. Threepence. (*Maundy-money.*) Same type as preceding.

178. S. 1831. Twopence. (*Maundy-money.*) Same type.

179. S. 1831. Penny. (*Maundy-money.*) Same type.

180. C. 1831. Penny. Obv. Undraped bust. "GULIELMUS IIII DEI GRATIA.......1831." Reverse same as No. 164.

181. C. 1831. Half penny. Same type.

182. C. 1831. Farthing. Same type.

VICTORIA.—1837. *Reigning Sovereign.*

183 and 184. G. 1838. Sovereigns. Obv. Head, engraved by *Wyon*, from a wax model taken by himself from the life.* "VICTORIA

---

* Humphrey, p. 144.

14

DEI GRATIA.......1838." Rev. Simple shield, surmounted by a crown, and bearing the arms of Great Britain, *quartered*, (the arms of Hanover being omitted; Queen *Victoria*, although the next heir to William IV., was prevented by the *Salique* law from assuming the scepter of Hanover—see *Introduction to Hanover*,) inclosed between two sprigs of laurel, crossed. "BRITANNIARUM REGINA FID. DEF.;" the rose, thistle, and shamrock beneath. Value $4.86.1 each. (See Plate XIX. No. 1.)

—. S. 1844. Crown. Obv. Wyon's head of Victoria. "VICTORIA DEI GRATIA"......"1844." Rev. Crowned shield, bearing the arms, *quartered*, between two branches of laurel, crossed. "BRITANNIARUM REGINA. FID. DEF." On the edge is "DECUS ET TUTAMEN," etc. (See *Division XV.*, "*Selections*.") Value $1.12.4.

185. S. 1847. Crown. Obv. A finely engraved bust of the queen, crowned. "VICTORIA DEI GRATIA BRITANNIAR REG. F. D." Rev. Four crowned shields arranged as a cross, with the star of the *garter* in the center, and the rose, thistle, and shamrock in the angles. "TUEATUR UNITA DENS. ANNO. DOM. MDCCCXLVII." "DECUS ET TUTAMEN ANNO REGNI UNDECIMO," on the *edge*. Value $1.12.4. (See Plate XIX. No. 2.)

186. S. 1840. Half crown. Obv. *Wyon's* head. "VICTORIA DEI GRATIA.......1840." Rev. Crowned shield inclosed between two laurel branches, crossed; the rose, thistle, and shamrock beneath. "BRITANNIARUM REGINA. FID. DEF. Value 56.2 cts. (See Plate XIX. No. 3.)

187. S. 1849. One florin.* Obv. Bust, crowned. "VICTORIA REGINA. 1849." .Rev. Four crowned shields arranged as a cross, with a rose in the center, and the thistle, rose, and shamrock in the angles. "ONE FLORIN, ONE TENTH OF A POUND." Value 45 cts. (See Plate XIX. No. 4.)

188. S. 1853. Florin. Obv. Bust, crowned. "VICTORIA D. G. BRIT. REG. F. D. MDCCCLIII. Rev. Device similar to preceding. "ONE FLORIN, ONE TENTH OF A POUND."

189. S. 1838. Sixpence. Obv. *Wyon's* head. "VICTORIA DEI

---

* The issue of this piece was considered as the first step toward a decimal system of money, a subject which has agitated the English mind for some time.

GRATIA BRITANNIAR. REG. F. D." Reverse same as No. 174. Value 11 cts.

190. S. 1838. Fourpence (2 *pieces*). Obv. Same as preceding, with the legend more abbreviated. Rev. Britannia, as in the copper coinage of the preceding reign. "FOUR PENCE," with the date "1838" beneath.

191. S. 1838. Threepence. (*Maundy-money.*) Obverse same as preceding. Rev. Crowned numeral, and the date inclosed between two branches of oak, crossed.

192. S. 1838. Twopence. (*Maundy-money.*) Same type.

193. S. 1838. One-and-a-half pence. (*Maundy-money.*) Same type.

194. C. 1839. Farthings (two pieces). Obv. Wyon's head. "VICTORIA DEI GRATIA."......"1839." Rev. Same device as No. 190. "BRITANNIAR. REG. FID. DEF." (See Plate XIX. No. 5.)

195. C. 1839. Half farthing. Obverse same as No. 190. Rev. "HALF FARTHING. 1839," surmounted by a crown; the rose, thistle, and shamrock beneath.

196. C. 1839. Quarter farthing. Same type.

197. C. 1848. Model quarter farthing. Obv. Head, "VICTORIA REG." Rev. "MODEL QUARTER FARTHING. 1848." Much reduced in size from the preceding piece (196).

198. C. 1848. Model eighth farthing. Obv. Head, and the letters "V......R." Rev. "MODEL EIGHTH FARTHING 1848."

199. B. 1848. Model quarter farthing. Obverse same as preceding. Rev. "D ¼" with the word "MODEL" at one side, and the date "1848" at the other.

200. C. and S. Model penny. Made of copper, with a plug of silver in the center. On the copper is inscribed "ONE PENNY MODEL." Reverse the same. On the silver: Obv. Wyon's head. "VICTORIA REG." Rev. The numeral "I."

201. C. and S. Model half penny. Same as preceding.

COINS OF AUSTRALIA.

203. G. 1852. One pound. Obv. A crown, with the date beneath. "GOVERNMENT ASSAY OFFICE, ADELAIDE." Rev. "VALUE ONE POUND,"

inscribed in three lines. Legend. "WEIGHT 5 DWT. 15 GRS."......"22 CARATS." Edge grained. Value $5.32. (See Plate XX. No. 3.) For a duplicate see *Division XV.*, "*Selections.*"

204 and 205. G. 1853. Two-ounce piece and half ounce of PORT PHILLIP. Obv. A Kangaroo; beneath is the date "1853." Legend. "PORT PHILLIP."......"AUSTRALIA," inscribed in sunken letters. Upon the reverse of the larger piece is a large figure 2, upon which is inscribed "TWO OUNCES." Legend. "PURE AUSTRALIA GOLD."......"TWO OUNCES." The smaller piece is of the same type, with the fraction $\frac{1}{2}$ substituted for the figure 2. They have grained edges. (See Plate XX. No. 1.)

206. G. 1855. Sovereign, of the SYDNEY MINT. Obv. Head of Victoria. "VICTORIA D. G. BRITANNIAR. REGINA F. D."......"1855." Rev. "AUSTRALIA," inscribed beneath a crown, and between two branches of laurel, crossed. "SYDNEY MINT."......"ONE SOVEREIGN." Edge grained. (See Plate XX. No. 2.)

COINS OF CANADA.

The new coins of Canada, which are upon a decimal footing, are the pieces of twenty, ten, and five cents, in silver, and one cent in copper. The silver coins have upon the obverse a head of her majesty, *laureated*, and the legend "VICTORIA DEI GRATIA REGINA." ......"CANADA." On the reverse the denomination, in cents, and the date, are inscribed between two branches of grape; above is suspended a crown. The edges are grained. The value of the larger piece is about 18$\frac{2}{3}$ cents. The cent differs slightly in type from the silver, having the head on the obverse inclosed in a beaded circle, and on the reverse the denomination and date are encircled by a similar circle and a grape-vine. (See Plate XX. Nos. 4 to 7.)

BRITISH GUIANA.*

That section of country lying on the northern coast of South America, and bearing the general name of *Guiana*, is now divided

* The coins of this colony have been temporarily placed in the Division of "Oriental Coins," in the west room.

into three sections, belonging respectively to Great Britain, Netherlands, and France. There appears to be little if any coinage for the two latter portions at the present day. British Guiana has long enjoyed the use of a complete series of coins, issued by the mother country. This was based upon the *guilder*, as a unit, divided into twenty stivers, up to the year 1839. But by an ordinance of February of that year, it was "deemed advisable to establish dollars and cents as the denomination of moneys of account of British Guiana, in the place of guilders and stivers."*

British Guiana consists of the two countries or districts of Essequebo and Demarara. There appears to have been a distinction made between them before the year 1816. Up to that year there was issued a series of coins consisting of the pieces of three, two, one, one-half, and one-quarter guilder, in silver, and the half stivers in copper. These were all of the same type, and bore upon the obverse a bust of George III., *laureated,* and adorned with drapery. Legend. "GEORGIUS III. DEI GRATIA." On the reverse was a figure denoting the value in guilders, surmounted by a crown, and inclosed by two oak branches, crossed. Legend. "COLONIES OF ESSEQUEBO & DEMARARY TOKEN." and the date. The copper piece differed slightly from the silver in having the legend, "GEORGIUS III D. G. REX," on the obverse, and on the reverse the inscription, "HALF STIVER," was placed beneath the crown. (See Nos. 1 to 6, *Division IV. of Oriental Coins.*) In 1816 a new set of silver coins, consisting of the pieces of two, one, one-half, and one-quarter guilder, were issued, of the same type as the previous coinage, but having the legend, "GEORGIUS III D. G. BRITANNIARUM REX," on the obverse, and the legend, "UNITED COLONY OF DEMARARY & ESSEQUIBO," on the reverse. These coins also have the edge plain instead of grained, as in the previous issues. (See Nos. 7 to 10.) After the accession of William IV. a third series of coins was issued, embracing a full set, from the piece of three guilders down. These had upon the obverse a simple head of William, and the legend, "GULIELMUS IIII D. G. BRITANNIAR. REX F. D." The reverse remained unaltered, and the edges were plain as in the

* Manual of Coins and Bullion.

last coins of George III. (See Nos. 11 to 16.) Whether there have been any coins issued under the ordinance of 1839, we are unable to state, none having yet appeared at this Mint.

BRITISH TOKENS.*

1. S. 1812. Three shillings. Obv. Head of George III., *laureated.* "GEORGIUS III DEI GRATIA REX." Rev. "BANK TOKEN. 3 SHILL. 1812." inscribed within a wreath of oak and laurel.

2. S. 1812. Three shillings. Obv. Bust, *laureated.* "GEORGIUS III DEI GRATIA REX." Rev. Same inscription as preceding, in a wreath of oak.

3. S. 1812. One shilling-and-sixpence. Same as No. 1.

4. S. 1815. Same.

5 and 6. S. 1804. Five shillings. Obverse same as No. 2. Rev. Britannia seated, holding an olive branch in one hand and a spear in the other, her left arm resting upon a shield, beneath which is a *cornucopia;* a bee-hive in the background; the whole surrounded by an oval band, bearing the inscription, "FIVE SHILLINGS......DOLLAR." Outside is "BANK OF ENGLAND......1804."

7. S. 1804. Six shillings. Obverse same as preceding. Rev. Britannia seated, holding a palm branch, extended, in her right hand, her left arm resting upon a harp. "BANK OF IRELAND TOKEN...... 1804......SIX SHILLINGS."

8. S. 1808. Thirty-pence. Obverse same as preceding, with a slight difference in the head. Rev. Same device as preceding. "BANK TOKEN......XXX PENCE......IRISH."

9. S. 1813. Tenpence. Obverse same as No. 1. Rev. "BANK TOKEN. 10 PENCE. IRISH. 1813," inclosed in a wreath of shamrock.

10. S. 1805. Fivepence. Obverse same as No. 1. Rev. "BANK TOKEN. FIVE PENCE. IRISH. 1805."

---

* The coins answering to the following description have been temporarily placed in the Division of "Oriental Coins," in the west room, where will also be found a quantity of British copper tokens (forty-one pieces). These were struck by traders and others as advertisements, and are of little consequence.

11. S. 1811. Shilling, of York. Obv. Shield, between branches of palm and laurel, crossed; above "YORK," beneath "1811." Rev. "CATTLE AND BARBER." "ONE SHILLING SILVER TOKEN."

12. S. 1811. Sixpence. Same type.

13. S. 1811. Shilling, of Bristol. Obv. A castle, and the prow of a vessel, surrounded by a *garter*, bearing the inscription "VIRTUTE ET INDUSTRIA." Above are two arms, crossed, one holding a pair of scales, and the other a serpent. "BRISTOL TOKEN, FOR XII PENCE." Rev. "PAYABLE BY MESSRS FRANS GARRATT, WM TERRELL, EDWD BIRD, SANT BECK & FRANS H. GRIGG." inclosed in a circular line. "TO FACILITATE TRADE. ISSUED IN BRISTOL AUGT. 12 1811."

14. S. 1811. Shilling, of Bristol. Obv. Shield, supported by two unicorns; two arms, as in No. 13. "ONE SHILLING TOKEN, GENUINE DOLLAR SILVER, 3 DWT." Rev. "SOMERSET, WILTS, DEVON, GLOUCESTERSHIRE, NORTH AND SOUTH WALES, AND BRISTOL TOKEN." "ISSUED BY E. BRYAN, BRISTOL."

15. S. 1811. Sixpence, of Bristol. Obv. Line, bearing the denomination. Legend. "R. TRIPP & CO. BRISTOL......1811." Rev. "PAYABLE BY ONE DOLLAR FOR 10 TOKENS & 2D OR 20 TOKENS FOR 2 DOLLARS & 4D, AND 40 FOR A ONE POUND NOTE."

16. S. 1811. Shilling, of Bristol. Obv. A bridge. "BRISTOL & WILTSHIRE......1811......TOKEN." Rev. Same device as the obverse of preceding. "PAYABLE BY NIBLACK & LATHAM AT THEIR WAREHOUSE, BRIDGE ST & TROWBRIDGE."

17. S. 1811. Shilling, of Bristol. Obv. Same device as No. 14. "LET TRADE AND COMMERCE FLOURISH. BRISTOL. ISSUED BY W. SHEPPARD. EXCHANGE."......"SEPT. 6, 1811." Rev. "VALUE 12 PENCE," in a wreath of oak. "SOMERSETSHIRE, WILTSHIRE, GLOUCESTERSHIRE, SOUTH WALES AND BRISTOL TOKEN."

18. S. 1811. Shilling, of Flintshire. Obv. A shield, surmounted by the Welsh feathers, and bearing two keys in *saltiere*. "FLINTSHIRE BANK. AUGUST 12, 1811." Rev. "FLINTSHIRE BANK TOKEN ONE SHILLING." The initials "I. O. S. & D."

19. S. 1812. Shilling, of Lincoln. Obv. A shield, bearing the cross of St. George, between two oak branches, crossed. "LINCOLN SILVER TOKEN. 1812." Rev. "MILLSON AND PRESTON." encircled by

a garter, bearing the inscription, "DOLLAR SILVER." "A ONE POUND NOTE WILL BE GIVEN FOR 20 OF THESE."

20. S. 1812. Shilling, of STOCKPORT. Obv. The goddess of Commerce seated upon a cotton bale, and holding a pair of scales, extended, in her left hand, and a *cornucopia* in her right, a sword lying at her feet, a ship in the distance. "ONE SHILLING SILVER TOKEN. 1812." Rev. A bee-hive and bees. "T. CARTWRIGHT D. G. & R. FERNS ......STOCKPORT."

21. S. 1811. Shilling, of the SHAFTESBURY BANK. Obv. Shield, between two laurel branches, crossed. "SHAFTESBURY BANK...... LICENSED 14 MARCH, 1811." Rev. "DORSETSHIRE, WILTSHIRE, AND SHAFTESBURY BANK TOKEN. VALUE ONE SHILLING."

22. S. 1811. Shilling, of SELWOOD. Obv. Bust, at full-face, crowned. "FRAME SELWOOD. TOKEN. FOR 12 PENCE." Rev. Cross. "A ONE POUND NOTE GIVEN FOR 20 TOKENS. 1811."

23. A Spanish dollar, bearing the stamp of "I. & A. MUIR, GREENOCK."

DIVISION XI.

GERMAN STATES.

In A.D. 1500, the Empire of Germany was divided, under Maximilian I., into the six *circles* of *Franconia, Bavaria, Suabia, Upper Rhine, Westphalia,* and *Saxony;* and twelve years later, the number was increased to twelve, by dividing the *circles* of the *Upper Rhine* and *Saxony,* and adding the *circles* of *Austria* and *Burgundy.* Each *circle* had, at its head, a lay and an ecclesiastical *prince,* who assembled the legislative bodies of the States of the *circle,* and communicated between them and the emperor. In addition to these, they also had a military chief, or *Field Marshal,* as he was called, who commanded the military forces, and made all the necessary provisions of stores, ammunition, etc., for their maintenance and support. With some modifications, this was the state of affairs up to 1806, when the Empire was dissolved and transformed into the present *Germanic*

Confederation. This Confederation was first composed of forty different States or Sovereignties, including the four *free cities* of *Lubeck, Frankfort, Bremen,* and *Hamburg;* but was afterward reduced to thirty-five. The government consists of a "*permanent Diet,*" of seventeen votes, which holds it sittings at Frankfort, and is presided over by the Plenipotentiary of Austria. This body regulates all the affairs of the Confederation, which would properly come under the jurisdiction of the Executive. In the apportionment of representatives to the Diet, *Austria, Prussia,* and the larger States have *one* each; while only *six* are allotted to the smaller States and cities. Whenever any important measures or changes in the existing laws are to be considered, they convene what is called the *General Assembly,* a body consisting of sixty-nine votes,* of which *Austria* and *five* of the larger States have *four* each; *five* others *three* each; three *two* each; and the rest *one* each.

Any one who has attempted to trace out the history of the German States in all its details, can possibly form some idea of the labor attending the study of their coins. There is not a State in Germany, in whose history divisions and subdivisions, and reunions of these divisions, have not taken place to a greater or less extent, thus producing a dire confusion among the titles and devices on the coins; in fact, it not unfrequently requires as much ingenuity as industry, to be able to state, with any degree of accuracy, to what Sovereign, or even to what *State,* a coin properly belongs.

Many of the northern German States have upon their coins a figure emblematic of the "*wild men of the Hartz Mountains,*" as they are called. In the time of the first Roman emperors, the north of Germany was peopled by many brave and hardy barbaric nations or tribes, who paid but little attention to the arts of agriculture, but appear to have derived their principal sustenance from the spoils of the chase and of conquest.† It is a curious fact that these hardy

---

* Including the votes of the two *Hohenzollerns* and *Saxe-Gotha,* which houses have become extinct.

† Cæsar, speaking of the *Suevians,* whom he accounts to be by far the most warlike and considerable of all the German nations, says: "They allow of no such thing as property or private possession in the distribution of their lands; their residence, for the sake of tillage, being confined to a single year. Corn is not

people, though of such a warlike character that they were never satisfied unless engaged in making war upon their neighbors, possessed the crowning virtue of chastity to an eminent degree. Infidelity among the wives of the warriors was a thing seldom known. Polygamy was not permitted among the common people, and seldom resorted to by the princes for the purpose of increasing their alliances. And it is said that whenever the fortunes of war turned the tide of conquest against them, their wives and daughters, who always accompanied them in battle, usually resorted to the alternative of self-destruction, rather than suffer the embraces of the victors. For these reasons the people of the northern States hold the memory of their ancient and barbarous progenitors in much reverence; and the princes have considered their image an emblem of sufficient virtue, stability, and prowess, to grace their coinage even in latter times.

At the Diet of Augsburg, in 1559, two standards were recognized for the gold coins of Germany. The first was $18\frac{1}{2}$ carats fine; and from a mark weight of such gold 72 *florins*, 36 *maximilians*, or 24 *carolins* were to be coined. This standard was continued until 1740. The *second* was $23\frac{2}{3}$ carats, or 986 thousandths fine; 67 *ducats* to be coined from a mark weight. This would be equivalent to 53.87 Troy grains per ducat. This coinage was continued in Austria and other southern States until a very recent date.

In 1740 a third standard originated in Brunswick, and soon became general through the northern States. The fineness was at first $21\frac{2}{3}$ carats, or 903 thousandths fine; but was afterward reduced to $21\frac{1}{2}$ carats, or 896 thousandths fine; and from a mark weight of such gold $17\frac{1}{2}$ pieces of ten thalers, 35 pistoles or five-thaler pieces, or 70 half pistoles were to be coined. This would place the weight of

---

much in use among them, because they prefer a milk or flesh diet, and are greatly addicted to hunting. Thus the quality of their food, their perpetual exercise, and free unconfined manner of life (because being from their childhood fettered by no rules of duty or education, they acknowledge no law but will and pleasure), contribute to make them strong and of an extraordinary stature. They have likewise accustomed themselves, though inhabiting a climate naturally very cold, to bathe in their rivers, and clothe themselves only with skins, which, as they are very small, leave a great part of their bodies quite uncovered." (*Cæsar's Commentaries*, book iv. sec. 2.)

the ten-thaler piece at 206.26 Troy grains; but they are seldom found to weigh more than 205 grains.

Subsequent to the year 1819, pieces of ten and five gulden, nine-tenths fine, have been coined in Baden; but these, with the other systems above noticed, have been superseded, as will be shown presently.

Most of the German States have conformed in their silver coinage to the different conventions which have been held for the purpose of equalizing the standards of German silver coins. The first convention for this purpose was held at Leipsic in 1690. The second was convened in 1753, and its standards are known as the "Convention rate." The third was held at Dresden, in 1838, at which meeting all the States were represented except Austria, Hanover, Brunswick, and a few States of less importance. Below will be found a table giving the weight, fineness, value, etc. of the principal pieces, according to each convention, together with the crown and florin of the southern States. The values here set down are the *legal*, and not the *current* values, and are computed according to the present price of silver ($1.21 per Troy ounce.)

Description.		No. of pieces to the Cologne mark, fine.	Wt. in Troy grains.	Fineness. thous.	Value.
Leipsic rate, 1690.	Specie thaler............	9	451.1	889	$1.12.3
	Specie florin*..........	18	Various.	Various.	56.1
Convention rate, 1753.	Specie thaler............	10	433.2	833	1.01.0
	Specie florin	20	216.6	833	50.5
	Half florin...............	40	108.3	833	25.2
	Twenty kreutz. (B.S.)	60	103.2	583	16.8
Crown of Southern States	....	9 8-100	456.	872	1.11.6
Florin	do do	24	200.6	750	42.1
Dresden rate, 1838.	Two thaler, or three-and-a-half gulden...	7	572.9	900	1.44.4
	Thaler.....................	14	343.8	750	72.1
	Two-third thaler.......	21	229.2	750	48.1
	One-third thaler........	42	114.6	750	24.0
	One-sixth thaler........	96	72.2	521	10.5
	Florin......................	24½	163.7	900	41.2
	Half florin...............	49	81.8	900	20.5
	One-tenth florin (six kreutzers)	270	40.	333	03.7
	One-twentieth florin (three kreutzers) ...	540	20.	333	1.9

* Called *zweydrittel*, or two-third piece, because it was two-thirds of the thaler of account, though only half of the specie thaler. It was sometimes coined of fine silver, sometimes only three-fourths fine, the weight varying accordingly.

On the 24th of January, 1857, a convention was concluded between the principal German States, including Austria and the free city of Frankfort, by which a new system of coinage was established. It was agreed that the half of one kilogram, (equal to 500 grammes, or 7717.5 Troy grains,) called "*zollpfund*," should serve as a standard at the mints of all the States who were parties to the convention. This zollpfund, or half kilogram, was divided into 1000 parts, each equivalent to one-half of a gramme.

The convention provided for the issue of two denominations of gold, the crown and half crown. These were to be nine-tenths fine; forty-five crowns to be coined from the zollpfund of standard gold, the half crown in proportion. These were called "trade coins," being struck to facilitate trade between the different States.

Of the current silver coins there were to be five denominations, (not including the two "union coins.") These were the pieces of two and one florin, nine-tenths fine; the former to be coined at the rate of $20\frac{1}{4}$, and the latter at $40\frac{1}{2}$ pieces to the zollpfund of standard silver; the quarter florin, 520 thousandths fine, $93\frac{6}{10}$ pieces to the zollpfund; the piece of ten new kreutzers, 500 fine, 250 pieces to the zollpfund; and the piece of five new kreutzers, 375 fine, 375 pieces to the zollpfund. The values of the latter pieces appear ridiculously small to an American citizen.

The "union coins" which, like the two gold pieces, were intended to facilitate commercial intercourse between the States, were the pieces of two and one thaler, nine-tenths fine; the first to be coined at the rate of $13\frac{1}{2}$, and the latter at 27 pieces to the zollpfund of standard silver.

The copper coins were of three denominations: the pieces of three, one, and one-half new kreutzers. These were coined respectively at the rate of 50, 150, and 300 pieces to the zollpfund, and were to be of pure copper.

Annexed is a table in which the standards of the gold and silver coins are set forth in a more clear and comprehensive manner. We also introduce a column containing the weight of the different pieces in Troy grains, and another containing the values, in our money, according to the legal standards.

DESCRIPTION.	No. of pieces to the zollpfund weight of fine metal.	Standard fineness in thous.	No. of pieces to the zoll-pfund wt. of standard metal.	Weight in Troy grains.	Value in U. S. currency.
Gold trade coins:					$
Crown	50	900	45	171.05	6.64.7
Half crown...............	100	900	90	85.75	3.32.3
Silver "union" coins:					
Two thalers..............	15	900	13½	571.06	1.44.0
One thaler................	30	900	27	285.08	72.0
Silver current coins:					
Two florins...............	22½	900	20¼	38.01	09.6
One florin.................	45	900	40½	19.08	04.8
One-quarter florin......	180	520	93 6-10	8.24	01.2
Ten new kreutzers......	500	500	250	3.08	0.43
Five new kreutzers.....	1000	375	375	2.05	0.21

SECTION I.—PRUSSIA.*

Prior to the fourteenth century Prussia was but an inconsiderable duchy. But since the accession of FREDERICK VI. of Nuremburg, in 1415, on which occasion it was raised to the rank of an electorate, it has been steadily augmenting both in extent and influence, and now ranks among the first powers of Europe. It was raised to the rank of a kingdom during the reign of FREDERICK III., in 1701, upon which occasion FREDERICK dropped the "III." and assumed the title of FREDERICK I., he being the *first* of the royal house. It now consists of several States, the principal of which are: the Dukedom of Prussia, which gives name to the whole; the Electorate of Brandenburg, which contains BERLIN, the capital; Silesia, and parts of Poland and Saxony. FREDERICK, after his adoption of royalty, continued the title of Elector upon his coins, styling himself "*King of Prussia and Elector of Brandenburg.*" But upon the accession of FREDERICK II., in 1740, the title of elector was omitted, and the sovereigns have since used the simple title "*King of Prussia.*"

1. S. 1688. Thaler, (dollar,) of FREDERICK II. (as elector.) Obv. Bust, "FRID. WILH. D. G. M(archio) B(randenb.) S(acri) R(omani)

---

* We have omitted the plates in this portion of the work. The coins of the German States are of such a multifarious character that we have found it impossible to do them justice without exceeding our limits, and therefore omit them altogether.

I(mperii) ARC(hithesarius) & EL"(ector) Rev. Shield, surmounted by a crown. "CHURF. BRAND. LANDMUNZ. 1688."

2. S. 1689. Thaler. Obv. Bust, in armor. "FRIDER. III D. G. M. B. S. R. I. ARC. & EL." Rev. Crowned shield. "MONETA NOVA BRANDENB. 1689."

3. S. 1692. Same.

4. S. 1714. Thaler, of FREDERICK I. (king). Obv. Bust, in armor, *laureated.* "FRID. WILH. D. G. REX. BORUSSIÆ." Rev. Crowned shield. No legend.

5. S. 1720. Thaler. Obv. Bust, in armor. "FRID. WILH. D. G. REX BORUSS. EL. BRAND." Rev. Crowned shield. No legend.

6. G. 1750. Double frederick d'or, or ten-thaler piece of FREDERICK II. Obv. Bust, in armor. "FRIDERICUS BORUSSORUM REX." Rev. Eagle, surrounded by flags, etc.: a crown suspended above. No legend. Value $7.91.

7. S. 1750. Thaler. Obverse same as preceding. Rev. Flags and martial emblems, surmounted by a crowned eagle; above is "EIN REICHS THALER;" beneath, "1750." Value 71.3 cts.

8. G. 1752. Frederick d'or. Same type. Value $3.96.

9. G. 1753. Half frederick d'or. Obv. Undraped bust. Same legend as No. 6. Rev. An eagle in flight, carrying flags, etc.; the date above. Value $1.98.

10. G. 1763. Frederick d'or. Same type.

11. S. 1764. Thaler. Obverse same as preceding. Reverse same as No. 7. Value 71.4 cts.

12. S. 1764. Florin. Obv. Bust, *laureated.* "FRIDERICUS BORUSSORUM REX." Reverse same as No. 7, with "2 EINEN R. THALER." Value 35.7 cts.

13. G. 1767. Double frederick d'or. Same type as No. 9. Value $3.96.

14. S. 1771. One-third thaler. Obverse same as No. 9. Rev. "3 EINEN REICHS THALER. 1771," inclosed in a wreath composed of a palm and laurel branch, crossed. Value 23.6 cts.

15. S. 1774. Same.

16. G. 1776. Frederick d'or. Same as No. 9. Value $3.96.

17. S. 1785. Thaler. Same as No. 12. Value 71.4 cts.

18. S. 1786. Same. (Frederick II. died in this year, and was succeeded by Frederick William II.)

19. S. 1791. Thaler, of FREDERICK WILLIAM II. Obv. Bust, in armor. "FRIED. WILHELM KOENIG VON PREUSSEN." Rev. A crowned eagle, with a scepter in the dexter, and the imperial globe, or mound, in the sinister talon; above a pedestal, from which depends a portion of a laurel wreath; beneath are two palm branches, crossed. "EIN REICHS THALER" above, and the date beneath. Value 71.3 cts.

20. G. 1795. Half frederick d'or. Obverse same as preceding. Rev. Martial emblems surmounted by a crowned eagle. No legend. Value $1.97.

21. G. 1796. Same.

22. S. 1796. Thaler. Obverse same as No. 19, with the bust in civil dress. Rev. Shield, bearing the Prussian eagle surmounted by a crown and supported by two "*wild men*,"* each holding a club; beneath is "EIN THALER, 1796." Value 71.3 cts.

23. S. 1796. Florin, of FREDERICK GEORGE. Obv. A crowned shield, with the Prussian eagle on a shield of pretence. "F. G. REX. BOR(russiæ) PR(inceps) SUP(remus) NOVIE(astri) & VAL"(angini). Rev. *Fleur de leuced* cross, with a sun in the center. "SUUM CUIQUE. 1796." Value 35.7 cts.

24. S. 1796. One-third thaler. Same as preceding. Value 23.6 cts.

25. S. 1799. Florin, of FREDERICK WILLIAM III. Obv. Bust, in civil dress. "F. W. III REX BOR. PR. SUP. NOVIE & VAL." Rev. Crowned shield, with the Prussian eagle on a shield of pretence, supported by two wild men. "SUUM CUIQUE." Value 35.5 cts.

26. G. 1801. Double frederick d'or. Same as No. 20. Value $7.93.

27. S. 1801. Two-third piece. Obv. Crowned shield, between branches of laurel. "FRIEDR. WILH. KOENIG V. PR. M(arkgraf) ZU BRAND. D(anzig) H(aldenstein) R. R. E(lbing) K(onig) U(nd) KURF"(urst). Rev. "$\frac{2}{3}$" "18 STUCK EINE MARK FEIN......1801." Struck for Brandenburg. Value 55.6 cts.

---

* Emblematic of the ancient inhabitants of the Hartz Mountains, in the north of Germany. (See *Introduction to the German States.*)

28. S. 1801. Same.

29. S. 1802. Thaler. Obverse same as No. 26. Reverse same as No. 22. Value 71 cts.

30. S. 1803. Same.

31. G. 1803. Frederick d'or. Same as No. 26. Value $3.96.

32. S. 1814. Thaler. Obv. Undraped bust. Same legend as No. 26. Rev. "EIN REICHS THALER, 1814," inclosed in a wreath of two oak branches, crossed. "VIERZEHN EINE FEINE MARK."* Value 71.4 cts.

33. S. 1815. Same.

34. G. 1817. Half frederick d'or. Obv. Bust, in uniform. "FRIEDR. WILHELM III KOENIG V. PREUSSEN." Reverse same as No. 20. Value $1.98.

35. S. 1818. Thaler. Same type, with "EIN THALER" above the device on the reverse. Value 71.4 cts.

36. S. 1819. Same.

37. S. 1822. One-sixth thaler. Obv. Head. Same legend as No. 34. Rev. Shield, surmounted by a crown and encircled by an order chain. "LXXXIV EINE F. M. VI EINEN THALER." Value 12 cts.

38. S. 1826. Same.

39 and 40. B.S. 1821. One silver groschen. Obverse same as preceding. Rev. "1 SILBER GROSCHEN 1821," occupying the field. "30 EINEN THALER.—SCHEIDE MÜNZE." Value 3.3 cts.

41. S. 1824. Thaler. Same type as No. 37, with "EIN THALER, XIV EINE F. M." on the reverse, and "GOT MIT UNS" on the edge.

42. S. 1829. Same. Value 72 cts.

43. G. 1825. Frederick d'or. Obverse same as No. 37. Rev. The Prussian eagle perched upon a cannon, the date beneath. Value $3.96.

---

* The *Cologne mark* is a standard weight, and is equivalent to 3609.5 *Troy grains;* and the rate of coinage is usually expressed as so many pieces to the *fine mark*, as in this case the *thaler* is coined at the rate of "14 *to the fine mark;*" that is, the *thaler* is equivalent *in value* to the *one-fourteenth* of the fine mark, or *standard weight of pure silver*, aside from the alloy of copper. The *Cologne mark* weight of pure silver is worth at the present mint rate ($1.21 *per ounce*) $10.11, lacking the twentieth of a *mill.*

44. G. 1831. Double frederick d'or. Same type. Value $7.97.

45. B.S. 1831. Half groschen (2 *pieces*). Same type as No. 39.

46. S. 1832. Thaler. Obverse same as No. 37. Rev. "SEGEN DES MANSFELDER BERGBAUES" (seed of the Mansfield mines) occupying the field. "EIN THALER XIV EINE FEINE MARK......1832." Edge same as No. 41. Value 72 cts.

47. G. 1835. Frederick d'or. Same type as No. 43. Value $3.96.

48. S. 1840. Two-thaler piece. Obverse same as No. 37. Rev. Shield, surrounded by an order chain, a mantle of *ermine* suspended from a crown and forming a canopy over the shield. "2 THALER. VII EINE F MARK. $3\frac{1}{2}$ GULDEN."......"VEREINS——MÜNZE," "GOTT MIT UNS," on the edge. Value $1.44.4.

49 and 50. S. 1841 and 42. Two-thaler piece, of FREDERICK WILLIAM IV. Same type as preceding. Value $1.44.4.

50. S. 1855. Thaler. Obverse same as preceding. Rev. Crowned shield, encircled by a laurel wreath and an order chain. Value 72.1 cts.

BRUNSWICK.

In the early part of the middle ages, Brunswick, with Hanover, formed part of ancient Saxony. And in the reign of HENRY, *the Lion*—twelfth century—it comprised the united duchies of Bavaria and Saxony; but Henry having refused to aid the emperor, Frederick Barbarossa, in his wars with the pope, he was deprived of both duchies by a decree of the Diet in 1180, and only left the possession of his alodial domains of Brunswick and Luneburg. ERNEST, *the Confessor*, who died in 1546, left three sons, the eldest of whom died in 1559; whereupon the duchy was divided between the two surviving brothers, *Augustus*, the eldest, receiving Brunswick-Wolfenbüttel or Brunswick, and *William*, Brunswick-Luneburg or Hanover. In 1806 the reigning prince—the Duke Charles William Frederick—commanded the Prussian troops at the battle of *Auerstädt*, where he was wounded and soon after died. His possessions were immediately seized by the conqueror, and formed part of the kingdom of *Westphalia*, till 1813. After the battle of *Leipsic*, the duchy was restored to its rightful possessor, Frederick William, youngest son of the preceding duke.

60. S. 1643. Crown. Obv. "AUGUSTUS HERTZOG ZU BRAUNS. UND LU." (Augustus, Duke of Brunswick and Luneburg;) the duke dressed in armor, with his head uncovered, and evidently in the act of returning thanks to Heaven for his success. Rev. "ALLES MIT BEDACHT. 1643," (all is accomplished by prudence;) the device represents a broadsword, sheathed, leaning against a square block, the former bearing the inscription "13 K. MAII," and the latter "AP. 13. XI. 10. IN. F."

61. S. 1643. Crown. Obv. "AUGUSTUS HERTZOG ZU BRAUNS. U. LU." Shield surmounted by four helmets. Rev. "TANDEM PATIENTIA VICTRIX. ANNO. 1643." (Perseverance is at last victorious;) the device represents the ringing of a bell, which bears an inscription (abbreviated) to the effect that "THIS BELL FIRST PROCLAIMED THE NEW PEACE."

These coins were probably struck to commemorate the battle of *Dutlingen*, in which the *Duke George*, of Brunswick, took part against the imperialists; having joined the standard of GUSTAVUS ADOLPHUS, of Sweden, soon after the battle of *Lutter*, in 1626. It was formerly the practice, in most of the German States, to strike *medallic coins* of this description to commemorate any important national event. Many of the old German *ducats* are found to be of this character.

62. G. 1661. Ducat, of CHRISTIAN LEWIS. Obv. Horse *courant.* "SINCERE ET CONSTANTER; 1661." Rev. Crowned shield, the letter "S." at one side, and "W." at the other. "CHRIST. LUD. D. G. DUX BR. ET LUNEB."

63. B S. 1684. Two marien groschen, (two pennies,) of RUDOLPH AUGUSTUS. Obv. The device represents a wild man in the act of lopping the limbs from a yew-tree. "D. G. RUDOLPH AUGUSTUS DUX BR ET L." Rev. "II MARIE GROS.," occupying the field. "REMIGIO ALTISSIMI. 1684."

64. S. 1691. Crown, of AUGUSTUS and ANTHONY ULRIC. Obv. Shield, surmounted by five helmets. "RUD. AUG. & ANTH. ULR. D. D. BRUN. & LUN." Rev. Two wild men holding in their hands two olive

branches intwined. "UT. FRONTIBUS ITA FRONDIBUS CONJUNCTISIMI." (Thus face to face as the branches are intwined.)

65. S. 1692. Twenty-four marien groschen, of same. Obv. Horse *courant.* Same legend as preceding. Rev. "FURSTL. BR. LUNEB. LANDT MÜNTZ. 1692." (Princes of Brunswick and Luneburg. Provincial coin;) the denomination occupying the field.

66. S. 1694. Twenty-four marien groschen, of same. Obverse same as preceding. Rev. "NACH DEN LEIPZIGER FUS," (according to the Leipsic rates;) the denomination occupying the field.

67. S. 1695. Florin, of same. Obverse same as preceding. Rev. Shield, surmounted by a crown. "REMIGIO ALTISSIMI UNI."

68. S. 1698. Twenty-four marien groschen, of same. Same as No. 66, with "FURSTL. BRUNS. LUNEB. MÜNTZ. 1698," on the reverse.

69. S. 1704. Twenty-four marien groschen, of ANTHONY ULRIC. Obv. Device same as No. 63. "D. G. ANTHON. ULRICH. DUX BR. & LUN." Rev. "LABORE ET CONSTANTIA. 1704;" the denomination in the field.

70. S. 1712. Twenty-four marien groschen, of same. Obv. Device same as No. 63. "CONSTANTER." Rev. "D. G. ANTONI ULRIC DUX BR. & LUN," with the denomination in the field.

71. G. 1749. Five thalers, of CHARLES, *Duke of Brunswick.* Obv. Bust, "CAROLUS D. G. DUX BR. ET LUN." Rev. Horse *courant.* "NUNQUAM RETRORSUM. 1749;" the denomination beneath. Value $3.97.

72. G. 1760. Ten thalers. Same type. Value $7.81.

73. S. 1764. Florin. Same type. Value 55.3 cts.

74. S. 1768. Twenty-four marien groschen. Obv. "D. G. CAROLUS DUX BRUNSVIC & LUNEB. 1768," with the denomination occupying the field. Reverse same as preceding.

75 and 76. S. 1790. Specie thaler, of CHARLES WILLIAM FERDINAND. Obv. Crowned shield, hung with laurel; horse *courant* on a shield of pretence. "CAROLUS GUIL. FERD. D. G. DUX BRUNSV. ET LUN." Rev. "X EINE FEINE MARK. CONVENTIONS M.;" the denomination in the field. Value 99.8 cts.

77. G. 1795. Five thalers, of same. Obv. Device same as preceding. "CAROLUS GUILIELMUS FERDINANDUS." Rev. "D. G. DUX BRUNSVICENS. ET LUNEBURG," and the denomination. Value $3.97.

78 and 79. S. 1800. Twenty-four marien groschen. Same type as No. 66.

WESTPHALIA.

81. S. 1808. Two francs, of NAPOLEON. Obv. Bust, *laureated.* "HIERONYMUS NAPOLEON." Rev. "2 FRANCS," inclosed in a wreath of laurel. "KOENIG V. WESTPHALEN FR. PR......1808." "GOTT ERHALTE DEN KOENIG," on the edge. Value 38 cts.

82. G. 1810. Ten thalers. Obv. Crowned shield, hung with an order chain and badge. Same legend as preceding. Rev. Same type as preceding, without the laurel wreath. Value $7.87.

83. S. 1810. Florin. Obv. Bust. Rev. "$\frac{2}{3}$" in the field "N. D. REICHS FUSS. FEIN SILBER." Same legend as preceding. Value 55 cts.

84. G. 1811. Ten thalers. Same as No. 81, with the wreath on the reverse omitted. Value $7.87.

85. S. 1812. Thaler. Same type as preceding, with "X EINE FEINE MARK. 1812," in the field of the reverse. Value $1.00.

86. S. 1813. Same.

87. S. 1813. Florin. Obv. Bust, *laureated.* Otherwise same as No. 83.

88. G. 1813. Ten thalers. Same type as No. 84.

89. G. 1813. Ten francs. Same as No. 84, with the legends more abbreviated. Value $1.92.

* * * * * * *

91. S. 1813. One-sixth thaler. Obv. Horse *courant.* "FRIDERICUS GUIL. D. G. DUX BR. ET L." Rev. No device. "LXXX EINE FEINE MARK. CONV. M." "VI EINEN THALER. 1813," in the field. Value 12 cts.

92. G. 1813. Ten thalers. Obv. Shield, draped with laurel and crowned. "FRIDERICUS GULIELMUS." Rev. "D. G. DUX BRUNSVICENS. ET LUNEBURG." "X THALER. 1813," in the field. Value $7.89.

93. G. 1817. Ten thalers. Obv. Shield, same as preceding. "GEORGIUS D. G. PRINC. REGENS." Rev. "TUTOR NOM CAROLI DUCIS BRUNS. ET LUN." "X THALER. 1817," in the field. Value $7.89.

FREDERICK WILLIAM fell, at the head of his troops, at *Quatre Bras*, and was succeeded by CHARLES FREDERICK, his oldest son, who, being a minor, was placed under the tutilage of George IV., then Prince Regent of England, who continued to act in this capacity until October, 1823, when Charles assumed the reins of government in his own right.

94. B.S. 1819. Three marien groschen. Obv. "160 EINE FEINE MARK." "3 MARIEN GROSCHEN, 1819," in the field. Rev. Horse *courant.* "KÖN. HANNOVERSCHE CONVENTIONS MÜNZE." (Royal Hanoverian convention money.)

95. B.S. 1819. One marien groschen. Obv. "GEORG. T. N. CAROLI. D. BR."

96. B.S. 1820. One twenty-fourth thaler. Obv. "GEORGIUS D. G. R. T. N. CAROLI D. BR. ET. L."

97. B.S. 1823. Four pfenning. Same as preceding.

98. C. 1824. Two pfenning. Obv. Horse *courant.* "CARL. HERZOG ZU BRAUNSCHW. U. L." Rev. "II PFENNING SCHEIDE MUNZE. 1824."

99. G. 1825. Ten thaler. Obv. "CARL. HERZOG ZU BR. U. LUEN." Same device as No. 92. Rev. The denomination. Value $7.91.

100. S. 1828. Six pfenning. Same type.

101. S. 1830. One-twelfth thaler, of CHARLES. Same as No. 98.

102. G. 1831. Ten thalers. Obv. "WILHELM HERZOG V. BR. U. LUEN." Horse *courant.* Rev. The denomination. Value $7.80.

103. G. 1834. Ten thalers, of WILLIAM. Obv. Crowned shield, supported by two wild men; horse *courant,* on a shield of pretence. "WILHELM HERZOG Z. BR. U. L." Rev. "X THALER. 1834." inclosed in a wreath formed of two sprigs of oak, crossed. Value $7.89.

104. S. 1838. Thaler, of same. Obv. Bust, without the laurel. "WILHELM HERZOG. Z. BRAUNSCHWEIG U. L." Rev. Crowned shield, heavily draped; a portion of the *collar* and the *badge of the Guelphic** order beneath the shield. "EIN THALER. XIV EINE F. M."

---

* The Royal Guelphic Order was a Hanoverian order of knighthood, established by George IV., Prince Regent of England, in 1815. It probably derived its name from the *Guelphs* or *Guelfs*, a powerful faction of the middle ages, which was opposed to the German emperors and their adherents, the latter of whom were called *Ghibelines.* The antagonism between these two parties resolved itself into a struggle between the secular and spiritual powers, the *Ghibelines* sustaining the cause of the emperor, while the *Guelfs* stood by the pope. The wars between the two contending parties deluged *Italy* with blood for nearly

(One thaler, fourteen to the fine mark.) "NEC ASPERA TERRENT," on the edge. Value 72.2 cts.

105. S. 1838. Same as preceding, showing the reverse.

106. S. 1840. One-sixth thaler. Obv. Head, "WILHELM HERZOG," etc. Rev. "VI EINEN THALER. LXXXIV. EINE F. MARK." "4 GUTE GROSCHEN," (four good grosh-piece) in the field.

Of the *groschen* or *grosh-piece*, there are three different varieties: 1st. The *good groschen*, of 24 to the thaler, worth about *three* cents in our money. 2d. The *silver groschen*, of 30 to the thaler, worth about 2.7 cents. 3d. The *marien groshen, of* 24 *to the florin*, and consequently worth about 2.3 cents.

HANOVER.

Since the division of the house of Brunswick in 1559 into the two branches of Brunswick and Hanover, the systems of government have been entirely distinct, although it would seem that the *administration* of both has, for a portion of the time, been vested in the same individual; thus we find that from 1592 to 1648, the same persons who reigned as Dukes of Brunswick *proper*, were also Dukes of Hanover. But in the latter year, upon the death of Frederick II., CHRISTIAN LEWIS succeeds in Brunswick, while ERNEST AUGUSTUS appears as Duke of Hanover. ERNEST was made an elector in 1692, and continued to reign until his death in 1698, when he was succeeded by GEORGE LEWIS, who, upon the death of his uncle, GEORGE WILLIAM, in 1705, inherited the Dukedom of ZELL, and in 1714 ascended the throne of England as GEORGE I.; since which time the house of Hanover has continued to supply the throne of England with sovereigns; and the succession was the same in both countries until the death of William IV., when, by the *Salique** law, VICTORIA was prevented from assuming the crown of Hanover, and it consequently descended to the *next male heir*, who was the *Duke of Cumberland.*

---

three centuries. The order consists of *grand crosses*, *commanders*, and *knights*, and is both a civil and a military distinction. It is sometimes styled the "*Order of Merit.*"

* A fundamental law, which provides that *males only* shall inherit the throne.

Hanover was raised to the rank of a kingdom during the reign of George III., in 1814. It may be proper here to remark, that the same titles are found on the coins of Hanover as on those of Brunswick, until a very recent period, the princes of both houses styling themselves "*Dukes of Brunswick and Luneburg.*" The name of "*Hanover*" did not appear upon the coins until in the reign of GEORGE IV., when it was added to the old title. But in the following reign, of WILLIAM IV., the simple title "*King of Hanover,*" was adopted.

115. S. 1687. Crown, of ERNEST AUGUSTUS. Obv. His bust, "ERNESTUS AUGUSTUS D. G. EP. OSNAB. DUX BR. ET LUNEB." Rev. "SOLA BONA QUÆ HONESTA. 1687." (Honest things are the only good things.) Shield surmounted by five helmets.

116. S. 1690. Florin, of same. Obv. The wild man is here represented grasping in his right hand a pine-tree, which has been denuded of a portion of its verdure, and torn from the ground. Legend same as the reverse of 115. Rev. *Sword* and *crosier* in *saltiere,* through a crowned shield. "ERNEST AUG. D. G. EPISC. OSN. DUX B. & L."

117. S. 1713. Florin, of GEORGE LEWIS. (George I. of England.) Obv. Horse *courant.* "IN RECTO DECUS." "FEIN SILB." Rev. Crowned shield, name and titles.

118. S. 1714. Two marien groschen, of same. Obv. "IN RECTO DECUS," horse *courant,* "1714." Rev. "GEORG. LUD. D. G. D. B. & L. S. R. I. A. T. & E." "II MARIEN GROS." in the field.

119. S. 1729. Crown, of GEORGE II. Obv. Horse *courant.* "NEC ASPERA TERRENT." Rev. The royal arms; the arms of England, Ireland, and France occupying the first three quarters of the shield, and the arms of the house of Hanover, the fourth. "GEORG. II D. G. M. BRIT. F. & H. REX. F. D. BR. & L. DUX. S. R. I. A. TH. & EL." (Which, in unadulterated English, means: "*George II., by the Grace of God, King of Great Britain, France, and Ireland, Defender of the Faith, Duke of Brunswick and Luneburg, Arch Treasurer and Elector of the Holy Roman Empire.*")

120. S. 1733. Florin, of same. Rev. Crowned shield, bearing the arms quartered as before.

121. S. 1737. Crown of same. (Same as preceding.)

122. G. 1758. Five thalers, of same. Obv. Crowned shield; name and English titles. Rev. His German titles, with the denomination and date occupying the field. Value $3.93.

123. S. 1760. Florin, of same. Obv. *Device* same as 116, and his German titles. Rev. Crowned shield. Value 56 cts.

124. S. 1766. Crown, of George III. Obv. Crowned shield; name and English titles not so much abbreviated as in the former reign. Rev. *St. Andrew* and his cross; German titles. Value $1.12.

125. S. 1776. Four marien groschen, of same. Obv. Name and English titles. "IIII MARIEN GROSCH." occupying the field. Rev. (See No. 116) German titles.

126. S. 1783. Twenty-four marien groschen, of same. Obv. Crowned shield, name and titles arranged as before; the denomination occupying the field of the reverse.

127. S. 1797. Same reverse.

128. S. 1801. Florin, of same. Obv. Bust, *laureated;* name and titles. Rev. "18 STÜCK EINE MARK FEIN. 1801." "2–3" in the field. Value 56 cts.

129. S. 1807. Florin, of same. Obv. Shield encircled by the *garter*, and surmounted by a crown; arms of Hanover on a shield of pretence. "GEORGIUS III D. G. BRITANNIARUM REX F. D." Rev. The fraction "2-3" and German titles. Value 56 cts.

130. S. 1814. Florin, of same. Bust and English titles on the obverse. German titles on the reverse. Value 56 cts.

131. G. 1814. Ten thalers, of same. Obv. Horse *courant.* Rev. "X THALERS. 1814." English and German titles arranged as before. Value $7.84.

132. G. 1814. Same reverse.

133. G. 1814. Two-and-a-half thaler, of same type. Value $1.95.

134. G. 1815. Five thalers. Obv. Crowned shield, draped with the *garter;* arms of Hanover on a shield of pretence. "GEORGIUS III D. G. BRITANNIARUM. REX. F. D." Rev. "BRUNSVICENS ET LUNEBURG DUX. S. R. I. A. T. ET E.;" the denomination in the field. Value $3.91.

135. S. 1828. Florin, of George IV. Obv. Bust, "GEORG. IV

D. G. BRIT. & HANOV. REX. F. D. BR. & LUN. DUX." Reverse same as No. 128. Value 56 cts.

136. G. 1829. Ten thalers, of same. Obv. Bust, "GEORGIUS IV D. G. BRIT. & HANOV. REX F. D." Rev. "BRUNSVICENSIS & LUNEBURGENSIS DUX; the denomination in the field. Value $7.85.

137. G. 1832. Ten thalers, of WILLIAM IV. Obv. Bust, without the laurel. "GULIELMUS IV D. G. BRIT. ET HANOV. REX F. D.," etc. Rev. A crowned shield, bearing on its outward edge the legend "NEC ASPERA TERRENT;" arms of Hanover on a shield of pretence. "1832"......"ZEHN THALER." Value $7.89.

138. G. 1835. Five thaler, of same. Obv. Bust, "WILHELM IV KOENIG V. GR. BRIT. U HANOVER." Rev. Crowned shield, with the sides made concave, encircled by the *Guelphic* collar; sprigs of oak and laurel in the concavities; arms of Hanover on a shield of pretence. Value $3.91.

139. S. 1834. One-sixth thaler, of same. Same as preceding, with "VI EINEN THALER. "LXXXIV EIN F. M.," for *legend* on the reverse. "NEC ASPERA TERRENT," on the edge. Value 12 cts.

140. G. 1838. Ten thalers, of ERNEST AUGUSTUS (Duke of Cumberland). Obv. Bust, without the laurel. "ERNEST AUGUST. V. G. G. KÖENIG V. HANNOVER." Rev. Slightly modified from the preceding reign. "NEC ASPERA TERRENT," on the edge. Value $7.90.

141 and 142. S. 1838. Thaler. Obv. Head, "ERNST. AUGUST. V. G. G. KOENIG VON HANNOVER." Rev. Crowned shield and *Guelphic* collar, arranged as in No. 138, with the oak and laurel forming a wreath behind the shield. "EIN THALER. XIV EINE F. M."......"FEINES ——SILBER." "NEC ASPERA TERRENT," on the edge. Value 72 cts. each.

143. B.S. 1838. One-twelfth thaler. Obverse same as preceding. Rev. "CLXVIII EINE FEINE MARK."......"JUSTIRT;" the denomination in the field. Value 6 cts.

144. B.S. 1838. Four pfenning. Obv. Crowned shield, bearing a horse *courant*. "KÖN HANNOV. SCHEIDE M." Rev. "4 PFENN. 1838."

145. C. 1838. One pfenning. Obv. A crowned *monogram*. Rev. "1 PFENNIG 1838."

146. G. 1839. Two-and-a-half thaler. Obverse same as No. 140.

Rev. "KOEN BR. V. GR. BRIT. U IRL; H. V. CUMB. H. Z. BR. U L." (Prince Royal of Great Britain and Ireland; Duke of Cumberland, Duke of Brunswick and Luneburg;) the denomination occupying the field. Value $1.97.

147. S. 1839. Florin. Obverse same as No. 140. Rev. "NACH DEN LEIPZIGER FUSSE;" the fraction "2-3" occupying the field. Value 57 cts.

148. G. 1850. Ten thalers. Obv. Head. "ERNST. AUGUST. KOENIG VON HANNOVER." Rev. Crowned shield, bearing the British arms quartered, and the arms of Hanover on a shield of pretence. "ZEHN THAL."......"1850." Value $7.90.

149. S. 1852. Thaler, of GEORGE V. Obv. Bust, "GEORG. V. V. G. G. KOENIG V. HANNOVER." Rev. Shield, same as preceding, surmounted by the imperial crown. "EIN THALER. BERGSEGEN DES HARZES.——XIV EINE F. M." "NEC ASPERA TERRENT," *on the* edge. Value 72 cts.

NASSAU.

The Duchy of Nassau is one of the southern States of Germany, and derives its name from the Castle of Nassau, which is said to have been built by the *counts of Laurenburg*, in the beginning of the twelfth century. Upon the death of *Henry, the Rich*, in 1254, it was divided between his two sons, WALRAM IV. and OTHO, WALRAM taking the earldoms of *Nassau, Idstein,* and *Weilburg;* and *Otho*, the remainder. The former was the founder of the *house of Nassau;* and the descendants of the latter became earls of *Dillenburg* and *Liegen*, and founders of the house of *Orange*. WILLIAM III. of England was a member of the latter family. After various changes all the possessions of the *Walram* line devolved upon LEWIS II., a member of the *Nassau-Weilburg* family; but upon his death in 1625, his possessions were again divided into the three branches of *Laarbruck, Idstein,* and *Weilburg*. The former branches have since, however, become merged in the latter; and since 1816 have formed only one principality.

A 157. C. 1773. Quarter kreutzer. Obv. "1-4 KREUZ. 1773." No device. Rev. Crowned shield, bearing a lion *rampant* between "*C*" and "*P*."

B 157. S. 1805. One groschen. Obv. Pointed shield, with the lion *rampant;* a crown suspended above. Rev. "1 GROSCHEN F. R. P. GREIZER. L. M. 1805."

158. C. 1810. One kreutzer. Obv. Crowned shield. "HERZ. NASSAISCHE SCHEIDMUNZ." Rev. "1 KREUZER. 1810;" wreath of oak.

159. S. 1813. Thaler. Obv. Bust, "FRIEDRICH AUGUST HERZOG ZU NASSAU." Rev. Crowned shield, between sprigs of *laurel* and *palm.* "ZEHN EINE FEINE MARK."

160. S. 1815. Same.

161. S. 1817. Thaler. Obv. Shield; a mantle of ermine suspended from a crown, and forming a canopy over the shield. "HERZOGTHUM NASSAU." Rev. No device. "EIN KRONEN THALER," inclosed in laurel.

162. S. 1818. Thaler. Obv. Bust, "WILHELM HERZOG ZU NASSAU." Rev. Same device as the obverse of preceding. "KRONEN THALER."

163. S. 1825. Same.

164. S. 1823. Three kreutzers. Obv. Crowned shield. "HERZ. NASS. SCHEIDMUNZ." Rev. '"III KREUZER. 1823."

165. C. 1834. Kreutzer. Obv. Crowned shield. "HERZOGTHUM NASSAU." Rev. "EIN KREUZER. 1834."

166. S. 1838. One gulden. Obv. Bust, "WILHELM HERZOG ZU NASSAU." Rev. "1 GULDEN. 1838;" wreath of oak.

167. S. 1838. Six kreutzers. Obv. Crowned shield. "HERZOGTHUM NASSAU. Rev. "6 KREUZER. 1838;" oak wreath.

168. S. 1839. Half gulden. Obv. Bust, "WILHELM HERZOG ZU NASSAU."

169. S. 1840. Half gulden. Obv. Bust, "ADOLPH HERZOG ZU NASSAU."

SECTION II.—HESSE: HESSE-CASSEL, HESSE-HOMBURG, AND HESSE-DARMSTADT.

The ancient principality of Hesse has undergone various divisions. In the sixteenth century it was divided into several principalities, the princes of each of which retained the ancestral title of *Landgrave;* and after various changes and divisions it has, at last, been erected into the three sovereign States of—first, *Kur-Hessen,* or *Hesse-Cassel;* second, *Hesse-Darmstadt;* third, *Hesse-Homburg,* titles which are derived from the names of their respective capitals. The coins, however, can only be distinguished by the titles of their sovereigns, the first being "*Kurfurst*" (Elector), the second "*Grosherzog*" (Grand Duke), and the third "*Landgraf*" (Landgrave), of Hesse; and *this* distinction will not apply to coins of an earlier date than 1803, the year in which Hesse-Cassel was erected into an electorate.

1. S. 1636. Crown, of WILLIAM V. Obv. Lion *rampant.* "WILHELM D. G. LANDGAVI HASSIÆ COM. C. D. Z. ET N." Rev. A representation of a "*water spout;*" the wind, lightning, etc., issuing from the clouds; the rays of the sun above; buildings in the background. "JEHOVA VOLENTE HUMILIS LEVABOR."

2. G. 1761. Ducat, of FREDERICK II. Obv. Eight L's and crowns arranged as a cross, with "F. D." in the center. Rev. Shield, bearing a lion *rampant*, surmounted by a crown, and surrounded by seven smaller shields, bearing the arms of the different houses of Hesse.

3. S. 1766. Thaler, of same. Obv. Bust, "FRIDERICUS II D. G. HASS. LANDG. HAN. COM." Rev. Shield, encircled by the garter, and surmounted by a crown; supported by two lions. "X ST. EINE MARK FEIN."......"JUSTIRT." Value $1.00.6.

4. B.S. 1767. One-fourth thaler, of same. Obv. Crowned shield, bearing a lion *rampant.* "$53\frac{1}{3}$ ST. EINE MARK FEIN." Rev. Shield, with "IV EINEN REICHS THAL. 1767." inscribed upon it. "FURSTL HESS LANDM."......"JUSTIRT."

5. B.S. 1767. One-sixth thaler. Obv. A lion *rampant*, supporting a shield bearing the royal cipher. "30 STUCK. EINE MARK FEIN." Rev. Same legend as preceding, with the denomination in the field. Value 11.4 cts.

6. B.S. 1768. One-fourth thaler. Obverse same as No. 4. Reverse same as preceding.

7. G. 1771. Pistole. Obv. Head, "FRIDERICUS II D. G. HASS. L. H. C." Rev. A sun with a lion in the center, and "VIRTUTE ET FIDELITATE;" the date beneath. Value $3.88.4.

8. B.S. 1772. One-fourth thaler. Same type as No. 6.

9. G. 1785. Double pistole. Same as No. 7, with "FRIDERICUS II D. G. HASS. LANDG. HAN COM." Value $7.74.2.

10. S. 1785. Florin. Obverse same as preceding. Reverse same as No. 3.

11. S. 1789. Thaler, of WILLIAM IX. Obverse same as preceding. Rev. Crowned shield, hung with laurel, with "EIN THALER." above, and "1789" beneath. Value 72.1 cts.

12. B.S. 1791. One-sixth thaler. Obv. Crowned shield, bearing a lion *rampant*. Rev. "80 STUCK EINE MARK FEIN;" with the denomination in the field.

13. G. 1799. Five thalers. Obverse same as No. 11. Rev. Martial emblems, with a lion *couchant* in front. "5 THALER."......"1799." Value $3.88.4.

14. B.S. 1804. One-sixth thaler. Same type as No. 12.

15. B.S. 1807. Twenty kreutzers, of HESSE-DARMSTADT. Obv. Head. "LUDWIG GROSHERZOG VON HESSEN." Rev. Crowned shield. "60 STUCK EINE FEINE MARK;" the denomination "20." beneath the shield.

16. S. 1809. Thaler, of HESSE-DARMSTADT. Obverse same as preceding. Rev. Crowned shield, between branches of palm and laurel, crossed. "ZEHN EINE FEINE MARK."......"1809." Value $1.00.7.

17. G. 1817. Five thalers, of HESSE-CASSEL. WILLIAM I. Obv. Head, "WILHELMUS I. ELECT HASS LANDGR. M. D. FULD." Reverse same as No. 11. Value $3.90.8.

18. S. 1819. Thaler, of HESSE-CASSEL. Obv. Head, "WILHELM I. KURF. SOUV. LANDGRA. Z. HESSEN GR. H. U. FULDA." Rev. "EIN THALER, 1819," inclosed in a wreath of laurel. "KUR: HESS: LAND: MUNZE," on the edge. Value 72 cts.

19. B.S. 1821. Six kreutzers, of HESSE-DARMSTADT. Obv. Crowned shield. "GROSHERZOGTHUM HESSEN." Rev. "SCHEIDEMUNZE." ......"1821." "6 KREUZER," in the field.

20. B.S. 1824. One-third thaler, of HESSE-CASSEL. WILLIAM II. Obv. Bust, in uniform. "WILHELM II KURF. S. L. V. HESSEN G. H. U. FULDA." Rev. "3 EINEN THALER, 1824," inclosed in a wreath of laurel. Value 24.1 cts.

21. S. 1825. Thaler, of HESSE-DARMSTADT. Obv. Undraped bust, "LUDEWIG GROSHERZOG VON HESSEN." Rev. Shield, surmounted by a *cuirass;* a mantle of ermine suspended from a crown, and forming a canopy over the shield. "EIN KRONEN THALER......1825." "EHRE VATERLAND GOTT." on the edge. Value $1.00.7.

22. S. 1825. Reverse of same.

23. B.S. 1831. One-sixth thaler, of HESSE-CASSEL. Same as No. 20. Value 12 cts.

24. B.S. 1835. One-sixth thaler, of same. Obv. Crowned shield, surrounded by an order chain. "WILH. II KURF. U. FRIEDR. WILH. KURPR. U. MITREG." (William II. Elector, and Frederick William, Electoral prince and Coregent.) Rev. "KURFURSTENTHUM HESSEN ......84 EINE FEINE MARK." "6 EINEN THALER, 1835," in the field. Value 12 cts.

25. S. 1836. Thaler, of HESSE-DARMSTADT. LUDWIG II. Obv. Head. "LUDWIG II GROSHERZOG VON HESSEN." Reverse same as No. 21. "EHRE VATERLAND GOTT." on the edge. Value $1.00.7.

26. S. 1836. Thaler, of HESSE-CASSEL. WILLIAM II. and FREDERICK WILLIAM. Same type as No. 24. "GOTT BESCHINNE UNS." on the edge. Value 71.5 cts.

27. B.S. 1836. One-sixth thaler. Same as preceding.

28. S. 1838. One gulden, of HESSE-HOMBURG. Obv. Bust, in uniform. "LUDWIG. SOUV. LANDGRAF ZU HESSEN." Rev. "1 GULDEN 1838" inclosed in a wreath of oak. Value 41.3 cts.

29. S. 1838. Half gulden, of HESSE-DARMSTADT. LUDWIG II. Obv. Head, "LUDWIG II GROSHERZOG VON HESSEN." Reverse same as preceding. Value 20.6 cts.

30. S. 1839. Same.

31. S. 1839. Two thalers, of same. Obverse same as preceding. Rev. "VEREINS MÜNZE. 1839." inclosed in a wreath of oak. "3½ GULDEN. 2 THALER......VII EINE FEINE MARK." "CONVENTION VOM 30 JULY 1838." on the edge. Value $1.44.6.

32. G. 1840. Five thalers, of HESSE-CASSEL. WILLIAM II. Same type as No. 26.

33. G. 1840. Five gulden, of HESSE-DARMSTADT. LUDWIG II. Obverse same as No. 29. Reverse same as No. 21.

SAXONY.

Saxony is one of the principal States of Germany. It was originally a duchy, but was raised to the rank of an electorate at the accession of FREDERICK I., in 1423. Upon the accession of OTHO

III., DUKE OF SAXONY, to the imperial throne of Germany in 936, he resigned Saxony to the house of *Stubenskorn,* in which line it remained until 1106, but soon after passed, by marriage, to the house of Bavaria, and with the latter was added to the Duchy of Brunswick, where it remained until 1180. But in the latter year Brunswick was curtailed of both duchies, and Saxony was divided between BERNARD of *Asconia,* and the Bishop of *Cologne;* the eastern portion being assigned to the former, and the western to the latter. After its advancement to the electoral rank it remained in the family of Frederick until 1547, when JOHN FREDERICK, having joined the Protestant League of *Smalcalde* against the Emperor Charles V., was defeated and taken prisoner at *Muhlberg,* and compelled to renounce the electorate, and the Duke MAURICE, a descendant of ALBERT, the brother of ERNEST, was presented with the electoral crown by the emperor. (*See Note to No.* 45.) During the reign of FREDERICK AUGUSTUS II., in 1756, Saxony was invaded by the King of *Prussia,* and it remained under the *Prussian* yoke until the peace of *Hubersburgh* in 1763. FREDERICK AUGUSTUS III.,* who ascended the throne in the latter year, took part with Napoleon in his wars against *Austria, Russia,* and *Prussia,* and was advanced by Napoleon, in 1807, to the rank of a king, and was also invested with the newly created Duchy of *Warsaw.* But, after the downfall of Napoleon, he was compelled to renounce all claim to the Duchy of *Warsaw,* and a portion of his kingdom was cut off and annexed to *Prussia.*

37. S. Crown, of JOHN, *the Constant.* (1525–1532.) Obv. Bust, in armor. "JOAN ELEC. GEO. FIE. FE." Rev. Bust, "MONE NOVA DUCUM SAXO."

38. S. 1530. Crown, of GEORGE, *Duke of Saxony.* Obv. Bust, "NAW. MUNTZ. HERZOG GEORGEN ZU SAXE." Rev. Five shields, *in cross,* the central one bearing the arms of Saxony. "NACH. DEM ALTEN SCHROT. UND KORN. 1530."

39. S. Crown, of AUGUSTUS, *the Pious.* (1553–1586.) Obv. Bust, robed in *ermine* and crowned, carrying a sword. "AUGUSTUS D. G.

---

* FREDERICK CHRISTIAN was the successor of FREDERICK II., but reigned only two months and twelve days.

DUX SAXONIE SA(cri) ROMA(ni) IM"(perii). Rev. "ARCHIMARSCHAL ET ELECTO"(r). Shield bedecked with three helmets.

40. G. 1614. Ducat, of JOHN GEORGE I. Obv. Four busts at full-face. "JUL. CLIVI. ET MONTI. SINEÆ VINARI;" the date beneath the device. Rev. Same device as above. "MONETA NO. AUREA FRAT DUC SAX." It also has engraved upon it on one side "NAT 1672," and on the other the initials "W. C. S."

41. S. 1630. Florin, of same. Obv. The elector, in armor, carrying his sword in one hand and his helmet in the other. "JOHAN GEORG. D. G. DUX SAX. JUL. CLIV. ET MONT." Rev. Shield, arms of *Wettin* on a shield of pretence. "SACRI. ROMANI IMP. ARCHIMAR ET ELECT."

42. S. 1686. Crown, of JOHN GEORGE III. Obv. Bust, as in preceding. "JOHAN GEORG. III D. G. DUX SAX. JUL. CLIV. ET MONT." Rev. Shield, bedecked with eight helmets. "SAC. ROM. IMP. ARCHIM. ET ELECT."

43. S. 1696. Florin, of FREDERICK AUGUSTUS I. Obv. Bust, in armor. "FRID. AUGUST. D. G. DUX SAX. I. C. M. A. & W. Rev. Crowned shield, between two palm branches, interwoven with flowers and crossed; arms of *Wettin* and *Saxony.* Same legend as preceding.

44. S. 1696. Florin. Same type.

45. S. 1706. Florin, of same. Obv. Bust, in armor; a sash over the right shoulder. "D. G. FRID. AUGUST. REX POLONIARUM." Rev. Two shields, one bearing the arms of *Poland* and *Lithauania*, and the other the arms of *Saxony*, inclosed between palm branches and surmounted by a crown. "DUX SAX I. C. M. A. & W. S. R. I. ARCH. & EL. 1706."

In 1697 Frederick was elected King of Poland. But in 1704 he was deposed, through the influence of CHARLES XII. of Sweden, and STANISLAUS SESZCYNSKI was elected, at the Diet of Warsaw, to fill his place.* After the celebrated battle of *Pultowa*, in 1709, Frederick was restored, and continued to reign until his death, in 1733; and, after an interval of eight months, his son, FREDERICK AUGUSTUS II., succeeded him, and reigned until 1763, when he died, and another

* Frederick, however, continued to issue coins bearing the title of "*King of Poland.*"

interregnum of *eleven* months intervened, at the expiration of which Stanislaus Augustus Poniatowski was elected to succeed. It was during the latter reign that the shameful divisions of Poland took place; and at the third dismemberment in 1795, when poor Poland was finally apportioned out to the three powers of Russia, Prussia, and Austria, Stanislaus was forced to abdicate, and made a formal resignation of his crown to the Russian minister at *Grodno.*

46. G. 1711. Ducat, of Frederick I. Obv. The king on horseback; no legend. Rev. Two altars, one bearing the *imperial vestment, scepter, crown,* and the *imperial globe;* while the other bears the *sword* and *crown,* with the *king's mantle.* "FRID. AUG. REX ELECTOR, VICARIUS, POSTMORT. JOSE IMPERAT." Frederick claimed the succession to the imperial throne upon the death of Joseph I.; but it was finally determined in favor of Charles VI., the brother of Joseph.

47. S. 1755. Crown, of Augustus III., *King of Poland.* Obv. Bust, in armor, crowned. "D. G. AUGUSTUS III REX POLONIARUM." Rev. Crowned shield, bearing the arms of Poland and Lithauania, quartered; and a shield of pretence surmounted by the electoral crown and bearing the arms of Saxony; the whole inclosed between two *palm* branches, crossed. "SAC. ROM. IMP. ARCHIM. ET ELECT 1755."

Frederick Augustus II. assumed the title of Augustus III., as did his father (Augustus I.) that of Augustus II., as *King of Poland.* This title did not, however, appear upon the coins of Saxony. They continued the simple titles of "FREDERICK AUGUSTUS," as *Electors of Saxony,* upon their own coins.

48. G. 1756. Ten thalers, of same. Same as preceding, with the exception that "10 TH." (the denomination) is substituted for the initials "E. D. C." beneath the shield.

49. S. 1763. Thaler, of same. Obv. Bust, "D. G. FRID. AUGUST. REX POL. D. S. J. C. N. A. & W." Rev. Double shield; arms of Saxony on one side, and those of Poland and Lithauania on the other, surmounted by a crown. "SAC. ROM. IMP. ARCHIM. ET ELECTOR 1763." "X EINE FEINE MARCK."

50. B.S. 1763. Twelfth thaler. Obv. Double shield, similar to preceding. "D. G. FRID. AUG. REX POL. EL. SAX." Rev. "CLX EINE FEINE MARCK, 1763." "12 EINEN THALER" in the field; no device.

51. B.S. 1763. One-forty-eighth thaler. Obv. Crowned shield, bearing the arms of *Poland* and *Lithauania,* the arms of Saxony on a shield of pretence. No legend. Rev. "48 EINEN THALER. 1763."

52. S. 1763. Thaler, of FREDERICK CHRISTIAN. Obv. Bust, "D. G. FRID. CHRIST. PR. R. POL. & L. DUX SAX." (Christian was *regent* of Poland during his short term as Elector of Saxony.) Rev. "JUL. CL. MONT. A. & W. S. R. I. ARCHIM & ELECTOR. 1763." Crowned shield, bearing the arms of Saxony; a shield of pretence, and a *heart shield.* The *first* bearing the arms of *Poland* and *Lithauania;* the *second,* the arms of the *younger* or *Albertine* branch of the house of *Wettin,* surmounted by the electoral crown.

53. S. 1764. Thaler, of FREDERICK AUGUSTUS III. Obv. Bust, "FRID. AUGUST. D. G. SAXONIA ELECTOR." Rev. Shield, surmounted by the electoral crown, bearing two fields, one containing the arms of *Wettin,* and the other the arms of *Saxony;* the whole inclosed between two *olive* branches, crossed. "X EINE FEINE MARCK. 1764."

54. S. 1764. One-sixth thaler, of same. Obv. "F. A. D. SAX" (for "*Fred. Aug., Duke of Saxony*") in *monogram,* surmounted by a crown. Rev. Crowned shield; arms of Saxony on a shield of pretence. "F. S. W. U. E. C. V. M., 1764." "80 EINE FEINE MARCK."

55. B.S. 1764. One-twelfth thaler. Obv. Crowned shield, (same as No. 52.) "FRID. AUGUST D. G. SAXONIÆ ELECTOR." Rev. "CLX EINE FEINE MARCK." "12 EINEN THALER. 1764," in the field.

56. B.S. 1764. One-twenty-fourth thaler. Same as preceding.

57. S. 1765. Thaler. Obv. "FRID. AUGUST. D. G. DUX SAX ELECTOR." Rev. Device same as No. 52 "DER SEGEN DES BERGBAUES," (the art of mining.) "X EINE FEINE MARCK. 1765."

58. S. 1766. Florin. Obverse same as preceding. Rev. *Two* shields, each encircled with a wreath of laurel; one bearing the arms of *Wettin,* the other of Saxony, surmounted by the electoral crown. "XX EINE MARCK F."

59. S. 1767. Thaler, of XAVIER, *Prince Regent.* Obv. Bust, "XAVERIUS D. G. REG POL. & LITH. DUX SAX." Rev. Crowned shield,

bearing the arms of the various houses of Saxony, Poland, etc., with the arms of *Wettin* on a shield of pretence. "ELECTORATUS SAXONIÆ ADMINISTRATOR." "X EINE MARCK F."

FREDERICK III. succeeded to the throne in 1763, at the age of thirteen years, and his uncle, FRANCIS XAVIER, assumed the regency during the minority of the young prince. The titles and effigy of Frederick were, however, placed upon the coinage as a general rule, although some pieces seem to have been struck bearing those of XAVIER. This piece is the only specimen of the latter contained in this collection. *Bonneville* gives only one specimen of the date of 1768; and it is highly probable that this coinage was continued in small amounts during the whole of Xavier's regency.

60. S. 1776. Thaler, of FREDERICK III. Obv. Bust, "FRID. AUGUST D. G. DUX SAX ELECTOR." Reverse same as No. 52. "X EINE MARCK. F."

61. G. 1777. Five thalers, of same. Obverse same as preceding. Reverse same as No. 57. "5 THALER 1777."

62. G. 1783. Ten thalers. Same type.

63. S. 1790. Thaler. Same as No. 59.

64. S. 1790. Thaler. Obv. Bust, "FRID. AUG. D. G. DUX SAX ELECTOR & VICARIUS IMPERII." Rev. The double-headed eagle, bearing upon its breast a crowned shield, with the arms of *Wettin* and *Saxony* borne as in No. 52. "X EINE MARCK F."

Like the two preceding monarchs of his name and house, FREDERICK III., upon the death of JOSEPH II. in 1790, claimed the succession to the imperial throne of Germany, and was equally unsuccessful in his efforts to attain that dignity.

65. G. 1794. Ten thalers. Obv. "FRID. AUGUST D. G. DUX SAX. ELECTOR." Rev. Crowned shield, bearing the arms of *Wettin* and *Saxony*, hung with laurel and inclosed between two *palm* branches. "10 THALER. 1794."

66. S. 1806. Thaler. Same type as preceding.

67. S. 1806. Same, with the addition of "DER. SEGEN DES BERGBAUES" on the reverse.

68. S. 1807. One-forty-eighth thaler. Obv. Shield, surmounted by the *royal electoral* crown as heretofore, and bearing the arms of

Saxony. Rev. "48 EINEN THALER. 1807." From this date up to the present time, the arms of *Wettin* have been uniformly omitted in the coinage of Saxony.

69. S. 1809. Thaler. Obv. Head, "FRID. AUGUST D. G. REX SAXONIÆ." Rev. Shield, same as preceding. "ZEHN EINE FEINE MARK. 1809."

70. S. 1813. Florin. Same as preceding. Rev. "ZWANZIG EINE FEINE MARK. 1813."

71. G. 1817. Ten thalers. Obv. Head, "FRID. AUGUST D. G. REX SAXONIÆ." Rev. Same device as preceding. "1817. ZEHN THALER."

72. G. 18. Ten thalers. Obv. Bust, in uniform. "FRIEDRICH AUGUST KOENIG V. SACHSEN." Reverse same as before, except that the device is somewhat smaller.

73. S. 1819. Thaler. Same pattern as preceding. "ZEHN EINE FEINE MARK." "GOTT REGNE SACHSEN." (God reigns in Saxony) on the *edge*. This is the first inscription found upon the *edge* of the coins of this kingdom, and has been continued upon all the larger pieces up to the present time.

74. S. 1820. Same reverse.

75. S. 1821. Thaler. Same type. Rev. "DER SEGEN DES BERGBAUES."......"ZEHN EINE FEINE MARK. 1821."

76. S. 1823. Thaler. (The face of the king appears considerably older on the coinage of this date than in the former years; the style, however, continues the same.)

77. S. 1824. Thaler. The shield on the reverse, which has heretofore been of an oval shape, now undergoes a change and appears nearly square, with the sides and top made *concave;* while the base is arched or made *convex.* "ZEHN EINE FEINE MARK."

78. S. 1824. Thaler. Obv. Bust, slightly enlarged. Rev. The field containing the shield and date "1824" (the latter being divided by the shield, "18" appearing at one side and "12" at the other,) is inclosed by a circular line, outside of which is the motto "DER SEGEN DES BERGBAUES," and "ZEHN EINE F. M."

79. S. 1827. Florin, of ANTHONY. Obv. Head of Anthony. "ANTON V. G. G. KOENIG. VON SACHSEN." Rev. Crowned shield, like that on the last coins of the preceding reign, inclosed between two olive branches. "ZWANZIG EINE FEINE MARK."

80. B.S. 1828. One-twenty-fourth thaler. Obv. Same device as the reverse of preceding. "ANTHON V. G. G KOEN V. SACHS." Rev. "320 EINE FEINE MARK." "24 EINEN THALER. 1828," in the field.

81. B.S. 1829. One-sixth thaler. Same as No. 78, with "ACHTZIG EINE FEINE MARK," on the reverse. In the bust on this and the succeeding coins of this reign Anthony is represented as being considerably older than before; and for this reason it is probably a much better likeness than that on his first coins, as Anthony was seventy-two years of age at the time of his accession in 1827.

82 B.S. 1830. One-third thaler. Same type.

83. G. 1830. Ten thalers. Same type.

84. G. 1834. Five thalers. Same type.

85. S. 1835. Thaler. Same type.

86. S. 1836. Same.

87. B.S. 1836. One-twelfth thaler, of FREDERICK AUGUSTUS IV. Obv. Crowned shield, (the olive branches omitted.) "FRIEDRICH AUGUST KOENIG V. SACHSEN." Rev. "160 EINE FEINE MARK." "12 EINEN THALER" and the date occupying the field.

88. S. 1836. Thaler. Obv. Head of FREDERICK. "FRIEDRICH AUGUST V KOENIG V. SACHSEN." Same reverse as the coins of Anthony.

89. C. 1837. Three pfenning. Obv. Square shield, crowned. "KÖNIGL. SÄCHS SCHEIDE MÜNZE." Rev. "3 PFENNIGE. 1837." No device.

90. S. 1838. Thaler. Same as No. 87.

91 and 92. C. 1838. One pfenning. Same as No. 88, with the *legend* on the obverse omitted.

93. G. 1839. Five thalers. Obverse same as No. 87. Rev. Square shield, crowned and inclosed in branches of laurel; denomination and date. No legend.

94 and 95. S. 1839–41. Thalers. Obverse same as No. 87. Rev. Shield, draped with the order-band and star of the order of the "*White Eagle*" or "*Polish Eagle;*" a mantle of *ermine* suspended from a crown, and forming a canopy over the shield. "EIN THALER. XIV EINE F. M." and the date.

96 and 97. B.S. 1841. One-sixth thaler. Same type as preced-

ing, with "FUNF. N. GR." (*five new groschen,*) and "6 EINEN THALER. 84 EINE F. M." on the reverse.

98. B.S. 1841. Two new groschen. Obv. Square shield, crowned. "K. S. SCHEIDE MÜNZE.......1841." Rev. "2 NEW GROSCHEN 20 PFENNIGE."

99. B.S. 1841. One new groschen. Same type.

100 and 101. B.S. 1841. Half new groschen. Same type.

102 and 103. C. 1841. Two pfennings. Same type.

104. S. 1856. Thaler, of JOHN. With the exception that the bust is turned to the observer's *left,* this is of the same type as the coins of this denomination in the preceding reign.

INDEPENDENT DUKEDOMS OF SAXONY.

Lying to the west of Saxony, but having no connection whatever therewith, are several small "Dukedoms of Saxony," (as they are commonly called,) consisting of *Saxe-Altenburg, Saxe-Coburg, Saxe-Meiningen,* and *Saxe-Weimar-Eisenach.* As a general rule, they depend upon the coinage of Prussia for their currency, except in the smaller denominations, or "*Scheide münze,*" which each prince coins within his own territory; *Saxe-Meiningen* and *Weimar* are, however, exceptions to this rule, having, at different periods, coined a few pieces of the larger denominations. We have one coin of *Saxe-Gotha* (described hereafter), but this house, as before noticed, has now become extinct. It will be seen that the small coins of these provinces are not represented in the cabinet collection. They are of very little interest either from a numismatic or commercial point of view, except as they partake of the *base* character which attaches to the lesser coins of most of the German States, and consequently would only occupy space which can be much more profitably appropriated.

SAXE-MEININGEN.

110. S. 1854. Two thalers, of BERNARD. Obv. Head of the duke. "BERNARD HERZOG ZU SACHSEN MEININGEN." Rev. Draped shield, surmounted by six helmets, bearing the arms of various houses; the arms of *Saxony* on a shield of pretence. "$3\frac{1}{2}$ GULDEN. VII EINE F. MARK. 2 THALERS."......"VEREINS MÜNZE."

111. S. 1838. One gulden. Obv. Bust, "BERNARD HERZOG ZU SACHSEN MEININGEN." Rev. "1 GULDEN. 1838," inclosed in a wreath of oak.

112. S. 1829. Six kreutzers. Obv. Crowned shield between "S." and "M." (for "Saxe-Meiningen") and the date "1829." Rev. "LANDMÜNZE. 6 KREUZERS." the "6" occupying the field.

SAXE-WEIMAR-EISENACH.

114. S. 1815. Thaler. Obv. Pointed shield, crowned. "GROSHERZOGTHUM SACHSEN."......"10 EINE FEINE MARK." Rev. "DEM VATERLANDE. 1815." inclosed in a wreath, formed of two oak branches, crossed.

115. S. 1841. Thaler. Obv. Bust. "CARL. FRIEDRICH GROSHERZOG Z. SACHSEN. W. E." Rev. Crowned shield, bedecked with the collar and badge of the order of the *Polish Eagle;* a shield of pretence surmounted by a crown, and bearing the arms of Saxony. "EIN THALER. XIV EINE F. M." and the date.

SAXE-COBURG.

117. S. 1765. Thaler, of ERNEST FREDERICK, *Duke of Saxe-Coburg-Saalfeld.* Obv. Bust, in a *cuirass.* "ERNESTUS FRIDERICUS D. G. D. S. COBURG SAALFELD." Rev. Shield, surmounted by a crown; arms quartered; a shield of pretence bearing the arms of Saxony. Saxe-Coburg was divided into four districts, consisting of *Saxe-Saalfeld, Saxe-Meiningen, Saxe-Gotha,* and *Saxe-Hildburghausen.*

118. B.S. 1805. Six kreutzers. Obv. Shield, inclosed between branches of *palm* and *olive,* crossed; a crown suspended above. No legend. Rev. "H(erzogthum) S(achsen) COBURG. LAND. M"(ünze). ......"VI KREUZER. 1805." in the field.

SAXE-GOTHA.

120. S. 1836. Twenty kreutzers, of ERNEST. Obv. Bust, "ERNEST HERZOG ZU SACHSEN COBURG GOTHA." Rev. Shield, bearing the arms of Saxony, inclosed between branches of laurel; a crown suspended above. "60 EINE F. MARK." and the date and denomination together, thus: "18-20-36."

WÜRTEMBERG.

Upon the decline of the Roman Empire, Würtemberg was erected into a dukedom, under the jurisdiction of the Franks; but near the end of the eleventh century the dukedom was dissolved, and apportioned out to a number of *counts*, who declared themselves independent. One of these was the Count of *Beutelsbach-Würtemberg*, whose family gradually absorbed all the other provinces, until, at the end of the fifteenth century, Würtemberg was again united into a single duchy, under the *Beutelsbach* dynasty. During the reign of FREDERICK WILLIAM, who succeeded his father as Duke of *Würtemberg* in 1797, the duchy became the theater of war, and was overrun by the French armies. WILLIAM, however, afterward gained the favor of the EMPEROR, together with a large accession of territory, and, in 1803, was raised, by Napoleon, to the rank of an elector, and in 1806 was still further honored by the title of *king*. Upon the final arrangement of the German States by the Congress of Vienna, the territorial accessions were confirmed, and the kingly title finally recognized.

122. S. Medallic coin, (probably current at about twenty kreutzers.) Obv. Bust, in civil dress. "FRID. CARL. D. G. D(ux) WIRT(tembergensis) ET TALMIN. ET T"(ecensis). Rev. The device represents St. George on foot,* fighting the dragon. "DURA PLACENT FORTIBUS." Not dated.

123. G. 1732. Quarter carolin, of EBERHARD LOUIS. Obv. Bust, in armor. "EBER. LUD. D. G. DUX WUR. & T." Rev. Shield, surmounted by a crown, and encircled with the order chain of the order of the "*Golden Eagles.*" "CUM DEO ET DIE." "17......32."

124. B.S. 1759. Fifteen kreutzers, of CHARLES EUGENE. Obv. Bust, "CAROLUS D. G. DUX WUR." Rev. Crowned shield. "WURTEMBERG LANDMUNZE, 1759......15 K."

125. S. 1760. Thaler, of same. Obv. Bust, in armor, ornamented with the band and star of the order of the *golden eagles*, and the

---

* He usually appears mounted.

badge of the *golden fleece*. "CAROLUS D. G. DUX WURT. & T." Rev. Shield, surmounted by the electoral crown, and inclosed between branches of *palm* and *laurel*, crossed. "PROVIDE ET CONSTANTER." ......17*10 F. M.*60."

126. S. 1781. Thaler, of same. Obverse similar to preceding. Rev. Oval shield, surmounted by the electoral crown, and draped with the band and star of the order of the *golden eagles*, inclosed between branches of palm and laurel, crossed. Legend same as preceding.

127. G. 1790. Ducat, of same. Obv. Bust, "CAROLUS D. G. DUX WIRT & T." Rev. Shield draped with the collar and star of the *golden eagles*, and surmounted by the electoral crown. "PROVIDE ET CONSTANTER......1790."

128. B.S. 1808. Six kreutzers, of FREDERICK WILLIAM. Obv. "F. R." (Frederick Rex) interlaced. "KÖNIGL. WURT. SCHEIDE MÜNZE......VI KREUZER." Rev. Circular shield, bearing the arms in two fields, surmounted by the royal crown, and inclosed between two branches of palm, crossed. "1808."

129. S. 1810. Thaler, of same. Obv. Head, "FRIDERICH I. KOENIG. VON WURTEMBERG." Rev. Shield, surmounted by the royal crown, and supported by a *lion* and *stag*, each carrying a flag; the date beneath. "KOENIGL. WURTTEMB. KRONEN THALER," on the edge.

130. S. 1817. Thaler, of WILLIAM, (son of the preceding monarch.) Obv. Undraped bust. "WILHELM KOENIG. VON WÜRTTEMBERG." Rev. The denomination and date, surmounted by a crown, and inclosed in a wreath formed of a single branch of laurel.

131 and 132. G. 1818. Ducat, of same. Obverse same as preceding. Rev. Crowned shield, supported by a lion and stag; the date beneath.

133. S. 1824. Gulden, of same. Obverse same as No. 30. Rev. Circular shield, surmounted by a crown and inclosed in a wreath of oak. "EIN-GULDEN ST. KÖN. WÜRTTEMB." and the date. "FURCHTLOS UND TREU." (fearless and true) on the edge. Value 39.4 cts.

134. G. 1825. Five gulden. Obverse same as No. 30. Rev. Pointed shield, surmounted by a crown, and inclosed between branches of oak and laurel, crossed. "FUNF GULDEN."......"1825."

135 and 136. S. 1825–1837. Thaler, of same. Obv. Bust, "WIL-

HELM KOENIG VON WURTTEMBERG." Rev. Same type as preceding. "FURCHTLOS UND TREU" on the edge. Value $1.11.

137. S. 1833. Thaler. Obverse same as preceding. Rev. Aquarius; the goddess of Trade; and a cornucopia. The former is in a reclining posture, leaning upon his jug, from which the water is running, while the goddess is represented carrying a *caduceus*, or wand of Mercury, in her left hand, and a sealed packet, extended, in the other; the cornucopia appearing to the right of the field. "HANDELSFREIHEIT DURCH EINTRACHT." and the date.

Thus, taking the legend in connection with the device, it would seem to be a commemoration of, or rather an allusion to the Zollverein, or *Customs League*, a treaty or compact which exists between a portion of the German States, by which a *freedom of trade* is permitted between the different States of the League, no duties being charged upon merchandise transported from one State to another, after it has passed the frontiers of the first State, and having paid a duty there. The significance of the device being that "TRADE WILL PROSPER UNDER THE AUSPICES OF THIS TREATY,"—the treaty being the document which the goddess holds in her right hand.

138. G. 1841. Ducat, of same. Obv. Head, "WILHELM KOENIG. V. WÜRTTEMBERG." Rev. An oval shield, surmounted by a crowned helmet, and supported by a lion and stag, with their hind feet resting upon a scroll, which bears the motto "FURCHTLOS UND TREU." Legend. "1 DUCATEN. 67 EINE M. Z. 23$\frac{2}{3}$ K," and the date.

SECTION III.—BAVARIA.

Shortly after the fall of the Roman Empire, which had swallowed up nearly all of Germany, the government of Bavaria was assumed by CHARLEMAGNE, who deposed THISSILO II. and governed Bavaria by legates. In one of these (Leopold) the ducal title was restored; and, after remaining three generations in his family, it was disposed of at the will of the German emperors until 1180,* when OTHO I.

* In that year it was detached from the house of Brunswick, by a decree of the Diet. (See *Introduction to Saxony.*)

succeeded to the ducal crown. But a century later, upon the death of LOUIS II. in 1294, his possessions were divided between RODOLPH I., *the Stammerer*, and LOUIS III.; the former receiving the Palatinate of the Rhine, and the latter the Duchy of Bavaria. After this date it underwent various changes, and at one time comprised a number of petty sovereignties, the principal of which were the Duchies of Upper and Lower Bavaria (which were, however, soon united); the Palatinate of the Rhine; the Margraviate of Brandenburg-Baireuth, and various Bishoprics and Free Cities, all of which coined their own money. Upon the death of MAXIMILIAN JOSEPH, Elector of Bavaria, in 1777, without issue, his possessions passed over to CHARLES THEODORE, Elector of the Palatinate. The latter likewise dying without issue in 1799, MAXIMILIAN JOSEPH, *of Deux-Ponts*, became sole possessor of the *Palatinate, Bavaria,* and *Deux-Ponts.* Bavaria was made an Electorate in 1623, and was advanced to the rank of a Kingdom, by Napoleon, in 1806, which rank it still retains.

BRANDENBURG-BAIREUTH.*

1. S. 1550. Crown, of ALBERT. Obv. Bust, in armor. "ALBERT D. G. MARCHIO BRANDENBU." Rev. An ornamented cross, with a small shield bearing an eagle in the center, and four large shields in the angles. "SI. DE^{S} PRONOBIS QUIS CONTRA NOS."

2. G. 1601. Ducat, of FREDERICK ALBERT and CHRISTIAN. Obv. Three busts in full-face, with "16—1" beneath, (which is probably intended for "1601," the cipher being omitted.) "D. G. FRID. ALB. ET CHRISTI. FR. MARCH. BR. DUCES." Rev. Shield, "PRUSS. ST. POM. CAS. VAN. LAG. BURG. I. NURNB. PR. R."

3 and 4. S. 1766. Thaler, of FREDERICK CHRISTIAN. Obv. Bust, in armor. "FRID. CHRIST. D. G. M. B. D. B. ET S. B. N." Rev. Shield, surmounted by the electoral crown and supported by two lions. "ZEHEN EINE FEINE MARK" and the date.

---

* This province was at one time a dependency of Prussia, and was known as *Rhenish Prussia.* Numismatists and others are often apt to confound Baireuth with the Electorate of Brandenburg, which constitutes a large portion of Prussia; whereas there is no connection between them.

5. G. 1767. Ducat, of same. Obv. Frederick, dressed in uniform and mounted upon a horse *salient.* "FRID. CHRIST. D. G. M. B. D. B. ET. S.;" the date beneath. Rev. An order-star, with a small eagle in the center, suspended from an electoral crown. "SINCERE ET CONSTANTER."

6. G. Ducat, of SCHWABACH—FREDERICK and SIGISMUND. Obv. Full-length figure of a saint. "FRID. & SIGISM. MARCH BRAND." Rev. An ornamented cross, with shields in the angles. "MONETA NOVA. AUR. SWABACH." No date.

7. S. 1754. Thaler, of SCHWABACH—CHARLES WILLIAM FREDERICK. Obv. Bust, in armor. "CAR. WILH. FRID. D. G. M. B. D. P. & S. B. N. C. S." Rev. A crowned eagle, with a shield upon its breast. bearing the arms of Zollern, with "SCHWABACH" beneath. "ZEHEN EINE FEINE MARK."

ANSPACH.

8. B.S. 1762. Twenty kreutzers, of ALEXANDER. Obv. Bust, inclosed in a wreath composed of two branches of laurel, crossed. "ALEXANDER D. G. MARCH BRAND." Rev. A pedestal, bearing the denomination, with a palm branch at each side, and surmounted by a crowned eagle, with a small shield upon its breast bearing the arms of Zollern; the date beneath. "LX EINE FEINE MARK."

9. G. 1769. Ducat, of same. Obv. A knight dressed in armor, placing a heart upon an altar on which a fire is burning. "PATRI PATRIÆ DICATISSIMUS." Rev. "S. P. D. D. CHR. FRID. CAR. ALEXANDRO. MARCH BR. PR. DUCI. BURG. NOR. SUP. A. 1769. TUT. LEG. TRANSLATA ORD. EQU. C. W. R." inscribed in ten lines. Value $2.24.

BRANDENBURG-ANSPACH-BAIREUTH.

10. S. 1769. Thaler, of ALEXANDER. Obv. Bust, "ALEXANDER D. G. MARCH BRAND D. B. & S. B. N." Rev. An eagle in flight, carrying a *band,* the ends of which are united in a bow-knot beneath; to the band are suspended two shields, one at each side; the whole forming a circle which incloses the date "MDCCLXIX," inscribed in three lines. "FELIX CONJUNCTIO." A series of coins of this type were struck in 1769, to commemorate the union of the two houses of

Anspach and *Culmbach* (*Baireuth*), under ALEXANDER, of *Anspach.* Value $1.00.

11. S. 1774. Thaler, of SCHWABACH—ALEXANDER. Obv. Undraped bust, "ALEXANDER D. G. MARCH BRAND." Rev. Crowned shield, surrounded by martial emblems and supported by a lion; arms of *Culmbach* and *Zollern* in the second and third quarters, and the Bavarian eagle in the *first* and *fourth.* "SCHWABACH," and the date beneath. "ZEHEN EINE FEINE MARK." Value $1.00.

BAVARIA PROPER (*Upper and Lower.*)

12. G. Ducat, of LEWIS, *Prince Regent.* (1314–1349.) Obv. Three shields joined together and forming a triangle in the center, which contains a star. "MONETA NOVA AUREA. BA." Rev. A cross, with its limbs extending to the edge; a shield in the center. "LUDWIG P. R. (Prince Regent) DUX BAVAR." Value $2.24.

LEWIS III. who succeeded in the Duchy of Bavaria in 1294, was elected Emperor of Germany in 1314, and continued to reign in that capacity until his death in 1349. This piece was consequently struck under the regency.

A 13. G. 1500. Ducat, of ALBERT II., "*the Wise.*" Obv. The duke, in a kneeling posture, praying to the Virgin Mary. "MARIA ORA PRO MEA." Rev. Shield, surmounted by the date; the initial H. at one side, and A. at the other. "ALBERTI AURUM BAVARIE DUCIS." Value $2.24.

B 13. G. 1674. Ducat, of FERDINAND MARY. Obv. Bust, "F(erdinandus) M(aria) U. B. & P. S. D. C. P. R. S. R. I. AR. & EL. L. L." Rev. Shield, surmounted by the Virgin and child. "CLYPEUS OMNIBUS INTESPERANTIBUS." Value $2.24.

14. B.S. 1717. Fifteen kreutzers, of MAXIMILIAN EMANUEL. Obv. Bust, "MAX. EMA. H. I. B. C. D." Rev. Shield, encircled with the order chain of the *golden fleece,* and supported by a lion. "LANDMUNZ," and the date and denomination (15.) Value 9 cts.

15. G. 1734. Double Ducat, of CHARLES ALBERT. Obv. Bust, "C(arolus) A(lbertus) D(ei) G(ratia) U(triusque) B(avariæ) & P(alatinatus) S(uperioris) D(ux) C(omes) P(alatinus) R(heni) S(acri) R(omani) I(mperii) A(rchidopifer) & E(lector) L(andgravius L"(euchten-

bergæ). Rev. Virgin and child; the former holding a scepter in her left hand, and supporting a shield, which is encircled by the order chain of *St. George.* "CLYPEUS OMNIBUS IN-TE-SPERANTIBUS," and the date. Value $4.48.

16. G. 1747. Ducat, of MAXIMILIAN JOSEPH. Obv. Two busts in profile, one over the other. "D. G. M(aximilian) J(oseph) U. B. & P. S. D. C. P. R. S. R. I. A. & E. L. L. & M(aria) A(nna) R(egia) P(rinceps) P(oloniæ) & S"(axoniæ). Rev. A landscape, with the sun rising in the background. "DESIGNANT AMBO. SERENUM." Beneath the device is inscribed "BAVAR. DUPL. CONNUBIO FELIX 1747." Value $2.24.

17. S. 1755. Thaler, of MAXIMILIAN JOSEPH. Obv. Bust, bedecked with the order star of *St. George.* "D. G. MAX. JOS. U. B. & P. S. D. C. P. R. S. R. I. A. & E. L. L." Rev. Crowned shield, bearing the Bavarian arms, draped with the order chains and badges of *St. George* and the *golden fleece,* and supported by two lions; the date beneath; no legend. Value $1.00.

18 and 19. S. 1768–71. Thaler, of same. Obv. Bust, bedecked with the order star of *St. George* and the badge of the *golden fleece.* Same legend as preceding. Rev. Virgin and child; the former with her foot resting upon the *crescent,* and a scepter in her right hand; the latter holding the imperial globe in one hand, and pointing upward with the other, surrounded with clouds and diverging rays; the date beneath. "PATRONA BAVARIAE." Value $1.00.

20. B.S. 1773. Twenty kreutzers, of same. Obv. Bust, inclosed in a wreath composed of two laurel branches, crossed. Same legend as preceding. Rev. A pedestal, surmounted by a crowned shield, draped with the order chains and badges of *St. George* and the *golden fleece;* branches of palm and laurel at the sides. "IN DEO. CONSILIUM," and the date.

21. B.S. 1774. Ten kreutzers. Same type.

PALATINATE OF THE RHINE.

22. S. 1660. Florin, of CHARLES LEWIS. Obv. Bust, in armor, "CARL. LUD. D. G. C(omes) P(alatinatus) RH(eni) S. R. I. ARCHITH (esaurius) ET EL(ector) BA(variæ) DU"(x). Rev. The arms curiously

arranged on three shields, above which is a helmet, surmounted by a lion *sejant.* "PROVIDEBIT DOMINUS."

23. G. 1721. Ducat, of CHARLES PHILIP. Obv. The count, dressed in armor, and mounted; the initials "J. G. W." on the ground beneath the horse. "CAR. PHIL. D. G. C. P. R. S. R. I. ARCHIT ET EL." Rev. A crowned shield, surrounded by an order chain, to which is attached four other crowned shields, thus forming a cross, with "CP" also crowned, in the angles, the whole surrounded and united by the order chain of the *golden fleece.* Value $2.24.

24. G. 1773. Carolin, of same. Obv. Undraped bust, "CAR. PHILIP D. G. EL PALATINUS." Rev. A circular shield, with C's reversed, interlaced, and surmounted by crowns, placed at opposite sides; P's similarly arranged at the two remaining angles, the whole forming a cross. "MONE. NOVA. AUREA. PALATI. Value $4.78.

25. S. 1758. Thaler, of CHARLES THEODORE. Obv. Bust, "D. G. CAR. THEOD. C. P. R. S. R. I. A. T. & EL." Rev. Two joined shields, surmounted by the electoral crown, and draped with the order chain and badge of *St. Hubert.* "EX VISCERIBUS RODINAE WILDBERG, 1758." "FEIN SILBER," in italic scrip beneath. Value $1.11.

26. S. 1765. Thaler, of same. Obv. Bust, "CAR. THEODOR. D. G. C. P. R. S. R. I. A. T. & EL." Rev. Three shields, two connected by a band, and the third hung from the connection by a ring, the whole surmounted by the electoral crown, and the date; branches of palm and laurel at the sides. "10 EINE FEINE MARCK." Value $1.00.

27. S. 1765. Florin. Same type as preceding. Value 50 cts.

28. S. 1766. Thaler. Obverse same as No. 26. Rev. A shield, surmounted by the electoral crown and the date; a crowned lion at one side and a stalk of *maize* at the other. "X EINE FEINE MARK." Value $1.00.

29. B.S. 1767. Ten kreutzers. Obverse same as No. 26. Rev. Crowned shield, between two branches of laurel, crossed. "AD NORMAM CONVENTION;" the date and denomination beneath. Value 7.5 cts.

30. S. 1774. Thaler. Obverse same as No. 26. Rev. Highly ornamented shield, between branches of palm and olive, surmounted by the crown and date. "10 EINE FEINE MARCK." Value $1.00.

BAVARIA (*After the Union.*)

31. S. 1778. Thaler, of CHARLES THEODORE. Obv. Bust, ornamented with the order bands and badges of *St. George* and the *golden fleece.* "CAR. TH. D. G. C. P. R. U. B. D. S. R. I. A. & EL. D. J. C. & M." Reverse same as No. 18. Value $1.00.

32. S. 1792. Thaler, of same. Obv. Undraped bust, "CAR. THEOD. D. G. C. P. R. U. B. D. S. R. I. A(rchi) D(apifer) & EL. PROV. & VICAR." Rev. Double-headed eagle, bearing an oval shield upon its breast, surmounted by the electoral crown, and draped with the order chain and badge of the *golden fleece;* the imperial globe occupies one field, and the arms of the *Palatinate* and *Bavaria* the other two. "IN PART RHENI. SUEV. ET JUR. FRANCON." and the date. Value $1.00.

33. S. 1799. Thaler. Same as No. 31.

BAVARIA (*Kingdom.*)

34. S. 1807. Thaler, of MAXIMILIAN JOSEPH. Obv. Bust, in uniform. "MAXIMILIAN JOSEPH. KÖNIG VON BAIERN." Rev. Shield, surmounted by the royal crown, and supported by two lions; a shield of pretence, bearing a sword and scepter in *saltiere,* surmounted by a crown, the date beneath. "FUR GOTT UND VATERLAND." "ZEHEN EINE FEINE MARK." on the edge. Value $1.00.

35. S. 1809. Thaler, of same. Obv. Undraped bust, "MAXIMILIANUS JOSEPHUS BAVARIAE REX." Rev. A sword and scepter in *saltiere,* surmounted by a crown, the date beneath. "PRO DEO ET POPULO." "BAIERISCHER KRONTHALER." on the edge. Value $1.00.

36. S. 1818. Thaler. Obv. Bust, *laureated.* Same legend as preceding. Rev. A square block resting upon a tiled floor, and bearing the inscription "CHARTA MAGNA BAVARIAE;" beneath is the date "XXVI MAII MDCCCXVIII." "MAGNUS AB. INTEGRO SÆCLORUM NASCITUR ORDO." "ZEHEN EINE FEINE MARK." in raised letters on the edge. (Struck to commemorate the "Constitutional Act," passed in May, 1818—an instrument of great length, which made material changes, both in the form of government and the laws.) Value $1.00.

37. B.S. 1819. Six kreutzers, of same. Obv. Undraped bust,

"MAX JOSEPH KONIG VON BAIERN." Rev. Crowned shield, between branches of laurel and palm, crossed; "6" at one side, and "K." (six kreutzers) at the other, and the date beneath. "LAND-MÜNZ."

38. B.S. 1819. Three kreutzers. Same type.

39. S. 1822. Thaler. Same as No. 34. Value $1.00.

40. S. 1825. Thaler. Same as No. 35. Value $1.00.

41. S. 1826. Thaler, of LUDWIG I. Obv. Head, "LUDWIG KOENIG VON BAYERN." Rev. The royal crown, inclosed in a wreath composed of an oak and laurel branch, crossed. "GERECHT UND BEHARRLICH." and the date. "BAYERISCHER KRONTHALER." on the edge. Value $1.12.

42. S. 1827. Thaler. Obv. Bust, "LUDWIG I KŒNIG VON BAYERN." ......"ZEHN EINE FEINE MARK." Rev. Star of the order of *Theresa*, inclosed in a wreath, composed of two branches of *white lily*, crossed. "DIE KŒNIGIN VON BAYERN STIFTET DEN THERESIEN ORDEN." and the date. Edge grained. Value $1.12.

43. S. 1828. Thaler. Same as No. 41.

44. S. 1833. Thaler. Obverse same as No. 42. Rev. The goddess of Commerce leaning against a pedestal, and holding a *caduceus* in her right, and a *cornucopia* in her left hand; an anchor at one side and the prow of a *galley* at the other; the date beneath. "ZOLLVEREIN MIT PREUSSEN SACHSEN. HESSEN. U. THURINGEN." (Bavaria joined the Zollverein, or Customs League, in this year.) Value $1.02.

45. S. 1834. Thaler. Obverse same as No. 42. Rev. "LANDTAG 1834." inclosed in a heavy wreath of oak, intwined with a band. "EHRE DEM EHRE GEBÜHRT." Finely engraved.

46. S. 1835. Thaler. Obverse same as No. 42. Rev. A *caduceus*, between two branches of laurel, crossed. "BEYTRITT VON BADEN ZUM TEUTSCHEN ZOLLVEREIN." and the date.

47. S. 1835. Thaler. Obverse same as No. 42. Rev. A monument. "DENKM DER TRENNUNG DER KŒN THERESE VON IHREN SOHNE DEM KŒN. OTTO. ERRICHTET BEI AIBLING BAYERISCHEN FRAUEN." inscribed in two concentric lines; the date beneath.

48. S. 1836. Thaler. Obverse same as No. 42. Rev. A church. "BAYERN ERRICHTETEN DIE H. OTTOKOPELLE ZU KIEFERSFELDEN. ZUM ANDENKEN AN KŒN OTTO'S ABSCHIED V. SEINEM VATERLANDE." inscribed in two concentric lines, with the date beneath.

49. S. 1838. Three gulden. Obv. Undraped bust, "LUDWIG I KŒNIG VON BAYERN." Rev. "DIE EINTHEILUNG D. KÖNIGREICHS AUF GESCHICHTL GRUNDLAGE ZURÜCKGEFÜHRT. 1858." inscribed in seven parallel lines, and surrounded by a circle of eight small wreaths, united by bands, and containing the names of the different provinces of Bavaria. "DREY EINHALB. GULDEN**VII E. F. M." on the edge. Value $1.18.

50. B.S. 1838. One half gulden. Obverse same as preceding. Rev. "1-2 GULDEN. 1838." inclosed in a wreath of oak. Value 20 cts.

51. B.S. 1839. Three kreutzers. Obv. Crowned shield, arms of Bavaria on a shield of pretence. "KŒNIGR. BAYERN." Rev. "3 KREUZER. 1839." inclosed in a wreath of oak. Value 2 cts.

52. B.S. 1839. One kreutzer. Same type as preceding.

53. B.S. 1833. One kreutzer, (2 *pieces.*) Obverse same as No. 47. Rev. Crowned shield, like No. 34, between branches of palm and laurel, crossed. "LAND-MÜNZ." and the denomination and date.

54. C. 1839. One pfenning, (2 *pieces.*) Obv. Crowned shield, like No. 51, between two branches of oak, crossed. Rev. "1 PFENING. 1839."

55. C. 1839. One heller. Same type as preceding.

56. S. 1841. One gulden. Same type as No. 50. Value 40 cts.

57. S. 1847. Two gulden. Obverse same as No. 49. Rev. Crowned shield, supported by two lions; arms of Bavaria on a shield of pretence. "ZWEY GULDEN." and the date. Value 79 cts.

58. S. 1854. Two thalers, of MAXIMILIAN II. Obv. Undraped bust, "MAXIMILIAN II KŒNIG V BAYERN." Rev. Same device as preceding, with "3 1-2 GULDEN. VII EINE F. MARK.......2 THALER." above, and "VEREINS MÜNZE, 1854." beneath. "CONVENTION VOM 30 JULY, 1838." on the edge.

59. S. 1853. Two gulden. Same type as preceding.

BADEN.

Baden first came under the house of *Zähringen* in 1052, by the accession of HERMAN, third son of BERTHOLD, (the founder of the house of *Zähringen,*) who acquired the ducal crown by marriage, and his son, HERMAN II., who succeeded him in 1073, and reigned until 1130, assumed the title of *margrave,* but not, however, until the last year of his reign. Subsequent to this period Baden experienced various changes, but the first permanent division took place in 1515, when the *Margrave,* CHRISTOPHER I., who succeeded to the throne in 1475, abdicated, having first divided his dominions among his three sons, BERNHARD, PHILIP, and ERNEST, and died, in a state of insanity, in 1527. But Philip dying soon after, his two surviving brothers divided the whole between themselves, BERNHARD taking *Baden-Baden,* and ERNEST *Baden-Dourlach.* In this divided state it remained until the death of AUGUSTUS GEORGE, of Baden-Baden, in 1771, without issue, when his possessions passed over to CHARLES FREDERICK, of Baden-Dourlach, by virtue of a treaty of mutual succession which existed between them. Baden was advanced to the rank of an electorate in 1803, and upon the formation of the present *Germanic Confederation* in 1806, the elector received the title of GRAND DUKE (*Grösherzog.*) Baden has also been much increased in extent by several territorial additions since the treaty of Luneville in 1801. From 1813 to 1816 Baden was in a very unsettled condition, as will be readily seen by a reference to the coins of that period. They bear neither the name, bust, nor title of any sovereign, but merely the legend, "*Grand Duchy of Baden,*" and the arms; and again in 1819 coins of the same description appear. The latter, however, was probably caused by a short interregnum, occurring between the death of CHARLES LOUIS FREDERICK and the accession of his uncle LOUIS.

60. C. 1721. Twelve heller. Obv. An eagle and the date. Rev. "XII HELLER REICHS STADT. ACHEM," inscribed in five parallel lines. No device.

61. S. 1766. Thaler, of CHARLES FREDERICK. Obv. Bust, in armor, "CAROLUS FRID. D. G. MARCHIO BAD. ET. H." Rev. Crowned shield, with a griffin at each side, and an order star beneath; above is "ADNORMAM CONVENTIONIS," and beneath the date and "X EINE F. MARCK." Value $1.00.

62. B.S. 1773. Twenty kreutzers. Obv. Bust, "CAROLUS FRID. D.

G. MARCHIO BAD. & H." Rev. Crowned shield, between branches of palm and laurel. "LX EINE FEINE MARCK, 1773." Value 12 cts.

63. S. 1778. Thaler. Obv. Head, same legend as preceding. Rev. Oval shield, surmounted by a crown, and the date between branches of palm and olive, crossed. "X EINE FEINE MARCK," beneath. Value $1.00.

64. S. 1813. Thaler, of the INTERREGNUM. Obv. Shield, bearing the arms of Baden, displayed upon a mantle of ermine; the latter being suspended from a crown. "GROSHERZOGTHUM BADEN," and the date. Rev. "I KRONEN THALER," inclosed in a wreath, composed of two laurel branches, crossed. Value $1.12.

65. S. 1816. Thaler. Same type as preceding, with the obverse somewhat improved in appearance, the *mantle* being draped in a much more graceful manner. Value $1.12.

66. S. 1819. Thaler, of the SECOND INTERREGNUM. Same type as preceding. This piece is *four grains* higher in weight than the one preceding it. The coins of both epochs, however, were doubtless of the same standards and value, the difference in this case being easily accounted for.

67. G. 1819. Ten gulden, of LOUIS. Obv. Head, "LUDWIG GROSHERZOG VON BADEN." Rev. Crowned shield, between branches of laurel, crossed, bearing the arms of *Baden;* the denomination; "10" at one side, and "G." at the other; the date beneath. Value $4.09.

68 and 69. S. 1819. Thaler. Obverse same as preceding, with the date. Rev. Same device as No. 65, with "KRONEN THALER." beneath. Value $1.12.

70. S. 1825. Two gulden. Same as No. 67, with "WEM TRAU SCHAU." on the edge. Value 83 cts.

71. G. 1826. Five gulden. Same as No. 67. Value $2.05.

72. B.S. 1830. Ten kreutzers. Obverse same as No. 67. Rev. "ZEHN KREUZER 1830," inscribed in three lines between branches of laurel. Value 5.6 cts.

73. B.S. 1830. Three kreutzers. Same type as preceding.

74. S. 1831. Thaler, of LEOPOLD. Obv. Undraped bust, "LEOPOLD GROSHERZOG VON BADEN." Rev. Crowned shield, bearing the

arms of Baden, and supported by two *griffins.* "KRONEN THALER." and the date. Value $1.09.

75. S. 1834. Same.

76. B.S. 1834. Six kreutzers. Obverse same as preceding. Rev. "6 KREUZER 1834," between branches of laurel, crossed.

77. C. 1835. One kreutzer. Same type as preceding.

78 and 79. S. 1839. One gulden. Obverse same as No. 74. Rev "1 GULDEN, 1839," inclosed in a wreath composed of two oak branches, crossed. Value 41 cts.

MECKLENBURG.

Mecklenburg is one of the most ancient States of Germany. Its first inhabitants were the *Vandals,* who abandoned the country and migrated southward about the fifth century of the present era, and the duchy passed into the possession of the *Obotriti* and other *Sclavonic* nations. The ancestor of the present ducal family was *Niclot* or *Nicholas,* who was killed in 1159, in a battle against HENRY *the Lion, Duke of Brunswick and Luneburg,* who seized his possessions. But in 1164, PRIBISLAS,* son of Nicholas, took advantage of the absence of HENRY, who accompanied the Emperor FREDERICK BARBAROSSA on his first expedition to Italy, to recover his dominions; but *Henry* returned and defeated PRIBISLAS in a battle fought near Demmin, in 1167. The latter, however, afterward embraced Christianity and was restored, and continued to reign until his death in

* The *Encyclopedia Britannica* states, on page 420, vol. xiv., that "*the ancestor of the present ducal family of Mecklenburg was Pribislav, who was made a prince of the Empire by* CHARLES IV. *in* 1340." Upon reference to other authorities, it appears, in the first place, that *Charles* did not accede to the imperial crown until the death of LOUIS V. in 1347. And secondly, in the whole history of the house of Mecklenburg since the death of NICHOLAS, no person is found bearing the name of "*Pribislav;*" and the only name which approaches it in the most remote degree is that of *Pribislas* (above mentioned), who was doubtless the person indicated. Thus, in the first instance making a discrepancy of at least *seven years* in the time; and in the latter of *nearly two centuries.* (This work has been found to want accuracy in its historical statements.)

1178. Mecklenburg is at present divided into the two divisions of *Schwerin* and *Strelitz.* This division, as it now exists, took place upon the accession of FREDERICK WILLIAM in 1692, to the Schwerin branch, who, finding a competitor in ADOLPHUS FREDERICK I., *Duke of Strelitz,* a convention was entered into under the mediation of the imperial commissaries, and the present arrangement effected. Each branch has a distinct coinage, although it would appear that, further than the *administration* of the government, there is very little distinction between the two. The legislative bodies of each are annually convened together, and pass common laws and impose common taxes for the whole of Mecklenburg. During the reign of FREDERICK FRANCIS, the duchy was conquered by Napoleon. But, upon the downfall of the latter, it was again restored, and in 1815, was advanced to the rank of a *grand-duchy.* It appears to have had no part in the conventions of 1753 and 1838, for the equalization of silver coins; but the *grand-dukes* continue to coin money at the old *Leipsic* rate. No coins of *Strelitz* have yet appeared at this mint.

85. B.S. 1764. One schilling, of FREDERICK. Obv. His initial letter, surmounted by a crown. Rev. "1 SCHILLING COURANT. MECKLENB : SCHWERIN : MUNZE. 1764."

86. B.S. 1790. Same, of FREDERICK FRANCIS. Same type as preceding.

87. S. 1808. Florin, of FREDERICK FRANCIS. Obv. A shield, surmounted by a crown. "FRIED. FRANZ. V. G. G. HERZOG ZU MECKLENB. SCHWERIN." Rev. The fraction "2-3" occupying the field. "18 STUCK EINE MARK FEIN." and the date. Value 56 cts.

88. B.S. 1827. Eight schillinge, of same. Obv. The initials "F. F." interlaced and surmounted by a crown. "V. G. G. GR. HZ. V. M. S." Rev. "8 SCHILLINGE MECHL. SCHW. LAND MÜNZ, 1827." inscribed in parallel lines. No device. Value 12.6 cts.

89. S. 1828. Florin, of same. Obv. Head, "FRIEDR FRANZ. V. G. G. GR. HERZOG V. MECKLENBURG SCHW." Rev. Shield, surmounted by a helmet, and displayed upon a mantle of *ermine,* which is suspended from a crown; the fraction "2-3" beneath. "18 STUCK EINE MARK FEIN. 1828." Value 56 cts.

90 and 91. B.S. 1830. Four schillinge. Obv. Head, "FRIEDR.

FRANZ. V. G. G. GROSSHERZOG. V. MECKLENBURG SCHW." Rev. "4 SCHILLINGE. 1830" in the field; above is "12 EINEN THALER." beneath "LANDES—MÜNZE." Value 12 cts.

92. G. 1831. Ten thalers, of same. Obverse same as preceding. Rev. Crowned shield, supported by a *griffin* and *stag*, upon a mantle of *ermine*, draped from a crown; above is the denomination "ZEHN THALER," and beneath, the date "1831." Value $7.89.

93. G. 1839. Ten thalers, of PAUL FREDERICK. Obv. Head, "PAUL FRIEDR. GROSSHERZOG V. MECKLENBURG SCHWERIN." Reverse same as preceding. Value $7.89.

94. B.S. 1839. One schilling. Obv. The initials "P. F." interlaced and surmounted by a crown. "V. G. G. GR. HERZOG V. MECKLENBURG. SCH." Rev. "1 SCHILLING. 1839." occupying the field; above is "48 EINEN THALER," and beneath, "LANDES MUNZE."

95. S. 1840. Florin, of same. Obv. Undraped bust. Same legend as No. 93. Rev. Crowned shield, partially inclosed by a laurel wreath. "XVIII STUCK EINE MARK FEIN SILBER." and the date. Value 56 cts.

MISCELLANEOUS.

Under this head is comprised a number of coins belonging to various States, together with a number of medallic ducats, etc., which it is impossible to class under *any* particular division, as they were struck as a kind of *medallic money* to commemorate events of a general character; thus rendering the place of coinage, if it were a matter of importance, still one of great uncertainty.

WALDECK.

97. G. 1761. Quarter ducat, of CHARLES. Obv. Head, "CAROL. D. G. PR. WALD." Rev. Crowned shield bearing a star. "ARDUA AD. GLORIAM VIA." and the date. Value 56 cts.

98. S. 1810. Thaler, of FREDERICK. Obv. Crowned shield, bearing the arms of *Waldeck* and *Pyrmont*, (the former being a *star* borne on a field *or*, and the latter a *shin-bone in fess*, surmounted of another *in pale* on a field *argent*,) inclosed between two branches of laurel, *crossed*. "FRIDERICUS PR. WALDECCIAE COM. PYR." Rev.

"X EINE FEINE MARK. 1810.——T. W." inclosed in a beaded circle. "VIRTUTE VIAM DIMETIAR." Legal value $1.01.

99. S. 1824. Thaler, of GEORGE HENRY. Obv. "EIN KRONEN THALER. 1824," inscribed in four lines between two branches of palm, crossed, surmounted by a crown. "GEORG HENR. FURST Z. WALDECK U PYRMONT." Rev. A palm-tree with its top depressed by a weight; a shield bearing the arms of Waldeck and Pyrmont suspended against its trunk. "PALMA LUB. PONDERE CRESCIT." Legal value $1.01.

SCHWARZBURG-RUDOLSTADT.

100. S. 1812. Thaler, of FREDERICK GUNTHER. Obv. Undraped bust, "FRIEDRICH GUNTHER FURST ZU SCHWARZBURG RUDOLSTADT." Rev. "EIN SPECIES THALER, 1812," inclosed in a wreath composed of two oak branches, crossed. "X EINE FEINE MARK CONVENTIONS MÜNZE. Legal value $1.01.

101. S. 1841. Two-thaler piece, of same. Obv. Undraped bust, "FRIEDR. GUNTHER FURST ZU SCHWARZBURG." Rev. Shield, surmounted by six helmets, and supported by a *wild man* and a female, each holding a lance. "VEREINS MÜNZE" and the date beneath. "2 THALER VII EINE F. MARK. 3½ GULDEN." "GOTT MIT UNS" on the edge. Legal value $1.44.4.

ANHALT.

(Anhalt is composed of the three contiguous duchies of *Anhalt-Bernburg*, *Anhalt-Dessau*, and *Anhalt-Kothen.*)

102. S. 1834. Thaler, of ALEXANDER CHARLES. Obv. Shield, suspended upon a mantle of *ermine*, draped from a crown. "ALEXANDER CARL. HERZOG ZU ANHALT." Rev. "LEGEN DES ANHALT BERGBAUES. 1834." inscribed in four parallel lines. "EIN THALER XIV EINE FEINE MARK;" beneath are two hammers, or sledges, crossed. "GOTT MIT UNS," on the edge. Legal value $1.01.

BERNBURG.

103. C. 1794. One pfenning. Obv. A *bear*, with a collar upon its neck, on a wall, with an arched doorway beneath. Rev. "1 PFENING 1794."

104 and 105. B.S. 1827–31. One-twenty-fourth thaler. Obverse

similar to preceding, the doorway fitted with a closely barred door, and a crown upon the head of the bear. Rev. "24 EINEN THALER, 1827," occupying the field. "H(erzogthum) ANH. BERN. LAND MÜNZE."

OLDENBURG.

106. B.S. 1816. One-third thaler. Obv. Pointed shield, draped as in No. 102. Rev. "3 EINEN THALER. 1816," inscribed in the field; above is "OLDENB. COUR(ant) MÜNZE."

107. B.S. 1816. Twelve groschen. Obv. Crowned shield, draped with laurel. Rev. "12 GROTE. OLD. COUR. MÜNZE 1816."

REUSS.

108. S. 1812. Thaler, of HENRY, *Duke of Reuss.* Obv. Shield, draped as in No. 102. "HEINRICH D. LI JUNG. LINIE FURST REUSS VON EBERSDORF." Rev. "EIN SPECIES THALER 1812 —•+•— L." occupying the field. "X EINE FEINE MARK CONVENTIONS MÜNZE." Legal value $1.01.

HOHENLOHE.

109. S. 1770. Thaler, of LOUIS FREDERICK CHARLES. Obv. Bust, in armor, bedecked with the order-band and star of the order of the *Polish Eagle.* "LUD. FRID. CAROL. D. G. PRINC. AB. HOHENL. COM(es) DE GLEICH D(ux) IN. LANGENB. & CRANICHFELD." Rev. Shield, bearing two lions *current,* bedecked with the order-band and star as above, and draped as in No. 102. "X EINE FEINE MARCK," and the date. Legal value $1.01.

HOHENZOLLERN-HECHINGEN.

110. S. 1839. One gulden, of FREDERICK WILLIAM CHARLES. Obv. Head, "FRIEDRICH W. C. FURST ZU HOHENZ. HECH." Rev. "1 GULDEN 1839," inclosed in a wreath composed of two oak branches, crossed. Value 41 cts.

HOHENZOLLERN-SIGMARINGEN.

111. S. 1839. One gulden, of CHARLES. Obv. Head, "CARL. FÜRST ZU HOHENZOLLERN SIGMARINGEN." Reverse same as preceding. Value 41 cts.

Both of these States have become extinct, having been purchased by the King of Prussia.

LIPPE.

112. B.S. 1770. One-sixth thaler, of SIMON AUGUSTUS. Obv. Head, "SIM. AUG. COUR. & N. D. LIPP. S. D. V. & A." Rev. "VI EINEN THALER" in the field. "AD NORMAM CONVENTIONIS, 1770." Value 12 cts.

LORRAIN.

113. S. —. Crown, of CHARLES V., *Duke of Lorrain.* Obv. Full-length figure, crowned; a scepter in one hand, and the imperial globe in the other. "CAROLUS QUINT ROM. IMPERATOR." Rev. Double-headed eagle, with a small shield (bearing an eagle) upon its breast. "MONETA CIVIT IMPER. BISUNTINÆ." This is one of the most deceptive pieces in the collection. It would be supposed at first glance to be a coin of the EMPEROR CHARLES V.; whereas Charles V. of Lorrain was an entirely different person.

MEDALLIC DUCATS, ETC.

121. G. 1659. Ducat, of GEORGE LOUIS and CHRISTIAN. Obv. Three busts in armor, at full-face. "D. G. GEORGIUS LUDOVIC. & CHRISTIA FRAT." Rev. "DUCES SILESIA LIGNBREG. & WOLAU. 1659." Shield, surmounted by three helmets.

122. G. 1779. Half ducat. Obv. Shield, bearing a donkey. "REG. D. MAXIMILIANO CÆSARE P. F. AUG." Rev. A full-length image of the body of *St. Alban*, carrying his own head in his hands, the head having been severed from the body. "SANCTUS ALBANUS MARTYR," beneath; to the left is "MOG," and to the right "1779."

123. G. —. Ducat. Obv. St. George slaying the dragon. "S. GEORGIUS EQUITUM PATRONUS. Rev. A ship blown by the winds. "IN TEMPESTATE SECURITAS."

124. G. —. Ducat, of the SECRET ORDER OF ROSICRUCIANS. Obv. A cross, with a rose-bush in bloom, growing around it. "DAS CREUZ. ZUM BESTEN WENDE." Rev. "GOTT SEGNE DIS GEBÆNDE."

125. G. —. Ducat. Obv. Profile bust of CHRIST. "IN EINEM STEHET UNSERE SELIGKEIT." Rev. Implements of crucifixion. "SOLCH UNSERE SELIGKEIT ERWIRBT JESUS."

126. G. —. Ducat. Baptismal token. Obv. A group performing the baptismal ceremony. "WER. GLAUBL. UND GEZARIFIKWIRD DER WIRD FELIG WERDEN." Rev. A prayer in German verse.

127. G. —. Ducat. Obv. The Baptism of JOHN. No legend. Rev. "DIS WASSER BAD. GIBT HEIL UND GNAB," inscribed in four lines.

128. G. 1617. Lutheran Centennial ducat—just one hundred years after the beginning of the Reformation. Obv. Bust, in a mantle of *ermine*, carrying a sword; the lower portion being concealed behind a shield bearing the arms of the house of *Wettin* and of *Saxony*. "FRID" at one side of the head, and "III" at the other. "SECUTUM LUTHERANUM," and the date "1517" beneath. Rev. Bust, as above, with a shield, bearing the arms of the four houses of Saxony, *quartered*, and the arms of *Wettin* on a shield of pretence. "JOH" at one side of the head, and "GEOR" at the other. "VERBUMDNI MANET IN ÆTERNUM," and the date "1617" beneath. Coined by JOHN GEORGE I., *Duke of Saxony*.

129. G. —. Ducat. Obv. A vessel containing fire and a heart. "BETHE UND." Rev. "ARBEITE GOTT WIRDS WOHL MACHEN." (Bees and industry perform God's work.) A beehive and bees. This piece was probably struck for distribution among the pupils of the royal schools, as an incentive to assiduity in their studies.

130. G. —. Half ducat. Obv. Sword and crosier, in *saltiere*, through a crowned shield. "HERB : SOLA." Rev. An upright sword, draped with a sash, and a cord and tassels. "DEFENDIT NON LAEDIT."

131. G. —. Quarter ducat. Obv. Crowned shield. "OMNIBUS VIRTUTIS LAUDANTUR." Rev. "SOLA CONSTANTIA CORONATUR."

SECTION IV.—HANSE-TOWNS: BREMEN.

The only characteristic for which the coins of the City of Bremen are remarkable is their extreme *baseness*, as compared with the coins of other governments, in the smaller denominations. In fact, the coins of Bremen, for this reason, are not current outside of the city limits; a fact which explains their character without further comment, as it is notorious that the small coins of all the German States are very *base*, being seldom as high as 550 thousandths fine. However, in the coins of the larger denominations, although the average fineness is somewhat below the German standard, they compare very favorably with other German coins, some of the pieces being coined at a remarkably high standard, as will be found to be the case in the piece 36 *grote*, of the new issue of 1840, which was coined at 15 *loths* 14 *grains*, or 986 thousandths fine; but at the same time the *one-groten* piece, of the same series, was only 281 thousandths fine, that is to say, there was only 281 parts of *pure* silver to 719 parts of *base metal.* And as the principal coinage of money in Bremen consists of the smaller denominations, it is easy to conceive how the city can soon be flooded with a coinage which is not current, at any price, outside of its own gates; consequently the luckless traveler who, in passing through Bremen, is compelled to step into its shops and purchase any article necessary for his comfort or convenience while a sojourner in the city, and receives in change (as he will invariably do if he is not posted) a quantity of its worthless "*scheide-münze*," will find, the moment he turns his back upon the Weser, that his wallet is only depressed by a useless burden. Bremen reckons by dollars of 72 grote, the *groten* consisting of *five schwaren.* In 1753 the principal coin was the piece of 48 *grote*, which was coined at 750 thousandths fine, and worth 56.4 cents. After that date, until 1840, there appears to have been but little money coined. At the latter time the new issue above mentioned took place, consisting of the pieces of 36, 12, and 6 *grote*, and the *one-groten* piece. The small copper pieces have since been added. The city formerly coined gold of the denominations of the ducat and double ducat, but these were long ago discontinued. Many of the two and three *grote* pieces bear the numerals 24 and 36, respectively, which means so many pieces to the dollar of 72 *grote*, twenty-four *three-grote* pieces making a dollar, and thirty-six of the former. The figures in question are usually inclosed in small brackets or circles, and sometimes appear upon the eagle's breast.

1. G. Ducat, of FREDERICK, *Archbishop of Bremen.* Obv. Image of the bishop carrying a key; his lower extremities hidden by a shield bearing a lion *rampant.* "FRIED DEI GRA A(rchi) EP(iscopus) B"(remensis). Rev. A shield, with a cross *potent* extending to the

edge, two keys *in saltiere*, and a lion *rampant*, (borne double). "MONE NOVA BREMEN."

2. B.S. 1512. Six grote. Obv. The bishop, seated; his lower extremities hidden by a shield, bearing two keys *in saltiere*. "E. STAE. D. G. ADMI(nistrator) S(anctus) T. B." Rev. A key. "MONETA NOVA BREMENSIS, 1572."

3. B.S. Half groten. Obv. Full-face bust of a saint, with a roll of parchment and a key. "SANCT. PETRUS." Rev. A key. "MO. NO. REIP. BREM."

4. B.S. 1635. Three grote. Obv. Double-headed eagle, with the imperial globe upon its breast, surmounted by a crown. "FERD(inandus) D. G. RO(man) IMP(erator) S(emper) AU"(gustus). Rev. A shield, bearing a key and the date. "MON. NO. REIP. BREMENSIS."

5. B.S. 1640. One grotten. Obv. A cross *pattée*. "CRUX CHR. NOS. SAL." Rev. A key and the date, inclosed in a single circle. "MONE. NO. REIP. BREM."

6. B.S. 1642. Two grote. Obv. Double-headed eagle. "FERD. III D. G. RO. IMP. SE. AU." Reverse similar to preceding.

7. S. 1643. Forty-eight grote. Obv. Same device as No. 4. "FERDIN. III D. G. ROM. IMP. SE. AUGUS." Rev. A shield, bearing a key, and supported by two lions; the date above. "MONE NOVA ARG. REIPUB. BREMENSIS."

8. B.S. 1657. Twelve grote. Obverse same as preceding. Rev. A key, surmounted by a crown. "STAT. GELT BREMER." "XII GROT." in the *exerque*.

9 and 10. S. 1660. Thaler, of 72 grote. Obv. Double-eagle, as in No. 4. "LEOPOLD D. G. ROM. IMP. SEM. AUGUST." Rev. Shield, bearing a key, surmounted by a crown, and supported by two lions; the date beneath. "MON NOVA. ARG. REIPUB. BREMENSIS."

11. S. 1661. Forty-eight grote, of LEOPOLD. Same type as preceding.

12. B.S. 1666. Twenty-four grote. Obverse same as preceding. Rev. Crowned shield with the date, "16" at one side, and "66" at the other; and the denomination "24 GROTE;" beneath "BREMER STAT. GELT."

13. B.S. 1666. Twelve grote. Same type as preceding.

14. G. 1667. Double ducat. Obv. A full-length portrait of the emperor, dressed in armor and crowned; the imperial globe extended in the left hand and a scepter in the right. "LEOPOLD D. G. ROM. IMP SEM. AUGUST." Rev. Crowned shield, supported by two lions. "DUCAT NOV. AURE REIPUBL. BREMENSIS."

15. G. 1672. Ducat. Obv. Bust, *laureated.* "LEOP. D. G. ROM IMP. SEMP AUG." Rev. A key, surmounted by a crown, with the date inclosed in a wreath composed of two olive branches, crossed. "DUCAT NOV. AURE REIP BREMENS."

16. B.S. 1671. Three grote. Obv. Double-eagle. "LEOP. D. G. ROM. IMP. SEMP. AUG." Rev. Crowned shield, bearing a key, and the date; the denomination beneath. "BREMER STAT GELT."

17 and 18. B.S. 1733–1739. Two-grote pieces, of CHARLES VI. Same type as No. 4, with the imperial globe omitted.

19 and 20. B.S. 1749. Twenty-four grote. Obv. Double-eagle, crowned, a sword and scepter in the dexter, and the imperial globe in the sinister talon, (the latter being omitted from the breast.) "FRANCISCUS D. G. ROM. IMP. SEMP. AUG." Reverse same as No. 16.

21. S. 1753. Forty-eight grote. Obverse same as preceding. Rev. Crowned shield, bearing a key, and supported by two lions. "MONETA NOVA REIPUBL. BREMENSIS."

The following specimens were presented to the UNITED STATES MINT by the City of BREMEN, and includes a set of the new issue of 1840, and many specimens of older dates, some of which have been described in the preceding pages.

23. B.S. 1646. Four grote, of FERDINAND II. Obverse same as No. 4. Rev. Shield, bearing a key, and the date; and backed by a cross, with its limbs extending to the edge. "MONE. NO. REIP. BREMENSIS."

24. B.S. 1657. Eighteen grote, of FERDINAND III. Obverse same as No. 4. Rev. Same device as No. 21. "MONE NOVA ARG. REIPUB. BREMENSIS."

25. B.S. 1657. Twelve grote, of same. Same type as No. 8.

26. S. 1668. Double dollar, of LEOPOLD. Obv. Same device as No. 4. "LEOPOLD. D. G. ROM. IMP. SEM. AGUS." (Augustus.) Rev.

Crowned shield, bearing a key, and supported by two lions; the date beneath. "MONETA NOVA REIPUBLICÆ BREMENSIS." Value $2.50.

If we except the pound sterling, of CHARLES II., (which can hardly be considered as a regular coin, having been issued merely from necessity, and therefore partaking of the character of a "*siege piece*,") this is the largest of silver coins, and bears the evidences of a very high standard of fineness. (It has not been assayed, the *value* above stated being assumed.) It is a very rare and curious piece. *Weight* 841.5 *Troy grains*.

27 and 28. B.S. 1671–1672. Six grote, of LEOPOLD. Same type as No. 4.

29. B.S. 1749. Twenty-four grote. Same as No. 19.

30. C. 1781. One schwaren. Obv. A key and the date. Rev. "I. SCHWAREN."

31. B.S. 1674. One groten, of LEOPOLD. Same type as No. 17.

32 and 33. B.S. Two-schwaren pieces. Same type as No. 3.

34. C. 1697. One schwaren. Same type.

35 and 36. 1846. Thirty-six grote. Obv. Crowned shield, bearing a key and supported by two lions. "FREIE HANSESTADT BREMEN." Rev. "36 GROTE 1846. 15 L(oths) 14 G"(rains) inscribed between two oak branches, crossed.

37, 38, and 39. B.S. 1841–1846. Twelve grote. Obv. Crowned shield. Same legend as preceding. Reverse same as preceding, with "12 GROTE 1841. 11 L. 15 G."

40 and 41. B.S. 1840. Six grote. Same type as preceding, and same standard of fineness, (11 *loths* 15 *grains*.)

42. B.S. 1840. One groten. Same type as preceding, with "I GROTEN 1840," on the reverse; the fineness being omitted.

43. C. 1853. Two-and-a-half schwaren. Obv. A key, and the date. Rev. "2½ SCHWAREN."

NUREMBERG.

49. G. Ducat. Obv Image of St. Lawrence. "SANCTUS LAURENCIUS." Rev. A rudely executed eagle, with the initial "N." upon its breast. "MONETA COHUNIS D. NUREMBERG."

50 and 51. G. 1521, 1523. Ducats. Obv. St. Lawrence, and the date. "SANCTUS LAURENTIUS." Rev. Same device as preceding. "MONETA REIPU. NURENBERGENSIS."

52. G. 1617. Ducat. Obv. St. Lawrence. "SANCTUS LAURENTIUS." Rev. Shield. "MONE REIPUB. NURENBERG 1617."

53. G. 1618. Ducat. Obverse same as preceding. Rev. A shield, supported by a cherub. "MONETA NOVA. REIP. NORINBERG. 1618."

54. G. —. Ducat. Obv. An eagle. "DUCATUS REIPUB. NORIMBERG." Rev. Two shields, supported by a saint. "SIT DEUS AUXILIUM TUTA SIT IPSE SALUS."

55. G. —. Ducat. Obv. Three joined shields, with a dove, holding an olive branch in its beak, perched upon the top. "SECULUM NOVUM CELEBRAT RESP(ublicæ) NORIBERGENSIS." Rev. A hemisphere, surmounted by a lamb, carrying a banner, which bears the word "PAX." "TEMPORA NOSTRA PATER DONATA PACE CORONA."

56. G. —. Half ducat. Same type.

57. G. 1700. Quarter ducat. Obv. Crowned shield, between two palm branches, crossed. "MON. REIP. NORIMB.......1700." Rev. Same device as preceding. No legend.

58. G. 1700. Half ducat. Same as preceding. Struck on a square planchet.

59 and 60. G. —. Quarter ducats. Same as preceding.

61. S. 1611. Thaler, of RUDOLPH II. Obv. Double-eagle, surmounted by a crown, with the imperial globe upon its breast, bearing the numeral "60." "RUDOLPH II. ROM(an) IMP(erator) AUG(ust) P. F. DEC"(us). Rev. Two shields, with "RESPUB. NURENBERG.—F. F." above, and the date beneath.

62. S. 1621. Florin, of FERDINAND II. Obv. Double-eagle, surmounted by a crown. "FERDINANDUS II D. G. ROMAN. IMPER. SEMP. AUGUST." Rev. Three shields, and the date, inclosed in a beaded circle. "MONETA ARGENTEA REIPUB. NURENBERG."

63 and 64. S. 1757–59. Thaler, of FRANCIS I. Obv. Bust, in armor, bedecked with the order chain and badge of the *golden fleece* and a sash; the head *laureated.* "FRANCISCUS D. G. ROM. IMP. SEMP. AUG." Rev. A crowned eagle, in flight, grasping a scepter in the dexter, and a sword in the sinister talon, two shields beneath, joined

at the *chef*, and suspended from the talons of the eagle by ribbons; beneath is inscribed "X EINE FEINE MARK." "MONETA NOVA REIP'BL. NORIM——BERGENSIS."

65. S. 1765. Thaler, of JOSEPH II. Obv. Double-eagle, with the imperial globe upon its breast, a sword in the dexter, and a scepter in the sinister talon. "JOSEPHUS D. G. ROM. IMP. SEMP. AUG." Rev. The City of Nuremberg, with a *Gloria Dei* above. "X EINE FEINE MARCK 1765." Beneath is the word "NÜRNBERG," and the letters "S. R."

HAMBURG.

The coinage of this city is based upon the mark *current*, which is divided into sixteen *schillings*. The only gold coin is the ducat, at the German rate; but these are very rare, and seldom seen, being struck more for show (*schaumünze*) than for general circulation. In the silver coinage the specie dollar of the Leipsic basis was formerly the principal piece, but it has been discontinued since 1764. It was reckoned at $3\frac{3}{4}$ marks *current*. Since that time, until the year 1808, the coinage consisted of the pieces of two marks current; one mark, and eight, and four schillings. Since 1833 the pieces of one schilling, half schilling, or *secksling*, and the quarter schilling, or *dreiling*, have been added to the coinage.

73 and 74. S. 1789. One mark of JOSEPH II. Obv. Same device as No. 65, in the preceding section. "JOSEPHUS II. D. G. ROM. IMP. SEMP. AUGUSTUS. 1789." Rev. A square shield, bearing the city arms (a castle), and surmounted by a helmet. "16 SCHILLING HAMBURGER COURANT."

75 and 76. S. 1795. Two marks, of FRANCIS II. Same type as preceding.

77. B.S. 1797. Eight schillings, of same. Obverse same as preceding. Rev. A castle. "8 SCHILLING HAMBURGER COURANT;" the initials "O. H. K," beneath the castle.

78. B.S. 1797. Same. With the devices considerably reduced in size.

79. B.S. 1797. Four schillings, of same. Same type as No. 77.

80 and 81. S. 1808. Two marks. Obv. Shield, bearing a castle,

and surmounted by a helmet. "17 EINE MARK FEIN." Rev. "32 SCHILLINGE HAMBURGER COURANT. 1808." No device.

82. B.S. 1726. Two schillings, of CHARLES VI. Obv. Same device as No. 73. "CAROLUS VI. D. G. ROM. IMP. SEMP. AUG." Rev. A shield, bearing the denomination "11 SCHILL:" above is a castle inclosed between two branches of olive. "HAMBURGER CURRENT, 1726."

83. B.S. 1836. Secksling. Obv. A castle, with the initials "H. S. K." beneath. Rev. "1 SECKSLING 1836."

84. B.S. 1837. One schilling. Obverse same as preceding. Rev. "1 SCHILLING HAMB. COUR. 1837."

FRANKFORT.

This city "reckons with the southern German States, in florins or *gulden* of sixty kreutzers. As late as 1796, ducats were coined of the usual weight and fineness; but no gold coinage seems to have been executed since that date. Of the silver coins, the convention-dollar was the principal, of which, from 1763 to 1796, there are six different impressions. Frankfort was a party to the southern convention of 1837, at which the rate of 24½ florins to the fine mark was agreed upon. Consequently, since 1838 there has been a new coinage of pieces of one gulden, one-half, six kreutzers, and three, and one kreutzer." The gulden weighs 164 grains, and is nine-tenths fine; value 41.1 cents. The six-kreutzer piece weighs 39 grains, is 333 thousandths fine; value 3.5 cents.

85. G. 1612 Ducat, of MATTHIAS. Obv. The emperor, seated upon his throne, with a male and female, standing at either side. "MATTHIAS IM REGEM ROMA ELECTUS. A. 1612." Rev. A winged saint, seated upon a bank, and blowing a trumpet; above is an eagle descending with a chaplet in its beak, and a palm branch in its sinister talon. "MONETA NOVA AN. FRANCO-FURTENSIS."

86. S. 1843. Three-and-a-half-gulden piece. Obv. A view of the River *Main*, with the City of Frankfort on the left shore, and the bridge across the river; several vessels and small boats are seen in different parts of the harbor, while the sun is just appearing beyond the bridge; beneath are two *cornucopias*, crossed, with a *caduceus*, and the engraver's name, "ZOLLMAN." Above is inscribed "FREIE

STADT FRANKFURT." Rev. "3½ GULDEN. 2 THALER. 1843," inclosed in a wreath, composed of two oak branches, crossed; above are the words "VEREINS MÜNZE," and beneath, "VII EINE F. MARK. "CONVENTION VOM 30 JULY, 1838," on the *edge*.

87. S. 1838. One gulden. Obv. Crowned eagle. "FREIE STADT FRANKFURT." Rev. "1 GULDEN, 1838," inclosed in a wreath of oak.

88. B.S. 1838. Half gulden. Same type.

89. B.S. 1838. Six kreutzer. Same type.

90 and 91. B.S. 1838. Three kreutzer. Same type.

92 and 93. B.S. 1838. One kreutzer. Same type.

COLOGNE.

97. G. —. Ducat. Obv. Shield, backed by a cross, with its limbs extending to the edge. "THEO(dia) ARCH(iepiscopus) COLONIEN"(sis). Rev. Three shields joined and forming a triangle in the center, which contains a crescent. "MONETA NOVA AUREA BI"(lensis).

98. G. —. Ducat. Obv. The arms. "THEODIA AR(chi) EPI(scopus) COLONI." Rev. A full-length figure. "MONETA BUINSIS."

99. G. —. Ducat. Obv. The bishop, seated in his chair of state, with his feet behind a small shield. "ROPERTUS ARCHI. CO"(loniensis). Rev. A cross, with small shields in the angles. "MONE NOVA AUREA BURME."

100. G. —. Ducat. Obv. Same device as preceding. "THEODIA AR. EPI. COL." Rev. Same device as preceding. "MONETA NOVA RILENSIS."

101. G. —. Ducat. Obv. Full-length figure of the bishop with his crosier. "THEODIA AR. EPI. CO." Rev. The arms. "MONETA NOVA AUREA BU."

102 and 103. S. 1666–69. Thaler. Obv. Bust, "MAX(imilianus) HAN (Henricus) D. G. ARC. COL. PRIN(ceps) EL"(ector). Rev. Crowned shield, with the date "1666" above the crown. "EP(iscopus) ET PRINC(eps) LEOD. DUX. BUL(ensis) MAR(chio) FR(anciæ) CO(loniensis) LO. HO."

BAMBERG AND WURTZBURG.

104. G. —. Ducat. Obv. Bust, in a mantle of *ermine.* "AD. FRI. D. G. EP(iscopus) BAM(burgæ) ET WIR(ceburgi) S(acri) R(omani) I(mperii) P(rinceps) F(ranciæ) O(rientalis) D"(ux). Rev. A full-length figure crowned, and supporting a shield with the left hand; a dove descending with a palm branch in its beak. "F-LOREBORE DIVIVO. HOC GERMINE PACIS." Beneath is inscribed "S. P. Q. W." (meaning "*Senatus populus—que Wirceburgensis.*")

A 105. G. —. Ducat. Obv. Shield, bedecked with three helmets, and backed by a sword and crosier in *saltiere.* "JOAN PHILIP. D. G. EPISC. HERB(ioplensis) S. R. I. P. FR. O. DUX." Rev. Shield, bearing a key. "ORE ET CORDE. S. P. Q. W. SUBM. OFFERT."

B 105. G. —. Ducat. Obv. Crowned shield, backed by a sword and crosier *in saltiere,* and displayed upon a mantle bedecked with five helmets. "ANSEL FRANC(iscus) D. G. H. S. R. I. PR. FR. OR. DUX." Rev. In the lower part of the field is a shield, bearing a key, above which is inscribed at one side, "S. P.," and at the other, "Q. W.;" while in the *upper* part of the field are two hands, issuing from the clouds, and grasping three links, from which a cross depends. "LUX PATRIÆ SIGNUMQUE SALUTIS."

106. G. —. Ducat, Obv. Bust, at three-quarter face; the lower portion hidden by a small shield, surmounted by a crown, and backed by a sword and crosier *in saltiere.* "JO(an) PH(ilip) D. G. S. S. M. A(rchi) E(piscopus) S. R. I. AE. P. E. E. H(erbioplensis) F. O. DUX." Rev. "ORE ET CORDE S. P. Q. W. SUBM. OFFERT," inscribed in four lines; a *divine glory* above, and a shield, bearing a key, beneath; a *laurel* and palm branch at either side.

107. S. 1693. Crown. Obv. A shield, bedecked with three crowned helmets, and a sword and crosier. "JOHANNES GODEFRID D. G. EPS (Episcopus) HERBIP. (Herbioplensis) FRANC. OR. DUX." Rev. A full-length figure of the bishop in canonicals, a crosier in the left hand, and a sword in the right; the initials "I. M." appear to the right of the field, and "W" to the left. "SANCTUS KILIANUS," and the date "1693." This piece has a ring attached to the edge, evidently for the purpose of wearing it about the person as an ornament. The custom of

wearing coins of a religious or irregular character (such as are here termed "*medallic coins*") as ornaments or charms, has prevailed extensively, in times past, among the Germans, and was, doubtless, handed down to them from the ancient Greeks, as we find that the same custom was in vogue among the latter as long ago as the beginning of the MACEDON EMPIRE.

SALISBURG.

109. G. 1640. Square ducat. Obv. The bishop in canonicals, seated in his chair, with the salt-basket on his right arm, and a crosier in his left hand. "SANCTUS RUDBERTUS EPS. (Episcopus) SALISB. 1640." Rev. Shield and cross-staff, bedecked with the hat and tassels of the bishopric. "PARIS D. G. ARCHI EPS. SAL(isburgensis) SE(dis) AP(ostolicæ) L"(egatus).

110. G. 1668. Half ducat. Obv. Same device as preceding. "S. RUDBERTUS EPS. SALISBURG. 1668." Rev. Shield, bearing the arms of the bishopric in six fields, surmounted by the cross-staff and bedecked with the hat and tassels. "MAX GAND D. G. AR. EP. SAL. SE. A. L." The fraction "1-2" (half ducat) beneath the shield.

111 and 112. G. 1714–19. Quarter ducat. Obverse same as preceding, with the fraction "1-4" beneath the bishop. Rev. Shield, backed by a sword and crosier *in saltiere,* and surmounted by a crown, and the cross-staff bedecked with the hat and tassels of the bishopric. "FRAN. ANT. D. G. ARCHI. EP. SALISB."

113. G. 1776. Half ducat. Obv. Bust, "HIERONYMUS D. G. A(rchi-Episcopus) & P(rinceps) S(alisburgensis) A(postolicæ) S(edis) L(egatus) N(atus) G(ermaniæ) PRIM"(as). Rev. Shield, surmounted by the cross-staff, and displayed upon a mantle draped from a crown; a sword and crosier appearing at either side of the crown; the date "1776" beneath.

114. G. 1794. Ducat. Obverse same as preceding. Rev. Shield, surmounted by the cross-staff, bedecked with the hat and tassels, and displayed upon a mantle arranged as in preceding; arms of the bishopric quartered; a shield of pretence, bearing the family arms of the bishop; the date "1794" beneath.

115. S. 1628. Crown. Obv. Eight bishops, carrying a *catafalque.*

"S. S. RUPERTUS ET VIRGILIUS PATRONI TRANSFERUNTUR 24 SEPT." Rev. The front of the cathedral at Salisburg, supported by two bishops (St. Rupert and St. Virgil); beneath is a shield, surmounted by a cross-staff, bedecked with the hat and tassels of the bishopric. "ECCLES(iasticus) METROP(olis) SALISB(urgensis) DEDICATUR 25 SEPT. APARIDE ARCHIE." The date "1628" in the field above the bishops.

116. S. 1785. Thaler. Obverse same as No. 113. Rev. Oval shield, surmounted by the cross-staff, bedecked with the hat and tassels of the bishopric; draped as in No. 113, with the date beneath.

STRALSUND.

118. S. 1707. Florin. Obv. Arms of the city, (a "*broad arrow*,") with the fraction "2-3" beneath. "MONETA NOVA STRALSUNDENSIS. 1707." Rev. A cross *moline*. "IN TUO——SALVA NOS DEUS."

METZ.

119. S. 1650. Thaler. Obv. Bust, "S(anctus) STEPHANUS PROTO MARTIR." Rev. Arms of *Metz*. "MONETA CIVITA METENSIS. 1650."

MUNSTER.

120. S. 1693. Twenty-four marien groschen. Obv. Crowned shield, backed by a sword and crosier *in saltiere*. "FRIDER. CHRIST D. G. EP(iscopus) MONAST." Rev. The denomination inscribed in three lines. "BURGGR. STROMB. S(acri) R(omani) I(mperii) PRIN(ceps) D(ominus) IN BORCK. 1693."

RATISBON.

121. G. —. Ducat. Obv. Bust in armor, *laureated*, and bedecked with an order chain and sash. "FRANCISC(us) I. D. G. ROM. IMP(erator) SEMP(er) AUG"(ustus). Rev. A view of the City of Ratisbon, with a *Gloria Dei*, and the inscription "SIBI CONSCIA RECTI" above, and the name "RATISBONA," beneath.

122. S. 1787. Thaler. Obv. A vessel, sailing upon the water, and containing a figure, seated, with two keys in his left hand, and his right resting upon a book; beneath is a shield, bearing the city arms (a dexter *bend argent*, on a field *gules*, red), surmounted by a head bedecked with a cardinal's hat, and backed by a sword and

crosier *in saltiere;* the whole surrounded by fifteen small oval shields arranged in a circle. Rev. "REGNANS CAPITULUM ECCLESIÆ CATHEDRALIS RATISBONENSIS SEDE VACANTE M.D.CCLXXXVII," inscribed in seven parallel lines. "10 EINE F. MARK," beneath.

LOWENSTEIN.

123. S. —. Crown. Obv. Shield, bedecked with four helmets; the arms of Bavaria on a shield of pretence. "GEILDORF. & MONT S. PR. IN CHASS. D(ominus) IN SEHAR. BR. HERB. & NEUCH." Rev. In the upper half of the field is a tree with two branches, each branch encircled by a crown, and grasped and held asunder by two arms; above the tree is a scroll with "DUM SCINDITUR FRANCOR." In the lower half is the same tree, with its branches sustained and united by a brace (formed by two bars united with pins at their ends), and a crown; above is a scroll, with "ME CONJUNCTIO SERVAT." These devices are *reversed;* the one in the upper half of the field having its top turned downward. "EUCH CASIM CŌ. IN LEWENST. WERTH. ROCHEF. VIREB."

124. S. 1769. Thaler. Obv. Bust, in armor. "CAROL. D. G. S(acri) R(omani) I(mperii) PRIN(ceps) DE LÆWENST. WERTH." Rev. Crowned shield, draped with an order chain and star; a lion at each side. "X EINE FEINE MARCK." Beneath is inscribed "W.—17—W.—69.—E."

HILDESHEIM.

125. S. —. One-sixth thaler. Obv. Shield, backed by a sword and crosier *in saltiere,* and displayed upon a mantle of ermine, draped from a crown. "FRID. WILH. D. G. EPISC HILDES(heimi) S(acri) R(omani) P"(rinceps). Rev. "VI EINEN THALER 1764," inscribed in the field. "80 EINE FEINE MARCK."

HENNEBERG.

126. S. 1693. Florin. Obv. Shield, bearing the arms of Saxony, and surmounted by the electoral crown. "SAXONIA MONETA COMMUNIS HENNEBERGENSIS." Rev. A crowned hen, standing upon one leg. "FELIX FODINARUM ILM—EN AVIENSIUM REPARATIO."

STOLBERG.

127. B.S. 1673. Twelve marien groschen. Obv. A stag. "GUSTAV. G(rafen) Z(u) S(tolberg) W(ernigerode) U(nd) KÖNSTEIN H(erzog) Z. H. U(nd) N. L(anterberg U(nd) CL"(ettenberg). Rev. "XII MARIEN GROSCH," occupying the field.

128. B.S. 1764. One-sixth thaler. Obv. Shield bedecked with three helmets. "FRID. BOTHO. U. CARL. LUDW. GR(afen) Z(u) ST(olberg) K(önigstein R(ochefort) W(ernigerode) U. H"(ohenstein). Rev. A stag, standing beside a crowned pillar. "LXXX EINE FEINE MARCK. 1764."

AUGSBURG.

129. G. 1623. Ducat. Obv. A double-eagle, surmounted by a crown; a small shield upon its breast. "FERDINANDUS II. ROM. IMP. P. F. AUG." Rev. The arms of Augsburg, (*a fir cone,*) with the date MDCXXIII." beneath. "AUGUSTA VINDELIC."

130. G. 1651. Ducat. Obv. Bust, in armor, *laureated,* and bedecked with the order chain and badge of the *golden fleece.* "FERDINAND. III D. G. R. I. S. A. P. F." Rev. Shield, bearing the city arms. "AUGUSTA VENDELICORUM," and the date "1651."

TREVES.

131. G. 1619. Ducat. Obv. A full-length figure, carrying a key. "LOTHARIUS D. G. AR(chi-Episcopus) TR(evitis) PR(inceps) EL"(ector). Rev. The arms, on four shields, inclosed in a *trefoil* compartment. "MO. NO. A CON 1619."

MAGDEBURG.

132. G. 1677. Ducat. Obv. Double-eagle, with the imperial globe upon its breast, surmounted by a crown; the date above. "FERINAND II. D. G. RO. I. S. A." Rev. A man, in armor, upon the city wall; the buildings of the city in the background. "MO. NO. AUR. CI(vitas) MAGD"(eburgensis).

MENTZ.

133. G. —. Ducat. Obv. The bishop, in canonicals, seated in his chair, with a crosier in his left hand. "JOHIS AR(chi) EP(iscopus) MAGU." Rev. A shield, bearing the arms of the city, and inclosed in a *trefoil* compartment. "MONETA I. HOEST SUP. MOGEN."

134. G. —. Ducat. Obv. A full-length figure, with a cross-staff in the left hand. Rev. A shield, bearing the arms in two fields; small shields suspended at each side. Same legend as preceding.

135. G. 1730. Ducat. Obv. Bust, "D. G. FRANC. LUD. ARCHIEP. MOG(ensis) PR(inceps) EL"(ector). Rev. A hand, issuing from the clouds, and leading a lion with a cord, thrown loosely over his head. The date "1730" beneath. "DEO DUCE."

136. S. 1766. Thaler. Obv. Bust, in a mantle of *ermine*. "EMERIC JOSEPH D. G. A. EP. MOG. S. R. I. P. G. A. C. P. EL." Rev. Two joined shields surmounted by a crown, and backed by a sword and crosier *in saltiere*. "X EINE FEINE MARK 1766."

BACHERACH.

137. G. —. Ducat. Obv. A full-length figure, with a double-eagle perched upon the right hand, and a cross-staff in the left. "S(anctus) JOHEIS BRAJATS." Rev. Five shields *in cross*, and inclosed in a *quarterfoil* compartment, the uppermost bearing the arms of Bavaria, and the central one a lion *rampant*. "MONETA OPIDI BACHERACH."

WESEL.

138. G. —. Ducat. Obv. A full-length figure, with a cross-staff in the left hand. "WERNER AR(chi) EP(iscopus) TRE"(vensis). Rev. The arms, on three shields, inclosed in a *trefoil* compartment. "MONETA NOVA WESAL."

SPIRES.

139. G. —. Ducat. Obv. Three joined shields, supported by two *wild men*, displayed upon a mantle of *ermine*, draped from a crown, and backed by a sword and crosier *in saltiere*. "AUGUSTUS D. G. EP(iscopus) SP(irensis) S. R. I. P(rinceps) ET P(ræpositus) W(eissenburgensis) EL(ectus) 29 MAI. CONSECR(atus) 16 SEPT. 1770." Rev.

Minerva, helmeted, with a spear and laurel branch in her right hand, and the shield of *Medusa* on her left arm. To the right of Minerva is a *Genius* holding a pair of scales in its right hand, and a plumet line in its left. To her left is another *Genius* carrying a *cornucopia* on its right arm, and an olive branch in its left hand, a bee-hive and bees appearing in the background; while a third *Genius* is descending toward the goddess; and the sun, with his diverging rays, surmounts the whole. "DEO O(ptimo.) M(aximo) AUSPICE. SUAVITER ET FORTITER SED JUSTI NEO SIBI SED SUIS."

COBLENTZ.

140. G. —. Ducat. Obv. A bishop, seated in his chair, his feet hidden by a shield. "WERNER AR(chi.) EP(iscopus) TR"(evensis). Rev. A shield, bearing the arms in two fields, and inclosed in a *trefoil* compartment, outside of which is a beaded circle "MONETA NOVA COVELENSIS."

"GOLD MONEY OF THE SILVER CITY."

141. G. —. Ducat. Obv. The emperor, crowned, and seated upon his throne, with a glory around his head, and both hands extended, and grasping the beaded circle, which incloses the field; beneath is a small shield. "URBEM CHRISTE TUAM SERVA." Rev. A circular shield, with its edge indented, so as to form six sections, in each of which is a skull; charged with an imperial globe. "AUREUS URBIS ARGENTINAE NUMMUS." (Gold money of the silver city.) This is one of the most remarkable pieces in the collection, as it bears neither date, name, nor other mark, from which its authorship can be deduced—the obverse being a prayer to "*Christ to save the city*," which, as we are informed on the reverse, is the *Silver City*.

JUNGSTEIN (*Yungstein.*)

142. S. 1516. Small piece. Obv. Two joined shields, above which is the date "MDXVI." and beneath, the letter "A." "EBERHARD COM (es) IN JUNGSTEIN." Rev. An eagle. (The legend is partially defaced.) "——AE MAXIMILI. URB. AUG. DEF——."

ITALIAN STATES.

SECTION V.—SARDINIA.

The nucleus around which the present kingdom of Sardinia has been gradually formed was the Duchy of Savoy.* In the year 933 Savoy was incorporated with the kingdom of ARLES, and with the latter was annexed to the Empire of Germany; its different provinces being governed by counts, who were appointed by the German emperors. The Emperor SIGISMUND I. erected it into a duchy in 1417, and annexed to it the territories comprised in the Principality of Piedmont. AMADÆUS VIII., who was the first duke of Savoy, abdicated in 1440, and the same year was elected pope by the Council of Basil, with the title of FELIX V., but renounced the *tiara* in 1449, to put an end to the schism, and died two years after, (1451.) During the reign of VICTOR AMADÆUS II., who ascended the throne in 1675, a war broke out between France and Germany, in which he became involved, and in 1703 declared against France, in the war for the succession of Spain, in which he lost Savoy and nearly all of Piedmont. But, afterward, in 1706, he defeated the French before Turin, and reconquered Piedmont; and, by the peace of *Utrecht*, in 1713, recovered Savoy, and was, at the same time, created *King of Sicily;* but, in 1718, exchanged the latter for the Island of Sardinia. In the reign of VICTOR AMADÆUS III., Sardinia was again invaded by the French, and by the treaty of *Paris*, in 1796, *Savoy* and *Nice* were annexed to the French Republic, and Piedmont became the *Sub-Alpine Republic*, or *Eridania*. The king, CHARLES EMANUEL

---

* The origin of the house of Savoy has long been a controverted point among genealogists. But the most reliable authorities seem to concur in deriving its origin from the house of Saxony; and, it is asserted, that for this reason the counts of Savoy always sat, in the imperial diets, upon the same bench with the dukes of Saxony, and immediately after them. The first count of Savoy was BAROALD, who was descended, according to the same authorities, from WHITIKIND *the Great*.

IV.,* took refuge in the Island of Sardinia, which alone was left to him. In 1802 this prince was succeeded by EMANUEL V., and, in the same year, the *Sub-Alpine Republic* was suppressed, and the territories annexed to France. Upon the downfall of Napoleon, however, the king recovered his continental possessions, with the addition of Genoa.

The French system of money was adopted for *Eridania* in 1800, and since the restoration, in 1814, has been continued; the coins being of 80, 40, and 20 *lire,* or francs, in gold; and 5, 2, 1, $\frac{1}{2}$ and $\frac{1}{4}$ *lire,* in silver.

The ancient Duchy of Genoa, which, as before stated, now makes up a portion of the Sardinian monarchy, was converted into the *Ligurian Republic* in 1798, and issued gold and silver coins bearing the new title. The gold pieces were the *genovine,* of 96 *lire,* and its half; the silver were the *scudo,* of 8 *lire,* and its half, with the smaller denominations. Genoa retained its right of coinage after its annexation to Sardinia in 1814; but the only specimens of the new coinage which have yet appeared here, are the pieces of *ten* and *five soldi,* Nos. 14, 15, and 16.

1. S. 1755. Quarter scudo, of CHARLES EMANUEL III. Obv. Bust, with the date "1755" beneath. "CAR. EM. D. G. REX SAR(diniæ) CY(priæ) ET JER"(osalymæ). Rev. Circular shield, surmounted by a crown, and encircled by the order chain of the order of "*the Prophecy of Maria.*" The arms quartered; the arms of Sardinia occupying the first quarter, Cypria the second, Jerusalem the third, and Montferrat the fourth; a shield of pretence, bearing an eagle, with the cross of Savoy upon its breast. "DUX SABAUD(iæ) ET MONTISFER(rati) PRINC(eps) PEDEM(ontii) &"(cætera).

2. S. 1757. Scudo. Same as preceding. Value $1.37.

3. S. 1795. Twenty sols, of VICTOR AMADÆUS III. Obv. Bust, with the date "1795" beneath. "VICT. AMED. D. G. REX SARD." Rev. Crowned shield, bearing the arms quartered, with a shield of pretence like preceding.

4. S. 1802. Five francs, of ERIDANIA. Obv. *Justice,* leaning upon

---

* CHARLES EMANUEL IV. succeeded in 1796, in the midst of the troubles.

and encircling Liberty with her left arm; an olive crown in her left hand, and a palm branch in her right. Liberty holds in her right hand a staff, surmounted by the liberty-cap, and in her left a *quadrant*, her head surmounted by a helmet. On the base, which supports the device, is inscribed the *engraver's* name, "LAVY." "GAULE SUBALPINE." Rev. "5 FRANCS—L'AN 10," inclosed in a wreath, composed of *maize* and *laurel* branches, crossed. Beneath is inscribed the name "ERIDANIA," and above "LIBERTE EGALITE." This piece was struck after the annexation of Piedmont to France; the inscription "L'AN 10," meaning the tenth year of the French Republic, and not the year of the Republic of *Eridania,* which did not exist so long. Value 97 cts.

The following pieces, Nos. 5 to 13, were struck by the Duchy of Genoa, before its annexation in 1814.

5. S. 1653. Eight soldi. Obv. The Virgin Mary, seated upon a cloud, with a halo of stars around her head, and holding the infant Jesus on her left arm, and a scepter in her right hand. Beneath is the number "VIII." "ET REGE EAS. 1653. I. A. B." Rev. a cross *moline,* with mullets in the angles. "DUX ET GUB(ernator) REIP(ublicæ) GENU"(ensis).

6. S. 1675. Half lira. Obv. A full-length figure of Christ, holding in his left hand a cross-staff, around which a scroll is intwined, and pointing upward with his right hand. "NON SURREXIT MAJOR, 1675." Rev. Crowned shield, bearing a cross. "DUX ET GUB. REIP. GENU."

7. G. 1792. Genovine, of 96 lire. Obverse same as No. 5. Rev. Shield, bearing a cross, surmounted by a crown, and supported by two griffins. "DUX ET GUB. REIP. GENU." Value $15.17.

8. S. 1793. Two lire. Obverse same as No. 6. Rev. Crowned shield, bearing a cross, and supported by two griffins. "DUX ET GUB. REIP. GEN." Value 36 cts.

9. S. 1794. Two lire. Obverse same as preceding, with "ECCE AGNUS DEI," inscribed upon the scroll.* Rev. Two griffins, support-

* The preceding pieces, Nos. 6 and 8, doubtless have the same inscription, but being somewhat worn, it is rendered illegible.

ing a shield between them, and holding a crown above it. "DUX ET GUB. REIP. GENU."

10. S. 1794. One lire. Same type as preceding. Value 16 cts.

11. S. 1795. Four lire. Same type. Value 64 cts.

12. S. 1796. Scudo, of eight lire. Same type. Value $1.27.5.

13. G. 1798. Genovine, of the LIGURIAN REPUBLIC. Obv. The goddess of Liberty, with her head surmounted by the *mural crown*, seated upon a stone block, her left arm resting upon an oval shield, bearing the arms of Genoa, and grasping a spear in her right hand; in front of and leaning against the block is a *quadrant*, immediately beneath which is inscribed, on the *base* which supports the device, the engraver's name, "E. VASSALLO." Beneath is the denomination "L. 96." (96 *lire.*) "REPUBLICA LIGURE ANNO I." Rev. A fasces, surmounted by a liberty-cap, and inclosed between two branches of laurel; beneath is the date "1798." "NELL' UNIONE LA FORZA." On the edge is inscribed the weight and fineness. "BONTA KAR. 22. PESO GRANI 550." (22 carats fine; weight 550 grains.) Value $15.17.

14. B.S. 1814. Four soldi. Obv. A pointed shield, bearing the arms of Genoa, surmounted by a crown, and inclosed between two cornucopias, crossed; the initial "S." at one side, and the numeral "4" at the other; beneath is the date "1814." "RESPUBLICA GENUENSIS." Rev. St. George and the dragon. "EX PROBITATE ROBUR."

15 and 16. S. 1814. Ten soldi. Obverse same as No. 8. Rev. Same device as No. 9. "RESPUBLICA GENUENSIS." Beneath is inscribed "SOL. 10."

17 and 18. S. 1817. Five lire, of VICTOR EMANUEL. Obv. Undraped bust, with the date "1817" beneath. "VIC. EM. D. G. REX SAR. CYP ET JER." Rev. Crowned shield, bearing the arms of *Sardinia* in the first quarter, Cypria and Jerusalem in the second, Genoa in the third, the fourth being a cross *or*, on a field *argent*, surmounted of a *label azure;* a shield of pretence, bearing an eagle, with the cross of Savoy upon its breast; the whole encircled by the order chain of the order of the *Prophecy of Maria*; beneath is "L——5." (5 lire.) "DUX SAB. JANVAE. (Genoa) ET MONTISF. PRINC.

PED. D." On the edge is inscribed "FERT*—•+•—*FERT*—•+•—*FERT." Value 97.2 cts. each.

19. G. 1818. Twenty lire. Same as preceding. Value $3.83.

20. G. 1827. Eighty lire, of CHARLES FELIX. Obv. Undraped bust, with the date "1827" beneath. "CAR. FELIX D. G. REX SAR. CYP. ET HIER"(osolymæ). Rev. A heart-shaped shield, finely engraved, and bearing the arms, arranged as in the preceding piece, surmounted by a crown, and draped with the order chain of the preceding piece; the whole inclosed between two oak branches, crossed; beneath is the denomination "L. 80." "DUX SAB. GENUAE ET MONTIS. PRINC. PED. D." Edge like No. 17. Value $5.39.

21. G. 1831. Forty lire. Same type. Value $7.66.

22. G. 1827. Twenty lire. Same type. Value $3.83.

23 and 24. S. 1827–1828. Five lire. Same type. Value 97.2 cts.

25. S. 1825. Two lire. Same type. Value 31 cts.

26. S. 1828. Lira. Same type. Value 19.4 cts.

27. S. 1828. Fifty centimes. Same type, with the shield charged with the arms of Savoy, (the rest being omitted.)

28. G. 1836. Twenty lire, of CHARLES ALBERT. Obv. Undraped bust, with the date "1836" beneath. "CAR ALBERTUS D. G. REX SARD. CYP. ET HIER." Rev. Crowned shield, bearing the arms of Savoy, and draped with the order chain of the preceding pieces, the whole inclosed between two branches of laurel, crossed. Legend same as in the preceding reign. Edge grained. Value 3.85.

29. G. 1833. Ten lire. Same as preceding. Value $1.92.

30. S. 1833. Five lire. Same type as preceding, with the edge like No. 17. Value 97.2 cts.

LOMBARDY AND VENICE.

That region of country lying in the north of Italy, and bordering upon the Tyrol, which has been known, until recently, as the Lombardo-Venetian Kingdom, and which has so long been the battle-field on which the political destinies of Europe have been decided, the stage for the reception of those actors who, in times past, have been so potential in Europe in overturning dynasties and setting up usurpers, was acquired by the Austrian emperors at an early period, and soon after the extinction of the Western Empire. After its annexation to the Austrian Empire, the portion comprised in the division of Lombardy was ruled by viceroys appointed by the emperors, while the division of Venice was under the immediate jurisdiction of the doges of Venice. But when NAPOLEON BONAPARTE came upon the stage, as a competitor with Austria, for the domination in Italy, this state of affairs received an interruption which threatened the extinction of the Austrian rule in the Italian provinces. In 1797 the armies of the *French Republic*, under Napoleon, overran the State of Lombardy, and erected it into a separate government, with the title of the CISALPINE REPUBLIC; and coins bearing the new title were issued. But Lombardy was destined to undergo most rapid changes; and three years later, the "Cisalpine Republic" found its grave, and Lombardy reverted to the Austrian crown. But two years after, in 1802, it again escaped from the grasp of the Hapsburg dynasty, and became the ITALIAN REPUBLIC, with NAPOLEON as its president, and in 1805 was erected into a kingdom, under the same person, who established his capital at *Mantua*, where he was crowned "*King of Italy*," with the "Iron Crown," so famous, from the supposition that it was fashioned from one of the nails with which Christ was crucified. With the addition, from time to time, of Venice, Ragusa, and some of the Papal States, this was the state of affairs up to 1814–15, when Napoleon *descended*, as rapidly as he had before *ascended*, the wheel of fortune. Amid the rearrangement of Europe which then took place, Lombardy and Venice were restored to the Emperor of Austria, and were consolidated into the Lombardo-Venetian Kingdom, and a series of coins issued which were entirely distinct in appearance from the coins of Austria *proper*. (See introduction to Austria.) But since the revolution of the past year, under the auspices of a second NAPOLEON, there is likely to be another radical change in the coins of this territory; and, in anticipation of the changes which may take place, the coins of Lombardy and Venice have been removed from the division of Austria and placed among the "Italian States," this disposition of them being considered the most proper under all circumstances, as the Austrian provinces in Italy, although under the almost immediate dominion and supervision of the emperor, have always had a coinage which was as distinct from that of Austria as it was proper or practicable to make them, and being struck *specially* for circulation in those dependencies, they thereby acquire an *Italian* character, which it is hard to efface. One can scarcely look upon an Austrian coin of Lombardy without at the same time associating with it in his mind the name of "*Italy.*"

The monetary unit of this country is the *lira* or *livre*, divided into twenty *soldi*. This has been repeatedly changed in value. Before 1797, it was worth 14.7 cents; under NAPOLEON, 19.3 cents, and now 16.6 cents of our money. The system of coinage, from 1804 to 1815, was the same as that of France; the *lira* and the *franc* being interchangeable.

37 and 38. S. 1781–85. Thaler, of JOSEPH II. Obv. Bust, *laureated.* "JOSEPH II. D. G. R. IMP. S. AUG. G(ermaniæ) H(ungariæ) ET B(ohemiæ) REX. A(rchidux) A"(ustriæ). Rev. Crowned shield, between branches of palm and laurel, crossed, quartered with eagles and serpents; the arms of Austria and Lotharingia, on a shield of pretence. "MEDIOLANI ET MANT. DUX 1785." Values 88.5 cts.

39. G. 1814. Forty lire, of NAPOLEON. Obv. Head, with the date "1814," and the mint-mark "M"(antua) beneath. "NAPOLEONE IMPERATORE E RE." Rev. The French eagle, with a shield upon its breast, draped with an order chain and star; a shield of pretence, bearing the iron crown of *Mantua.* Behind the eagle are two spears *in saltiere;* the whole being displayed upon a mantle of *ermine*, draped from a crown; beneath is the denomination "40 LIRE." "REGNO D'ITALIA." On the edge is inscribed "DIO PROTEGGE LA ITALIA." Value $7.70.

40. G. 1808. Twenty lire. Same type as preceding. Value $3.85.

41. S. 1814. Five lire. Same type. Value 97 cts.

42. S. 1811. Two lire. Same type. Value 38.8 cts.

43. S. 1810. Lira. Same type, with stars upon the edge. Value 19.4 cts.

44. S. 1810. Ten soldi. Obverse same as preceding. Rev. The iron crown, with the denomination "10 SOLDI," and the mint-mark "M." beneath. "REGNO D'ITALIA." Value 9.5 cts.

19

45. S. 1811. Five soldi. Same type as preceding. Value 4.7 cts.

46. C. 1813. One soldi. Same type.

47. C. 1813. Three centimes. Same type.

48. G. —. Ducat, of ALOYSIUS MOCENIGO, *Doge of Venice*. Obv. St. Mark, with the doge kneeling before him, and holding a flag-staff in his left hand, one end resting upon the ground; above the doge are the letters "D U X," placed one under the other; while to the right is the name "ALOY MOCENI." On the left edge, behind St. Mark, and placed one under the other, are the letters "S. M. VENET" (*Sanctus Marcus Venetiæ*). Rev. A shield, bearing a saint, surrounded with stars. "SIT T(ibi) XPE, (an abbreviation of the Greek name '*XPIΣTE*,' *i.e. Christe*). DAT(us) Q(uem) TU —— REGIS ISTE DUCA"(tus).

49. G. —. Ducat, of LUDWIG MANIN, *Doge of Venice*. Same as preceding, with "LUDO MANIN" substituted for the name of "*Aloy Moceni.*"

50. G. —. Quarter ducat of VENICE. Obv. Same device as No. 48, with the legend "PET. LAU. DUX. S. M. VEN." Rev. Same device as No. 48, with "EGO. SUM. LUX MUN"(di).

51. S. —. Crown. Obv. A cross moline, ornamented, and inclosed in a beaded circle. "ANTON PRIOL DUX VEN"(etiæ); beneath are the initials "V. —— G." Rev. A shield, bearing a winged lion (arms of St. Mark) inclosed in a beaded circle; beneath are the numerals "140." "SANCTUS MARCUS VEN."

52. S. 1762. Lira. Obv. The doge, in a kneeling posture, holding a staff, surmounted by a cap and tassels; the date "1762" beneath. "MARE. —— FASCARENUS D"(ux). Rev. The arms of St Mark, or of Venice. "SANCT. MARCUS VEN." Value 14.7 cts.

53 and 54. S. 1789–95. Crown. Obv. A female bust, enveloped in a mantle of ermine. "RESPUBLICA VENETA." Rev. The lion of St. Mark; beneath is the date "1789." "LUDOVICO MANNIN DUCE."

55. C. 1822. Five centimes. Obv. A ducal crown, surmounted by the imperial. "REGNO. LOMBARDO-VENETO." Rev. "5 CENTESIMI. —— 1822."

56. C. 1822. Three centimes. Obverse same as preceding. Rev. "3 CENTESIMI —— 1822."

57. S. 1824. One lira, of FRANCIS I. Obv. Bust, *laureated.* "FRANCISCUS I D. G. AUSTRIÆ IMPERATOR." Rev. Austrian double-eagle, with a shield upon its breast, draped with the order chain and badge of the *golden fleece,* and surmounted by the ducal crown. Serpents and winged lions *quartered,* with the arms of Austria on a shield of pretence; beneath is the inscription "LIRA AUSTRIACA." "LOMB. ET VEN REX A(rchidux) A(ustriæ) 1824." Value 16.6 cts.

The following comprises a complete set of gold and silver coins struck by the Austrian government for Lombardy and Venice, since the re-establishment of the Austrian rule in these States in 1814.

58. G. 1838. Sovereign, of FERDINAND I. Obv. Bust, *laureated.* "FERD. I. D. G. AUSTR. IMP. HUNG(ariæ) BOH(emiæ) R(ex) H. N. V." Rev. Austrian double-eagle, with a shield upon its breast, surmounted by the ducal crown, and encircled with the order chain and badge of the *golden fleece,* and the order band and badge of the order of *Maria Theresia.* Under the shield, and inside of these, are three other order chains with their badges. The arms are serpents and winged lions *quartered,* with a shield of pretence, bearing the arms of Austria and Lotharingia. "REX LOMB. ET VEN. DALM(atiæ) GAL(iciæ) LOD (omeriæ) ILL(yriæ) A(rchidux) A(ustriæ) 1838." On the edge is inscribed, "TUERI RECTA." Value $6.77.

59. G. 1839. Half sovereign. Same as preceding, with the shield draped with the order chain and badge of the *golden fleece* (the others being omitted.) Value $3.38.

60. S. 1839. Scudo. Same type as No. 58. Value $1.01.5.

61. S. 1839. Half scudo. Same type. Value 50.7 cts.

62. S. 1839. Lira. Obv. Bust, *laureated.* "FERD. I. D. G. AUSTRIÆ IMPERATOR." Rev. Same device as No. 59, with "LIRA AUSTRIACA" beneath. "LOMB. ET VEN. REX. A. A. 1839." Value 16.6 cts.

63. S. 1839. Half lira. Obverse same as preceding. Rev. Shield, with the arms arranged as in No. 58, surmounted by the ducal and imperial crowns, the latter surmounting the former; beneath is the denomination "½ LIRA." "LOMB. ET VEN. REX A. A. 1839." Value 8.3 cts.

64. S. 1839. Quarter lira. Same type. Value 4.2 cts.

65 and 66. S. 1848. Fifteen soldi, of the PROVISIONAL GOVERN-

MENT *of Venice.* Obv. The lion of St. Mark, supporting an open volume. "GOVERNO PROVVISORIO DI VENEZIA." Rev. The denomination "15." inclosed in a beaded circle. "CENTESIMI DI LIRA CORRENTÉ;" the date "1848" beneath.

ROME.

The popes of Rome exercise not only spiritual, but temporal jurisdiction over that portion of the Italian territory which extends for nearly half its length in an irregular strip northward along the borders of the Grand-Duchy of Tuscany and the Duchy of Modena, until it strikes the southern boundaries of Lombardy and Venice, but comprising in its main portion a large part of the center of Italy—its western coast being washed by the waters of the Mediterranean, and the eastern bordering upon the Adriatic Sea. In times gone by, here has been the seat of a power which has exercised a greater influence over the destinies of the world than any mere temporal government could ever hope to do. It has not only held within its grasp, and moulded for its own purposes, the physical powers of men, but their superstitions likewise; their spiritual and their worldly interests have found a common center and a common head at *Rome.*

The papal government is hard to characterize under any title which has yet been applied to governmental forms; but it approaches nearer to an *elective monarchy* than any other—the pope, who must be a cardinal in the church, being elected by his fellow-cardinals, and holding his office during life.

The year 1754 marked an epoch in the papal coinage. Previous to this time, the *scudo* or crown, which was the integer, was coined at the weight of 491.89 *Troy grains,* and 913 thousandths fine; but was then reduced to 408.48 *Troy grains* in weight, the same standard of fineness being retained.

The gold coins were the *sequin,* which was coined of fine gold, at the rate of 99 to the *libra* or pound weight, (the *libra* weighing 5234 *Troy grains,*) and of the legal value of 2.15 scudi; there was also the *doppia d'oro,* and its double and half, which were coined at 917 thousandths fine, and at the rate of 62 *doppia* to the *libra.*

After the reduction in standard of 1754, the silver coins consisted of the six denominations, of the *scudo*, which was divided into ten *paoli* (pauls), or 100 *bajocchi* (cents); the half scudo; the testoon, of three pauls; the piece of two pauls (called a *quinto*); the paul, of ten *bajocchi*, and its half. This was the state of the coinage up to 1798, the twenty-third year of the pontificate of PIUS VI. This pope took an active part in opposing the French Republicans, in return for which his territories were invaded in 1797, and himself taken prisoner the year following. Rome was erected into a republic, according to the French order of the day, and gold and silver coins issued, bearing appropriate devices and inscriptions. These pieces were a large gold coin called the *scudo d'oro*, weighing 910 grains, and 833 thousandths fine, and a silver *scudo*, weighing the same as the papal coinage, but reduced to the French standard of fineness. This coinage, being short lived, has become quite *rare*. The papal government having been reinstated in 1800, in the person of PIUS VII., who held his office, by a precarious tenure, until 1809, when his territories were wrested from him and annexed to the French Empire. This state of things lasted until the overthrow of the EMPEROR NAPOLEON in 1814, when PIUS was restored to the pontifical chair, and retained peaceable possession until his death in 1823. He was succeeded by LEO X., who reigned until 1829. From this date there was an interregnum of two years, until 1831, when GREGORY XVI. was elected. In this reign an important change took place in the coinage, the old system having been cast aside, and the coinage placed upon a decimal footing, both in its divisions and fineness. The gold coins, under this system, were the pieces of *ten*, *five*, and *two-and-a-half* scudi, the legal weight of the larger piece being 267.7 Troy grains, the smaller in proportion, and all nine-tenths fine. The silver coins were of the same denominations as before, the weight of the scudo being 415 *Troy grains*, the smaller in proportion, and nine-tenths fine.

A portion of the papal territory is comprised in the city and district of BOLOGNA, which enjoys the sovereign prerogative of coinage. The coins are of the same denominations and value as the papal coinage, being distinguished from the latter by the abbreviations

"BAN." or "BANON." and sometimes by the Latin name "BANONIA" in full. For two or three years, however, subsequent to 1795, a scudo was coined by the "PEOPLE AND SENATE OF BOLOGNA," which was of a different alloy from the scudo of Rome *proper*, being somewhat higher in value, (see No. 134,) and weighing 449 *grains.*

73. S. 1620. Scudo, of PAUL V. Obv. Bust, "PAULUS V. BURGHESIUS P(ontifex) MAX(imus) 1620." Rev. St. George and the dragon. "S(anctus) GEORGIUS. FERRARIA PROTECTOR."

74. S. 1675. Scudo, of CLEMENT X. Obv. Shield, bearing the papal arms, surmounted by two keys *in saltiere*, and the papal crown. "CLEMENT X PONT MAX." Rev. A tomb, with a cross upon its front; at the right side is ST. PAUL, bearing a sword in his right hand, and pointing backward toward the tomb with his left; on the left side is ST. PETER bearing two keys; beneath is a small shield, bedecked with a hat and tassels. "DABIT FRUCTUM SUUM IN TEMPORE." Beneath is inscribed the date "MDCLXXV."

75. S. 1685. Half paul, of INNOCENT XI. Obv. Arms and insignia of the pope. "INNOC. XI. P. M." Reverse not legible.

76. S. 1689. Half paul, SEDE VACANTE. Obv. Shield and cross-staff, backed by the cross of *Malta*, surmounted by the cap and tassels, two keys, and the church-banner "SEDE VACAN(te) A(nno) MDCLXXXIX." Rev. The sacred dove, surrounded by diverging rays, with the word "ROMA" beneath. "UBI V. V. ET SPIRAT."

77. S. 1690. Testoon, of ALEXANDER VIII. Obv. Bust, "ALEXAN VIII PONT. M. A(nno.) I." Beneath is the engraver's name, "HAMERANUS." Rev. A yoke of cattle drawing a plow among stalks of grain; beneath is the date "CIↃIↃCXC," and a shield bedecked with the hat and tassels. "RE TRURUENTARIA RESTITUTA."

78. G. 1709. Half sequin, of CLEMENT XI. Obv. Bust of ST. PETER, surrounded by diverging rays. "SANCTUS PETRUS. AP"(ostolus). Rev. Insignia and arms of the pope. "CLEM. XI P. M. A. IX."

79. S. 1710. Half paul, of same. Obverse same as the reverse of preceding. Rev. A shield, bearing the inscription "DATE ET DABITUR."

80. C. 1723. Half bajocchi, of INNOCENT XIII. Obv. A shield, bearing an eagle, and surmounted by the keys and papal crown. "INN. XIII P. M. A. II." Rev. "MEZO BAJOCCO," inscribed in three lines.

81. S. 1726. Half paul, of Benedict XIII. Obv. Same device as No. 79. "BENE XIII P. M. A. II." Rev. A sepulcher. "ANNO JUBIL;" beneath is the date "1725."

82. S. 1735. Testoon, of Clement XII. Obv. Bust, "CLEMENS XII P. M. AN V." Rev. Insignia and arms of the pope, with the date "1735" above.

83. S. 1735. Testoon, of same. Obv. Arms and insignia of the pope. "CLEMENS XII PONT. M. AN. V." Rev. A shield bearing the inscription, "URBE NOBILITATA MDCCXXXV." Above is a cherubim, and beneath a small shield, bearing a castle, and surmounted by the hat and tassels.

84. S. 1735. Paul, of same. Obverse same as preceding. Rev. The inscription "A. A. A. F. F. RESTITUTUM COMMERC," in four lines, between two palm branches. Beneath is a small shield, bearing a castle, and bedecked with the hat and tassels.

85. S. 1735. Half paul. Obverse same as No. 83. Rev. Bust of St. Peter, with his head surrounded by a glory. "S. PETRUS AP."

86. S. 1736. Testoon Obverse same as No. 83. Rev. "URE NOBILITATA MDCCXXXV." inscribed between two palm branches; a small shield beneath.

87. S. —. Paul. Obverse same as No. 83. "CLEMENS XII PONT. M. AN——" (not legible). Reverse same as No. 84.

88. S. 1738. Half paul. Obverse same as No. 83. Rev. "IN CIBAS PAUPERUM, 1738," inscribed between two branches of palm.

89. S. 1740. Half paul. Obverse same as No. 83. Rev. Shield, bearing the inscription, "HABETIS PAUPERES, 1739."

90. S. 1740. Half paul. Obverse same as No. 83. Rev. Shield, bearing the inscription, "IMPLETI ILLUSIO NIBUS, 1739."

91. G. Quarter sequin, of Benedict XIV. (1740 to 1758.) Obv. "BEN. XIV." inscribed beneath the papal crown, and two keys *in saltiere;* beneath are two palm branches, crossed. Rev. Bust of St. Peter. "S. PETRUS."

92. G. 1744. Sequin, of same. Obv. The Virgin Mary, seated upon a cloud, and holding two keys in her right hand, and a lantern in her left. "BENED. XIV P. M. 1744." Rev. Arms and insignia of the pope, surmounted by the sacred dove. "REPENTE DE CŒLO."

93. S. 1744. Half paul. Obverse same as No. 83, with "BENED. XIV PONT. M. A. IV." Rev. "OCULI EJUS IN PAUPEREM, 1744," inscribed in five lines, between two branches of laurel.

94. G. 1746. Half sequin. Same as No. 92.

95. S. 1754. Half paul. Obverse same as No. 93. Reverse *not legible.*

96. S. 1756. Two pauls. Obv. Bust, "BEN XIV. PON. M. A. XVII." Rev. Same device as No. 92, with the date "MDCCLVI." Value 20 cts.

97. S. 1763. Paul, of CLEMENT XIII. Obv. A shield, bearing the pope's family arms, surmounted by the papal crown and keys. "CLEM. XIII PONT. M. A. V." Rev. "ABLECTAT JUSTOS MISERICORDIA, 1763," inscribed in five lines; beneath is a small shield, surmounted by the hat and tassels, and bearing two batons *in saltiere;* the whole surrounded by a wreath of laurel. Value 10 cts.

98. S. 1765. Half paul. Obverse same as preceding. Rev. The inscription, "UTERE QUASI MOMO FUIGI, 1764." Value 5 cts.

99. S. 1774. Testoon, of CLEMENT XIV. Obv. The arms and insignia of the pope. "CLEMENS XIV PONT. MAX A. V." Rev. St. Peter and St. Paul confronting each other, the former holding his keys aloft in his right hand, and the latter supporting a sword, with the point resting upon the ground, in his right hand, and carrying a volume under his left arm; above is the sacred dove, and beneath is a small shield, bedecked with the hat and tassels, and the date "1773." Above, to the left, is inscribed "S. PETRUS," and to the right "S. PAULUS." Value 30 cts.

100. S. 1774. Two pauls. SEDE VACANTE. Obv. Shield and cross-staff, backed by the cross of *Malta,* and surmounted by the hat and tassels, two keys, and the church banner. "SEDE VACANTE. MDCCLXXIV." Rev. The sacred dove. Beneath is inscribed "QUINTO DI SCU"(do), and above, "VENI LUMEN CORDIUM." Value 20 cts.

101 and 102. S. 1775. Paul, of PIUS VI. Obv. The insignia and arms of the pope. "PIUS VI. PONT. M. A. I." Rev. A sepulcher, with the date "1775" beneath.* "MUNDI REVER TUNTUR." Value 10 cts.

---

* This piece bears upon its face an *apparent* discrepancy. PIUS VI. succeeded in 1774, and, upon examining the *obverse* of this piece, we find that it

103. S. 1777. Half scudo. Obv. Bust, "PIUS SEXTUS, PONT. M. A. III." Rev. The Virgin Mary, seated upon a cloud, and holding two keys in her right hand, and a lantern in her left; beneath is a small shield, bedecked with the hat and tassels. "AUXILIUM DE SANCTO, 1777." Value 52 cts.

104. S. 1780. Scudo. Obv. Arms and insignia of the pope. "PIUS SEXTUS PONT. M. A. VI." Reverse same as preceding. Value $1.04.4.

105. S. 1784. Two pauls. Same type as preceding. Value 10 cts.

106. S. 1788. Half paul. Obverse same as preceding. Rev. The inscription, "AUXILIUM DE SANCTO." No device. Value 5 cts.

107. S. 1796. Testoon. Obverse same as No. 104. Rev. St. Peter and St. Andrew, the latter leaning upon his cross and weeping, while St. Peter stands by his side holding the keys in his left hand, and pointing upward with his right; the sun's diverging rays above; beneath is the date "1796," and a small shield, bedecked with the hat and tassels. "SANCTUS PETRUS. SANCTUS ANDREAS." Value 30 cents.

108. S. 1796. Two pauls. Same type as No. 104. Value 20 cents.

109. S. 1801. Half scudo, of PIUS VII. Obv. Arms and insignia of the pope. "PIUS VII PONT. M. A. II." Reverse same as No. 103. Value $1.04.4.

110. G. 1803. Doppia. Obverse same as preceding. Rev. St. Peter seated upon a cloud, holding the keys in his left hand, and

---

purports to be struck in the *first year of his reign,* whereas upon the *reverse* it bears the date 1775, which is the *true* date of the coin. The explanation is found in the fact that PIUS did not succeed until the latter part of the year, his predecessor having died September twenty-second, after which a short interregnum ensued, as will be seen by referring to No. 100. Therefore the *year of his pontificate* did not expire until the latter part of 1775; and a coin which was actually struck in 1774, and another struck in the year following, can both be of the *first year of his reign.* Most of the papal coins bear no other date than the year of the reign, but where the contrary is the case, this discrepancy will often be noticed.

pointing upward with his right. "APOSTOLOR PRINCEPS;" beneath is a small shield, bedecked with the hat and tassels. Value $3.28.

111. S. 1816. Half paul. Obverse same as No. 109. Rev. The inscription, "PAUPERI PORRIGE MANUM," in three lines; beneath which, and divided from it by a sectional line, is the date "MDCCCXVI," and the initial "B." Value 5 cts.

112. S. 1818. Scudo. Same type as No. 103, with the inscription "IN TERRA PAX" on the edge. Value $1.05.8.

113. C. 1826. Half bajocchi, of LEO XII. Obv. Arms and insignia of the pope, with two olive branches, crossed; beneath, "LEO XII P. M. A. III." Rev. The inscription, "MEZZO BAJOCCO. ROM. 1826," in four lines.

114. C. 1826. Quatrino (quarter bajocchi). Same type as preceding.

115. S. 1830. Testoon. SEDE VACANTE. Obv. A shield, bearing a cock and a star, and surmounted by a cross-staff, hat, keys, and tassels, and the church banner; beneath is the name "ROMA." "SEDE VACANTE MDCCCXXX." Rev. The sacred dove, with "BAJ. 30" (30 bajocchi) beneath. "VENI LUMEN CORDIUM." Value 31.6 cts.

116 and 117. C. 1831. Bajocchi, of GREGORY XVI. Obv. Arms and insignia of the pope. "GREGORIUS XVI PONT. MAX. AN. I." Rev. "BAJOCCO ROMANO, 1831," inclosed in a wreath of laurel. Value one cent.

118 and 119. C. 1831. Half bajocchi. Same type.

120. S. 1834. Scudo. Obv. Bust, with the date "1834," and the engraver's name, "NIC. GERBARA," beneath; "GREGORIUS XVI PON. MAX A. IV." Rev. The circumcision of Jesus, *Simeon* receiving the infant Jesus from the hands of his mother, the Virgin Mary. In the background, to the right, is Joseph, carrying a basket containing two doves. ("*To offer a sacrifice according to that which is said in the law of the Lord, a pair of turtle doves, or two young pigeons.*" Luke, ii. 24.) To the left is the prophetess, Anna, with clasped hands, looking upon Jesus. ("*And she coming in that instant gave thanks likewise unto the Lord, and spake of him to all them that looked for redemption in Jerusalem.*"—Luke, ii. 38.) Beneath is the word "ROMA," and above, "LUMEN AD REVELATIONEM GENTIUM."

This sentence is rendered in the Protestant Bible as "*A light to lighten the Gentiles*," (Luke, ii. 32); while the Catholic Bible renders it, as in the inscription above, "*A light to the revelation* (or enlightenment) *of the nations*." (See the Gospel of ST. LUKE, chapter ii., 21st to 39th verses.) Value $1.05.7.

121. G. 1835. Five scudi. Obv. Bust, with the letter "R." (*Roma*) and the initials of the engraver, "N. G." beneath. "GREGORIUS XVI PON. MAX AN V." Rev. The denomination and date, "5 SCUDI, 1835," inclosed in a wreath of laurel. Value $5.19.4.

122. G. 1836. Ten scudi. Same type. Value $10.36.8.

123. G. 1836. Two-and-a-half scudi. Same type. Value $2.59.7.

124 and 125. C. 1848–1849. Bajocchi, of PIUS IX. Obv. Arms and insignia of the pope. "PIUS IX PON. MAX. ANN. III." Rev. the inscription, "BAJOCCO, 1848," inclosed in a wreath of laurel.

126. S. 1850. Piece of two pauls. Obv. Bust, with the engraver's name, "N. GERBARA," beneath; "PIUS IX PONT. MAX. ANN. IV." Rev. "20 BAJOCCHI, 1850," and the initial "R." inclosed in a wreath of laurel. Value 20 cts.

127 and 128. C. 1850. Half bajocchi. Same type as No. 124.

129. C. 1851. Two bajocchi. Same type.

130. C. 1854. Five bajocchi. Same type.

131. S. 1856. Five bajocchi. Obv. Arms and insignia of the pope. "PIUS IX PON. MAX ANN X." Rev. "5 BAJOCCHI, 1856, R." inscribed within a wreath of laurel.

CITY OF BOLOGNA.

132. S. 1778. Half paul. Obv. Shield, with the arms quartered, the abbreviated word "LIBER"(tas) occupying the second and third; beneath is the date "1778." Rev. A lily, with the letter "B"(ologna) and the numeral "5" in the *exerque*. "PIUS VI PONT. MAXIM." Value 5 cts.

133. S. 1783. Half scudo. Obv. Bust of the pope. "PIUS SEXTUS PONT. MAX. AN. VIII." Rev. A chapel, with a shield at each side, one surmounted by the hat and tassels, and the other by a lion's head; beneath is the name and date, "BONONIA, 1783," and the

numeral "50," (50 bajocchi,) and above, "ADVENTUS OPTI MI PRINCIPIS."

134. S. 1796. Scudo. Obv. Shield, bearing the arms quartered; a cross in the first and fourth, and the word "LIBERTAS" in the second and third quarters, inclosed between branches of laurel, and surmounted by a lion's head; beneath is "P. 10, (ten pauls,) 1796," and above, "POPULUS ET SENATUS BONON." Rev. The Virgin and child, upon a cloud, floating above the city. "PRÆSIDIUM ET DECUS." Value $1.13.

134. S. 1796. Half scudo. Same type as preceding.

135. S. 1797. Scudo. Same type.

SECTION VI.—TUSCANY.

The territory embraced in the Grand-Duchy of Tuscany at one time formed a large portion of ancient *Etruria*. Etruria was composed of several different divisions or tribes (twelve in number), which were all leagued together for the common defense, each being governed by a king, or *lucumo*. One of these was PORSENA, so famous from the league into which he entered for the purpose of restoring TARQUIN to Rome. The Etruscan territories afterward fell successively under the Romans, the Goths, the Lombards, and the government of Charlemagne. After the extinction of the Western Empire, Tuscany underwent various changes until the year 1531, when the whole became united under ALEXANDER DE MEDICIS, (at which time it was called *Florence*, the name of its capital city,) whose successor, COSMO I., assumed the title of grand-duke. The Medicis family remained in undisturbed possession of the throne until 1737, when the family became extinct by the death of JOHN GASTON, and the Grand-Duchy passed to the Emperor CHARLES VI., who conferred it upon his son-in-law, FRANCIS, Duke of Lorrain, with the title of FRANCIS III. Upon the accession of the latter to the throne of the German Empire in 1745,* he retained the sovereignty of Tuscany, adding his new titles to the legend on the

* Francis claimed the succession in 1740, but was not the actual emperor until the death of his competitor, CHARLES VII. of Bavaria, in 1745.

Tuscan coins. In 1792, FERDINAND III., a grandson of Francis, succeeded to the throne of Tuscany, and at the same time the French Revolution, which afterward involved all Europe, broke out. By the treaty of Luneville, in 1801, FERDINAND was deposed, and the State erected into a Kingdom, with its ancient title of *Etruria*, and LOUIS, a son of the Duke of Parma, placed upon the throne. This prince died in 1803, and his infant son succeeded, under the regency of the queen-mother, MARIA LOUISA. In 1808, the kingdom was dissolved and the territory annexed to the French Empire, though subject to the nominal rule of ELIZA, the sister of NAPOLEON. This was the condition of the State up to the overthrow of the latter, when the Grand-Duchy was restored, and FERDINAND recovered the throne of which he had been deprived for thirteen years, and continued in possession until his death in 1824, when he was succeeded by LEOPOLD II.

The gold coins of Tuscany are the *ruspone*, and the *zecchino gigliato*, or sequin. They are both meant to be of fine gold; the *ruspone* being coined at the rate of $32\frac{4}{9}$ pieces to the *libra*, or pound, which would place it at the weight of 161.5 *Troy grains*—the Tuscan libra weighing 5240 *Troy grains*. The *sequin* is one-third of the ruspone in weight and value.

The silver coins are somewhat intricate, from the fact that they have three different units or integers. The first series is based upon the *paul;* the second upon the *lira;* and the third upon the *florin*. The first series originated in 1738, and consisted of five pieces; the largest being the scudo, or crown of ten pauls, which was called after the names of the grand-dukes, first *Franciscone*, and afterward *Leopoldone*. The smaller pieces were of five, two, one, and one-half paul; the latter being divided into 40 *quattrini;* the legal fineness was 917 thousandths, and the weight of the scudo, 424.7 *Troy grains;* the others in proportion.

The second series was introduced in 1803, and consisted of the pieces of ten, five, one, and one-half livre; they were coined at 958 thousandths fine; the piece of ten livres weighing 608.8 *Troy grains;* the others in proportion. Coins of this series are now rare.

The last series was commenced in 1826, and consists of the florin, with its half and quarter. There are also the *base silver*, or billon piece, called a *crozia*, and the piece of *ten quattrini*. The copper coins are the pieces of five, three, and one *quattrini*. There are also the larger silver pieces of the double and quadruple florin.

1 and 2. S. —. Pontine coins, of the middle ages. The first has on its obverse a full-length figure, holding a staff in one hand and a truncheon in the other, and on the reverse, a figure of St. John the Baptist; and the second, on the reverse, a *fleur de lis*, and the name "FLORENTIA" (Florence), and on the reverse, St. John, with his cross-staff, and his name "S. JOHANNE. B"(aptista).

3. S. —. Testoon,* or piece of three pauls, of ALEXANDER DE MEDICIS, head of the ducal line in Tuscany; acquired the crown in 1531. Obv. Bust, "ALEXANDER M(edici) R(omanus) P(rinceps) FLOREN(tiæ) DUX." Rev. St. Cosmus and St. Damianus, conferring together; the latter holding an open volume in his hand. "S(anctus) COSMUS. S. DAMIÆNUS."

4. S. —. Testoon, of COSMUS II.† Obv. Bust, "COSMUS MED. R. P. FLOREN DUX. II." Rev. St. John the Baptist, seated, and holding a cross-staff in his left hand, and pointing upward with his right. "S. JOANNES BAPTISTA."

5 and 6. S. —. Same. Obv. Bust, "COSMUS MED. FLOREN ET SENARUM DUX. II." Rev. The City of Florence, with the Virgin Mary upon a cloud above it. "SENAVETUS CIVITAS VIRGINIS."

7. S. 1567. Same. Obverse same as preceding. Rev. St. John, with the date "1567" beneath. "S. JOANNES BAPTISTA."

8 and 9. S. 1575–77. Testoon, of FRANCIS II. Obv. Bust, "FRAN(ciscus) MED(ici) MAGN(us) DUX ETRURIÆ II." Reverse same as preceding.

10 and 11. S. 1621–36. Testoon, of FERDINAND II. Obv. Bust in armor. "FERD. II. MAGN. DUX ETR. V."‡ (The latter number indi-

---

* This name is used for the purpose of brevity.

† The successor of Alexander was Cosmus I.

‡ Kelly states, on page 211, in his "*Explication of Coin*," that this number, placed at the end of the *legend*, means the *year of the reign;* and gives us as an example a piece of COSMUS III. (See Nos. 13 to 17.) Upon examining a num-

cates that Ferdinand was the fifth of his name in the family.) Rev. St. John, holding a cross-staff in his left hand, and pointing upward with his right. "S. JOANNES BAPTIST."

12. S. 1665. Scudo, (*pezza della rosa.*) Obv. Crowned shield, bearing the arms of Tuscany, with the date "1665" beneath. Rev. "FERDINANDUS II. MAG. D. ETR. V."

13. S. 1677. Testoon, of COSMUS III. Obv. Bust, "COSMUS III D. G. MAG. D. ETRU VI." Rev. St. John, with a lamb reposing at his feet. "S. JOANNES BAPTIST."

14. S. 1680. Scudo. Obv. Bust, "COSMUS III D. G. MAG. DUX ETRURI VI;" beneath is the date "1680." Rev. The baptism of John, with the date "1681" beneath; above is the sacred dove. "FILIUS MENS DILECTUS."

15. S. 1692. Scudo, of same Obv. Bust, surmounted by a crown. "COSMUS III D. G. MAG. DUX ETRUR VI." Beneath is the date "1692." Rev. A harbor, with shipping, lighthouse, etc., and a city in the background. "ET. PATET ET FAVET."

16 and 17. S. 1706–18. Scudo (*pezza della rosa.*) Obv. Crowned shield, with the date "1706" beneath. "COSMUS III D. G. M. DUX ETRURIÆ." Reverse same as No. 12.

18. G. 1725. Sequin, of JOHN GASTON. Obv. A *fleur de lis.* "JOAN. GASTO I. D. G. M. DUX ETR." Rev. St. John. "S. JOANNES BAPTISTA." Beneath is the date "1725."

---

ber of coins of the same monarch, of different dates, the fact appears that the same number was used upon all; thus proving conclusively that Kelly is wrong. Referring to No. 13 above, we find a coin of Cosmus III., bearing the date 1667, with the number VI. at the end of the *legend.* We also find another coin, of 1680 —*three years later*—with the same number; and still another, of the date 1692, with the same number, and all struck during the reign of Cosmus III. And as a still further proof, to show that this could not have occurred through any mistake or accident, we have three coins of FERDINAND II., bearing the several dates of 1621, 1636, and 1665, (see Nos. 10, 11, and 12,) all of which have the number "V." at the end of the legend. From this state of facts, the most probable conclusion, and the one which is adopted above is, that it was intended to signify that FERDINAND was the *fifth Ferdinand* of the Medicis family; and second, as Duke of Tuscany.

19 and 20. S. 1748. Scudo, of FRANCIS III., *Duke of Lorrain.* Obv. Bust, *laureated.* "FRANCISCUS D. G. R(omanus) I(mperator) S(emper) A(ugustus) G(ermaniæ) H(ungariæ) REX, LOT(haringiæ) BAR(ri) M(agnus) D(ux) ETR"(uriæ). Rev. The Austrian double-eagle. "IN TE DOMINE SPERAVI." Beneath is the date "1748," and the name "PISIS" (meaning *Pisa.* This is the mint-mark, and appears on all the coins struck at the Pisa Mint). Value $1.08 each.

21. S. 1767. Scudo, of LEOPOLD. Obv. Bust, "PETRUS LEOPOLDUS D. G. P(rinceps) R(omani) H(ungariæ) ET B(ohemiæ) A(rchidux) A(ustriæ) M(agnus) D(ux) ETRUR." Rev. Shield, backed by the cross of Malta, and surmounted by a crown; arms of Austria, Lotharingia, and Tuscany, on a shield of pretence. "DIRIGE DOMINE GRESSUS MEAS." Beneath is the date "1767." Value $1.08.4.

22. S. 1769. Same. The date on this piece has been altered so as to read "1100."

23 and 24. S. 1770–74. Scudo. Same type as preceding Value $1.08.4.

25. S. 1782. Piece of two pauls. Obverse same as preceding. Rev. Small oval shield backed by the cross of Malta, surmounted by a crown, and encircled by the order chain and badge of the *golden fleece,* bearing the arms of Austria, Lotharingia, and Tuscany. Same legend as before. Value 21.6 cts.

26. S. 1783. Paul. Same type. Value 10.8 cts.

27. S. —. Half paul. Same type, with the shield displayed upon a mantle of ermine draped from a crown. (The date is illegible, and the legends nearly so.) Value 5 cts.

28. S. 1784. Scudo. Same as No. 21. Value $1.08.4.

29. S. 1795. Scudo, of FERDINAND III. Obv. Undraped bust, "FERDINANDUS III D. G. P. R. H. ET B. A. A. M. D. ETRUR." Rev. Crowned shield, backed by the star of Malta, and encircled by the order chain and badge of the *golden fleece.* "LEX TUA VERITAS." Value $1.08.

30. S. 1798. Scudo. Same type.

31. S. 1803. Scudo, of LOUIS I. Obv. Undraped bust, "LUDOVICUS I. D. G. HISP(aniarum) INF(ans) REX ETRURIÆ &"(cætera). Rev. Crowned shield, backed by the star of Malta, and bedecked

with the order chain and badge of the *golden fleece*, and three order stars; a shield of pretence and a heart shield; the first bearing the arms of Spain, and the second those of Anjou and Tuscany. "VIDEANT PAUPERES ET LÆTENTUR." Value $1.07.8.

32. C. 1804. Two soldi, of CHARLES LOUIS. Obv. Crowned shield, backed by the star of Malta, and bearing the arms of Anjou and Tuscany. "CAR. LUD. R(ex) ETR(uriæ) & M(aria) ALOYSIA R. RECTRIX." Rev. "UN DECIMO DI LIRA." "2 SOLDI 1804."

33 and 34. S. 1806–07. Scudo, of same. Obv. Busts of Louis and Maria, placed *vis-à-vis*, or facing each other. "CAROLUS LUD. D. G. REX ETR. & M. ALOYSIA R. RECTRIX I. I. H. H." Rev. Same device as No. 31. "DOMINE SPES MEA A JUVENTUTE MEA." Value $1.07.8.

35. S. 1820. Five pauls, of FERDINAND III. Obv. Undraped bust, "FERD III. D. G. P(rinceps) I(mperii) A(ustriæ) P(rinceps) R(egalis) H(ungariæ) ET B(ohemiæ) A(rchidux) A(ustriæ) M(agnus D(ux) ETR"(uriæ). Rev. Crowned shield, bearing the arms of Austria, Lotharingia, and Tuscany, and draped with the order chain and badge of the *golden fleece*, the order band and star of *Maria Theresia*, and the order band and star of the Tuscan order of St. Stephen. "LEX TUA VERITAS." Beneath is the name of the mint, "PISIS," and the date. Value 54 cts.

36 and 37. S. 1823. Half lira. Obv. A shield like preceding, draped with the order band and star of *Maria Theresia*. "FERD. III A(rciduca) D'A(ustria) G. D. (Granduca) DI TOSC"(ana). Rev. "MEZZA LIRA.——10 SOLDI," and the date "1823." Value 7.6 cts.

38. G. 1824. Sequin, of LEOPOLD II. Obv. A *fleur de lis*. "LEOPOLDUS II D. G. A(rchidux) A(ustriæ) M(agnus) D(ux) ETR." Rev. St. John, seated, holding a cross-staff in his left hand, and pointing upward with his right. "S. JOANNES BAPTISTA." Beneath is the date "1824." Value $2.30.

39. S. 1826. Florin. Obv. Undraped bust, "LEOPOLDO II. A. D'A. GRANDUCA DI TOSCANA." Rev. A *fleur de lis*, with the words "FLORINO" beneath, and "QUATTRINI CENTO, 1826," above. Value 27.3 cts.

40. B.S. 1826. Ten quattrini. Obv. Circular shield, surmounted

by a crown, and backed by the star of Malta. "LEOP. II A. D'A. GRAND. DI TOSC." Rev. The inscription, "10 QUATTRINI, 1826." Value 3 cts.

41. S. 1827. Half florin. Obv. Pointed shield, surmounted by a crown, and backed by the star of Malta. "LEOP. II A. D'A. GRAND. DI TOSC." Rev. "QUATTRINI 50. ½ FLORINO, 1827." Value 13.5 cts.

42. S. 1829. Double florin. Obv. Undraped bust, "LEOPOLDUS II D. G. P. I. A P. R. H ET B. A. A. MAGN DUX ETR." Rev. A pointed shield, suspended upon the cross of Malta, which is surmounted by a crown, and backed by two flag-staffs *in saltiere*, encircled by the order chain and badge of the *golden fleece*, and the banners depending from the flag-staffs. "SUSCEPTOR NOSTER DEUS." Beneath is the mint-mark "PISIS," and the date; on the edge is inscribed "DUB. FLORIN. CINQUE PAOLI." Value 55 cts.

43. C. 1829. Five quattrini. Obv. Crowned shield. "LEOP. II. A. D'A. GRAND. DI TOSC." Rev. "5 QUATTRINI, 1829."

44. C. 1832. Three quattrini. Same type.

45. C. 1832. One quattrini. Same type.

46. S. 1834. Quadruple florin. Obv. Undraped bust, "LEOPOLDUS II. D G. P. I. A. P. R. H ET B. A. A MAGN. DUX ETR." Rev. Shield, surmounted by a crown, backed by the cross of Malta, and encircled by the order chain of the *golden fleece;* a shield of pretence, crowned, and bearing the arms of Austria, Lotharingia, and Tuscany. "SUSCEPTOR NOSTER DEUS." Beneath is the mint-mark and date, "PISIS—1834." On the edge is inscribed "QUATTRO FLORINI—DIECI PAOLI." Value $1.09.3.

47. S. 1843. Half florin. Obv. Undraped bust, "LEOP. II. D. G. P(rinceps) R(egalis) H. ET B. A. A. M. D. ETR." Rev. An oval shield, surmounted by a crown, backed by the cross of Malta, and encircled by the order chain and badge of the *golden fleece.* "SUSCEPTOR NOST DEUS." Beneath is the date "1843." Value 13.5 cts.

LUCCA AND PIOMBINO.

48. S. 1743. Scudo. Obv. Crowned shield, bearing the word "LIBERTAS;" two palm branches, crossed. "RESPUBLICA LUCENSIS." Beneath is the date "1743." Rev. A man, in ragged attire, beside a

mounted knight, who is in the act of throwing his mantle over the former. "SANCTUS MARTINUS."

49 and 50. S. 1807–08. Five francs, of FELICE and ELISA. Obv. Their busts in profile, the latter upon the former. "FELICE ED ELISA P. P. DI LUCCA E PIOMBINO." Rev. "5 FRANCS," inclosed in a wreath of laurel. "PRINCIPATO DI LUCCA E PIOMBINO." Beneath is the date "1807." Value 97 cts.

51. S. 1807. One franc. Same type. Value 19.4 cts.

PARMA.

56. S. 1628. Scudo, of ODOARDUS V. Obv. Bust in armor. "ODOARDUS. FAR(nese) PL(acentiæ) ET PAR(mæ) DUX V." Rev. St. Anthony, supporting a flag-staff. "S(anctus) ANTONINUS M(ajor) PROT(ector) PLAC"(entiæ). Beneath is the date "1628," and the initials "L.——X" (ten lire).

57. G. 1786. Doppia, of FERDINAND I. Obv. Head, "FERDINANDUS I. HISPANIAR(um) INFANS." Rev. Crowned shield, bearing the arms of Parma, with a shield of pretence; and a heart shield, bearing the arms of Spain and Anjou; branches of laurel at either side. "D. G. PARMA PLAC(entiæ) ET VASTAL(iæ) DUX 1786."

58. G. 1815. Forty lire, of MARIA LUCIA. Obv. Bust, with the date "1815" beneath. "MARIA LUICIA PRINC. IMP. ARCID. D'AUSTRIA." Rev. Shield, bearing the ducal arms, with the arms of Austria on a shield of pretence, displayed upon a mantle of ermine draped from a crown, and encircled by the order chain and badge of St. George. "PER. LA GR. DI DIO DUCH. DI PARMA. PIAC(enza) E GUAST"(ala). Beneath is a scroll, bearing in indented letters the denomination "40 LIRE." On the edge is inscribed "DIRIGE ME DOMINE." Value $6.66.

59. S. 1815. Five lire. Same as preceding. Value 97 cts.

60. S. 1815. Lira nuova. Same type. Value 19.4 cts.

61. S. 1815. Ten soldi. Obv. Bust, "M. LUICIA PRIN. IMP. ARCID D'AUS." Rev. The initials "M. L." interlaced, and surmounted by a crown. "PER. LA GR. DI DIO DI PARMA P. G." Beneath is the denomination "10 SOLDI."

62. S. 1815. Five soldi. Same as preceding.

NAPLES AND SICILY.

In order to gain a thorough knowledge of the coins of the two Sicilies, it is highly necessary to be perfectly familiar with their history. The various changes and divisions and reunions which they have experienced has produced a confusion in the devices and inscriptions on their coins which is well calculated to mislead the young numismatist; while at the same time it would appear that the relative value and relation of the pieces to one another has been but little affected by their political vicissitudes. The legend HISPANIARUM INFANS, which has always found a place upon the coin whenever the house of Aragon has found a seat on the throne, has, doubtless, often led unskillful persons into the error of classing Neapolitan coins among those of Spain.

The first division between the Island of Sicily and the Peninsular territory occurred near the end of the reign of CHARLES, of Anjou, who reigned from 1266 to 1285. In the year 1282, PETER III. of *Aragon*, invaded Sicily, on account of the massacre, called *the Sicilian* VESPERS, and was crowned *King of Sicily* at Palermo. They remained in this state, under the two houses of Anjou and Aragon, up to 1435, when ALPHONSO I—who inherited the crowns of Aragon and Sicily from FERDINAND, of *Castile*, in 1416—succeeded JANE II. in Naples. He was opposed, however, by RENATUS, *of Anjou*, but appealed to arms, and finally triumphed over his rival. Upon his death, in 1458, his dominions were divided, according to the provisions of his last will and testament, between his natural son FERDINAND, and his brother JOHN; the former receiving Naples, and the latter, Aragon and Sicily. This distinction lasted until 1504, at which time FERDINAND, *the Catholic*, King of Spain, whose reign commenced in Sicily and Aragon in 1479, also took possession of Naples, driving FERDINAND III. from the throne, and compelling him to take refuge in France, where he died. FERDINAND, *the Catholic*, died in 1516, and was succeeded by CHARLES I. of Spain. The latter afterward became the famous Emperor CHARLES V., and through him Naples and Sicily passed into the house of Austria, where they remained until 1700, when, by the will of CHARLES V., *King of Spain*, it passed, in common with the rest of the Spanish monarchy, to PHILIP IV. *of Bourbon,* grandson to LOUIS XIV. of France. This movement, however, met with a determined opposition from the house of Hapsburg. The "*war of the Spanish succession*" ensued; and in 1707, a conspiracy procured the throne of Naples for PRINCE CHARLES, Archduke of Austria, and son of the Emperor LEOPOLD. By the treaty of Utrecht, in 1713, Charles was confirmed as King of Naples, and VICTOR AMADÆUS II., Duke of Savoy, was made King of Sicily, under the protection of QUEEN ANNE, of Great Britain. But the King of Spain having invaded the island, a treaty of peace was made in 1718, by which AMADÆUS exchanged the Island of Sicily for that of Sardinia, and Sicily again returned to the house of Bourbon. Soon after, Naples fell to the same house, the ARCHDUKE having been deposed by CHARLES, second son of the King of Spain, in 1735, who ascended the throne of Naples and Sicily, with the title of CHARLES VII. In 1739, CHARLES being called to the throne of Spain, vacated that of Naples, and was succeeded by his son FERDINAND. This monarch bore the two titles of FERDINAND IV. of Naples, and III. of the Island of Sicily. The latter title did not, however, appear upon the coins before his first deposal by Napoleon in 1799, but simply the name FERDINAND. But this difference serves to distinguish the coins of Sicily from those of the Peninsula; the latter having always borne the title FERDINAND IV. up to the time of his second restoration. Having joined in the alliance against France, FERDINAND was expelled from Naples in 1799, and his kingdom erected into the *Neapolitan*, or *Parthenopian Republic*, and silver coins of the denominations of the *ducat royal of twelve carlini*, and its half were issued, bearing appropriate devices, but were not dated, having merely the year of the French Republic, as "ANNO SETTIMO DELLA LIBERTA." (*The seventh year of liberty.*) In 1801, Ferdinand made a treaty, by which he recovered his dominions, thus putting a period to the republican coinage. The currency having now become somewhat depreciated, Ferdinand determined to call it in for recoinage; but before the work had been fairly commenced, he again made war upon France, and, in 1805, was a second time driven from the Neapolitan throne and compelled to retire to the Island of Sicily, where he established his court, and was permitted to continue in power; Joseph Napoleon being placed upon the throne of Naples. The latter made no alteration in the composition of the coins, contenting himself with a change in the devices; his head being placed upon the obverse, with his name and a portion of his titles; and on the *reverse* the remainder of his titles and his family arms. In 1808, this prince was transferred to the throne of Spain, and Joachim, Prince Murat, was placed upon the Neapolitan throne. The old system of money was retained until 1813, when the French standards were introduced, (the *lira* corresponding with the *franc.*) Two years after, the power of Napoleon came to an end, and the re-arrangement of Europe, which then took place, not only deprived Joachim of his transitory title, but of his life also.

Ferdinand, finding himself again reinstated upon the throne of the Two Sicilies, assumed the title of Ferdinand I.; doubtless intending thereby to consolidate the two governments into one, and by rendering the union between the two parts more intimate, to strengthen his own title; thus the coins of this monarch are found to bear the several titles of Ferdinand, and Ferdinand III.,* IV., and I. He abolished the French system of moneys, and in 1818 a new system was established, restoring the former standards, with some modifications in the gold. Since this time no material change has taken place. In 1826, Ferdinand was succeeded by Francis I., who reigned until 1830, when he was succeeded by Ferdinand II. The latter continued to exercise a tyrannical rule until 1859, when he died amid the rejoicings of his subjects, and was succeeded by his son Francis II., the reigning monarch.†

The Neapolitan coins at present under consideration commence with those of Charles II. of Spain (or V. of Naples), who reigned

---

* A Sicilian coin of 1810 bears this title.

† The latter prince, who has proved to be as great a tyrant, without half the firmness and discretion of his father, is now threatened with expulsion from his throne at the hands of his outraged subjects, led on by Garibaldi; having already lost his dominion over Sicily.

from 1665 to 1700. At this time the gold coins consisted of the pieces of 6, 4, and 2 ducats. The principal silver piece was the ducat royal, or *ducato di regno* (the gold pieces being the multiples of this), which was divided into 12 carlini, the carlini consisting of 10 *grani* or grains, making the different denominations of the ducat and its half, or piece of six carlini, and the pieces of five, three, two, one, and one-half carlini. There has also been a ducat of 10 carlini issued. The ducat of 12 carlini is found to weigh about 442 *grains Troy*, as taken from the circulation. The smaller pieces appear to have been in proportion. This system, with various modifications in the weight and fineness of the pieces, was continued up to the time of the introduction of the French system before mentioned.

On the island the principal gold piece was the *onzia* of 30 *tari*, the tara being equivalent to the carlino of the peninsula. The silver was of the same denominations as the peninsular coinage, but are easily distinguished from them, as the different pieces bear the marks T. 12, T. 6, T. 2, etc., meaning so many *tari*, whereas the peninsular coins are generally found to bear the amount of their value in grains, as so many *grana*—the ducat royal being marked "G. 120."

67. S. 1680. Two carlini, of CHARLES V. (II. of Spain.) Obv. Crowned shield, with the arms of Spain in the first quarter, encircled by the order chain of the *golden fleece*. "CAROLUS II. D. G. HISP NEAP. REX." Rev. The world, with the date "1680" upon its lower edge; above is a fasces and a cornucopia, the whole being surmounted by a crown. "HIS VICI ET REGNO."

Charles, although the Fifth of Naples, struck coins for his Italian possessions bearing his Spanish title of CHARLES II. He was the last of the house of Austria upon the Spanish throne, Spain having passed, upon his death, in 1700, into the house of Bourbon.

68. S. 1789. Two carlini, of same. Obv. Bust, "CAROLUS II D. G. REX HIS." Rev. Crowned shield, with the badge of the *golden fleece* beneath. "UTRIUS(que) SIC(iliæ) HIERUS(olymæ) G(rana) XX."

69. S. 1691. Two carlini, of same. Obv. Bust, surmounted by a crown. "CAR. II. D. G. REX HISP. ET NEAP." Rev. A shield, bearing the badge of the *golden fleece*, and the date and value, "16-91," and "G. XX."

70. S. 1693. Five carlini. Same type.

71. S. 1696. Two carlini. Same type.

72. S. 1734. Half ducat, of PRINCE CHARLES, *Archduke of Austria* (Naples). Obv. Crowned shield, bearing the arms of Naples, Castile, Aragon, Parma, and Tuscany, with the arms of Anjou on a shield of pretence. "CAR. D. G. REX. NEAP. HISP. INFANS. ETC." Rev. Aquarius, with water, and a volcano in the background. "DE SOCIO PRINCEPS." Beneath is the date "1734."

73. S. 1735. Ducat. Same as preceding.

74. S. 1736. Ducat. Same type.

This coin, from its date, appears to have been struck by the Archduke CHARLES, after his deposal by the Spanish prince, CHARLES VII., which occurred in 1735......It is curious to note the various *charges* upon the shield of CHARLES (Archduke). He seems to have considered his claims to a throne, as well as the actual occupation of it, a sufficient reason for the adoption of the family arms. Thus, he places upon his Neapolitan coins the arms of Aragon and Castile, together with the title HISPANIARUM INFANS, because CLEMENT XI. had acknowledged his right to the crown of Spain (through compulsion). He assumes, upon the same coin, the arms of Tuscany, because he had conquered the sea-coasts of Tuscany. But why he should assume the arms of Anjou, is somewhat inexplicable, as he claimed descent, in the direct line, from CONTRAN, *Count of Hapsburg*, and therefore could have little claim to a Bourbon pedigree. At the same time, it is still more strange that on no Neapolitan coin which has yet been noticed here, does this prince acknowledge his Hapsburg descent, although he was afterward indebted to that descent for the emperorship of Germany.

75. S. 1736. Half ducat, of CHARLES VII. Obv. Bust, *laureated.* "CAROLUS D. G. SIC. ET HIER(osolymæ) REX HIS(paniarum) INF"(ans). Rev. A double cross *moline;* three limbs surmounted by crowns; *fleur de lis* in the angles. "FAUSTO CORONA–TIONIS ANNO......1736."

76. S. 1738. One tara (Sicily). Obv. Bust, *laureated.* "CAR. D. G. SIC ET HIER REX HIS. IN." Rev. A crowned eagle. "FAUSTO CORONAT. ANNO......1738."

77. S. 1750. Ducat. (Naples.) Obv. Bust, bedecked with the

cross of Malta. "CAR. D. G. UTR(iusque) SIC. ET HIER REX." Rev. A crowned shield, charged as in No. 72. "HISPANIAR INFANS, 1750."

78 and 79. S. 1750. Half ducat (Naples). Same type as preceding.

80. G. 1751. Ouzia. (Sicily.) Obv. Bust, *laureated.* "CAROLUS D. G. SIC. ET HIE. REX." Rev. A phœnix issuing from the flames; above are the sun's diverging rays. "RE-SU-RCIT." Beneath the phœnix is the date "1751."

81. G. 1768. Piece of six ducats (Naples), of FERDINAND IV. Obv. Bust, bedecked with the badge of the *golden fleece.* "FERDINAN. IV D. G. SICIL. ET HIER. REX." Rev. An oval shield, surmounted by a crown, and inclosed between branches of palm and laurel, crossed; the badge of the *golden fleece* and the star of Malta suspended beneath. "HISPANIAR INFANS." At either side of the shield, beneath the crown, are the initials C. R. and C. Beneath is the date "1768," and at one side, above the date, is the initial D., and at the other, the numeral "6," meaning *six ducats.* Value $5.19.

82. C. 1780. Grană. Obv. Bust, "FERDINAN. IV SICILIAR. REX." Rev. "UN GRANO CAVALLI, G.—12—C—1780."

83. S. 1785. Ducat, of 100 *grani.* Obv. Bust, "FERDINAN. IV D. G. SICILIAR. ET HIE. REX." Rev. Crowned shield, between branches of palm and laurel, crossed. "HISPANIAR. INFANS 1785." Beneath is the denomination. "DUCATO G(rani) 100." Value 82 cts.

84. S. 1791. Carlin. Obv. Bust, "FERDINAN IV SICIL. REX." Rev. A cross *rayonant botonè* (that is, a cross botonè, or budded, with rays issuing from its angles). "IN HOC SIGNO VINCES." Beneath is the date "1791." Value 8.2 cts.

85. S. 1795. Ducat. Obverse same as No. 83. Rev. A shield like No. 77, draped with laurel. Beneath is the value "G. 120," and a palm and laurel branch, crossed. "HISPANIAR. INFANS. 1795." Value 98.6 cts.

86. S. 1795. Two carlini. Obverse same as No. 83. Rev. A crown, inclosed between branches of laurel, crossed; above are the initials "A. P." and beneath, the value, "G. 20." "HISPANIAR. INFANS. 1795." Value 16.4 cts.

87. S. 1795. Carlin. Same type as No. 84.

88. S. 1796. Three tari. (Sicily.) Same type as No. 75. Value 24.6 cts.

89. S. 1798. Ducat. (Sicily.) Obv. Bust, "FERDINAN. D. G. SICIL. ET HIER. REX." Rev. An eagle, with the shield upon its breast. "HISPANIARUM INFANS." Beneath is the date "1798." Value 98.6 cents.

90. C. 1798. Ten tornesi. Obv. Undraped bust, "FERDINAN. IV SICILIAR. REX." Rev. "TORNESI 10," and the initials "R." and "C." surmounted by a crown. Beneath is the date "1798."

91. S. —. Ducat, of the REPUBLIC. (1799–1802.) Obv. The goddess of Liberty, holding in her right hand a staff, surmounted by the liberty-cap, and supporting a fasces with her left. "REPUBLICA NAPOLITANA." Rev. "CARLINI DODICI," inclosed in a wreath composed of two oak branches, crossed. "ANNO SETTIMO DELLA LIBERTA." Value 98.6 cts.

92. S. —. Half ducat. Same type. (Rev. "CARLINI SEI.") Value 49.3 cts.

93 and 94. S. 1805. Ducats, of FERDINAND. Obv. Bust, with the date "1805" beneath. "FERDINANDUS IV D. G. REX." Rev. A pointed shield, charged as in No. 72, and surmounted by a crown. Beneath, at one side of the shield, is the initial L. and D. at the other. "UTR. SIC. HIER. HISP. INF."......"G. 120." The rim of the pieces, bearing the legends, value, and date, is slightly raised above the surface of the field. On the edge is inscribed "PROVIDENTIA OPTIMI. PRINCIPIS." Value 98.6 cts.

95 and 96. S. 1808. Ducats, of JOSEPH NAPOLEON. Obv. Head, "JOSEPH NAPOL. D. G. UTR. SICIL. REX." Rev. A crowned shield, with two fields; two cornucopias, crossed, and a dolphin in the upper field, and three legs in the lower; a shield of pretence, surmounted by a crown, and bearing the French eagle; at either side is a mermaid, one holding an anchor, and the other the paddle or rudder of *Aquarius*. "PRINC. GALLIC. MAGN. ELECT. IMP." Beneath is the date "1808," and the value "G. 120." On the edge are six dolphins, and the inscription "CUSTUS REGNI DEUS." Value 98.9 cts.

97 and 98. S. 1809–1810. Ducat, of JOACHIM NAPOLEON. Obv. Undraped bust, "GIOACCHINO NAPOL. RE DELLIE DUE SICILIE." Rev.

"DODICI CARLINI 1809," inclosed in a wreath composed of wheat and laurel. "PRINCIPE E GRAN. D'AMMIRAGLIO DI FRANCIA." Value 98.4 cents.

99. S. 1810. Ducat, of FERDINAND. (Sicily.) Obv. Bust, "FERDINANDUS III D. G. REX." Beneath is the value "TARI 12." The legend is on a raised rim as in Nos. 93 and 94. Rev. An eagle, inclosed in an olive wreath. "UTR. SIC. HIER. INFANS HISP." Beneath is the date "1810." Value 98.2 cts.

100. C. 1810. Two grani, of JOACHIM NAPOLEON. Obv. Head, "GIOACCHINO NAPOLEONE RE DELL. DUE SICIL." Rev. "GRANA 2," inclosed in a wreath of laurel. "PRIN. E GRAN D'AMMI. DI FRAN." Beneath is the date "1810."

101. G. 1813. Twenty lire. Obv. Head, with the date "1813" beneath. "GIOACCHINO NAPOLEONE." Rev. "20 LIRE," inscribed between branches of olive and laurel, crossed. "REGNO DELLE DUE SICILIE." Value $3.84.8.

102. S. 1813. One lira. Same type as preceding. Value 19.4 cents.

103. C. 1815. One tara, of FERDINAND. (Sicily.) Obv. Head, surmounted by a crown. "FERD. III. P. F. A. SIC. ET HIER. REX." Beneath is the date "1815." Rev. A bunch of grapes, the initial V. at one side, and B. at the other. Beneath is the value "G. 1."

104 and 105. S. 1818. Ducats, of FERDINAND I. Obv. Head, surmounted by a crown. "FERD. I. D. G. REGNI SICILIARUM ET HIER. REX." Beneath is the date "1818." Rev. Crowned shield, draped with eight order chains. "HISPANIARUM INFANS," and the value "G. 120." On the edge is inscribed "PROVIDENTIA OPTIMI PRINCIPIS." Value 99.2 cts.

106. S. 1818. Half ducat. Same type as preceding. Value 49.6 cents.

107. S. 1818. Carlin. Obverse same as preceding. Rev. A crowned shield, with a stalk of wheat at each side, and bedecked with the order chains and badges of the *golden fleece*, *St. George*, and *Malta*, (the others being omitted.) Same legend as preceding. Value 8.2 cents.

108. C. 1825. Ten tornesi, of FRANCIS I. Obv. Head, "FRANCIS-

CUS I. D. G. REGNI UTR. SIC. ET HIER. REX." Rev. "TONESI DECI," surmounted by a crown. Beneath is the date "1825."

109. C. 1827. Five tornesi. Same type as preceding.

110. G. 1831. Piece of six ducats, of FERDINAND II. Obv. Head, with the date "1831" beneath. "FERDINANDUS II. DEI GRATIA REX." Rev. An angel standing beside an altar, on which she is placing a crown with her right hand, while she supports an oval shield, bearing three *fleurs de lis*, with her left. "REGNI UTR. SIC. ET HIER." Beneath is inscribed "ACINI 170. TITOLO MILLESIMI 996. DUCATI 6."

111 and 112. S. 1831–1837. Ducat, of same. Obverse same as preceding. Rev. Crowned shield, with the value "G. 120" beneath. "REGNI UTR. SIC. ET HIER." On the edge is inscribed "PROVIDENTIA OPTIMI PRINCIPIS." Value 98.8 cts.

113. S. 1840. Two carlini. Same type. Value 16.4 cts.

114. S. 1857. Ducat. Same as No. 111. Value 98.8 cts.

ISLAND OF MALTA.

This island was formerly under the dominion of the Knights of Malta, CHARLES V. of Naples and Sicily having granted it, in 1522, to the "*Order of St. John of Jerusalem.*" The Knights continued in possession until 1798, when it was seized by NAPOLEON. It was afterward conquered by Lord NELSON, and annexed to the crown of Great Britain, to which it now belongs.

115. S. 1737. Scudo, of 12 tarins, of FRANCIS XIMENES, *Grand Master.* Obv. Bust, "FR(ater) D(on) FRANCISCUS XIMENEZ DE TEXADA M"(agister). Rev. Crowned shield, with the arms quartered; above, at one side of the crown, is "17," and at the other side "73," and beneath, at one side, the letter S., and, at the other, J. (*Sanctus Johannes.*)

116. S. —. Half scudo, of 6 tarins, of EMANUEL DE ROHAN. Obv. An eagle, with his head and body hidden by a crowned shield, bearing the arms *quartered.* "F(rater) EMANUEL DE ROHAN. M(agnus) M(agister) H(ospitalis) S"(ancti). Rev. The denomination "T. VI." (six tari,) and the date, (illegible,) inclosed in a wreath composed of palm and laurel branches, crossed.

DIVISION XII.

RUSSIA.

It seems a little singular that a nation whose dominion extends over a greater area than any other power, and which is now ranked as one of the first of the great nations of the world, should have little or no ancient history. In fact, the authenticated history of Russia extends no farther back than the middle of the twelfth century. It is true, that glimpses of earlier periods are presented by various authors, but their statements and surmises are so much in dispute as to be of little credit. The only point in which all seem to concur is, that RURICK was "Prince of all Russia" about the year 862 of the present era. From this time until the accession of ANDREW I., who commenced the dynasty of the Princes of Wladimir in 1157, some seven generations elapsed, during which time the number of the princes and the order of their succession is so much in dispute that chronologers usually omit the whole period.

Before the accession of IVAN BASILOWITZ IV. in 1534, the different sovereigns bore the title of *Welike Knex*, "Great Prince;" but IVAN added the title of *Tsar* or *Czar*, "King." The title of *emperor* was first assumed by PETER I., *the Great*, near the close of his reign, in the year 1721.

The house of *Romanow* ascended the throne in 1613, and continued in possession until 1762, when the house of *Holstein* acquired the crown by the person of PETER III. The reign of this prince, however, was of short duration, lasting only six months, when he was succeeded by his wife, CATHERINE II., who had caused PETER to be murdered. The succession since this time has been as follows: CATHERINE II., from 1762 to 1796; PAUL I., to 1801; ALEXANDER I., to 1825; NICHOLAS, to 1855; ALEXANDER, reigning sovereign.

The unit of value in Russia is the *rouble*, which is divided into 100 cents, or *copecks*. The gold coins are the *imperial*, of ten roubles; the half-imperial, or piece of five roubles; the piece of three roubles, and the one-rouble piece. Formerly there was a still smaller piece called a *poltina*, or half rouble. The piece of three roubles, however, is the only piece found in circulation.* The legal standards of the imperial are 917 thousandths fineness, and 201.75 Troy grains in weight; the smaller pieces in proportion.

The silver coins are the denominations of the rouble and its subdivisions, which are the pieces of 75, 50, 30, 25, 20, 15, 10, and 5 copecks; and, since 1832, the piece of one-and-a-half roubles. Formerly there was also the double rouble, but this was long since discontinued. The legal standards of the coined silver rouble are 875 thousandths fineness, and 319.6 Troy grains in weight; the other denominations in proportion.

The copper coinage comprises the pieces of 10, 5, 3, 2, 1, $\frac{1}{2}$, and $\frac{1}{4}$ copecks.

In the third year of the reign of Nicholas (1828), a decree was issued, authorizing the coinage of *platinum* in pieces of three roubles; and in the following year the piece of six roubles, and in 1830, a third piece of the denomination of twelve roubles were ordered. This experiment in the art of coinage was looked upon at the time with much interest, as heralding the advent of a new circulating medium; the metal being at that time comparatively new, although its existence had long been known. It was first discovered by an assayer named Wood, in Jamaica, in the year 1741. The experiment, however, proved a failure, from the fact that *platinum*, although containing all the properties which should class it as a precious metal, is insensible to furnace heat, and could only be worked by welding, which facts rendered it quite unsuitable for the purposes of coinage. Another difficulty was also found in the scarcity of the metal, which rendered its market value very unsteady. The platinum for this coinage was obtained from the mines in the *Ural* Mountains. No coins of this metal have appeared here of a later date than 1837, about which time its use was doubtless discontinued.

In 1832 a new series of silver coins was decreed, which were intended for circulation both in Russia and her dependency, Poland.

---

* Letter of John Ralli, Esq., U. S. Consul at Odessa, to the Treasury Department, May, 1859.

The Russian rouble and the Polish zloty are in such a relation to each other that one-and-a-half roubles are equivalent to ten zloty; a relation which is not arbitrary or forced, but which, on the contrary, has long existed. In order to strengthen the union and render the intercourse between the two countries more intimate and simple, a series of coins were struck, of which the ten-zloty piece was the principal, bearing both their Russian and Polish value; the former being inscribed in Russian, and the latter in Roman characters.

The principal difficulty experienced by the American numismatist in the study of Russian coins, will doubtless be found in the fact that the inscriptions are all in Russian characters; and as the Russian is a language which is little known in this country, or, in fact, even in Europe (outside of the Russian Empire), it is difficult to understand the most interesting as well as the most necessary portion of the study in question. In the present instance, we have been relieved from this embarrassment, through the kindness of the HON. WM. D. LEWIS, formerly Minister to Russia, who has generously assisted us by translating the inscriptions; and as MR. LEWIS is known to be a thorough Russian scholar, the reader may rest assured that the translations given in the following pages are perfectly reliable.

1. S. —. Rouble, of PETER I., *the Great.* Obv. Bust, in armor, partially enveloped in a military mantle, *laureated.* "TSAR. (*Czar*) PETER ALEKSAIEVICH. (son of Alexander) AUTOCRAT OF ALL THE RUSSIAS." Rev. The imperial Russian eagle, surmounted by a crown, and grasping a scepter in the dexter, and the imperial globe in the sinister talon. "NEW COIN; VALUE OF ONE ROUBLE." This piece was struck prior to the year 1721, as all the coins of PETER since that date bear the title of *Emperor.* Value 88 cts.

2. S. 1722. Double rouble, of PETER, *the Great.* Obv. Bust in armor, as in the rouble (No. 1). "PETER A(leksaievich) EMPEROR AND AUTOCRAT OF ALL THE RUSSIAS." Rev. Four Russian P's and four crowns, arranged as a cross, with 1's in the angles; the date "1722;" (the 17 being inscribed in one P, and the remainder 22 in another.) "NEW COIN; VALUE OF TWO ROUBLES." Value $1.76.

3 and 4. S. 1725. Roubles, of PETER, *the Great.* Obv. Bust, in armor, as on the rouble No. 1. "PETER A. EMPEROR AND AUTOCRAT

OF ALL THE RUSSIAS." Reverse same as the reverse of the double rouble (No. 2). "NEW COIN; VALUE OF ONE ROUBLE." Value 88 cts. each.

5. S. 1729. Rouble, of PETER II. Obv. Bust, in armor, *laureated.* "PETER II EMPEROR AND AUTOCRAT OF ALL THE RUSSIAS." Reverse same as the reverse of the roubles of PETER, *the Great* (Nos. 3 and 4). "NEW COIN; VALUE OF ONE ROUBLE." Value 88 cts.

6 and 7. S. 1732 and '34. Roubles, of ANNA. Obv. Bust of the empress, surmounted by a small crown. "BY THE GRACE OF GOD, ANNA, EMPRESS AND AUTOCRAT OF ALL THE RUSSIAS." Rev. The imperial Russian eagle, with a shield upon its breast, bearing the arms —St. George and the dragon. "MONEY; ROUBLE, 1732—4." Value 88 cts each.

8. S. 1735. Ten copecks, or "*Grevenneek*," of ANNA. Obv. The imperial Russian eagle. Rev. Ten pellets, and the Russian name "GREVENNEEK." Beneath a sectional line is the date "1735."

The pellets found on many of the small coins of Russia, and which denote the value of the piece in copecks, are for the enlightenment of the serfs, and others who are unable to read. They can ascertain the value of the piece by counting the pellets.

9. S. 1739. Fifteen copecks, of ANNA. Obv. Bust of the empress. "ANNA, BY THE GRACE OF GOD, EMPRESS AND AUTOCRAT OF ALL THE RUSSIAS." Rev. Martial emblems, standards, cannon, etc., upon which is an eagle with expanded wings, holding in its beak a laurel wreath; above is inscribed, "GLORY TO THE EMPIRE;" and beneath are the mint-marks and date "1739."

10. S. 1747. "Grevenneek," of ELIZABETH I. Obv. Bust of the empress. "BY THE GRACE OF GOD, ELIZABETH I. EMPRESS, AND AUTOCRAT OF ALL THE RUSSIAS." Rev. A shield, between sprigs of laurel, surmounted by a crown, and bearing the Russian name "GREVENNEEK," and the date "1747."

11. S. 1752. Rouble, of ELIZABETH I. Obv. Bust of the empress. "BY THE GRACE OF GOD, ELIZABETH I. EMPRESS AND AUTOCRAT OF ALL THE RUSSIAS." Rev. The imperial Russian eagle, with a shield upon its breast, bearing the arms. "MONEY; ROUBLE, 1752." Value 88 cts.

12. G. 1756. Two roubles, of ELIZABETH I. Obv. Bust of the

empress. "BY THE GRACE OF GOD, ELIZABETH I. EMPRESS AND AUTOCRAT OF ALL THE RUSSIAS." Rev. The imperial Russian eagle, as in the rouble (No. 11). "COIN; VALUE OF TWO ROUBLES, 1756." Value $1.97.

13. Silver medalet. Struck to commemorate the death of ELIZABETH. Obv. A *cenotaph,* upon which is deposited the imperial crown, beneath a canopy of ermine; above, upon the front of the canopy, is the monogram of Elizabeth, being a Russian E *reversed,* and containing the numeral "I." Rev. A crown, beneath which is the inscription, in seven parallel lines, "ELIZABETH THE FIRST, EMPRESS AND AUTOCRAT OF ALL THE RUSSIAS, DIED 25 DECEMBER, 1761."

14. S. 1762. Rouble, of PETER III. Obv. Bust, in armor. "PETER III BY THE GRACE OF GOD, EMPEROR AND AUTOCRAT OF ALL THE RUSSIAS." Rev. Same type as the reverse of the double rouble of PETER I. (No. 2). "NEW COIN; VALUE OF ONE ROUBLE."

15. Silver medalet. Struck upon the occasion of the coronation of CATHERINE II. Obv. The imperial crown, suspended in the diverging rays of the sun; above is inscribed, "FOR LOVE TO COUNTRY;" and beneath a sectional line, "SEPT. 22d." Rev. A small crown, beneath which is inscribed, in seven parallel lines, "CATHERINE II. EMPRESS AND AUTOCRAT OF ALL THE RUSSIAS, CROWNED IN MOSCOW, 1762."

16. S. 1769. Quarter rouble, of twenty-five copecks, of CATHERINE II. Obv. Bust of the empress. "BY THE GRACE OF GOD, CATHERINE II. EMPRESS AND AUTOCRAT OF ALL THE RUSSIAS." Rev. The imperial Russian eagle; above is the date "1769," and beneath, the Russian name of the coin, "POLUPOLTINICK."

17. G. 1777. Half rouble, or *poltina,* of CATHERINE II. Obv. Bust of the empress. "CATHERINE II EMP"(ress). Rev. The letters "E. A." interlaced and surmounted by a crown. " POLTINA 1777." Value 38 cts.

18. G. 1778. Imperial, of CATHERINE II. Obv. Bust of the empress, crowned with laurel. "BY THE GRACE OF GOD, CATHERINE II. EMPRESS AND AUTOCRAT OF ALL THE RUSSIAS." Rev. A circular shield, bearing the imperial Russian eagle, with four other shields, each surmounted by a crown, arranged around the first, in the form of a cross.

The first bears St. George and the dragon, and is surmounted by the imperial crown, the remaining three being surmounted by royal crowns. The angles of the cross thus formed contain the numerals composing the date "1778," and four roses. "IMPERIAL RUSSIAN COIN OF TEN ROUBLES." Value $7.84.

19. G. 1779. Rouble, of CATHERINE II. Obv. Bust of the empress, crowned with laurel. "BY THE GRACE OF GOD, CATHERINE II. EMPRESS AND AUTOCRAT OF ALL THE RUSSIAS." Rev. The imperial Russian eagle, bearing a shield upon its breast. "MONEY: ROUBLE, 1779." Value 75 cts.

20. S. 1779. Fifteen copecks, of CATHERINE II. Obv. Bust of the empress, crowned with laurel. "BY THE GRACE OF GOD, CATHERINE II. EMPRESS AND AUTOCRAT OF ALL THE RUSSIAS." Rev. The imperial Russian eagle, with a shield upon its breast, bearing the value "15." Beneath is a scroll, bearing the date "1779." Around the edge are fifteen pellets. Value 12 cts.

21 and 22. S. 1784–1795. "Grevenneek," of CATHERINE II. Same type as the grevenneek of Elizabeth. (See No. 10.)

23 and 24. C. 1790–1795. Pieces of ten copecks, of CATHERINE II. Obv. The imperial Russian eagle, with the shield upon its breast. Beneath is a scroll bearing the denomination of the coin, "TEN COPECKS." Rev. The letters "T. E." and the number "II" interlaced, and surmounted by a crown. The first two figures of the date are inscribed to the left of the monogram, and the last two to the right. The whole inclosed between branches of palm and laurel.

25. S. 1799. Rouble, of PAUL I. Obv. Four Russian P's and four crowns, arranged as a cross, with the numeral I. in the center. "COIN; VALUE OF ONE ROUBLE, 1799." Rev. A square compartment or shield, containing the inscription, "NOT TO US! NOT TO US! BUT TO THY NAME." Value 79 cts.

26. S. 1807. Rouble, of ALEXANDER I. Obv. Bust in uniform. "BY THE GRACE OF GOD, ALEXANDER I. EMPEROR AND AUTOCRAT OF ALL THE RUSSIAS." Rev. The denomination and date, "ROUBLE, 1807," occupying the field; "COIN OF THE RUSSIAN EMPIRE." Value 78 cts.*

---

* The silver coins both of Alexander and Nicholas are very unsteady in weight and fineness.—*Manual of Coins and Bullion.*

27. S. 1808. Rouble, of ALEXANDER I. Obv. The imperial Russian eagle, with a shield upon its breast, bearing the arms, encircled by the order chain and badge of the military order of St. Andrew.* Beneath are the initials "M.—K." "MONEY. ROUBLE," and the date "1808." Rev. The imperial crown of Russia, beneath which is inscribed "IMPERIAL RUSSIAN COIN;" and beneath a dash line the Russian letters "S. P. B.," inclosed between branches of oak and laurel, crossed. Value 78 cts.

28. S. 1810. Ten copecks, of ALEXANDER I. Obv. The imperial Russian eagle, as on the rouble (No. 27). Beneath are the Russian initials F.—G." Rev. The denomination and date, "10 COPECKS, 1810," and the Russian initials "S. P. B." in four lines. Value 8 cents.

29. S. 1811. Ten copecks, of ALEXANDER I. Obv. The imperial Russian eagle, as in the rouble (No. 27). Beneath are the initials "F.—G." and the date "1811." Rev. The imperial crown of Russia, beneath which are inscribed the denomination, "10 COPECKS," and the initials "S. P. B." inclosed between branches of oak and laurel, crossed. Value 8 cts.

30. S. 1813. Rouble, of ALEXANDER I. Obv. The imperial Russian eagle, as in the rouble of 1808 (No. 27). Beneath is the date "1813," and the Russian initials "P.—G." "MONEY*ROUBLE." Rev. The imperial Russian crown, beneath which is inscribed "PURE SILVER 4 ZOLOTNIK 21 DOLYAH,"† and the Russian initials "S. P. B." between branches of oak and laurel, crossed. Value 78 cts.

31. C. 1813. Two copecks, of ALEXANDER I. Obv. The imperial Russian eagle, as in the rouble (No. 27). Beneath is the date "1813," and the initials "P. S." Rev. The imperial crown, beneath which is inscribed the denomination "2 COPECKS," and the Russian initials "E. M.," between branches of oak and laurel, crossed.

32. S. 1819. Half rouble, or *poltina,* of ALEXANDER. Obv. The

---

* This order was established by *Peter the Great* in 1698.

† The *zolotnik* is the *ninety-sixth* part of a Russian pound, and the *dolyah* the *ninety-sixth* part of the *zolotnik.* The Russian pound is *one-tenth* less than the pound *avoirdupois.*

imperial Russian eagle, as in the rouble (No. 27). Above is inscribed "MONEY*POLTINA," and beneath, the date "1819" and the initials "P.—S." Rev. The imperial crown, beneath which is inscribed "PURE SILVER. 2 ZOLOTNIK $10\frac{1}{2}$ DOLYAH," and the initials "S. P. B." between branches of oak and laurel, crossed. Value 39 cts.

33. *Platina.* 1828. Three roubles, of NICHOLAS. Obv. The imperial Russian eagle, with a shield upon its breast, bearing the arms, encircled by the order chain and badge of the military order of St. Andrew. On each wing of the eagle are three smaller shields. *No legend.* Rev. The value "3 SILVER ROUBLES," inscribed in three lines, and beneath an ornamental dash is the date "1828," and the Russian initials "S. P. B." "2 ZOL(otnik) 41 DOL(yah) OF PURE URAL PLATINA." Value $2.39.

34 and 35. C. 1830. Pieces of ten copecks, of NICHOLAS. Obv. The imperial Russian eagle, with a pointed shield upon its breast, bearing the arms and grasping a thunderbolt in the dexter, and a laurel crown and scroll in the sinister talon. Beneath is the date "1830." Rev. The denomination "10 COPECKS," and, beneath an ornamental dash, the initials "S. P. B."

36 to 39. C. 1830. Pieces of five, two, and one copecks, of NICHOLAS. Same type as the ten-copeck piece (No. 34).

40 and 41. *Platina.* 1831–1832. Six roubles, of NICHOLAS. Same type as the piece of three roubles (No. 33). Rev. "6 SILVER ROUBLES, 1831. S. P. B." "4 ZOL. 82 DOL. OF PURE URAL PLATINA." Value $4.78.

42. S. 1835. Piece of one-and-a-half roubles, or ten zlotych of NICHOLAS. Obv. The imperial Russian eagle, as in the platina coins. (See No. 33) Beneath are the initials "N.—G." inclosed in a beaded circle. "PURE SILVER 6 ZOLOTNIK $31\frac{1}{2}$ DOLYAH." Rev. "$1\frac{1}{2}$ ROUBLE," in Russian characters, and 10 ZLOT," in Roman characters, beneath which is the date "1835;" the whole inscribed between branches of oak and laurel. Value $1.19.

43. S. 1837. Piece of three-quarter roubles, or five zlotych, of NICHOLAS. Obv. Same type as the obverse of the ten-zlotych piece (No. 42), with the Roman characters "M.—W." substituted for the Russian initials "N.—G." "PURE SILVER 3 ZOLOTNIK 15 DOLYAH."

Rev. "$\frac{3}{4}$ ROUBLE," in Russian, and "5 ZLOT." in Roman characters, with the date, between branches of oak and laurel.

44. S. 1837. Half rouble, or *poltina*, of NICHOLAS. Obv. Same type as the piece of ten zlot. (No. 42). "PURE SILVER. 2 ZOLOTNIK $10\frac{1}{2}$ DOLYAH." Rev. The imperial Russian crown, beneath which is inscribed "MONEY. POLTINA.—•+•—1837. S. P. B." between branches of oak and laurel. Value 40 cts.

45. *Platina.* 1837. Piece of three roubles. (See No. 33.) Value $2.39. (See Plate XXI. No. 5.)

46. G. 1838. Piece of three roubles, or twenty zlot.* of NICHOLAS. Obv. The imperial Russian eagle, as in the platina coins. (See No. 33.) Beneath are the initials "P.—D." Rev. "PURE GOLD. 81 DOLYAH.* 3 * ROUBLE," in Russian, and "20 ZLOTYCH" in Roman characters. The date "1838," and the initials "S. P. B." Value $2.39.

47. S. 1838. Rouble, of NICHOLAS. Obv. Same type as the piece of ten *zlot.* (No. 42). "PURE SILVER 4 ZOLOTNIK 21 DOLYAH." Rev. The imperial Russian crown, beneath which is inscribed "MONEY. ROUBLE—•+•—1838. S. P. B." between branches of oak and laurel. Value 79 cts.

48. S. 1838. Thirty copecks, or two zlot., of NICHOLAS. Obv. Same type as the platina coins. (See No. 33.) Beneath the eagle are the initials "M.—W." Rev. "PURE SILVER 1 ZOL(otnik) $25\frac{1}{2}$ DOL (yah) 30. COPECKS," in Russian, and "2 ZLOTE" in Roman characters, with the date "1838." Value 23 cts.

49. S. 1838. Fifteen copecks, or one zlot., of NICHOLAS. Obv. Same type as the *platina* coins. (See No. 33.) Beneath the eagle are the initials "N.—G." Rev. "PURE SILVER $60\frac{3}{4}$ DOL(yah) ●15● COPECKS," in Russian, and "1 ZLOTY." in Roman characters, with the date "1838." Value 11.5 cts.

50. S. 1838. Five copecks, of NICHOLAS. Obv. Same type as the *platina* coins. (See No. 33.) Rev. The imperial Russian crown, beneath which is inscribed "5 COPECKS—•+•—1838. S. P. B." inclosed in a wreath of oak and laurel. Value 4 cts.

51. G. 1839. Five roubles, or half imperial, of NICHOLAS. Obv.

---

* This piece was added to the coinage in 1834.

Same type as the platina coins. (See No. 33.) Beneath the eagle are the Russian characters "A—CH." Rev. "5 ROUBLES—•—1839. S. P. B." inclosed in a beaded circle. "PURE GOLD. 1 ZOLOTNIK 39 DOLYAH." Value $3.97. (See Plate XXI. No. 1.)

52. S. 1839. Twenty-five copecks, or quarter rouble, of NICHOLAS. Obv. The imperial eagle, as on the *platina* coins (see No. 33), inclosed in a beaded circle. "PURE SILVER. 1 ZOLOTNIK $5\frac{1}{4}$ DOLYAH." Rev. The imperial Russian crown, beneath which is inscribed "25 COPECKS—•—1839. S. P. B." between branches of oak and laurel. Value 20 cts.

53. S. 1839. 20 copecks, of NICHOLAS. Same type as the quarter rouble, No. 52. Value 16 cts.

54. S. 1851. Rouble, of NICHOLAS. Obv. The imperial eagle, as on the *platina* coins. (See No. 33.) Beneath are the Russian initials "P.—A." inclosed in a beaded circle. "PURE SILVER. 4 ZOLOTNIK 21 DOLYAH." Rev. The imperial crown of Russia, beneath which is inscribed "MONEY. ROUBLE—•—1851. S. P. B." between branches of oak and laurel. Value 79 cts. (See Plate No. XXI. No. 4.)

55 to 59. S. 1847 to 1853. Pieces of 50, 25, 20, 10, and 5 copecks. All same type and relative value of the rouble, No. 54.

POLAND.

69. G. 1697. Half ducat, of FREDERICK AUGUSTUS, *Elector of Saxony.* Obv. A mounted knight, grasping a baton. Rev. Two branches of palm, crossed, and surmounted by a crown. "D. G. F. A. E. S. EL. IN. REG: POLONIARUM D $\frac{17}{27}$ JUN: A° 1697." (By the grace of God, Frederick Augustus, Elector of Saxony, elected in the Kingdom of Poland on the 17th or 27th [old or new style] of June, Anno 1697.)

70. S. 1761. One-third thaler, of ELIZABETH I. *of Russia.* Obv. Bust of the empress, enveloped in a mantle of ermine. "ELISAB. I. D. G. IMP. TOT. RUSS. (Elizabeth I. by the grace of God, Empress of all the Russias.) Rev. The Polish eagle, "17—61," (*seventeen* at one side of the eagle, and *sixty-one* at the other.) Beneath a sec-

tional line is inscribed the denomination, "3 EIN R(eichs) TH(aler) COUR"(ant), (three to the rixdollar, current.)

71. S. 1776. Thaler, of STANISLAUS AUGUSTUS PONIATOWSKI. Obv. Bust, with the head encircled by a band. "STANISLAUS AUGUSTUS D. G. REX POL(oniæ) M(agnus) D(ux) LITU." (Lithauaniæ). Rev. A crowned shield, bearing the arms of Poland and Lithauania, *quartered*, with a shield of pretence bearing the arms of Poniatowski inclosed between two branches of palm and laurel, crossed, and intwined with the order band of the *Polish* or *white eagle*, from which depends the star of the order. The order band bears the motto, "GREGE ET PRO FIDE LEGE." Beneath are the initials "E—B," "X EX MARCA PURA COLONIEN, 1776," (ten from the mark fine Cologne weight). On the edge is inscribed "PIGNUS FIDEI PUBLICÆ." Value $1.00.

72. S. 1817. Two zlotych, of ALEXANDER I. *of Russia.* Obv. Undraped bust, "ALEXANDER I CESARZ SA W. RUS. KROL POLSKI," (Alexander I. Czar of all the Russias, and King of Poland.) Rev. The imperial Russian eagle; upon its breast is a mantle of ermine surmounted by a crown, and forming a canopy; beneath which is displayed a shield bearing the Polish eagle; above is inscribed "2 ZLOTE POLSKIE" and the date "18—17," and beneath "43 $\frac{43}{125}$ Z. GRZ CZ. KOL." (43 $\frac{43}{125}$ pieces to the fine mark.)

73. S. 1831. Five zlotych, of INDEPENDENT POLAND. Obv. A crowned shield bearing the arms of Poland and Lithauania in two fields, "KROLESTRO POLSKIE," (Kingdom of Poland). Rev. "5 ZLOT. POL." inscribed between two branches of oak, crossed. Beneath is the date "ROKU 1831" (year 1831) and the initials "K.—G.," and above "17 $\frac{211}{625}$ Z. GRZYW. CZYST KOL." On the edge is inscribed "BOZE ZBAW POLSKE," (God save Poland). Value 59 cts.

74. S. 1832. One zlotych, of NICHOLAS I. Obv. Bust of ALEXANDER I. *of Russia, laureated*, brother of Nicholas, (died in 1825). "ALEXANDER I CES ROS WSKRZESICIEL KROL POLS. 1815." Rev. "1 ZLO. POL. 1832," inscribed between two branches of oak, crossed. Beneath are the initials "K. G." "MIKOTAY (Nicholas) I. CES WSZ. ROSSYI. KROL. POLSKI PANULACY."

GREECE.

A particular interest attaches to the coins of Greece, from the fact that, if she were not the actual mother, she at least played *foster-dam* to the infant art of coinage, and was the first to start it upon its high mission into the wide world. She it was who first gave it that impulse, from which it has gradually developed itself, until it has risen from an obscure and rude art into an almost absolute science.

But Greece, notwithstanding the fact that she once produced and fostered the arts and sciences to a greater extent than any other country of a contemporaneous period, has sadly fallen from her high place among the nations of the world. From holding a position in the East, which was not surpassed, at a later time, in brilliancy by the extensive power of Rome, she has so far fallen, that her total annihilation would leave but a small gap in the present history of the world. During the time that Greece remained beneath the Turkish yoke, her existence was as little felt as though she had been submerged beneath the Egean wave. Although scholars in all portions of the globe were busily engaged in the perusal of her ancient authors, and in studying her ancient sculpture, it was almost impossible to realize that she still formed a portion of the world. But, happily, the present century has marked the first step in advance of this utter nothingness; and the success with which Greece emancipated herself, after a revolutionary struggle of nine years, from the Turkish rule, and assumed her place as an independent kingdom, in 1829, once more brought upon her the eyes of the world, and revealed the fact that, though fallen, she still retained a portion of that vitality which once made her so famous.

After the termination of her struggle for freedom, in 1829, some four years elapsed before any form of government was settled upon. But, in 1833, Otho of Bavaria was called to the throne, and honored with the title of "King of Greece."

The unit of Greek money is the *drachmè*, which is divided into 100 *lepta*. It appears to be about the value of the ancient coin of the same name, from which it was, doubtless, derived.

The gold coins are the pieces of 40 and 20 drachmè. Only the smaller piece has yet appeared here. The legal fineness is *nine-tenths*, and the weight of the twenty-drachmè piece 89 Troy grains.

The silver coins are the pieces of five, one, one-half, and one-fourth drachmè. The fineness is *nine-tenths*, and the weight 69 Troy grains to the single drachmè—the others in proportion.

The gold and silver coins are quite rare. Greece produces none of the precious metals, and is, therefore, dependent upon importation to supply her coinage; and from this cause, coupled with the fact that most of her coinage very soon finds its way to the melting-pot after its issue, has conspired to produce a scarcity, even within her own borders, which has rendered it necessary to adopt various coins of other countries, in order to supply the demand. Thus, various foreign coins have been *legalized*, at certain rates: such as the five-franc piece of France, at 5.58 dr.; the Austrian rixdollar, at 5.78 dr.; the Holland ducat, at 13 dr., etc.

The copper coinage consists of the pieces of ten, five, two, and one *lepta*. The latter coin may be said to represent the ancient *lepton*, more popularly known as the "*widow's mite*," but only so in name, as it is, in fact, a much larger piece.

89. G. 1833. Twenty drachmè, of OTHO. Obv. Undraped bust, "*ΟΘΩΝ ΒΑΣΙΛΕΥΣ ΤΗΣ ΕΛΛΑΔΟΣ*," (Otho, King of Greece). Beneath is the engraver's name, "*ΦΟΙΓΤ*," (Voight). Rev. A crowned shield bearing the arms (*azure; a cross argent*), with the arms of Bavaria in the center of the cross (*Barry bendy, azure and argent*), inclosed between two branches of laurel. Beneath is inscribed the denomination and date, "20 *ΔΡΑΧΜΑΙ*' (drachmè) 1833". Value $3.45. (See Plate XXI. No. 2.)

90. S. 1833. Five drachmè, of OTHO. Same type as the twenty-drachmè piece (No. 89), with a slight alteration in the reverse, the denomination and date being divided from the shield, etc. by a sectional line. Value 87 cts.

91 to 94. S. 1833–4. Pieces of one, one-half, and one-quarter drachmè, all the same type and relative values of the five-drachmè piece (No. 90). (See Plate XXI. No. 5.)

95 and 96. C. 1837. Ten lepta, of OTHO. Obv. Crowned shield bearing the arms, as in the twenty-drachmè piece (No. 89). "*ΒΑΣΙ-*

ΛΕΙΑ ΤΗΣ ΕΛΛΑΔΟΣ," (Kingdom of Greece). Rev. "10 *ΛΕΠΤΑ* (lepta) 1837" inclosed in a wreath of laurel.

97 to 102. C. 1837 to 1841. Pieces of five, two, and one lepta, all same type as the piece of ten lepta (No. 95). The name on the reverse of the smallest piece is in the singular, as—"1 *ΛΕΠΤΟΝ*," (1 lepton).

DIVISION XIII.

DENMARK.

The house of Holstein, which now occupies the throne of Denmark, acquired the crown in 1448 by the person of Christian, third son of the Count of Oldenburg, since which time it has continued in possession, and, in fact, furnished monarchs for several European thrones. At the time of the accession of Christian, Denmark comprised the three kingdoms of Denmark, Sweden, and Norway; for this reason, the Danish coins of the Holstein family always bear the arms of Sweden upon the same shield with those of Denmark, even at the present day, notwithstanding the fact that Sweden has never been under the Danish rule, since it was acquired by the venturesome and fortunate Gustavus Wasa, and totally severed from Denmark, in the year 1528. A branch of the Holstein family, however, has since occupied the Swedish throne.

Some confusion is occasioned among the coins of Denmark, from the fact that there have been three contemporary series of coins struck within its borders: one series being for Denmark *proper;* another for Holstein; and a third for Norway—the latter kingdom appears to have exercised the right of coining money at a remote period, and has retained it through all its political changes down to the present time. Its coins, however, have always borne a close resemblance to those of the country to which it belonged. During the time that it existed under the Danish sway, its coins were to be distinguished by the difference in the shield, which was only charged with the arms of Norway, to the exclusion of those of Denmark and Sweden; the arms of Norway being a lion rampant surmounting a battle-ax;* there were also beneath the shield two hammers, crossed; but the latter is not a safe mark by which to distinguish, as many of the pieces struck at Copenhagen bear the same mark. The hammers are the regular mint-mark of Norway, and are significant of the silver mines at Konigsberg, from which all the metal for the silver coinage is obtained. This may account for their use upon the Copenhagen coins; this mark having served to distinguish the Norway silver from that obtained from other sources. Some of the Norway coins had a legend on the *reverse* in the Norwegian language. The old riksdaler of Norway had, on the *reverse*, the lion rampant, with a battle-ax, and the following *legend* inscribed in two concentric circles: "MOD TRASKAB DAPPERHED. OGHVAD DER ÆRE GIVER DEN HEELE VERDENRAND BLANT NORSKE KLIPPER LOERE;" meaning, "Spirit, loyalty, valor, and whatever is honorable, let the whole world learn among the rocks of Norway." On the same piece of a later date, the legend is: "TROE LOVE MOD OGHVAD DAN KONGENS GUNST KAND VINDE, MENS NORGE KLIPPE HAR MAND SKAL HAS NORMAND FINDE;" meaning, "True lion's heart and whatever can win a Danish monarch's love, whilst Norway has rocks, shall be found among Norwegians."

The coins of Holstein are easily distinguished; and being interchangeable with those of Denmark, require no further notice in this place.

The earliest coins of Denmark, now under consideration, are those of CHRISTIAN IV., who reigned from 1588 to 1648. At this time the gold coinage consisted of the specie ducat of the German standards; the current ducat, 875 thousandths fine; and the *Christian d'or*, at 903 thousandths fine, and weighing 103 grains Troy per piece.

The silver was based upon the old *species daler*, as a unit, which was coined in each section of the monarchy, but was differently rated; its legal standards were: 875 thousandths fine, and weighing 445.8 Troy grains. This standard is said to have been adopted in the be-

---

* The lion of Norway, as at present depicted upon the coins, is somewhat different from the old lion. Formerly the lion was represented *upon the handle of the ax*, which was long and curved; but latterly the handle is shortened, so that he appears "rampant, grasping a battle-ax."

ginning of the sixteenth century, by FREDERICK I., who reigned from 1523 to 1533.* The smaller denominations were the pieces of one-half, two-thirds, and one-third of the same standards; the two last were coined for Holstein, being the pieces designated as *forty* and *twenty schillings.* The one-sixth piece was only 687 thousandths fine; and the pieces of one-twelfth, and one-twenty-fourth were still lower in fineness, the last being only 375 thousandths.

This was the state of the coinage up to the year 1813, when a royal edict was promulgated, making an entire change. Under this system the gold coinage comprises only the double and single *Frederick d'or*, or pieces of ten and five thalers; their legal fineness is 896 thousandths, and the weight of the ten-thaler piece 205 Troy grains; the other in proportion. The integer established by the provisions of this edict for the silver coinage is the *rigsbank daler*, or dollar of the National Bank, which is just half the weight and value of the old unit, the *specie daler.* The smaller denominations of 32, 16, and 8 rigsbank skillings, are equivalent to the $\frac{1}{6}$, $\frac{1}{12}$, and $\frac{1}{24}$ pieces of the old system. In 1836 the pieces of 4, 3, and 2 skillings were added to the coinage, and are coined at the fineness of 250 thousandths; the one-skilling piece has since been added. The *specie daler*, although no longer the unit, or integer, still exists as a coin at its former standards.

Denmark holds sway in the islands of St. Croix, St. Thomas, and St. John in the West Indies, and coins are issued for circulation in these possessions. But a division having been established, containing all the coins of the West Indies, those of Denmark will be found under that head.

1. S. 1608. Eight skillings, of CHRISTIAN IV. Obv. Bust, surmounted by a crown. "CHRISTIANUS IIII D. G. DAN. 1608." Rev. "VIII + SKILLIN + K. DANSK," inscribed in three lines; beneath is a shield, bearing the arms of Denmark (*or three lions current, and nine hearts argent*), a branch of laurel at one side, and palm at the other. "NORVE. VAND(alorum) GOTO(rum) Q. REX."

2. S. 1619. Specie daler, of same. Obv. Full-length image of

---

* Note in "Manual of Coins and Bullion."

the king, crowned, and attired in armor, grasping a scepter in his right hand, his left resting upon the hilt of his sheathed sword. "CHRISTIANUS IIII D. G. DANI." Rev. A crown, above which are the numerals composing the date "1619." Beneath are the initials "R. F. P.;" the whole inclosed in a beaded circle. "NORVEGI. VANDAL. GOTORU. Q. REX."

3. G. 1645. Ducat, of same. Obv. Image of the king, crowned, and attired in armor, a scepter in his right hand, and the imperial globe in his left. "CHRISTIANUS 4 D. G. D. N. V. G. Q. R." Rev. The inscription "IUSTUS יהוה IUDEX. 16—45."

4. S. 1660. One-third daler, or piece of two marks, of FREDERICK III. Obv. An F. and a 3. interlaced and surmounted by a crown. "11*MARCK*DANSKE*1660." Rev. A crowned shield, bearing the arms of Denmark, suspended upon a cross *potent.* "DOMINUS FROVIDEBIT."

5. S. 1666. One-sixteenth thaler. Obv. Bust, surmounted by a crown. "FRIDERIC 3. D. G. D. N. V. G. REX." Rev. "XVI E REICHS THA. 1666." inscribed in four lines within a beaded circle. "MONETA NOVA GLUCKSTADI."

6. S. 1676. One mark, of CHRISTIAN V. Obv. The initial "C." and a "5" interlaced and surmounted by a crown. "PIETATE ET JUSTITIA." Rev. "*1* MARCK DANSKE 1676," inscribed in four lines.

7. S. 1695. Eight skilling. Obv. Bust, "CHRIST(ianus) V. DEI GRA"(tia). Rev. A crown, with the numeral "8" at one side, and the initial "S." at the other (8 skilling). "DAN. NOR. VAN. GOT. REX," and the date "1695."

8 and 9. S. 1703–08. Eight skilling, of FREDERICK IV. Same type as preceding.

10. S. 1711. Twelve skilling, of FREDERICK. Obv. The royal cipher (F's and 4's interlaced), surmounted by a crown. "DEI G. REX DAN. NORV. G"(othorum). Rev. "TOLF SKILLING DANSKE 1711," inscribed in four lines.

11. S. 1712. Eight skilling. Obv. Bust, "FRID. IIII DEI GRAT." Reverse same as No. 7.

12. S. 1715. Sixteen skilling. Obv. Bust, "FRID. IIII D. G. REX

DAN. NOR. V. G." Rev. "*XVI* SKILLING DANSKE 1715;" two hammers, crossed, the initials "H. C. M," and a sprig of olive.

13. S. 1716. Two skilling. Obverse same as No. 10. Rev. Crowned shield, bearing the arms of Denmark. "II SKIL. DANSKE 1716."

14. S. 1716. Sixteen skilling. Obv. Bust, "FRID. IIII. D. G. REX DAN. NOR. V. G." Rev. "*XVI* SKILLING DANSKE 1716;" with a heart and the initials "C" and "W."

15. S. 1724. Twelve skilling, of FREDERICK IV. Obv. The royal cipher or monogram, crowned. "DOMINUS MIHI ADJUTOR." Reverse same as No. 12.

16. S. 1729. Eight skilling. Same type as No. 14.

17. S. 1733. Twenty-four skilling, of CHRISTIAN VI. Obv. The royal monogram, surmounted by a crown (two C's and two 6's interlaced). "D. G. REX DAN NORV. VAN. G." Rev. A shield, bearing the arms of Denmark, Norway, and Sweden (three crowns) suspended upon a cross, the upper limb surmounted by a crown; to the left is inscribed "17," and to the right "33," "24 SKILLING DANSKE COUR. M."

18. G. 1749. Specie ducat, of FREDERICK V. Obv. An equestrian image of the king. "FRID. V. D. G. DAN. NOR. V. G. REX." Beneath is the date "1749." Rev. Crowned shield, bearing the arms of Denmark, Norway, and Sweden; beneath is a trident, caduceus, globe, etc., and the initials "V. H." "PROVIDENTIA ET CONSTANTIA." Value $2.28.

19. G. 1757. Current ducat, of same. Obv. Bust, in armor, surmounted by a *laureated* helmet. "FRIDERICUS V. D. G. DAN. NOR. V. G. REX." Rev. A royal crown, beneath which is inscribed "XII M(arck) 17 57," and the initials "V. H." "PRUDENTIA ET CONSTANTIA." Value $1.82.

20. G. 1761. Current ducat. Same as preceding, with a simple uncovered head substituted for the bust. Same value.

21. S. 1762. Twenty-four skilling, of same. Obv. The royal monogram, surmounted by a crown. "D. G. DAN. NOR. VAN. GOT. REX." Rev. A crowned shield, bearing the arms of Denmark, Norway, and Sweden, draped with the order band and badge of the elephant

order. "24 SKILLING DANSKE COUR. M." Beneath are the initials "H. S. K." Value 44 cts.

22. G. 1775. Christian d'or, of CHRISTIAN VII. Obv. Bust, "CHRIST. VII D. G. REX DAN. NORV. V. G." Beneath is the date "1775." Rev. A *Gloria Dei*, with three royal monograms, each surmounted by a crown. "GLORIA EX AMORE PATRIÆ." Value $4.01.4.

23 and 24. S. 1776–77. Specie daler, of same. Obv. The royal monogram, crowned. "D. G. DAN. NORV. VAND. GOTH. REX." Rev. Crowned shield, bearing the arms of Denmark, Norway, and Sweden, inclosed between branches of olive, crossed; beneath are the two crossed hammers, the date, and the initials "H. J.—A. B." "GLORIA EX AMORE PATRIÆ." Value $1.09 each.

25. S. 1798. One-third daler, of same. Obv. Head, "CHRISTIANUS VII D. G. DAN. NORV. V. G. REX." Rev. A crowned shield, bearing the arms of Denmark, Norway, and Sweden; beneath are the two crossed hammers, the date "17—98," and the initials "C. M." "$\frac{1}{3}$ RIGSDALER SPECIES." Value 36.4 cts.

26. S. 1798. One-fourth rigsdaler courant, of same. Obv. The royal monogram, crowned. "5 STYKER. 1 RIGSDALER SPECIES." Rev. "*4* STYKER. 1 RIGSDALER COURANT." The date "1798," two crossed hammers, and the initials "J. G. M." Value 21 cts.

27. B.S. 1800. Two skilling, of same. Obv. The royal monogram, crowned. Rev. "2 SKILLING DANSKE SKILLEMYNT," the date "1800," the two crossed hammers, and the initials "J. G. M."

28. S. 1801. One-fourth rigsdaler courant, of same. Same type as No. 26.

29. G. 1802. Specie ducat, of same. Obv. A wild man, leaning with his right hand upon an oval shield bearing the arms of Denmark, and supporting with his left hand a club, the large end resting upon the ground; at one side is inscribed "18," and at the other "02." "MONETA AUREA DANICA." Rev. A square compartment, or shield, containing the inscription "1 SPECIES DUCAT. 23$\frac{1}{2}$ KARAT. 67. STYKKER 1 MARK BRUTO." Value $2.26.4.

30 and 31. S. 1808. One-sixth daler, of FREDERICK VI. Obv. The royal monogram, surmounted by a crown. "GANGBAR FOR $\frac{1}{6}$ RIGSDALER DANSK. COURANT." Rev. "FRIVILLIGT OFFER TIL FŒDRENE=

LANDET. 1808. M. F." inscribed in seven lines, and inclosed in an oak wreath. Value 17.4 cts.

32. C. 1809. Two skilling. Obv. Head, "FRIDERICUS VI DEI GRATIA". Rev. Crowned shield, bearing the arms of Denmark, Norway, and Sweden. At one side is the numeral "2," and at the other the initial "s," and beneath, the date "1809." "DANIÆ NORWEGIÆ VAN. GOTH. REX."

33. C. 1810. Two skilling courant, of same. Obv. The royal monogram, crowned. Rev. "*2* SKILLING COURANT, 18—10," inscribed in four lines.

34. S. 1813. Rigsbank daler. Obv. Head, "FRIDERICUS VI DEI GRATIA REX." Rev. A crowned shield, quartered by a cross, and bearing the arms of Denmark, Norway, Sweden, Schleswick, Gothen, and Wenden. Upon the cross is suspended a smaller shield, bearing the arms of Holstein, Stormarn, and Ditmarsen, with a shield of pretence, bearing the arms of Oldenburg and Delmenhorst. Value 55 cts.

35. C. 1815. Four skilling. Obv. A heart-shaped shield, surmounted by a crown, and bearing the arms of Denmark, Norway, and Holstein. *No legend.* Rev. "RIGSBANKTEGN FOR 4 SKILLING 1815."

36. C. 1815. Two skilling. Obv. An oval shield; otherwise same type as No. 35.

37 to 39. 1818. Two and one rigsbank skilling, all of the same type. The two-skilling piece has, on the obverse, an oval shield, bearing the arms of Denmark, Norway, and Sweden, surmounted by a crown; above is inscribed "$\frac{1}{48}$ RIGSBANK DALER." Rev. The inscription "2 RIGSBANK SKILLING 1818."

40. B.S. 1819. Eight rigsbank schilling. Obv. The royal monogram, crowned. *No legend.* Rev. "*8* REICHSBANK SCHILLING 1819." inscribed in five lines, with the initials "I. F. F." beneath.

41. S. 1820. Specie daler. Obv. Undraped bust, "FRIDERICUS VI D. G. DAN. V. G. REX." Rev. The crowned shield and arms of No. 34. Above is inscribed "EN RIGSDALER SPECIES," and beneath, the date "1820" and the initials "F F." Value $1.09.

42. S. 1820. Thirty-two rigsbank skilling. Obv. The royal monogram, surmounted by a crown. *No legend.* Rev. "*32* RIGSBANK

SKILLING 1820," inscribed in four lines, and the initials "I. F. F." Value 18 cts.

43. G. 1827. Double Frederick d'or. Obv. Head, "FREDERICUS VI REX DANIÆ." Rev. "2 FREDERICKS D'OR 1827," and the initials "I. F. F." *No device.*" Value $7.88.

44. G. 1831. Frederick d'or. Obverse same as No. 43. Rev. The crowned shield and arms of No. 34, with "1 FR." at one side and "D'OR" at the other. Beneath are the initials and date "F. 1831. F." Value $3.93.

45. B.S. 1831. One-twelfth daler. Obv. The royal monogram, crowned. At one side is the fraction "$\frac{1}{12}$," and at the other "SP." (*one-twelfth species*). Rev. "*16* REICHSBANK SCHILLING 1831." inscribed in five lines; the initials "I. F. F." beneath. Value 8.7 cts.

46. G. 1835. Double Frederick d'or. Same type as No. 43. Value $7.88.

47 to 49. B.S. 1836. Pieces of four, three, and two skilling, all same type. Obv. The royal monogram, crowned. Reverse of No. 47. "*4* RIGSBANK SKILLING 1836," and the initials "I. F. F."

50. G. 1837. Double Frederick d'or. Obv. Undraped bust, "FREDERICUS VI REX DANIÆ." Beneath the bust are the initials of the engraver, "G. G." Rev. The shield and arms of No. 34. At either side is a wild man, each carrying a club, and leaning upon the shield; the whole displayed upon a mantle of ermine, draped from a crown. Above is inscribed the denomination, "2 FR. D'OR," and beneath, the initials and date, "F. 1837. F." Value $7.88.

51. S. 1837. Specie daler. Same type as No. 41. Value $1.09.

52. G. 1838. Double Frederick d'or. Same type as No. 50. Value $7.88.

53. S. 1838. Rigsbank daler. Same type as No. 41, with the fraction "$\frac{1}{2}$" at one side of the shield, and "SP" at the other, (*half species*); and beneath, the initials "W. S." substituted for "F. F." Value 54.7 cts.

54. C. 1838. Half rigsbank skilling. Obv. The royal monogram, crowned; the date beneath. Rev. "RB. $\frac{1}{2}$ SK." *No device.*

55 and 56. S. 1840. Specie dalers, of CHRISTIAN VIII. Obv.

Undraped bust, "CHRISTIANUS VIII D. G. DANIÆ V. G. REX." Reverse same as No. 50, with the mantle suspended from a dome, studded with small crowns, and surmounted by a larger one, the shield encircled by the order chain and badge of the elephant order. On the *base* which supports the device is the name of the designer, "H. CONRADSEN." Above is inscribed "1 SPECIES," and beneath, the initials "F. F." and the date. Value $1.09.

57. S. 1848. Specie daler, of FREDERICK VII. Obv. Undraped bust, "FREDERICK VII KONGE OF DANMARK FOLKETS KJÆSLIGHED MIN STYRKE." Beneath is the date "1848." Rev. Bust of the preceding monarch, *Christian VIII.* (father of Frederick), the head bound with a chaplet of oak and laurel. "CHRISTIAN VIII KONGE AF DANMARK DOD DEN 20 JANUAR, 1848." Beneath is inscribed the denomination "1 SPECIES." Value $1.09.

58. S. 1854. Specie daler, of FREDERICK. Obv. Head, "FREDERICUS VII D. G. DANIÆ V. G. REX." Beneath is the date "1854." Rev. "2 RIGSDALER—9¼ ST:=1 M. F. S." (9¼ to the one mark [weight] of fine silver) inclosed in a wreath of oak. Value $1.09.

59. G. 1857. Two Fredericks d'or, of same. Obv. Head, "FREDERICUS VII D. G. DANIÆ V. G. REX." Rev. A shield, bearing the arms of No. 34, surmounted by a crown, and supported by two "wild men," displayed upon a mantle of ermine, draped from a crown. Above is inscribed "2 FR. D'OR," and beneath, the date. Value $7.88. (See Plate XXI. No. 3.)

60. S. 1855. Two rigsdaler. Same as No. 58. Value $1.09.

61. S. 1854. One rigsdaler. Same type. (See Plate XXI. No. 6.)

62. S. 1855. Half rigsdaler. Same type.

63 and 64. S. 1856–57. Pieces of 16 and 4 skilling. Same type. (Rev. "16 SKILLING R(igs) M"(ont).

65 and 66. B.S. 1856–57. Pieces of one and one-half skilling. Same type. Obv. The royal monogram (F. VII.), surmounted by a crown between two branches of oak, crossed. Beneath is the date. Rev. A circular shield, bearing the denomination. *Legend.* "SKILLING......RIGSMONT." (See Plate XXII. No. 5.)

NORWAY.

67. S. 1695. Piece of four marks, CHRISTIAN V. Obv. The royal monogram, crowned. "PIETATE ET JUSTITIA." Rev. The arms of Norway, surmounted by a crown, and inclosed between two branches of laurel, crossed, and draped with the band and badge of the elephant order. "IIII MARCK DANSKE. 1695;" two hammers, crossed. Beneath are the initials "H. C. M."

68. S. 1740. Twenty-four skilling, CHRISTIAN VI. Obv. The royal monogram, crowned. "D. G. REX DAN. NORV. VA. GO." Rev. Same device as No. 68. "24 SKILLING DÀNSKE 1740." Beneath are the crossed hammers, and the initials "T. L."

69. S. 1750. Twenty-four skilling, of FREDERICK V. Same type as No. 68.

HOLSTEIN.

71. S. 1753. Thaler, of PETER, *Grand-Duke of Russia.* Obv. Bust, in armor. "PETRUS D. G. MAGNUS DUX TOTUS RUSSIÆ." Rev. The Russian double-eagle, surmounted by the imperial crown, two shields upon its breast, one bearing the arms of Russia (St. George and the dragon), and the other the arms of Norway, Holstein, Stormarn, Ditmarsen (a mounted knight*), Oldenburg, and Delmenhorst; arms of Schleswick (two lions current, proper) upon a shield of pretence, the order chain and badge of the Russian military order of St. Andrew suspended from the wings of the eagle. "HÆR(es) NORW(egiæ) DUX SLESV(ici) HOLS(atiæ) ST(ormariæ) & DITM(arsiæ) COM(es) OLD (enburgi) & DELM(enhorstii). 1753," (heir to Norway; Duke of Schleswick, Holstein, Stormarn, and Ditmarsen; Count of Oldenburg and Delmenhorst). Value $1.09.

72. S. 1787. Forty-schilling, or two-third piece, of CHRISTIAN VII. *of Denmark.* Obv. Head, "CHRISTIANUS VII D. G. DAN. NORW. V. G. REX." Rev. Crowned shield, bearing the arms of Denmark, Norway, and Sweden; the fraction "$\frac{2}{3}$" at one side, and "SP." at the other; "40 SCHILLING SCHLESW. HOLST. COURANT." Beneath is the date and initials, "17—M. F.—87." Value 72.5 cts.

---

* Similar to the arms of Lithauania.

73. S. 1787. Ten schilling, of CHRISTIAN VII. Obv. The royal monogram, crowned; the fraction "$\frac{1}{6}$" at one side, and "SP." at the other. Rev. "❦10❦ SCHILLING SCHLESW. HOLST. COURANT, 1787," inscribed in five lines. Value 17.5 cts.

74. S. 1787. Two-and-a-half schilling, of CHRISTIAN VII. Same type as No. 73.

75 and 76. S. 1788 and 1794. Specie dalers, of CHRISTIAN VII. Same type as No. 72; the legend on the reverse being "60 SCHILLING SCHLESW. HOLST. COURANT." Value $1.09.2 each.

77 and 78. S. 1789–94. Pieces of ten and five schilling. Same type as No. 73. Value of the ten schilling 17.5 cts.

79. S. 1808. Twenty-schilling, or one-third piece. Same type as No. 72. Value 36.5 cts.

80. S. 1812. Two-and-a-half schilling, of FREDERICK VI. Same type as No. 73.

SWEDEN.

As before noticed, Sweden formerly constituted a portion of the Danish territory, having been conquered in 1389 by the armies of MARGARET, *Queen of Denmark.* In 1396, MARGARET caused her grandnephew to be acknowledged "Sovereign of the three kingdoms;"* and this title was confirmed by the treaty of Calmar, in 1397. This union subsisted until 1528. In 1518, GUSTAVUS WASA was sent as a hostage into Denmark; but, upon hearing of the treacherous seizure and execution of the ninety-four senators, who were beheaded at the order of the tyrannical CHRISTIAN II.—one of whom was ERICK WASA, the father of *Gustavus*—he made his escape, and arrived at *Dalecarlia,* in 1523. Here he harangued the people, on a Fair Day, and induced them to support his claims to the crown. From this time he experienced a series of triumphs, which ended, at last, in his being crowned *King of Sweden,* at Stockholm, in 1528. The family of *Wasa* continued in possession of the throne until 1654, when CHRISTIANA, daughter of GUSTAVUS ADOLPHUS, abdicated in

* Denmark, Sweden, and Norway.

favor of her cousin, CHARLES AUGUSTUS, *of Deux Ponts*, who assumed the crown, with the title of CHARLES X. The house of *Deux Ponts* was, in turn, succeeded by the house of *Holstein Huttin*, in 1751. ULRICA ELENORA, having married FREDERICK, son of the Landgrave of Hesse, resigned the throne to her husband, in 1720; and upon his death, in 1751, the house of Holstein commenced to reign, by the accession of ADOLPHUS FREDERICK. CHARLES XIII., brother of GUSTAVUS III., was the last prince of this house upon the Swedish throne. He was called to the throne upon the deposal of his nephew, GUSTAVUS IV., in 1809; and, soon after, the heir-apparent suddenly died, (1810). Consequently, BERNADOTTE, *Prince of Ponte Corvo*, and Marshal of France, was *elected Crown Prince*. He succeeded, upon the death of CHARLES, in 1818, without opposition. It was during the reign of CHARLES (in 1813) that Norway was annexed to the Swedish crown.

The unit of Swedish money, from ancient times, has been the *riksdaler** (government dollar) of 48 schillings. It was formerly coined at 878 thousandths fine, and at the weight of 451.7 Troy grains, and was subdivided into the pieces of two-thirds and one-third, of the same fineness; and the pieces of one-sixth, one-twelfth, and one-twenty-fourth, at a lower standard. But, in 1830, a law was enacted, by virtue of which the riksdaler is now coined at 750 thousandths fine, and at the weight of 525 Troy grains. This change, it will be noticed, makes no apparent difference in the value. The lower denominations are the pieces of one-half, one-quarter, one-eighth, and one-sixteenth, of the same standard of fineness.

The only gold coin, prior to 1840, was the ducat, coined at 976 thousandths fine, and of the usual weight; but since 1840 there has been issued a *four-ducat* piece, which appears to be of the same standard of fineness as the ducat. In addition to these, the National Bank is said to be issuing gold of the denomination of the ducat.† It is a curious fact, however, that gold is not a legal tender in the

---

* Report of American Consul at Stockholm to the Department of State, March 15, 1858.

† Letter of A. W. Frestadius, U. S. Consul at Stockholm, to the Treasury Department, July, 1859.

payment of debts, being merely considered as bullion, and is bought and sold at fluctuating prices, the value being regulated by the price of gold in England and Hamburg.*

The copper coinage was formerly represented by a piece called an *öre*, or *aere*. This piece bore the same relation to the *riksdaler* that the United States cent does to the dollar, the *daler* having consisted of one hundred *öre*. This was superseded by the skilling and its subdivisions, which were, doubtless, the half and quarter, although only the quarter skilling has yet appeared here. At the present time, copper is issued in large quantities by the National Bank, and consists of the pieces of two, one, two-thirds, one-third, and one-sixth *skilling*. The skilling of this series, it will be noticed, is only half the size of the government skilling. This discrepancy is accounted for by the following reasons: The government or mint skilling represented the *specie standard*, being a subdivision of the *specie daler*, or riksdaler; while the *skilling banco* represents the standard of *paper money*, its *intrinsic valuation* depending upon the *nominal* value of the *paper* daler, which is about *half the value* of the *specie daler*.

The parliament of 1854, however (as appears from the report of Mr. Frestadius), abolished the skilling system, and reinstated the old öre and its subdivisions, the half and quarter, so that the riksdaler is now subdivided into one hundred öre, instead of 48 schillings, as before. Whether this law makes any alteration in the copper coins of the National Bank, which is an institution distinct from the Royal Mint, being under the control of persons appointed by the parliament, we are unable to say; but the copper coinage of the bank being based upon the *paper circulation*, instead of the *specie basis*, as before noticed, would render very little change necessary, as the *skilling banco* would naturally be nearly equivalent to the öre, or one-hundredth part of the *specie daler*.

Norway, as before noticed, still continues to exercise the prerogative of coinage. The coins, however, are easily distinguished from those of Sweden *proper*, not only by the arms, but by the legend

---

* Letter of A. W. Frestadius, before quoted.

on the obverse. In the former the word *morges* comes before *Sveriges*, whereas in the latter this order is reversed. No changes having taken place in the composition of the Norway coins—either upon its change of masters in 1813 or the revision of Swedish coins in 1830—they still retain the ancient Danish standard. (For which see *Denmark*.)

81. S. 1610. Riksdaler, of CHRISTIAN IX. Obv. The king, attired in regal robes and crowned; a drawn sword in his right, and the imperial globe in his left hand. To the left of the king is a table, upon which are deposited a scepter and a key. Beneath, to his right, is a small shield, bearing the arms of Sweden, and to his left a similar shield, bearing the arms of Gothland (*bendy, azure and argent, a lion rampant proper*); above each is inscribed the abbreviations "SVER." and "GOTH." Between his feet is a still smaller shield, bearing the arms of Vandalia. Above is a glory, containing, in Hebrew characters, the word "JEHOVAH." "CAROLUS IX D. G. SVEGOR(um) GOTHOR(um) VANDALOR(um) &C. REX." Rev. An image of Christ, carrying the imperial globe. "SALVATOR MUNDI SALVANOS," inclosed in a circle, outside of which is inscribed "JEHOVAH SOLATIUM MEUM."

82. S. 1617. Four marks* of GUSTAVUS ADOLPHUS. Obv. Bust, in armor, *laureated.* Above is a glory, containing the Hebrew word "JEHOVAH." "GUSTAVUS ADOLF. D. G. —— REX SVECIÆ PRINCEPS HÆR.;" and in an inner circle "GLORIA ALTISSEMO SUORUM REFUGIO." Rev. Three shields, beneath a crown, one bearing the arms of Sweden, another of Gothland, and the third of Vandalia. "IIII SVENSKE MARKR. 1617."

83. S. 1632. Two marcks, of GUSTAVUS ADOLPHUS. Obv. Portrait profile of the king, attired in the robes of state, holding a baton in the right, and the imperial globe in the left hand. Above is a glory, containing the Hebrew word "JEHOVAH." "D. G. GUSTAVUS ADOLPHUS SVE(ciæ) GOT(horum) VAN(dalorum) REX." Rev. A crowned shield, bearing the arms of Sweden and Gothland *quartered*, with the

---

* Anciently the Swedish daler was divided into *six marks*, and each mark into sixteen schillings, after the example of the Danish *daler of account*, which is subdivided in a like manner.

arms of Vandalia on a shield of pretence, inclosed between branches of laurel, crossed. Above is inscribed "GOTT MIT UNS."

84. G. 1633. Ducat, of GUSTAVUS ADOLPHUS. Obv. Bust, in armor, at three-quarter face, *laureated.* "GUSTAV. ADOLPH. D. G. SVEGO(rum) GOTHO. VANDALO. REX MAG"(nus). Rev. A crowned shield, bearing the arms of No. 83. "PRINC(eps) FINLAND DUX ETHO. CAR. DOM(inus) ING."

Gustavus was killed at the battle of Lutzen in 1632, so that this piece must have been coined *after his death.* It bears the same legends and is of the same type as the last coins of his reign. His *specie daler* of 1732 was exactly the same pattern.

85. S. 1642. Riksdaler, of CHRISTIANA. Obv. Bust of the queen, at full-face. "CHRISTINA D. G. SVE. GOT. WAN(vandalorum) Q DE REGE HÆ." Rev. An image of Christ, with the imperial globe. To the left of the field is a crowned shield, bearing the arms of Sweden, Gothland, and Vandalia, in three fields. "SALVATOR MUNDI SALVANOS MDCXLII."

86. B.S. 1688. One marck, of CHARLES XI. Obv. Bust, in armor, partially enveloped in a military mantle. "CAROLUS XI D. G. REX SVE." Rev. The three golden crowns of Sweden, with the date "16—88," and the denomination "1—M."

87. S. 1695. Riksdaler, of CHARLES XI. Obv. Bust, as in No. 86. "CAROLUS XI D. G. REX SVE." Rev. Crowned shield, bearing the arms of Sweden. At one side is the numeral "8," and at the other the letter "M." "DOMINUS PROTECTOR MEUS 1695." On the edge is inscribed "MANIBUS*NE****LÆDAR*AVARIS."

88. B.S. 1701. One marck, of CHARLES XII. Obv. Bust, as in coins of CHARLES XI. "CAROLUS XII D. G. REX SVE." Reverse same as No. 86.

89. S. 1718. Riksdaler, of CHARLES XII. Obv. The royal monogram, surmounted by a crown. Beneath is the date "1718." "DOMINUS PROTECTOR MEUS." Rev. Four crowned shields, bearing the arms of Sweden and Gothland, arranged as a cross, with the arms of Vandalia in the center, and the characters "Q.—D.—S.—M.," each surmounted by a crown in the angles. "CARO—LI NER—FYRA."

90 and 91. S. 1736–1740. Riksdalers, of FREDERICK, *of Hesse-*

Cassel. Obv. Bust, "FRIDERICUS D. G. REX SVECIÆ." Rev. A crowned shield, supported by two lions, and bearing the arms of Sweden and Gothland, *quartered*, with a shield of pretence, and a heart shield, the latter bearing the lion *rampant* of Hesse, upon a blue field. An oval compartment, in the pedestal which supports the device, contains the date. Beneath are the initials "G. Z." Above is inscribed "GUD MITT HOPP." Value $1.10 each.

92. C. 1758. One öre, of ADOLPHUS FREDERICK, *of Holstein.* Obv. The royal monogram, crowned; the three golden crowns of Sweden, one at each side, and one beneath the monogram. Rev. Two arrows *in saltiere*, beneath a crown. "1 ÖR. S. M." (one öre, specie coin.)

93 and 94. S. 1781–1782. Riksdalers, of GUSTAVUS III. Obv. Undraped bust, "GUSTAVUS III D. G. REX SVECIÆ." Rev. The arms of Sweden upon a circular shield, surmounted by a crown, and encircled with the order chain and badge of the order of the *Seraphim.* "1—RD." (1 riksdaler.) Beneath are the initials "O. L." and the date. Above is inscribed "FÄDEMES LANDET." (The land of our fathers.) Value $1.10 each.

95. S. 1797. Riksdaler, of GUSTAVUS ADOLPHUS IV. Obv. Undraped bust, "GUSTAF. IV. ADOLPH SV. G. OCH. W. KONUNG." (Gustavus Adolphus IV., King of Sweden, Gothland, and Westmanland.) Rev. Same type as No. 93, with the inscription, above the shield, "GUD OCH. FOLKET." (God and the people.) Value $1.10.

96. S. 1804. One-sixth riksdaler, of GUSTAVUS ADOLPHUS IV. Obv. Bust, in armor, bedecked with an order band. "GUSTAF. IV. ADOLPH. SV. G. OCHR V. KONUNG." Rev. Same type as No. 95. Value 18.3 cts.

97 and 98. C. 1819. Skilling and quarter skilling, of CHARLES XIV. Obv. The royal monogram, crowned. The three crowns of Sweden, arranged as in No. 92. "FOLKETS KÄRLEK MIN BELÖNING." (The people's love is my recompense.) Rev. Two arrows *in saltiere.* "1 SKILLING, 1819."

99 and 100. G. 1838–1843. Pieces of one and four ducats, of CHARLES XIV. Both of the same type. Obv. Undraped bust, "CARL. XIV. SVERIGES NORR. G. OCH. V. KONUNG." Rev. The three crowns of Sweden upon an oval shield, encircled by the order chain

and badge of the order of the *Seraphim*, and displayed upon a mantle draped from a crown. Beneath are the initials "A. G." and the date. "FOLKETS. KÄRLEK MIN BELÖNING." Edge grained. *Value of the four-ducat piece* $9.07, *and of the ducat* $2.26. (See Plate XXII. No. 1.)

101. S. 1838. Riksdaler species, of CHARLES XIV. Obv. Same type as the ducat (No. 100). Rev. A crowned shield, encircled by the order chain and badge of the order of the *Seraphim*, and bearing the arms of Sweden, Norway, and Gothland, in three fields, with a shield of pretence, bearing the arms of Vandalia and Bernadotte. Beneath is the denomination "1 R.—SP." (1 riksdaler species), the initials "A. G.," and the date "18—38." "FOLKETS. KÄRLEK MIN BELÖNING." On the edge is inscribed "75∽100 DELAR FIN SILFVER." Value $1.10.

102 to 104. 1830–1832. Half, quarter, and eighth riksdalers, of the same type and relative value as the riksdaler No. 101.

105 to 107. C. 1837–1839. Pieces of two, one, and two-thirds skilling banco, of CHARLES XIV. Obv. Bust enveloped in a Roman mantle. "CARL. XIV. SVERIGES NORR. G. O. V. KONUNG." Rev. Two arrows *in saltiere*. Above is inscribed the denomination, as "2 SKILLING BANCO," and beneath the date, inclosed in a wreath of oak.

108 and 109. C. 1837 and 1836. Pieces of one-third, and one-sixth skilling banco, of CHARLES XIV. Obv. The royal monogram, crowned. The three crowns of Sweden, arranged as in the öre, No. 92. "FOLKETS KÄRLEK MIN BELÖNING." Rev. Same type as No. 105.

110. S. 1844. Riksdaler, of OSCAR. Obv. Undraped bust, "OSCAR SVERIGES NORR. GOTH. OCH. VEND. KONUNG." Rev. A crowned shield, supported by two lions, and bearing the arms of Sweden and Gothland, *quartered*, with a shield of pretence, bearing the arms of Vandalia and Bernadotte. On the base which supports the shield is the date "1844," and the denomination "1 R.—SP." (1 riksdaler species). Beneath are the initials "A.—G." Above is inscribed "RÄTT OCH. SANNING," and on the edge "75—100 DELAR FIN SILFVER." Value $1.10. (See Plate XXII. No. 2.)

NORWAY.

119. S. 1831. Specie daler, of CHARLES XIV. Obv. Bust, enveloped in a Roman mantle. "CARL. XIV. JOHAN NORGES SVER. G. OG. V. KONGE." Rev. A crowned shield, bearing the arms of Norway. "1—SP^{S}." (one species). Beneath is inscribed "9¼ ST. 1 MK. F. S." (nine and a quarter to one mark of fine silver), the date "18—31," and the mint-mark.

120 to 122. B.S. 1827 and 1825. Pieces of twenty-four and eight skilling, all of the same type as the daler (No. 119), with the inscription, denoting the number to the fine mark, omitted.

123. B.S. 1825. Four skilling. Obv. Crowned shield, bearing the arms of Norway. "CARL. XIV. JOHAN NORGES SVER. G. OG. V. KONGE." Rev. "4 SKILLING SPECIES. 18—25. J. M. K." inscribed in five lines.

124 and 125. C. 1833 and 1827. Pieces of two and one skilling. Obv. A crowned shield, bearing the arms of Norway. "CL. XIV.—JOH." (*Charles John XIV.*) Rev. "2. (or "1.") SKILLING SPECIES, 1833," inscribed in four lines.

126. S. 1850. Specie daler, of OSCAR. Obv. Undraped bust, "OSCAR NORGES SVER. G. OG. V. KONGE.+RET OG SANDHED." Rev. The arms of Norway, upon a crowned shield; and the denomination "1—S^{PS}," inclosed between two branches of oak, crossed. Above is inscribed "9¼ ST. 1 MK. F. S.," and beneath, the date "18–50." (See Plate XXII. No. 3.)

DIVISION XIV.

SWITZERLAND.

Before the year 1798 the Republic of Switzerland consisted of a confederacy of nineteen different States, or *Cantons*. But in that year they were consolidated into one government, called the HELVETIAN REPUBLIC (*Republik Helvetische*). This constitution, however, did not survive the French Republic, under whose example and influence it had been established, but was dissolved in 1803 by what is known as the Act of Mediation, and reduced to a kind of French Protectorate. They remained in nearly this state until 1815, when the Congress of Vienna re-established the old Confederacy, at the same time adding three new Cantons to it, so that it now consists of *twenty-two Cantons*, as follows:—1. Bern. This is one of the most populous, as well as the largest of the Cantons. 2. Zurich. 3. Vaud.* 4. Lucerne. 5. St. Gall. 6. Ticino.† 7. Basel. 8. Friburg. 9. Soleure (Solothurn). 10. Uri. 11. Schweitz (Schwyz). 12. Grisons (Graubündten). 13. Aargau. 14. Unterwalden. 15. Glarus. 16. Thurgau. 17. Schaffhausen. 18. Appenzell. 19. Zug; with the following three added by the Congress of Vienna: 20. Geneva, before 1815 a separate republic. 21. Valais (Wallis). 22. Neufchatel (Neuenburg). The latter is under the *dominion* of the King of Prussia, but forms no part of that kingdom.

Prior to the union of 1798, each Canton exercised the right of coinage; from that date until the fall of the Republic in 1803, coins were issued only in the name of the Helvetian Republic; but in 1803 the Cantons regained the right of coinage, which they retained until the formation of the Federal Constitution of 1847–48.

Previous to the year 1798, the gold coinage consisted of the denominations of the *ducat* and *pistole*. The ducat was not accurate or very regular in its value, but approached to the German standard. The pistole was coined at the standard of the French *louis d'or* of the law of 1785 (916.7 thousandths in fineness, and weighing 118 grains Troy to the piece).

The principal silver coin was the *ecu*, or crown of four Swiss francs, which was further subdivided into forty batzen. The smaller pieces were the half crown, the franc of ten batzen, and the pieces of five and one batzen. After the formation of the Helvetian Republic and the transfer of the right of coinage to the central administration, by the law of March 19th, 1799, a uniform currency was agreed upon, making the Swiss franc of ten batzen or ten rappen the unit. After the dissolution of the Republic in 1803, in consequence of the

* The *legends* on the coins of this Canton are in French.

† Legends in Italian.

Mediation Act, the right of coinage was restored to the sovereign Cantons, *subject to the regulations of the Senate as to fineness;* but after the restoration in 1815 the latter restriction was removed. In the year 1819, nineteen Cantons made a concordat for the regulation of the coinage, re-establishing the Swiss franc as the unit. But this regulation seems not to have been well observed; and "at several conferences afterward for the better regulation of Swiss mint matters, no resolutions could be agreed upon, and even existing actual resolutions and concordats were not strictly adhered to. It was only at the new federal organization (1847 to 1848), that the realization of a long-looked-for uniform and secure mint system found hope of success. Article thirty-sixth of the Federal Constitution withdrew the right of coinage from the Cantons, and conferred it exclusively upon the Federal Council; on the 7th of May, 1850, the Assembly framed a law which constitutes the French standard the lawful standard of Switzerland."* As some time was necessary to accomplish the redemption of the old coins, this law was not established *in full force* until the end of 1852. The new coinage, however, appeared in small quantities soon after the passage of the law. Under this system the coinage consists of the pieces of 5, 2, 1, and $\frac{1}{2}$ francs at 900 thousandths fine. The billion, or small coins, are the pieces of 20, 10, and 5 rappen, or centimes; the latter pieces are very base, the 20 rappen piece being only 150 thousandths; the 10 rappen only 100 thousandths; and the 5 rappen only 50 thousandths fine—in fact, making the proportion of silver so small as to render them no longer silver coins, the silver being merely lost in a proportionate amount of copper, zinc, and nickel. The copper† coins are the pieces of two and one rappen, or centimes. No gold coins were provided for by this law, as Switzerland depends entirely upon France and the Italian States for her gold currency. There appears to have been no gold coins issued by any of the Swiss Cantons since the dissolution of the Republic of 1798.

---

* Letter of John Endlich, Esq., U. S. Consul at Basel, to the Treasury Department, May 23, 1859, from which most of the data for this article are obtained.

† Strictly speaking, these are not *copper* coins, being an alloy of copper, zinc, and nickel. The term *copper* is used for the sake of convenience.

BERN.

1. B.S. 1756. Twenty kreutzers. Obv. A crowned shield, bearing the arms of the Canton (*Gules; a bear on a bend or, proper*). "MONETA REIPUB. BERNENSIS." Rev. A shield, bearing the denomination and date, "20 KREUTZER, 1756," inscribed in four lines. "DOMINUS PROVIDEBIT."

2. G. 1794. Ducat. Obv. The arms of the Canton. "RESPUBLICA BERNENSIS." Rev. The inscription "1 DUCAT, 1794," inclosed in a wreath of laurel. "BENEDICTUS SIT JEHOVA DEUS." Value $2.20.

3. S. 1795. Crown. Obv. The arms of the Canton. "RESPUBLICA BERNENSIS." Rev. A Swiss soldier,* armed and plumed, holding a long sword, the point of which rests upon the ground; beneath is the date "1795." "DOMINUS PROVIDEBIT." Value $1.14.

4. S. 1796. Two franken, or francs, of the same type as the crown (No. 3). Value 57 cts.

5. S. 1797. One franc. Obv. Crowned shield, draped with laurel, and bearing the arms of the Canton (the color of the metals omitted); beneath is the date "1797." "RESPUBLICA BERNENSIS." Rev. Eight B's interlaced and arranged as a cross, each limb surmounted by a crown; a *Gloria Dei* in the center. "DOMINUS PROVIDEBIT." Value 28.5 cts.

6. S. 1798. Crown. Obv. Crowned shield, bearing the arms of the Canton, inclosed in an oval compartment. "RESPUBLICA BERNENSIS." Rev. A Swiss soldier, armed and plumed, supporting a long sword as in No. 3; beneath is the date "1798." The whole inclosed in an oval compartment as on the obverse. "DOMINUS PROVIDEBIT." Value $1.14.

7. S. 1811. One franc. Obv. The arms of the Canton, upon an oval shield, surmounted by a crown, and inclosed between two branches of palm, crossed; beneath is a scroll bearing the inscription "DOMINUS PROVIDEBIT." Beneath the scroll is the date "1811." "CANTON BERN." Rev. A Swiss soldier, holding a long sword in his

---

* One of the three chieftains who were the founders of ancient *Helvetia*, called by the Swiss peasantry the *three Tells*.

right hand, and supporting with his left an oval shield, bearing the inscription "XIX CANTONE." "SCHWEIZ EIDSGENOSS." Value 28.5 cts.

8. B.S. 1818. Four kreutzers. Obv. Arms of the Canton upon a shield inclosed in a beaded circle; beneath is the value "CR.—4." "MONETA REIPUB. BERNENSIS." Rev. A *cross-flory*, with double limbs. "DOMINUS PROVIDEBIT," and the date "1818."

ZURICH.

10. S. 1727. Crown. Obv. Two lions *rampant*, combatant, one grasping a sword, and the other a palm branch, supporting an oval shield bearing the arms of the Canton (*party, per bend, proper; azure and argent*). "MONETA REIPUBLICÆ TIGURINÆ." Rev. The City of Zurich; above is the legend "DOMINE CONSERVA NOS IN PACE." Beneath, upon a small oval, is the date "1727." Value 93 cts.

11. S. 1736. Half crown. Obv. A lion *rampant*, wielding a sword, and supporting a shield bearing the arms of the Canton. On the ground, beneath the lion, is a small oval containing the fraction "1–2" "MONETA REIPUBLICÆ TIGURINÆ." Rev. The City of Zurich; above is inscribed the Latin name "TIGURUM," and on a scroll beneath is the date "1736." Value 46 cts.

12. S. 1776. Half crown. Obv. Same device as No. 11, with the *legend* "MONETA REIPUBLICÆ TURICENCIS." Rev. The inscription "JUSTITIA ET CONCORDIA 1776" encompassed by palm branches and flowers; beneath are two cornucopias, crossed. Value 46 cts.

13. S. 1810. Eight batzen. Obv. Shield, bearing the arms of the Canton, between branches of palm and laurel, crossed. "CANTON ZURICH." Rev. "8 BATZEN, 1810," inclosed between two branches of laurel, crossed.

VAUD.

15. S. 1810. Five batzen. Obv. A shield, bearing the arms of the Canton (*party per fess; argent and vert*, "LIBERTE ET PATRIE," inscribed upon the first,) surmounted by a chaplet of oak, and inclosed between two branches of laurel; beneath is the date "1810." "CANTON DE VAUD." Rev. "5 BATZ." inscribed within a wreath of grape and wheat. Value 12 cts.

16. B.S. 1831. One batzen. Obv. A shield, bearing the arms of the Canton, inclosed between branches of laurel; beneath is the denomination "1 BATZ." "CANTON DE VAUD. 1831." Rev. A cross, with the initial "C." in the center. "LES CANTONS CONCORDANTS DE LA SWISSE." Value 1.8 cts.

LUCERNE.

18. S. 1793. Ten batzen. Obv. Crowned shield, bearing the arms of the Canton (*party per pale; azure and argent*), draped with laurel, and inclosed between branches of laurel and palm. "MON(eta) NOV(a) REIP(ublicæ) LUCERNENSIS." Rev. Eight L's interlaced, and arranged as a cross, with the number "40" in the center. "DOMINUS SPES POPULI SUI," and the date "1793." Value 28 cts.

19. S. 1793. Five batzen. Same type as No. 18. Value 14 cts.

20. S. 1795. Twenty batzen. Obv. Arms of the Canton, upon a crowned shield, between two branches of laurel. Beneath is the denomination "20 BAZ." "RESPUBLICA LUCERNENSIS." Rev. Eight L's arranged as a cross, with a small wreath of olive in the center. "DOMINUS SPES POPULI SUI," and the date. Value 57 cts.

21. B.S. 1808. One batzen. Obv. Arms of the Canton upon an oval shield, draped with laurel. Beneath is the date "1808." "CANTON LUCERN." Rev. The inscription "1 BATZEN X RAPPEN," between two branches of oak.

22. S. 1812. Ten batzen. Obv. Arms of the Canton upon a crowned shield, between two branches of palm, crossed. Beneath is the date "1812." "CANTON LUZERN." Rev. A Swiss soldier, armed with a sword and spear, and supporting a shield, bearing the inscription "XIX CANTONE." Beneath is the denomination "10 BATZ." "SCHWEIZERISCHE EIDSGENOSSENSCHAFT." Value 28 cts.

23. S. 1814. Four franken. Obv. Arms of the Canton upon a crowned shield, between branches of palm. "CANTON LUZERN," and the date. Rev. A Swiss soldier, supporting a spear with his right hand, and leaning with his left upon a shield, bearing the inscription "XIX CANT." Beneath is the denomination "4 FRANKEN." "SCHWEIZER[E] EIDSGENOSSEN[T]. Value $1.14.*

* Assumed.

ST. GALL.

27. S. 162–. Crown. Obv. A bear. "MO(neta) NO(va) CIVIT(as) SAN GALLENSIS 162–." Rev. A double-eagle, surmounted by the imperial crown. "SOLI DEO OPT: MAX: SANS ET GLORIA."

28. S. 1777. Twenty batzen. Obv. A bear carrying a log of wood, with the date beneath, inclosed between branches of palm and olive. "ABB. S(an) G(allensis) E. S. J. A. V. E." Rev. A shield, bearing the arms of the bishopric, bedecked with the regalia of the church. Beneath the shield is a scene representing a female surmounted by a glory, and seated upon an altar, to whom a winged angel is presenting an olive branch. (The spirit of God bringing peace to the church.) Branches of palm and laurel at either side. "BEDA D. G. S(acri) R(omani) I(mperii) P"(rinceps). Value 58 cts.

29. B.S. 1813. One batzen. Obv. A shield, bearing the arms of the Canton (a fasces upon a green field) between two sprigs of oak. "CANTON ST. GALLEN," and the date. Rev. "1 BAZEN," and the mint-master's initial "K.," inclosed in an olive wreath. Value 2 cts.

TICINO.

31. B.S. 1835. Three soldi. Obv. A shield, bearing the arms of the Canton (*party per pale, gules and azure*), surmounted by a laurel wreath. "CANTONE TICINO." Rev. "SOLDI TRE.—1835," inclosed in a wreath of oak and lily.

BASEL.

33. G. 1702. Quarter ducat. Obv. A lion *rampant*, wielding a sword, and supporting a shield. "DOMINE CONSERVA NOS IN PACE." Rev. "ANNO DOMINE 1702," inscribed in three lines. *No legend.*

34. G. —. Ducat. Obv. Two palm and two laurel branches, crossed, with a staff surmounted by a liberty-cap. "FLORENUS AUREUS REIPUB. BASIL." Rev. A shield, bearing the arms of the Canton. "DOMINE CONSERVA NOS IN PACE." Value $2.15.

35. G. 1795. Pistole. Obv. The arms of the Canton upon an oval shield, draped with laurel, and surmounted by a hat and plume.

"RESPUBLICA BASILIENSIS." Rev. "DOMINE CONSERVA NOS IN PACE," inscribed in four lines, between branches of oak, crossed. Value $4.50.

36. S. —. Crown. Obv. The City of Basel; on a scroll above is inscribed the name "BASILEA." Rev. A shield, bearing the arms of the Canton, supported by two griffins. "DOMINE CONSERVA NOS IN PACE."

37. S. 1740. Quarter crown. Obv. The City of Basel. Above are eight small shields in an arch, and the name "BASILEA." Beneath is the date, a cornucopia, and an olive branch. Rev. A cockatrice supporting a small shield, bearing the arms of the Canton. "DOMINE CONSERVA NOS IN PACE."

38 and 39. S. 1765. Thalers. Obv. A cockatrice supporting a shield, bearing the arms of the Canton. "DOMINE CONSERVA NOS IN PACE." Rev. The denomination "1 THALER," inclosed in a wreath of laurel. "MONETA REIPUB. BASILENSIS," and the date. Values 83.2 cents.

40. S. 1765. Half thaler. Same type as No. 38. Value 42 cts.

41. S. 1765. Three batzen. Obv. The arms of the Canton. "DOMINE CONSERVA," etc. Rev. The inscription "'III BATZEN, 1765." "MONETA REIPUB. BASILENSIS."

42. S. 1766. One-third thaler. Same type as No. 38. Value 28 cents.

43. S. 1766. One-sixth thaler. Same type as No. 38. Value 14 cents.

44. B.S. 1810. One batzen. Obv. A shield, bearing the arms of the Canton, between two laurel branches, crossed. "CANTON BASEL." Rev. The inscription "1 BATZEN, 1810," between two oak branches, crossed. Value 2 cts.

SOLEURE.

46. S. 1794. Ten batzen. Obv. A crowned shield, bearing the arms of the Canton (*party per fess, gules and argent*), between two branches of laurel. "RESPUBLICA SOLODORENSIS." Rev. The initial "S." interlaced with a cross. "CUNCTA PER DEUM," and the date. Value 20 cts.

AARGAU.

48. S. 1809. Twenty batzen. Obv. A shield, bearing the arms of the Canton (*party per pale, sable and azure; a fess wavy azure, of the first, and three mullets argent, of the second*), between branches of laurel and palm, crossed. "CANTON ARGAU." Rev. A Swiss soldier, seated upon a stone block, holding a palm branch extended in his left hand, supporting a spear, and leaning with his right arm upon a shield, bearing the inscription "XIX CANT." From behind the shield protrudes a branch of oak. Beneath is the denomination "20 BATZ." "SCHWEIZERISCHE EIDSGENOSSENSCHAFT, 1809." Value 57 cts.

49. S. 1811. Five batzen. Obv. (See No. 48.) Rev. The inscription "5 BATZEN*1811*" between two branches of oak, crossed. Value 13 cts.

50. S. 1826. Five batzen. Obverse same as No. 48, with the denomination "5 BATZ." beneath the shield. "CANTON AARGAU, 1826." Rev. A cross, with the initial "C." in the center, inclosed in a wreath of laurel. "DIE CONCORDIER CANTONE DER SCHWEIZ."

APPENZELL.

52. B.S. 1808. One batzen. Obv. A shield, bearing the arms of the Canton (*argent, a bear sable, erect, proper*), between branches of palm and laurel, crossed. "CANTON APPENZELL," and the date, and initials "V.—R." Rev. The inscription "1 BATZEN—•+•—10" (rappen) inclosed in a wreath of olive. "JEDEM DAS SEINIGE."

UNTERWALDEN.

54. S. —. Twenty kreutzers. Obv. A shield, bearing the arms of the Canton. "MONETA REIP. SUBSYLVANIÆ SUPERIORIS." Rev. A double-eagle, surmounted by a crown. An oval shield upon its breast, upon which is inscribed the value "20." "DILEXET DOMINUS DECORUM JUSTITIA."

55. S. 1726. Same, with the date "1726" on the obverse.

GLARUS.

57. B.S. 1812. Three schilling. Obv. A shield, bearing a saint, with a staff and book, upon a red field, draped with laurel. "CANTON GLARUS," and the date. Rev. "III SCHILLING—9 RAPPEN," inclosed in a wreath of laurel.

GENEVA.

59 and 60. B.S. 1590. Six sols, or sous. Obv. A sun, with the arms of the Canton in the center (*party per pale; a demi-eagle of the first, and a key of the second field*). Rev. "SIX*SOLS * POUR LES SOLDATS DE GENEVE, 1590."

61 to 67. S. 1677–1685. Pieces of six, five, and three sols. Obv. Arms of the Canton, and the legend "CIVITAS (or "RESPUB.") GENEVENSIS." Rev. A cross and a sun, the latter containing the letters "I. H. S." (*Jesus Hominum Salvator.*) Legends "POST TENEBRAS LUX."

68. S. 1723. Crown. Obv. A shield, bearing the arms of the Canton, surmounted by a sun containing the letters "I. H. S." "RESPUBLICA GENEVENSIS." Rev. A double-eagle, surmounted by a crown. "POST TENEBRAS LUX," and the date. Value $1.12.

69 to 71. S. 1710–1714. Pieces of one, and one-half livre, of the same type as the crown. (No. 68.)

72 to 74. S. 1794. Pieces of fifteen sols. Obv. The French eagle, between branches of oak, crossed. "POST TENEBRAS LUX," and the date. Rev. "15 SOLS," surrounded by diverging rays. "EGALITE* LIBERTE*INDEPENDANCE."

75 to 77. B.S. 1795–1797. Pieces of three and six sols. Obv. Arms of the Canton. "GENEVE REPUBLIQUE"+"L'AN 6 DE L'EGALITE." Rev. "THREE (or "SIX") SOLS," inscribed between two branches of oak. "POST TENEBRAS LUX," and the date.

78 to 81. B.S. 1819–1833. Pieces of one sou. Obv. Shield, bearing the arms of the Canton. Above are the letters "I. H. S.," surrounded by diverging rays. "REP. ET CANTON DE GENEVE." Rev. The denomination, and the legend "POST TENEBRAS LUX."

82 to 88. B.S. 1839. Pieces of 25, 10, 4, 2, and 1 centimes. Obv.

Arms of the Canton, with the legend "POST TENEBRAS LUX." Rev. "REP: ET CANT. DE GENEVE," and the denomination and date, as "25 CENTIMES, 1839."

NEUFCHATEL.

90. C. 1807. Half batzen. Obv. A crowned shield, bearing the French arms, encircled by the order chain of the Legion of Honor. "ALEXANDRE PR. & DUC DE NEUFCHA^{L}." Rev. "$\frac{1}{2}$ BATZ.," inscribed between branches of oak and laurel. "PRINCIPAUTE DE NEUCHATEL," and the date.

REPUBLIC OF 1798.

92. S. 1801. Franc, of ten batzen. Obv. A Swiss soldier, carrying a standard. "HELVETISCHE REPUBLIK," and the date "1801." Rev. The denomination and mint-mark, "10 BATZEN—B." (Bern), inscribed within a hoop intwined with oak. Value 28.2 cts.

93 and 94. C. 1799. Half batzen. Obv. "HELVET. REPUBL. 5," inscribed between two branches of oak, crossed. Rev. "$\frac{1}{2}$ BATZEN, 1799," inclosed in a wreath of lily.

The pieces above described were not the only coins issued by the Republic of 1798. Full sets of the coins, provided for by the law of 1799, were issued, but, as the coinage was short lived, they have now become so scarce as to be seldom met with except in the cabinets of coin collectors. For the benefit of coin collectors, and others feeling an interest in the subject, the remaining pieces are noticed below, although not falling within the prescribed limits of the present work.

The *gold* coinage consisted of the *thirty-two* and *sixteen* franken pieces, both of the same type. On the obverse was a Swiss soldier, at front face, attired in armor and plumed, grasping a standard in his right hand, the end of the flagstaff sticking in his belt. Beneath was the mint-mark "B." (Bern), and above, the legend "HELVETISCHE REPUBLIK." On the reverse, inclosed in a wreath formed of a series of hoops, or concentric lines, bound together with a band, and intwined with oak, was inscribed the denomination and the date, divided by a dash line. The *silver* coins were the pieces of *four franken*, or one thaler (commonly designated "*the new thaler*," or new dollar), and its half of *two franken*. They were of nearly the same pattern as the *franken* piece described above (which see).

HELVETIA.

Constitution of 1848.

96 to 99. S. 1850. Pieces of five, two, one, and one-half franken, all of the same type. Obv. A device, emblematic of Helvetia; a female seated amid emblems of agriculture, with her right arm extended, and supporting with her left hand a pointed shield bearing the arms (*gules, a cross argent*). Above is the name "HELVETIA." *Reverse of the five franken.* The denomination "5 FR.," and the date "1850," inclosed in a wreath, composed of oak and white lily branches, crossed. Values same as the French coinage of this date. (See Plate XXII. No. 4.)

100 and 101. B.M. 1850. Ten centimes or rappen. Obv. A shield, bearing the arms, backed with oak branches. Above is the name "HELVETIA," and beneath, the date "1750." Rev. The value "10," inclosed in a wreath of oak. Contain only fifteen per cent. silver.

102. B.M. Five centimes. Same type. Only one-tenth silver.

103. C. 1850. Two centimes. Obverse same as No. 100. Rev. The numeral "2" inscribed between two branches of laurel, crossed. Contain no silver; an alloy of copper, zinc, and nickel. (See Plate XXII. No. 6.)

DIVISION XVI.

MEXICO.

The regular coins, as well as the history of Mexico, are so familiar to the American reader as to require, in this place, but a passing notice. The unit of value being the same in Mexico as in the United States, our dollar having, in fact, been derived from the Spanish dollar, and the fact that the coinage of Mexico has formed so large a portion of our currency, has served to render them nearly as familiar, among our dealers and traders, as our own lawful coins, especially in the smaller denominations. The quarters, eighths, and sixteenths of the Mexican dollar, the two last being known by the various names of "*shillings, levies, ninepence, sixpence, fips, bits*," etc., according to locality, have, in former times, had more effect upon our prices of small articles than our own small coins, which are much more simple in their subdivisions. Thus, until quite a recent date, our postages were regulated to the awkward sums of 6¼ and 12½ cents, instead of *five* and *ten;* and, even at the present time, notwithstanding the fact that recent legislation has nearly banished these coins from our circulation, our small dealers find it much more convenient, from long usage, to speak of "*shillings*, fips," etc., than of *dimes* and *cents.*

Mexico has always been a large producer of silver, and, in former times, it was always the practice to convert the silver into coins, prior to exportation, a custom which was, in fact, compelled by law, until within the last quarter of a century. This policy has served to give the currency of Mexico a great prominence abroad. The bulk of the famous coinage known as the *pillar dollar* emanated from Mexico; and before the revolution of 1821–22, by which she freed herself from Spanish thraldom, a large portion of the Spanish coins, bearing the effigy and insignia of the King of Spain, were actually executed in Mexico. For this reason, all Spanish coins which have been minted in Mexico, although conforming pretty nearly to the lawful standards of the mother country, and having been coined by the royal authority, have been comprised in the present division, as it would be difficult to draw a distinction between the Spanish and Mexican coins *proper*, without thereby confusing the reader.

The "*cob*" money of Mexico, which first claims our attention, not only in point of time, but also in style of execution, consists both of gold and silver, and is an unsightly coinage, of so rude a character as to scarcely deserve the name of coin. The larger portion of this coinage appears to have been issued before the year 1740, but a few specimens are found to bear date as late as 1768 and 1770. In the date, the *thousandth* place is usually omitted, so that the characters 738 (for example) are intended to signify 1738. It is evident, from their appearance, that they were struck with a hammer, as they are generally found to be of any form except that of a true circle; thus presenting a standing invitation for the practice of clipping. In Mexico these coins are known as "*máquina de papalote y cruz*," or "windmill and cross money;" the cross which appears in the impression being thought to bear a striking resemblance to the fans of a windmill.* There were full sets of these coins, from the doubloon down, differing, however, in type. They appear to have conformed to the lawful standard, or nearly so, as is evinced by the fact that they are found, even at the present time, to be within a few grains of the proper weight, notwithstanding their liability to clipping, before mentioned.

From 1810 to 1822, while the revolution was in progress, various coins appeared, among which were the well-known *cast* and *hammered dollars*, and the *Vargas* and *Morelas* pieces.

The *hammered dollars* appeared about the close of the year 1810. The communication between the capital and the interior being cut off, it was found necessary to establish mints at some of the provincial towns. As these could not be furnished with the necessary machinery, they were obliged to prepare the *planchets* by hand, and give them the impressions by means of a hammer. To the latter circumstance they are indebted for their name. They are found to be much inferior to the regular coinage, and are easily distinguished therefrom by their crude appearance.

The *cast dollars* are said to have been issued at Chihuahua, in the years 1811, '12, and '13; some of them, however, bear the mint-mark of the National Mint (M°), and are of various dates, ranging from 1804 to 1813.† But this circumstance is readily accounted for by the fact that they are *casts*, and that the molds were made from any Spanish dollars which happened to be at hand, without much regard to their dates or places of mintage. The fact of their being *cast*, renders it quite easy to distinguish them from the genuine *struck* dollars, as the impressions have a blurred or coarse appearance, which proceeds from the fact that silver, like gold, always *contracts* while cooling in the mold, and, therefore, presents an imperfect proof, wanting the fullness and sharpness of outline which is always observable in a

---

* The cross in question is usually designated "a cross potent" (crutch-shaped).

† Many of them bear the effigy and titles of CHARLES IV., who abdicated in 1808, in favor of his son, FERDINAND VII.

stamped coin. The cast dollars are very irregular in their weight, but the fineness averages about 916 *thousandths*. They range from 94 to 127 cents in value.

The *Vargas dollars* were coined at Sombrerete, by the republican general VARGAS, whose name appears in the impression. They bear the dates of 1811 and 1812, and are struck with a hammer. They are now quite rare, and are only to be met with in the cabinets of coin collectors. They were somewhat higher, both in weight and fineness, than the hammered dollars, noticed above.

The *Morelas* coins were issued by General Morelas, another general of the patriot forces. The pieces were cast in molds, and are very rude. There was a complete set of these coins, from the dollar to the sixteenth, but they are now extremely scarce. They were about the same standards as the *hammered dollars.*

There is another kind of currency (which may be classed as "irregular") at present circulating in Mexico, with which the reader is doubtless more familiar as an application in his daily ablutions than as a circulating medium. "In the small interior towns, and among the laboring people, *soap* is held as a legal tender, of which there is a large amount in circulation."*

The standards of Mexican coins issued since the revolution are the same as those adopted for the Spanish coins in 1772. The gold coinage consists of the doubloon, of sixteen dollars, and its subdivisions, the half, the quarter, or pistole, the eighth, or escudo, and the sixteenth, or gold dollar; the fineness, which is always inscribed upon the piece, should be 21 *quilates* (karats), or 895 thousandths, and the weight of the doubloon 418 Troy grains; the smaller pieces in proportion.

Of the silver there are six denominations: the dollar, or *peso*, of eight reals, and the pieces of four, two, one, and one-half reals (the latter being called a *medio*), and the quarter real, or half medio.

---

* Letter of EDWARD CONNOR, U. S. Consul at Mazatlan, to the Treasury Department, July 29, 1859. Rather a sad commentary upon the present state of civil society in Mexico! If report speak truly, we should judge this to be the only use to which soap is ever applied among the lower classes.

These are professedly 10 *dineros*, 20 *granos*, or 903 thousandths fine; and the dollar, or *peso*, should weigh the same as the doubloon; the others in proportion.

The National Mint of Mexico, which is located at the capital, was established in 1535; the mint-mark is M[o]. (the o. surmounting the M). After the breaking out of the revolution in 1810, several mints sprung into existence; whether these are all continued to the present time we are unable to say, but deem it expedient to state, in this connection, the location of each, with the dates at which they commenced operations—as far as practicable—and the marks by which their coins are to be distinguished.

The Mint of ZACATECAS appears to have commenced in 1810; mark Z[s]. Mint of DURANGO, 1811; mark D[o]. Mint of GUANAXUATO, 1812; mark G[o]. Mint of CHIHUAHUA, 1811 to 1814, recommenced in 1832; mark C[a]. Mint of GUADALAXARA, 1814; mark G[a]. Mint of SAN LUIS POTOSI,* 1829; mark P[i]. The Mint of the State of Mexico, at TLALPAN, the date of the original establishment of which is unknown, appears to have been discontinued, and revived again in 1829, and finally abolished about two years after; the mint-mark is ME. Mint of GUADALUPE Y CALAO, 1844; mark G.C. Mint of CULIACAN, in Sinaloa, 1846; mark C.

"COB" MONEY.

1. G. 1738. Doubloon, of PHILIP V. Obv. Two crowned columns standing in the water, the initials "L.—N." and "P—U—A" (plus ultra) and "7—3—8" (1738) are inscribed promiscuously at the sides and between the pillars. Rev. The arms of Spain, quartered by a *cross potent*. Value $16.00.

2–4. G. —. Pieces of one-half, one-quarter, and one-eighth of the doubloon; upon the obverse is a shield, bearing the arms of Spain and the royal arms. Rev. A *cross potent*, inclosed in a *quarterfoil* compartment. These pieces bear no dates.

5–11. S. 1693 to 1768. Cob dollars, and pieces of four, two, and

---

* This should not be confounded with the Mint of POTOSI, in Bolivia, which has a different mark.

one real. These coins are all of the same pattern; the dollars have on the obverse two crowned columns rising out of the water, as in the doubloon. The denomination "8." (meaning 8 reals) is inscribed between the crowns, and between two parallel lines are the letters "P L U S U L T R A" (plus ultra), crowded in without much attention to order; beneath is the date, inscribed as in the doubloon, omitting the thousandths place. Value of the dollar $1.05.

SPANISH-MEXICAN COINS.

12. S. 1629. Dollar, of PHILIP IV. Obv. Crowned shield, bearing the royal arms. "PHILIPUS IIII DEI G. 1629." Rev. The arms of Spain, quartered by a *cross-flory*, inclosed in a tressure of eight arches. "HISPANIARUM ET INDIARUM REX."

13. S. 1637. Dollar, of same. Obv. The royal arms upon a crowned shield. "PHILIPUS IIII D. G. HISPANIAR." Reverse same as No. 12, with the legend "ET INDIARUM REX. ANNO 1637."

This piece has been washed with gold, which accounts for its *brassy* appearance; the mint-mark is T. It is doubtful whether it belongs to Mexico.

14. S. 1714. Dollar, of PHILIP V. Obv. A crowned shield, bearing the royal arms; the arms of Anjou on a shield of pretence. "PHILIPPUS V. DEI G. 1714." Reverse same as No. 12.

15. S. 1733. Half dollar, or four reals, of PHILIP V. Same type as No. 14. This piece has been badly clipped.

17–20. S. 1737–44. "Globe" dollar, and its half, quarter, and sixteenth, or medio, all of the same type. Obv. A crowned shield, bearing the arms of Spain, with a shield of pretence bearing the arms of Anjou. "PHILIP V. D. G. HISPAN. ET IND. REX." Rev. Two crowned pillars, encircled with scrolls, bearing the letters "P L U S" and "U L T R" (plus ultra). Between the pillars are two hemispheres, surmounted by a single crown; above is inscribed "UTRAQUE UNUM." Beneath is the date and mint-mark (the latter being repeated, one appearing before, and the other after the date). Value of the dollar $1.04.

21. G. 1745. Pistole, or quarter doubloon. Obv. Bust, in armor. "PHILIP V. D. G. HISPAN. ET IND. REX," and the date "1745." Rev. A crowned shield, bearing the arms of Spain, quartered; a shield of

pretence bearing the arms of Anjou. "INITIUM SAPIENTIÆ TIMOR DOMINI." Value $4.03.2.

22 and 23. S. 1749–57. "Globe" dollars, of FERDINAND VI. Same type as No. 17. Value $1.04 each.

24. S. 1749. Medio, or sixteenth. Same type as No. 22.

25. G. 1759. Half doubloon. Obv. Bust, in armor. "FERDINAND. VI D. G. HISPAN. ET IND. REX."......"1759." Rev. Crowned shield, bearing the arms of Spain, with the arms of Anjou on a shield of pretence. "NOMINA MAGNA SEQUOR." Value $8.13.

26 and 27. G. 1762–69. Half doubloon and pistole, of CHARLES III. Same type. Obv. Bust, in armor. "CAROLS III D. G. HISPAN. ET IND. REX," and the date. Rev. Same type as No. 25.

28 and 29. S. 1762–71. "Globe" dollar and quarter dollar, of CHARLES III. Same type as No. 17. Value of the dollar $1.04.

30 and 31. S. 1779–85. "Pillar" dollar and quarter dollar, of CHARLES III. Obv. Bust, *laureated*, and enveloped in a Roman mantle. "CAROLUS III DEI GRATIA," and the date. Rev. A crowned shield, bearing the arms of Spain, *quartered*, the arms of Anjou on a shield of pretence, between two pillars, around which floats a scroll bearing the motto "PLUS ULTRA." "HISPAN. ET IND. REX." Value of the dollar $1.03.7.

On the pillar dollar and its parts, after this time, the mint-mark, the denomination in reals, and the initials of the mint-master, are placed immediately after the *legend* on the *reverse;* the mint-mark coming first, the denomination next, and the initials last. This is not the case with the gold coinage, the mint and mint-master's initials being inscribed *beneath*, while the denomination appears at the *sides* of the shield.

32. G. 1805. Doubloon, of CHARLES IV. Obv. Bust, in armor, bedecked with the badge of the *golden fleece*, and partially enveloped in a military mantle. "CAROL. IIII D. G. HISP. ET IND. R." and the date. Rev. A crowned shield, encircled by the order chain of the *golden fleece*, and bearing the royal arms in ten fields, with a shield of pretence bearing the arms of Spain, and a heart shield bearing the arms of Anjou. "AUSPICE DEO. UTROQ. FELIX." Value $15.57.

33. G. 1789. Escudo. Same type as No. 32.

34 to 38. S. 1791–1809. Pillar dollar and its parts (the half, quar-

ter, eighth, and sixteenth), of CHARLES IV. Obv. Bust, *laureated*, and enveloped in a Roman mantle. "CAROLUS IIII DEI GRATIA," and the date. Rev. Same type as Nos. 30 and 31. Value of the dollar $1.03.7.

39 and 40. G. 1809–11. Doubloon, and escudo or eighth, of FERDINAND VII. Same type. Obv. Bust, in armor, bedecked with the badge of the *golden fleece*, and draped with a military mantle. "FERDIN. VII D. G. HISP. ET. IND. R." Reverse same as No. 32. (The *legend* on the *reverse* of the smaller piece is much abbreviated.) Value of the doubloon $15.57.

41. S. 1810. Dollar, *of the* MINT OF THE STATE OF MEXICO (at Tlalpan). Obv. Bust of Ferdinand, enveloped in a Roman mantle, and *laureated*. Poorly executed. "FERDIN. VII DEI GRATIA," and the date. Reverse same as No. 30. Value $1.04.

42. S. 1814. Half pillar dollar, of GUADALAXARA. Same type as No. 41, with a somewhat different head—not much of an improvement, as far as the likeness is concerned. Value 51.5 cts.*

43 and 44. C. 1814–16. Pieces of two and one *quartino*. Same type. Obv. The royal monogram, crowned. "FERDIN. VII D. G. HISP. REX," and the date. Rev. The arms of Spain and Anjou, encircled by a wreath of laurel. Struck at the National Mint.

45. C. 1820. Quartino. Obv. The word "PROVISIONAL," with the fraction "$\frac{1}{4}$," and the date. Rev. A sun.

46. G. 1821. Doubloon, of GUADALAXARA. Obv. Bust of Ferdinand, *laureated*. "FERDIN. VII D. G. HISP. ET IND. R.," and the date. Rev. Same type as No. 39. Value $15.57.

HAMMERED COINS.

47 and 48. S. 1812. Hammered dollars, of ZACATECAS. Obv. Bust of Ferdinand, *laureated*. "FERDIN. VII.—8 R(eals)—DEI GRATIA." Rev. A device similar to the pillar dollar. "MONEDA PROVISIONAL DE ZACATECAS."

49. S. 1811. Quarter dollar, of ZACATECAS. Obv. A crowned shield, between two pillars. "FERDIN. VII.—2 R.—DEI GRATIA." Rev. Device not legible. "MONEDA PROVISIONAL DE ZACATECAS."

50. S. 1822. Hammered dollar, of DURANGO. Obv. Bust of Fer-

* The coins of this mint are very unsteady in value.

dinand, *laureated.* "FERDIÑ. VII DEI GRATIA," and the date. Rev. Same type as the pillar dollar of the regular series.

51. S. 1814. Half dollar, of the same type as the regular coinage; place of mintage not known. All the hammered dollars are very rude, the devices and legends being but half visible.

CAST DOLLAR.

52. S. 1812. This dollar is of the same type as the regular pillar dollar. It bears at the end of the legend, on the reverse, the mint-mark "CA.," which is doubtless intended for *Chihuahua*, at which place this coinage is said to have been executed.

VARGAS DOLLARS.

53 and 54. S. 1811–12. Dollars, of GEN. VARGAS. These pieces are very imperfect, the only visible portion of the obverse being the name "VARGAS," which appears in the legend, and the date which occupies the center of the piece. The reverse is somewhat more plain, being a crowned shield, bearing the arms of Spain and Anjou, as in the royal coinage; and in a circle around the shield, the legend "R. C. A X A. DE SOMBRETE." These have the appearance of having been struck over a former impression, as portions of various letters appear around the edge of the piece.

MORELAS COINS.

55 to 58. S. 1812–13. Dollar, and pieces of two, one, and one-half real, of GEN. MORELAS. Obv. A bow and arrow, between two palm branches, and the word "SUD," meaning "*the army of the South.*" Rev. The mint-mark "M°" and the denomination and date, as "8 R(eals) 1813." This is inclosed by a rude wreath; the two smaller pieces vary somewhat from this description, but not enough to render a separate description necessary.

CONSTITUTIONAL COINAGE.

59. G. 1823. Half doubloon, of ITURBIDE, or AUGUSTIN I. Obv. Undraped bust, "AUGUSTINUS DEI PROVIDENTIA," with the date and mint-mark. Rev. A shield, bearing the Mexican eagle; beneath are the emblems of authority. "MEX. I IMPERATOR CONSTITUT." The

denomination (in escudos) appears at the end of the legend. Value $7.74.9. (See Plate XXIII. No. 1.)

60 and 61. S. 1822. Dollars, of AUGUSTIN. Obv. Same type as the half doubloon. Rev. An eagle perched upon a cactus plant, and crowned. "MEX. I. IMPERATOR CONSTITUT." Value $1.04.6 each.

62 to 66. S. 1822–23. Dollar, and pieces of two, one, and one-half real. These are all of the same type as Nos. 60 and 61, with the exception of a material improvement in the style of the eagle on the reverse.

REPUBLICAN COINAGE.

67 to 70. G. 1824–48. Doubloon, and its half, eighth, and sixteenth, all of the same type. On the obverse is an open book, upon which is inscribed the word "LEY." Upon the book rests a hand, which grasps a staff surmounted by a liberty-cap. "LA LIBERTAD EN LA LEY." Beneath is inscribed (on the doubloon) "8 E(scudo) M° (Mexico) 1824. J. M.—21 Q"(uilates). Rev. An eagle perched upon a cactus plant, and holding a serpent with its beak and one talon; beneath are branches of oak and laurel. "REPUBLICA MEXICANA." (See Plate XXIII. No. 2.)

71 and 72. S. 1824. Dollar and quarter dollar. Obv. A liberty-cap, bearing the word "LIBERTAD" surrounded by diverging rays; beneath is inscribed (on the dollar) "8 R(eals) G° (Guanaxuato) 1824 J. M. 10 D(ineros) 20 G"(ranos). Rev. An eagle perched upon a cactus plant, and grasping a serpent; beneath are branches of oak and laurel. "REPUBLICA MEXICANA."

These piece were coined at Guanaxuato and Durango, respectively, and are known as *agachados*, or "hooked," a name which they derive from the position of the eagle's head, which is bent downward. Pieces of the same type are said to have been coined at the Mint of Mexico. An impression formerly prevailed in Mexico, that these pieces were of less value than the coins of a different type. Assays made at the Philadelphia Mint have proved this to be a fallacy.*

73 to 78. S. 1826–39. Dollars, and their subdivisions, the half,

* See "Manual of Coins and Bullion."

quarter, eighth, and sixteenth, all of the same type. Obv. A liberty-cap surrounded by diverging rays, as in the *agachados;* beneath is inscribed the denomination, mint-mark, date, mint-master's initials, and the fineness, "10 D(ineros) 20 G"(ranos). Reverse same as the gold coinage, the head of the eagle being erect. Value of the dollar $1.04.6. (See Plate XXV. No. 3.)

79. S. 1820. Half medio, or quarter real. Obv. A castle, with the letter "L." at one side, and "$\frac{1}{4}$" at the other; beneath is the date "1820." Rev. A lion *rampant.*

80. S. 1845. Half medio. Head of Liberty; beneath is the mint-mark Gº (Guanaxuata) and the initials of the mint-master. Rev. "$\frac{1}{4}$." "REPUBLICA MEXICANA," and the date "1845."

81. C. 1830. Quartino. Obv. "$\frac{1}{4}$.——Mº—A—1830" inscribed between two branches of palm. Rev. Same type as the silver coinage.

82. S. 1858. A proof dollar, of the *Mint of Mexico.* Same type as No. 73. Value $1.04. (See Plate XXV. No. 1.)

MINT OF "N. R."

99 to 103. These pieces—consisting of the doubloon, three-quarter doubloons, and a quarter dollar—are all of the same type as the regular coinage, and bear dates ranging from 1759 to 1816; they bear the mint-mark "N. R." Where this mint is located, we are not prepared to say; but, judging from the dates on the different pieces, it has evidently been in operation for a long series of years. They are, undoubtedly, an American coinage, but whether of Mexico or South America, is uncertain. They have been placed under Mexico, for want of a more *certain* arrangement.

PROCLAMATION PIECE.

105. S. 1790. Proclamation quarter dollar, of ORIZAVA. Obv. A device similar to the reverse of the pillar dollar. "CARLOS IV. REY. DE ESPANA Y D LOS YNDIAS." Rev. "LA MUI LELA VILLA DE ORIZAVA EN 11 D'ABRIL DE 1790," inscribed in five lines. "ENSU PROCLAMACION."

DIVISION XVII.

CENTRAL AMERICA.

Central America comprises all that narrow neck of land which connects North and South America, but which properly belongs to the former, extending from Mexico to the territories of New Granada, and comprising the following States: *Guatemala, San Salvador, Honduras, Nicaragua,* and *Costa Rica.*

Up to 1821 this country all belonged to Spain, but by the revolution which terminated in that year, by which most of its American colonies were lost to the crown of Spain, it became an independent province. During the reign of Iturbide it was incorporated with Mexico, but upon his deposal in 1823, became a distinct government, consisting of a confederation of the States above named, and began to coin money in that capacity in 1824.

This Confederacy lasted until 1839, since which time the country has been continually embroiled in internal as well as external trouble, which has had the effect to overturn the Confederacy, so that it now consists of several distinct parts. In the present chapter, however, these different parts are all included under the common head of "Central America," as it is neither easy nor desirable to arrange them under distinct heads.

The monetary system continues the same as that of Spain (*which see*), and, until recently, the coinage was executed at Guatemala, the mint-mark of which is N. G. The coins of this mint are never seen here in any quantity, a few specimens only now and then finding their way into this market.

The doubloon of the Guatemala Mint is found to be considerably below the Spanish standard, so much so as to reduce its value to about $14.96,* the fineness being about 833 thousandths, and the weight 417 grains. The dollars, before 1836, average 415 grains in weight, and are 896 thousandths fine, and are consequently worth about $1.04.1, at the

* And since 1838 still lower.

present rate for silver. Since 1836, however, the coinage has been very much depreciated, the dollars of recent coinage averaging only 85 or 86 cents in value. In fact, it is almost impossible to keep track of the different changes in either the monetary or political system of this country, as nearly every year brings some unlooked-for change.

1 to 4. G. 1828–1848. Doubloon and its parts—the half, quarter, and sixteenth. All of the same type. Obv. A range of mountain peaks, from behind which the sun is just risen. "REPUBLICA DEL CENTRO DE AMERICA," and the date. Rev. A tree, and the denomination "8—E"(scudo), inclosed by a circular line. "LIBRE CRESCA FECUNDO." Beneath is the mint-mark, and the fineness, "21 Q.s" (21 quilates). (See Plate XXIII. No. 3.)

5. S. 1825. Piece of two reals. This is similar in type to the gold, but is rather rude in appearance, and the legends are much abbreviated. The circular lines inclosing the fields are omitted.

6 to 10. S. 1824–1839. Dollars, and pieces of two and one real. All of the same type as the gold coinage, except that the sun, instead of being fully risen, just appears above the mountain to the left of the field. (See Plate XXV. No. 2.)

COSTA RICA.

11. G. 1842. One escudo. Obv. A star surrounded by diverging rays. Beneath is a palm and laurel branch, crossed. "EST D'COSTA RICA." Rev. A tree. Above is inscribed the fineness, "21 Q"(quilates), and beneath, the mint-marks and date. Value about $1.76. (See Plate XXIII. No. 5.)

12 and 13. S. 1846. Pieces of two reals. These are somewhat after the pattern of the Guatemala coinage. They are very rude, and appear to have been fashioned with the hammer and punch. It is a curious fact that, while the gold coinage is very perfect, the silver is no better than the Mexican cob money.

NEW GRANADA.

This country was formerly a vice-royalty of Spain, but in the year 1819 it declared independence and united with Venezuela, under the name of Colombia. After a struggle, which terminated in 1822, New Granada succeeded, with the assistance of Venezuela, in throwing off the royal authority. This union continued until 1831, when it was dissolved, and divided into the three republics of New Granada, Venezuela, and Ecuador. New Granada, however, continued the name of Colombia upon its coins up to 1836.

In the following classification, the coins of Colombia struck during the union are included under the head of New Granada, although many of them were actually coined in the adjoining State.

The mints of New Granada are at BOGOTA and POPAYAN, which have been long established. The coins usually have the name of the mint in full. The coins of Bogota, however, are occasionally marked Bª..

Their system of money is the same as that of Spain, and therefore requires no further notice here. But it may be remarked that the gold coinage of Popayan was formerly very irregular in fineness, being very much below the Bogota standards. There have also been several changes in the types, as will appear by the following description:—

19. S. —. One real, of FERDINAND VII. Obv. Bust of Ferdinand, with the characters "F.—7." Rev. A crowned shield, bearing the arms of Spain and Granada* in five fields, and the denomination "1—R."

20. S. 1819. Dollar, or *peso*, PATRIOT. Obv. Bust of an Indian chief, surmounted by a double crown of feathers. "LIBERTAD AMERICANA," and the date "1819." Rev. A pomegranate, and the denomination "8—R." "NUEVA GRANADA." Value 74.2 cts.

21. C. 1820. Quartino, PATRIOT. Obv. A cross *potent*, with the letters "S.—M." in the upper angles, and the arms in the two lower angles. Rev. A rude crown, beneath which is inscribed the denomination "$\frac{1}{4}$," and the date "1820," with the arms. This piece bears no other marks indicating its origin. It is probably a coin of the Revolutionary party.

---

* *Argent, a pomegranate, in pale slipt, proper.* These were the arms of the City of Granada, in Spain, and were probably adopted, along with the name, by the American colony.

22 to 26. G. 1823–1836. Doubloons and their subdivisions—the quarter, eighth, and sixteenth. All of the same type. Obv. A female bust—Liberty. The hair is confined by a band, on which is inscribed "LIBERTAD." "REPUBLICA DE COLOMBIA," and the date. Rev. A *fasces* in pale, crossed by a bow and arrows *in saltiere*, between two cornucopias. The name of the mint is inscribed in full above the device, and the denomination (in escudos) and the initials of the mint officers beneath. Value of No. 22, $15.61.7. The *second* doubloon was struck at POPAYAN, and is worth only $15.39.

27 to 29. S. 1820–1821. Dollars, and piece of two reals. Same type. Obverse same as No. 20. Rev. A pomegranate, and the denomination "8—R." "CUNDINAMARCA." The mint-mark is B^{a}. Value of the dollar 74.2 cts.

30. S. 1827. One real. Obv. Same device as the reverse of the gold coinage. "REPUBLICA DE COLOMBIA," and the date "1827." Rev. "B(ogota) 1 REAL R. R.," inscribed beneath a scroll bearing the word "LIBERTAD," and between two branches of laurel, crossed.

31 and 32. S. 1835. Dollars. Same type as No. 30, with the inscription "B^{A}. COLOMBIANO OCHO REALES R. S." on the reverse. Value 74.2 cts.

33. G. 1837. Doubloon. Obv. A female bust, enveloped in a Roman mantle. The hair confined with a band, bearing the name "LIBERTAD." "REPUBLICA DE LA NUEVA GRANADA," and the date "1837." Rev. A pointed shield, bearing the arms in three fields. Above is a condor and a scroll, upon the latter is inscribed "LIBERTAD L ORDEN." "DIEZ I LEIS PESOS. BOGOTA R. S." Value $15.61.7.

34. S. 1837. Dollar. Obv. A pointed shield, bearing the arms in three fields. "REPUBLICA DE LA NUEVA GRANADA," and the date. Rev. "8 REALES," inscribed within a wreath of laurel. "BOGOTA." Value 74.2 cts.

35. S. 1839. Dollar. Obv. A cornucopia, above which is a condor *volant*, holding in its beak a scroll, bearing the inscription "LIBERTAD L ORDEN." "REPUBLICA DE LA NUEVA GRANADA," and the date "1839." Rev. "LEI OCHO DINEROS," inscribed within a wreath of laurel. "VALE OCHO REALES."......"BOGOTA." Value 67.8 cts.

36. S. 1846. Half real. Obv. A pomegranate between two cor-

nucopias. "REPUBLICA DE LA NUEVA GRANADA," and the date. Rev. "$\frac{1}{2}$ REAL," inscribed within a wreath of laurel. "POPAYAN."

37. S. 1847. One real. Obv. A pomegranate between two cornucopias. "NUEVA GRANADA," and the date. Rev. "UN REAL," inclosed by a heavy wreath of laurel, intwined with a scroll or ribbon. Above is inscribed "BOGOTA," and beneath, "LEY 0,900."

38. S. 1848. Dollar. Obv. A shield, suspended upon four standards, and surmounted by a condor, with expanded wings. "REPUBLICA DE LA NUEVA GRANADA," and the date "1848." Rev. "DIEZ REALES," inscribed within a wreath of laurel. Beneath is inscribed "LEY 0,900." Value 67.8 cts. (See Plate XXV. No. 4.)

39. S. 1849. Two reales. Obv. A shield, bearing the arms, between branches of laurel, crossed. "REPUBLICA DE LA NUEVA GRANADA," and the date "1849." Rev. Same type as No. 37. ("*Dos reales.*")

40 and 41. G. 1849–56. Doubloon, and its half. Both of the same type. Obv. A female head—Liberty, encircled by a band bearing the word "LIBERTAD." "REPUBLICA DE LA NUEVA GRANADA," and the date. Rev. The arms, upon a pointed shield, suspended upon four standards. Upon the top of the shield is perched a condor, holding laurel in its beak. Beneath the condor floats a scroll, bearing the words "LIBERTAD L ORDEN." "BOGOTA PESO—25,8064 G(rames, equivalent to 398.31 Troy grains). LEI 0,900." The value of the doubloon No. 40 is about $15.31, and is alloyed almost entirely with silver. Large quantities will yield $15.36.* (See Plate XXIII. No. 4.)

CARTAGENA.

42. C. 1813. Small piece, of the City of CARTAGENA. Very rude. On the obverse is a figure seated beneath a tree; a building appears in the background. On the reverse are various inscriptions, including the value, date, etc., all of which are nearly obliterated. The name "CARTAGENA" appears in the legend. This piece was evidently struck by hand, and appears to have been an irregular and unauthorized

---

* Coins, Coinage, and Bullion.—*Dubois.*

coinage, probably called forth by the scarcity of small change, a want which is seriously felt by many of the South American States and the West Indies.

VENEZUELA.

When Ojeda and Vespucci approached the coast of South America in 1499, they were greeted with the sight of an Indian village, apparently built upon the waters of the Lake Maracaybo. The houses or huts having been built upon piles set in the water some distance from the shore of the lake, they called this insular village—which was so much of a novelty in the eyes of Vespucius that he allowed it to remain unmolested—*Venezuela* (the diminutive of *Venezia*, or Venice), and this name was afterward extended to the lake, and finally to the surrounding country.

After its conquest and settlement, Venezuela was established as a Captain-Generalship of Spain, and afterward included the Kingdom of Quito (now Ecuador). The country continued subject to the crown of Spain until 1811, when it gained its independence. In 1819 it united with New Granada, in the Republic of Colombia, and became a party to the Constitution adopted by the Congress of *Rosario de Cúcuta* in 1821; but upon the dissolution of this Constitution in 1831, Venezuela regained its former position as an independent Republic.

Down to 1824 there was issued at CARACAS, the capital, a rude coinage, consisting of the *peseta* of two reals, and its half. These were issued both under the royal and the republican authority. Specimens of the former are found to bear date from 1781 to 1821; while the republican coinage appears to have commenced in 1815. They were very much after the style of the Mexican "cobs," and are much below the lawful standards both in weight and fineness. In 1829 and 1830, there was also coined at Caracas, a half medio, or $\frac{1}{32}$ of the dollar.

Venezuela has no regular coinage at the present day, and the only coins which we have ever seen of that Republic are the copper pieces—the cent and its subdivisions the half and quarter. They have a *nominal* dollar, or peso, in which accounts are kept, which is divided into reals and cents; ten cents making one real, and ten reals one dollar. This dollar, however, is only worth about 74.4 cents of our money. The coins of various countries, including the United States, England, and France, are made current there at certain rates, which are established by law.*

57. S. 1821. Two reals, *cob money*, of FERDINAND VII. Obv. The arms of Spain, quartered by a *cross potent;* the initials of the king, "F.—7." Rev. Two upright pillars, with the inscription "2 (2 reals) PLU—SUL—TRA. B.—1821.—S." Beneath is the name "CARACAS."

58 and 59. S. 1824. Pieces of two and one real, of the PATRIOTS. Obv. Arms of Spain, quartered by a *cross potent.* Rev. Two upright pillars, with the characters "2.—U—SUL—TR.—'24" (1824).

The cobs of the Patriots appear to be much more rude than those of the Royalists; the latter having made some pretensions to a definite form in the execution of their pieces, if not a higher value.

60 to 63. C. 1843. Pieces of one, one-half, and one-quarter centavo, all of the same type. Obv. A female bust, surmounted by a cap, on the band of which is inscribed "LIBERTAD." "REPUBLICA DE VENEZUELA." Rev. (of the larger piece) "1 CENTAVO, 1843," inscribed between branches of laurel, crossed.

ECUADOR.

Ecuador, under the name of Quito (which it derived from its principal city, now the capital), having formerly been a part and parcel of Venezuela, was a sharer in the political changes of the latter province, and, after the union of 1819, which was effected between New Granada and Venezuela, Quito was incorporated as a portion of Colombia. But this incongenial and poorly organized union having come to an untimely end in 1831, the door was opened for Quito to acquire its independence and step into the world of petty nations as a sovereign power—an opportunity which was not disregarded. By the terms of the agreement through which this dissolution was effected, Colombia was divided into three republics,

* Letters of E. A. TURPIN, Consul at Caracas, and A. T. SMITH, Consul at Laguayra, to the Treasury Department, May 20 and 21, 1859.

each of which was to assume one-third of the Colombian debt. The province of Quito being one of the three parties to this agreement, immediately organized itself into a republic, under the name of *Ecuador*,* and established its capital at Quito.

A mint was soon after established at the capital, and in 1833 coins were issued, conforming in their divisions to the Spanish, the unit being the dollar of eight reals. Of the gold, there was the doubloon, and its half, quarter, and eighth; the gold coinage appears, however (by recent letters from that Republic), to have been discontinued, or nominally so.† The latest date we have seen is a doubloon of 1847, bearing the head of Bolivar.

The silver dollar has never been issued in any quantity, and is, consequently, seldom seen. The smaller coins are the pieces of four, two, one, and one-half reals. The four-real pieces are scarce, only making about three per cent. of the entire circulation; the two smaller pieces being used merely for change, are also issued in small quantities. The two-real piece is the principal coinage, composing nearly one-half of the circulation. The legal fineness is 666 thousandths; and the weight of the two-real pieces, which is very unsteady, averages about 92 Troy grains.

The remainder of the circulation is supplied from the coinage of adjoining States. The dollars and two-real pieces of Colombia, issued in 1821 and previously, are circulating in small quantities, making about three per cent. of the circulation. New Granada silver dollars, and two-real pieces issued at Bogota and Popayan, of the dates from 1839 to 1846, which are now uncurrent in New Granada, make about *thirty* per cent. Bolivian two-real pieces, all deeply cut, with a round hole in the center, make about *three* per cent. The latter bear the effigy of Bolivar, and are of the same standard of fineness as the Quito coins (666 thousandths), and average about 92.5 grains in weight, their value being about the same as the Quito pieces of the same denomination. The remainder of the cir-

* Its territories lie immediately beneath the equator.

† Gold doubloons have occasionally been coined, but were all sent off, and form no part of the circulation, which is exclusively of silver coins. (*Statement of Dr. Wm. Jameson, Assayer of the Quito Mint, to Hon. Chas. R. Buckalew.*)

culation consists of the Spanish "cut quarters." These, however, are merely a local currency, circulating only at Quito and some portions of the interior.*

The coinage of the Quito Mint is seldom seen in this country, the coins never finding their way here unless by the hands of travelers or visitors from that Republic to this.

67 and 68. G. 1835. Pieces of one-quarter and one-eighth of the doubloon. Same type. Obv. A female bust, the hair confined by a band, on which is inscribed "LIBERTAD." "EL ECUADOR EN COLOMBIA." Beneath is the name of the mint "QUITO." Rev. Two mountain peaks, upon each of which is perched a condor; above is a sun. "EL PODER EN LA CONSTITUCION," and the date. (See Plate XXIII. No. 6.)

69. G. 1836. Half doubloon. Obv. Bust, same as No. 67. "EL PODER EN LA CONSTITUCION." Beneath is inscribed "21 Q(uilates) 1836. 4 E"(scudo). Rev. Two mountains; upon one is a castle, and upon the other a condor; in the background appears a volcano; above is the sun, with the signs of the zodiac, and seven stars. "REPUBLICA DEL ECUADOR," and the name of the mint "QUITO."

70. S. 1838. One real. Obv. A fasces, crossed by a bow and arrows, between two cornucopias. "REPUBLICA DEL ECUADOR."...... "QUITO." Rev. Same type as the gold pistole No. 67.

71. G. 1847. Doubloon. Obv. Bust of Bolivar, with his name inscribed immediately beneath. "EL PODER EN LA CONSTITUCION."...... "1847.—21. Qs.." Rev. The arms and ensigns of the Republic. "REPUBLICA DEL ECUADOR."......"QUITO."

PERU.

This country declared its independence in 1821, but was not entirely freed from the Spanish yoke until the close of the year 1824. The Republicans began the coinage of money about the year 1822; but the Spanish monarch, still claiming dominion there, also issued coins, and, in fact, restruck many of the pieces issued by the Patriots.

---

* For the foregoing data we are largely indebted to an excellent statement made by HON. CHAS. R. BUCKALEW, U. S. Minister resident at Quito, to the Treasury Department, dated June 16, 1859.

This circumstance often tends to confuse the young searcher after numismatic knowledge. Patriot dollars of the year 1822 are frequently found impressed with the insignia of royalty—the crown—and the date 1824, which render their character rather ambiguous at first sight.

In 1836, the Republic was divided into the two nations of North and South Peru. This change was for some time exhibited in the coinage, but afterward entirely disappeared.

The coinage is executed at three different mints. The Mint of Lima is situated in North Peru, and has been long in operation; the mark is M, an involution of the letters L I M A.* The Mints of Cuzco and Arequipa are in South Peru; the mint-mark of the first is CUZCO, or CUZ., and of the latter, the abbreviation AREQ.

The coinage of Peru was formerly of the same standards as the Spanish, but the National Convention passed an act in September, 1851, providing for a decimal system, which, with the exception of one or two pieces, was the same as our own. The largest gold piece was called a "SOL" (sun), and was to weigh 569 Spanish grains; value $20. This was divided into pieces denominated respectively "MEDIO SOL," "DOBLIN," "ESCUDO," and the "MEDIO ESCUDO," of proportionate value. All nine-tenths fine.

The silver was to consist of the dollar, half dollar, peseta (20 cents), dinero, and the medio dinero. The dollar was to be nine-tenths fine, and to weigh 475 Spanish grains; the smaller pieces in proportion. The dollar, which was to be considered as the unit, was to consist of one hundred *centavo* (cents); the latter piece and its half were to be represented in the copper coinage.

In order to carry out the provisions of this act, the Government of Peru entered into contracts with parties in this country for the necessary machinery and the dies. These were all completed in due time and forwarded to Peru; but it is exceedingly doubtful whether the dies or machinery were ever brought into active use. The proof set of these coins contained in this collection were struck at this

---

* In former times the mark of this mint was L̇M.

mint prior to the shipping of the machinery, in order to test its capabilities, being merely trial pieces.

The actual coinage of Peru, at the present day, is very small, consisting only of half dollars. The bulk of the currency is represented by the Bolivian half dollar, though the coins of other States are also current.*

78. S. 1693. Dollar, of CHARLES II. Obv. The arms of Spain, quartered by a cross *potent.* "CAROLUS II D. G. HISPANI." Rev. The device is the same as the Mexican cobs, with the same inscriptions, and the legend "EL PERU—ANNO 1693." This piece has been struck with a hammer, and presents rather a curious appearance, especially on the obverse, from the fact that after having received one blow from the hammer, the position of the die has been slightly changed; so that the obverse has received two distinct impressions from the same die, the letters in the legend and the device being repeated.

79. G. 1851. Doubloon, of FERDINAND VI. Obv. Bust in armor, bedecked with the order chain of the *golden fleece.* "FERDND VI D. G. HISPAN ET IND. REX."......"1751." Rev. A crowned shield, bearing the arms of Spain and the royal arms in eight fields, with the arms of Anjou on a shield of pretence, encircled by the order chain and badge of the *golden fleece.* "INITIUM SAPIENTIÆ TIMOR DOMINI," and the mint-mark LM (repeated.) Value $16.26.5.

80. S. 1822. Patriot dollar, re-stamped by the Royalists. Obv. The arms and ensigns of the Republic, on which has been stamped a crown and the date "1824." "PERU LIBRE. M. 8 R. J. S."......"1822." Rev. A pillar encircled with a scroll. Upon one side is Virtue with a branch of olive, and upon the other the goddess of Justice, with the scales and sword. "POR LA VIRTUD Y LA JUSTICIA."

81 and 82. S. 1823. Patriot dollars. Same type as preceding, but not re-struck. Average values $1.05.

83. S. 1826. Dollar. Obv. The goddess of Liberty, in a Roman helmet, supporting a staff, surmounted by a liberty-cap, with one

---

* Letters of J. RANDOLPH CLAY, U. S. Minister resident at Lima, and CHAS. H. LAY, U. S. Vice-Consul at Callao, to the Treasury Department, July 18th, and September 1st, 1859.

hand, and a shield, bearing the inscription "LIBERTAD," with the other. "FIRME Y FELIZ POR LA UNION." Rev. The arms of the Republic, quartered upon a shield, surmounted by an oak wreath, between branches of palm and laurel. "REPUB. PERUANA. M. 8 R. J. M." ......"1826," and the mint-mark.

84. G. 1827. Doubloon. Same type as the dollar No. 83, except that the position of Liberty is slightly changed. Value $15.55.1.

85. S. 1826. Half medios. Obv. "LIMA.$\frac{1}{4}$.1826." Rev. The lama. (This animal appears in the arms of the Republic.)

86 to 89. S. 1826–1829. Dollar, and pieces of two, one, and one-half real. All of the same type as No. 83.

90. S. 1829. Half medio. Obv. "$\frac{1}{4}$," and the letters "C—S" inclosed in a wreath of laurel. Rev. A cornucopia and the date.

91 and 92. S. 1835–1836. Pieces of four and two reals. Both of the same type as No. 83. Struck at Cuzco.

NORTH PERU.

93. S. 1836. Dollar. Same type as No. 83, with the legend "EST NOR-PERUANO. M 8 R. T. M." on the reverse.

SOUTH PERU.

94. S. 1838. Dollar. Obv. A sun and four stars. "REPUB. SUD PERUANA."......"8 R. CUZCO, 1838." Rev. A volcano, a castle, and a cornucopia, with water in the background, and a ship sailing in the distance; the whole inclosed in a laurel wreath. "FIRME POR LA UNION."......"10 D(ineros) 20 G(ranos) CONFEDERACION R. A."

95. S. 1837. Piece of two reals. Obv. Same type as No. 94. Rev. "2 REALES B. A.," inscribed between two branches of laurel, crossed.

96 and 97. S. 1850–1855. Pieces of one and four reals. Same type as No. 83, with the legend "REP. PERUANA (mint-mark and denomination) 10 DS. 20 GS. M. B.," and the date on the reverse.

98. S. 1855. Dollar. Obv. The goddess of Liberty, supporting a spear in one hand, and a shield, bearing the word "LIBERTAD," in the other. "FIRME Y FELIZ POR LA UNION." Rev. The arms of the

Republic upon a shield, crowned with oak, between branches of palm and laurel, crossed. "REPUB. PERUANA. M.8 R. 10 D^{s} 20 G^{s} M. B."...... "1855."

The following are the *trial pieces* mentioned in the introduction as having been struck at this mint. They are exceedingly rare.

100 to 103. G. 1855. The "sol," and its subdivisions—the half, quarter, and eighth. All of the same type. Obv. A beautiful statue of Liberty, with the head at side-face, supporting the staff and liberty-cap in one hand, and a shield, bearing the word "LIBERTAD," in the other. "FIRME Y FELIZ POR LA UNION," and the denomination in *pesos*. Rev. The arms and ensigns of the Republic, surmounted by an oak crown. "REPUBLICA PERUANA LIMA. 9 DECIMOS FINO. M. B." ......"1855." (See Plate XXIII. No. 7.)

104 to 108. S. 1855. Dollar, and pieces of 50, 20, 10, and 5 *centimos*. All of the same type. Obv. A statue of Liberty at front-face, supporting a spear in one hand, and a shield, bearing the word "LIBERTAD," in the other. "FIRME Y FELIZ POR LA UNION."......"UN PESO. (On the smaller pieces the value is in "*centimos*.") Rev. The arms of the Republic on a shield, crowned with oak, between branches of palm and laurel. "REPUBLICA PERUANA. LIMA. 9 DECIMOS FINO. M. B."......"1855." (See Plate XXV. No. 5.)

109 and 110. C. 1855. Centimo and medio, or half centimo. Both of the same type. Obv. A sun. "REPUBLICA—PERUANA." Rev. "UN CENTIMO," or "MEDIO CENTIMO," inscribed within a wreath of laurel. "LIMA—1855."

DIVISION XVIII.

BRAZIL.

This country was first visited by VINCENT YAÑEZ PINCON, a Spaniard, in 1499, and in the year following by the Portuguese commander PEDRO ALVAREZ CABRAL, who took formal possession of the country in the name of the Portuguese monarch. He erected an altar, performed mass, in the presence of the natives, on Easter day, and set up a stone cross in commemoration of the event. Soon after this, settlements were commenced by the Portuguese, who thereby obtained absolute possession of the country, together with its rich deposits of gold, notwithstanding the prior visit of the Spaniards.

This acquisition afterward had rather a peculiar effect upon the condition of Portugal, which, from having been the *colonizer* of Brazil, became its *dependency.* This state of things was brought about during the reign of John Maria, as regent for the imbecile queen, Maria I., who, upon the invasion of Portugal by the French, in 1807, removed his court from *Lisbon* to *Rio de Janeiro.* In 1816 John became king, by the death of Maria, and assumed the title of John VI.

The removal of the court to Brazil gave great dissatisfaction to the Portuguese, who little relished the idea of changing places with their colony. This feeling afterward became so strong that John found it necessary to return to Lisbon in 1821, leaving his son, Don Pedro, *as regent.*

Some historians assert that the private instructions of the departing king to his son were, to oppose Brazilian independence (of Portugal, an event which he considered as imminent) as long as it was prudent, but, in the event of the tide becoming too strong, to place himself at its head, and thereby retain the scepter in his own hands rather than see it pass to the possession of an adventurer. However, be this as it may, it is certain that, upon the breaking out of the revolution, he made but little hesitation in adopting this line of policy. He immediately threw himself into the ranks of the independent party, and was proclaimed "Emperor of Brazil" in 1822, only one year after the departure of his father. Don Pedro continued to reign in this capacity until the year 1831, when he was compelled to abdicate the throne, leaving his infant son, Peter II., then only six years of age, as his successor. The rights of the latter were respected, and a regency immediately appointed to conduct the affairs of state during his minority. Peter assumed the reins of government upon arriving at his fifteenth year.

The mode of keeping accounts is the same in Brazil as in Portugal, both countries reckoning by *reis*. But there has long been a difference in the valuation of the *rei*, in the currency of the two countries. As long ago as 1747 it was decreed that a mark of such silver as was coined into 7500 *reis* in Portugal, should make *one-tenth* more in Brazil, that is, 8250 *reis*.*

At the present time, and since 1850, the unit of Brazilian money has been the *millrei*, of *one thousand reis*.

The *moidore*, of 4000 reis, and its half, constituted the gold coinage of Brazil up to 1822, but in that year a new coinage was instituted, to consist of the piece known as the half joe, of 6400 *reis*. This was to weigh 221.4 Troy grains, and to be 917 thousandths fine. By the law of October, 1833, another modification took place in the coinage; the only effect of this law upon the gold coinage, however, appears to have been to fix the value of the half joe at 10 *millreis*. The pieces of seventy,† twenty, and five‡ millreis appear to have been adopted at a more recent date.

The silver coins previous to 1833 were the pieces of three *patacs*, or 960 *reis*, and the two, one, one-half, and one-quarter patac,§—all professedly 917 thousandths fine. But by the law of 1833, these were displaced by a new series, consisting of the pieces of 1200, 800, 400, 200, and 100 *reis*, the largest piece being equivalent to the old 960 rei piece; they were all intended to be nine-tenths fine. This coinage was in turn superseded by the present series (apparently introduced about the year 1850 or 1851), which takes the *millrei* as its unit, and consists, as far as we are able to learn, of the two, one, and one-half millrei (or pieces of 2000, 1000, and 500 reis). There are doubtless other smaller pieces belonging to this series, but how many or of what value we are not yet advised. The legal standard of fineness

---

* Manual of Coins and Bullion.

† Letter of Geo. F. Upton, U. S. Consul at Rio Grand de Sul, to the Treasury Department, June 20, 1859.

‡ Ibid.

§ For the sake of convenience these pieces are designated, in the following description, by the number of *reis* represented in the several pieces; thus the two-patac piece is called "640 reis."

of all the new coins, both gold and silver, is *eleven-twelfths*, or $916\frac{2}{3}$ thousandths.*

A major portion of Brazilian currency consists of paper and copper, the latter being used principally for household purposes. Small ingots of gold, assayed and stamped at the government offices, are also used in the circulation, and are forbidden to be exported.

1 and 2. S. 1695–1699. Pieces of 640 reis, of PETER II. Obv. A crowned shield, bearing the arms of Portugal. "PETRUS II D. G. PORT. REX ET BRAS D"(ominus)......"640." Rev. A cross *potent*, upon which is a globe encircled by a belt. "SUBQ(uo) SIGN(o) NATA STAB" (it).

3 and 4. S. 1700. Pieces of 320 and 160 reis. Both same type as Nos. 1 and 2.

5. C. 1746. Twenty reis, of JOHN V. Obv. A crown, beneath which is inscribed the denomination and date. "JOANNES V. D. G. P. ET BRASIL REX." Rev. Belted globe. "PECUNIA TOTUM CIRCUMIT URBEM."

6. G. 1749. Moidore, of JOHN V. Obv. A crowned shield, bearing the arms of *Portugal.* "JOANNES V. D. G. PORTUG. REX."...... "4000." Rev. A cross, with double limbs, inclosed in a tressure of four arches. "ET BRASILIÆ DOMINUS ANNO 1749."

7–9. S. 1749–50. Pieces of 640 and 320 reis, of JOHN V. All of the same type as Nos. 1 and 2.

10. S. 1751. Piece of 320 reis, of JOSEPH I. Same type as No. 1.

11. S. 1752. Piece of 300 reis, of JOSEPH. Obv. A crown, beneath which is the initial "J." and the denomination and date. Rev. A cross *potent*, upon which is a globe, encircled by a belt, and bearing the initial "B." "SUBQ. SIGN. NATA STAB."

12. C. 1760. Forty reis, of JOSEPH. Same type as No. 5.

13 and 14. S. 1771. Pieces of 640 and 160 reis. Both same type as No. 1.

15. G. 1779. Moidore, of MARIA I. and PETER III. Same type as No. 6.

16 and 17. S. 1780. Pieces of 640 and 320 reis, of MARIA and PETER. Same type as No. 1.

* Report on the Finances, 1857, and letter of GEO. F. UPTON, before quoted.

18. C. 1790. Forty reis, of MARIA. Same type as No. 5, with the legend "MARIA I D. G. ET BRASILIÆ REGINA," upon the obverse. This piece has been restamped with the arms of Portugal.

19 and 20. S. 1802–04. Pieces of 320 and 640 reis, of MARIA. Same type as No. 1.

21. S. 1810. Piece of 960 reis, of JOHN, *regent.* Same type as No. 1. Obv. "JOANNES D. G. PORT P. REGENS. ET BRAS. D." (Prince Regent of Portugal, and Lord of Brazil.)

22. G. 1811. Moidore, of same. Same type as No. 6, with the legend "JOANNES D. G. PORT. E. ALG. P. REGENS," on the obverse.

23. S. 1812. Piece of 320 reis, of same. Same type as No. 21.

24 and 25. C. 1816. Ten reis, of same. Same type as No. 5, with the legend "JOANNES D. G. — BRAS. P. REGENS," on the obverse.

26–28. S. 1818. Pieces of 960, 640, and 80 reis, of JOHN VI. All of the same type. Obv. A crown, beneath which is inscribed the denomination and date, between branches of olive, crossed. "JOANNES VI D. G. PORT. BRAS ET ALG. REX." Rev. Same type as No. 1, with the arms of Portugal stamped upon the globe.

29. G. 1819. Moidore, of same. Obv. A cross, with double limbs, inclosed in a tressure of four arches. "JOANNES VI D. G. PORT BRAS ET ALG. REX."......"1819." Rev. The arms of Portugal, suspended upon a globe, surmounted by a crown, and inclosed between branches of olive and laurel, crossed. "4000." *No legend.*

30 and 31. S. 1820–21. Pieces of 320 and 640 reis, of same. Same type as No. 26.

32 and 33. C. 1821–22. Forty reis, of same. Obv. The denomination and date, inscribed beneath a crown. "JOANNES VI D. G. PORT BRAS ET ALG. REX." Rev. A belted globe, bearing the arms as in No. 26. "PECUNIA TOTUM CIRCUMIT ORBEM."

34 and 35. S. 1824–25. Pieces of 640 reis, of PETER I., *emperor.* Obv. The arms of Brazil, surmounted by the imperial crown, and inclosed between branches of olive and laurel, crossed. "IN HOC SIGNO VINCES." Rev. The denomination inclosed in a wreath of laurel. "PETRUS I. D. G. CONST. IMP. ET PERP. BRAS. DEF." (Peter I., by the grace of God, Constitutional Emperor, and Perpetual Defender of Brazil)......"1824 R"(io).

36. C. —. Forty reis. Same as No. 34.

37 and 38. C. 1824–25. Pieces of forty and twenty reis. Same type as preceding, but much reduced in size.

39 and 40. S. 1826. Pieces of 960 reis, of same. Same type as No. 34.

41 and 42. C. 1826–29. Pieces of twenty and eighty reis. Same type as No. 34.

The latter piece (eighty reis) appears to have been added to the copper coinage after the establishment of the empire.

43. G. 1833. Half joe, of PETER II. Obv. Head of the youthful emperor. "PETRUS II. D. G. CONST. IMP. ET. PERP. BRAS. DEF."...... "1833. R." Rev. The arms of Brazil, surmounted by the imperial crown, and inclosed between branches of laurel. "IN HOC SIGNO VINCES."......"6400."

The law of October, 1833, placed the value of the half joe at *ten millreis;* the old figures (6400), however, appeared upon that coin for several years after. But this piece may have been, and probably was struck before the passage of the law referred to.

44–49. S. 1837–38. Pieces of 1200, 800, 400, 200, and 100 reis. All of the same type. Obv. Arms of the empire, as in No. 43. "IN HOC SIGNO VINCES." Rev. The denomination inclosed in a wreath of laurel. "PETRUS II D. G. CONST. IMP. ET PERP. BRAS. DEF."......"1837."

50. G. 1838. Half joe. Same pattern as No. 43. Somewhat reduced in diameter, with a proportionate increase in thickness.

51. G. 1852. Piece of twenty millreis. Obv. Head of the emperor. "PETRUS II D. G. C. IMP. ET PERP. BRAS. DEF."......"1852." Rev. Same type as No. 50.

52. S. 1852. Half millrei. Obv. The arms, etc., with the inscription "IN HOC SIGNO VINCES," in a straight line above. Rev. The value in reis, inclosed in a wreath of laurel. "PETRUS II D. G. CONST. IMP. ET PERP. BRAS. DEF."......"1852."

53–55. S. 1854. Pieces of two, one, and one-half millrei. Same type as No. 52, except that the motto "IN HOC SIGNO VINCES" constitutes the legend. (See Plate XXVI. No. 1.)

56. G. 1857. Twenty millreis. Same as No. 51. (See Plate XXIV. No. 1.)

BOLIVIA.

This republic was established in 1825, from the five provinces of Upper Peru, which formerly belonged to the vice-royalty of Buenos Ayres, and which are known by the names of *Charcas*, *Potosi*, *La Paz*, *Cochabamba*, and *Santa Cruz de la Sierra*. These provinces, after having conquered their independence under the leadership of the famous SIMON BOLIVAR, assembled, by their delegates, at *Chuquisaca*, the capital, in August, 1825, and determined upon the establishment of the confederacy into a republic (it having been a question with the people whether they would take this course or annex themselves to the Argentine Confederacy), issued a declaration of national independence; and in order to display their gratitude to GEN. BOLIVAR for his eminent services in securing the liberties of the people, they decided upon calling the new republic *Bolivia*, in honor of his name.

Bolivia is a large producer of the precious metals, particularly of silver; and it is from the extent of the latter product that the country has attained a notoriety abroad. The famous Argentiferous mountain of *Potosi* alone is said to have yielded, from the time of its discovery in 1545 to the year 1800, a period of 255 years, the sum of $1,647,901,018. In the years 1846 and 1850, the entire yield of silver amounted respectively (by approximation) to $2,227,324.*

The coinage is not very important, consisting mostly of half dollars. The monetary system is nominally the same as that of Spain. At the present time no gold coins are issued for general circulation, and the largest silver piece is the half dollar mentioned above. This piece is two-thirds fine, and is valued at about thirty-three cents.† The smaller pieces, the two, one, and one-half real, are of the same standard of fineness, and of proportionate value. This standard of two-thirds fine was first adopted in 1830; previous to that time the coinage was of the Spanish standards.

---

* Ure's Dictionary.

† Letter of HON. J. COTTON SMITH, U. S. Minister at Chuquisaca, to the Treasury Department, June 13, 1859.

The mint is at Potosi, the mint-mark of which is a monogram representing the letters P T S I.

77 and 78. S. 1825. Dollar, and one-real piece, of FERDINAND VII. Both of the same type as the Mexican "pillar dollar," (which see.)

79–82. S. 1827–28. Dollar, and piece of four, one, and one-half real. All of the same type. Obv. Bust of Simon Bolivar, in uniform, and *laureated.* On the lower portion of the bust is inscribed the name "BOLIVAR." "LIBRE POR LA CONSTITUCION." Rev. A tree, beneath which are reposing two lamas; above are six stars in an arch. "REPUBLICA BOLIVIANA," and the date, mint-marks, etc. Value of the dollar $1.05.2.

83 and 84. S. 1830. Half and quarter dollar, of the depreciated standard, two-thirds fine. Same types as No. 79, with the exception of the quarter dollar, which has on the obverse the legend "FIRME POR LA CONSTITUCION." Value of half dollar 33 cts.

85. G. 1831. Doubloon. Obv. Bust of Bolivar, in uniform, with his name inscribed beneath. "LIBRE POR LA CONSTITUCION." Rev. A representation of the Argentiferous mountain of Potosi, above which the sun is rising; at one side is a lama, and at the other a sheaf of grain; beneath are six stars. "REPUBLICA BOLIVIANA," and the date, mint-marks, etc. Value $15.58. (See Plate XXIV. No. 3.)

86. S. 1841. Dollar. Obv. Bust of Bolivar, *laureated.* "LIBRE POR LA CONSTITUCION."......"BOLIVAR." Rev. Same type as No. 79. The dollars of this period are very unsteady in value, varying three or four cents, from 103 cents upward. (See Plate XXVI. No. 3.)

87. S. 1850. Half dollar. Obv. Bust of Belzu. "M. Y. BELZU PRESIDENTE CONSTITUCIO.[al] DE BOLIVIA."......"1850." Rev. A Hercules, with his club and a flambeau, treading upon a hydra-headed dragon. "LA FUERZA NATIONAL TRIUMFO DE LA ANARQUIA." Value 33 cts.

LA PLATA, OR ARGENTINE CONFEDERACY.

La Plata, formerly a vice-royalty of Spain, consists, at present, of a confederacy of fourteen States, including Buenos Ayres, which for some time has been independent of the Confederacy, but was united thereto in the latter part of the past year (1859). The government is very similar to our own, each State having a distinct constitution, and the whole being united under a central administration consisting of a congress and executive. The President, who is elected indirectly by the people, holds his office for six years.

Formerly the province of Potosi was included within the limits of this Confederacy, and it was from this silver-producing district that it first acquired the name of "*La Plata*," and afterward that of the "*Argentine Republic.*" The boundary line, however, has long been laid over on the La Plata side of this region; consequently these names are not as *apropos* as formerly. The whole country is more commonly known by the name of its principal sea-port city "*Buenos Ayres.*"

The monetary system is the same here as in Spain, but the standards are found to be much below those of the mother country, which renders it unsafe to take their coins at the professed valuation by count, as they usually range much lower. In fact, it is hard to determine the intrinsic values except by actual assay.

The principal mint appears to be located at RIOJA, capital of a State of the same name. The mint-mark is "R. A.," sometimes simply the initial "R." There is also a mint at Buenos Ayres, but as yet we have seen only one or two specimens from this mint. Some of the coins struck before 1817 bear the mark of the Potosi mint. (See Bolivia.)

101. S. 1815. Dollar of the Potosi mint. Obv. A sun. "PROVINCIAS DEL RIO DE LA PLATA." Rev. The arms of the Confederacy. "EN UNION Y LIBERTAD," and the date, mint-marks, etc. Value about 92 cts.

102 to 104. S. 1813–1815. Pieces of one and one-half real, of the Potosi mint. Same type as No. 101.

105. C. 1822. "Decimo," of Buenos Ayres. Obv. Arms of the Confederacy, between two branches of laurel, crossed. Rev. "BUENOS AYRES.—1822.—UN DECIMO," inscribed within a wreath of laurel.

106. S. 1826. Two reals, of RIOJA. Same type as No. 101.

107. C. 1827. Ten decim, of the National Bank of Buenos Ayres. Obv. A phœnix, encircled by a hoop or band, on which is an inscrip-

tion, but so much defaced as to be unintelligible. Rev. "10 DECIM," inscribed upon a shield, inclosed between branches of laurel. "BANCO NACIONAL."......"BUENOS AYRES, 1827."

108. S. 1828. Half dollar, of RIOJA. Same type as No. 101.

109. G. 1828. Doubloon, of RIOJA. Obv. A sun. "PROVINCIAS DEL RIO DE LA PLATA." Rev. The arms of the Confederacy decorated with martial emblems. "EN UNION Y LIBERTAD R. A. P. 8 S"(cudo)...... "1828." Value $15.51.

110. G. 1836. Doubloon, of RIOJA. Obv. Bust of ROSAS, Governor of Buenos Ayres. "REPUB. ARGENT CONFEDERADA."......"ROSAS." Rev. The Argentiferous mountain of Potosi, with martial emblems beneath. "POR LA LIGA LITORAL SERA FELIZ. R. 8 S."......"1836." Value about $15.50. (See Plate XXIV. No. 2.)

111 and 112. S. 1838. Dollars, of RIOJA. Obv. The mountain of Potosi, with martial emblems beneath. "REPUB. ARGENTINA CONFEDERADA R."......"1838." Rev. The arms of the Confederacy. "ETERNO LOOR AL RESTAURADOR ROSAS." Values, average $1.04. (See Plate XXVI. No. 2.)

URUGUAY.

By a treaty made between Brazil and Buenos Ayres in 1825, the territory bordering upon the *Rio de la Plata* and the River *Uruguay*, and lying at the southernmost extremity of the Brazilian empire, was erected into an independent Republic, with the sea-port city of *Montevideo* as its capital. The coinage, which is not important, appears to be executed at the latter place.

120. S. 1844. Dollar, or peso. Obv. The arms inclosed between two branches of oak, crossed. "REPUBLICA ORIENTAL DEL URUGUAY." ......"1844." Rev. "UN PESO FUERTE," surrounded by nine stars. "LITIO DE MONTEVIDEO."......"10½ Ds." (See Plate XXVI. No. 4.)

121. C. 1854. Twenty centesimos. Obv. A sun. "REPUBLICA ORIENTAL DEL URUGUAY."......"1854." Rev. A shield, bearing the figure "20," above which is a scroll, inscribed "CENTESIMOS," inclosed between branches of maize.

122 and 123. C. 1857. Forty and twenty centesimos. Same type as No. 121. There appears to have been a reduction in the size of the latter piece.

DIVISION XIX.

CHILI.

This country became an independent republic in 1817 (having previously been a dependency of Spain), and commenced the coinage of money in its new capacity in the same year.

Formerly the monetary system was the same as that received from the mother country; but in January, 1851, a law was passed establishing a decimal system. The gold coins were to consist of the *condor*, or ten-dollar piece, and its half and quarter, or *escudo*—the unit being the silver *peso*, or dollar of 100 centavo, which was subdivided into the half dollar, the twenty-cent piece, and the ten and five cent pieces, with the two copper coins, the centavo and its half, being in fact the same as the system adopted for Peru in the same year. The twenty-dollar piece, however, was not included. The standards of the gold coinage appear to be much below the standards of the United States, so much so, that the gold *condor* now sells in California for nine dollars.*

The mint is at Santiago, the mark of which is an S. surmounted by a small o.

Although Chili is a producer of the precious metals, the coinage has but little importance abroad, as the policy of that country is to export bullion unwrought.†

1. S. 1811. Two reals, of FERDINAND VII. Obv. Bust, in uniform, *laureated.* "FERDIN. VII DEI GRATIA."......"1811." Rev. Same device as the Mexican "pillar dollar." "HISPAN. ET IND REX." "S. 2 R(eals) F. I."

2. S. 1822. Dollar. Obv. A volcano; above is inscribed, within a wreath of laurel, the value, "UN PESO." "CHILE INDEPENDENTE." ......"SANTIAGO." Rev. A pillar, supporting a globe, above which

---

* Letter of G. R. BYCKMAN, U. S. Vice-Consul at Santiago, to the Treasury Department, July 20, 1859.

† Ibid.

is a star and a scroll, the latter bearing the word "LIBERTAD." "UNION Y FUERZA F. I."......"1822."

3. G. 1823. Doubloon, or "ounce." Obv. A pillar, crossed by two standards *in saltiere*, and surmounted by a globe and a star; the whole inclosed in a wreath of laurel. "POR LA RAZON, O LA FUERZA S̊. 8 E(scudo) F. I."......"1823." Rev. Two smoking volcanoes and a sun; beneath which is inscribed " A. D. 1818;" the whole inclosed in a wreath of laurel. "EL ESTADO D CHILE CONSTIT. INDEPENDIENTE." Value $15.57.

4. S. 1834. Two reals. Same type as No. 2.

5 and 6. C. 1835. Centavo, and a half centavo, both of same type. Obv. A star. "REPUBLICA DE CHILE."......"1835." Rev. "UN CENTAVO" or "MEDIO CENTAVO," inscribed within a wreath of laurel. "ECONOMIA ES RIQUEZA."

7. G. 1836. Doubloon. Obv. A hand resting upon a book, on the back of which is inscribed "CONSTITUCION." Above are the diverging rays of the sun. "IGUALDAD ANTE LA LEI. 8 E. I. J."......"21, Q^{s}." (Quilates). Rev. A shield bearing the arms of Chili (*party per fess, azure and gules; a star argent*), surmounted by a plume, and supported by a horse *rampant* and a condor, each crowned. "REPUBLICA DE CHILE S̊."......"1836." Value $15.66.

8. G. 1838. Two escudo. Same type as No. 7.

9. G. 1839. Doubloon. Obv. A statue of Liberty clad in mail, with her right hand resting upon the constitution, and supporting with her left the *fasces;* a cornucopia in the background. "IGUALDAD ANTE LA LEI. 8 E. I. J."......"21 Q^{s}." Rev. The arms, etc., as in No. 7, but much more artistic in appearance. Value $15.66. (See Plate XXIV. No. 4.)

It will be noticed that the color of the doubloon of 1836 (No. 7) is very different from that of the last piece, though the values are the same. This does not emanate, as might be supposed, from a difference in the standard of fineness, but from the fact that in the former the alloy is nearly all of *silver*, while in the latter *copper* is the principal metal used in alloying.

10. S. 1839. Dollar. Obv. A condor striving to break a chain by which he is confined. "POR LA RAZON Y LA FUERZA."......"10 D^{s}. 20 G^{s}." Rev. The arms of the Republic, surmounted by a plume,

and inclosed between branches of laurel, crossed. "REPUBLICA DE CHILE. S̊. I. J."......"1839." The denomination "8. R." appears within the wreath. Value $1.05.

11. S. 1853. Dollar. Obv. A condor, with pieces of broken chain; one piece being attached to its leg, and the other held in its beak, supporting an oval shield (*azure, a fasces, and thirteen mullets argent*). "POR LA RAZON O LA FUERZA."......"1853." Rev. The arms of the Republic, inclosed in a wreath of laurel. "REPUBLICA DE CHILE S̊."......"UN PESO." Value 97 cts.

12 and 13. S. 1856. Half dollars. Obv. A condor, in flight; one piece of chain in its beak, and another dangling from its talon. "POR LA RAZON O LA FUERZA."......"1856." Rev. The arms of Chili, between branches of laurel. "REPUBLICA DE CHILE. S̊."......"50 C"(entavo.) (See Plate XXVII. No. 1.)

14. S. 1852. Piece of twenty centavo. Same type as Nos. 12 and 13.

15. S. 1857. "Un decimo," or piece of ten centavo. Same type.

WEST INDIES.

With the exception of the Island of Hayti, or San Domingo, all the West India islands are dependencies of European nations. To *Great Britain* belong Jamaica, Bahamas, Barbadoes, Trinidad, and several smaller islands; to *Spain*, Cuba and Porto Rico; to *France*, Guadaloupe, Martinique, etc.; to the *Netherlands*, Curaçoa, etc.; to *Sweden*, St. Bartholomew; to *Demark*, St. Croix, St. Thomas, and St. John. These comprise the main portion of the islands. There are, however, some thirty other small islands, which are mostly owned by Great Britain; a few by France, and two or three by the Netherlands.

These islands have no gold coins of their own, and but a small amount of silver. They depend almost entirely upon the coinage of foreign nations for their metallic currency. The coins of Spanish countries especially, such as Colombia, Mexico, etc., are a large ingredient, and are a legal tender in most of the islands in payment of debts. United States coins, both gold and silver, are also current there, and in some localities are legal tenders; but are generally held at a discount against the Spanish.

The British, French, and Danish governments have, at times, issued coins of small denominations for circulation in their West India possessions. These issues, however, are very insignificant in their proportions, and deserve but little attention.

Some of the islands, including Hayti, Porto Rico, etc., have issued large quantities of paper, which is now circulating at very heavy discounts—the Haytian paper dollar being at 75 per cent. below par.

Formerly, and probably to some extent at the present day, "*cut money*" was extensively used. This currency consists of Spanish dollars cut into "bits;" each piece being stamped by the government authorities. This practice was first instituted by the government to supply the great lack of small change, a want which interfered very materially with the convenience of the people in their retail transactions. But very soon after its first commencement, the law began to be much abused by dishonest persons, who commenced the practice of cutting more pieces from the dollar than the law allowed and passing them at the government rates; frequently cutting the dollar into *five* pieces and passing them for *quarters*. A number of these pieces, bearing the marks of authority, will be found in the Cabinet collection. (See Nos. 37 to 44.)

In the Island of Trinidad, to prevent the exportation of dollars, the government resorted to the expedient of cutting a piece out of the center, equal to a real or one-eighth of the dollar, *more or less*, thus keeping the dollars at home and making them yield *nine reals*, which was a government profit, as the *cut* pieces were made current at their nominal values by the force of law. Such pieces are commonly called *cut dollars;* the whole pieces being denominated *round dollars*. (See Nos. 35 and 36.)

HAYTI.

Hayti, which is the second island in size, and ranks next, if not equal, to Cuba in population, was formerly a dependency of France and Spain, but is now an independent republic. On the breaking out of the French revolution in 1791, Hayti was thrown into a commotion which lasted for many years. In 1804 the French part of it became a kingdom or military despotism, consisting entirely of negro citizens, who had previously been slaves, with DESSALINES, a black man, for its monarch. Dessalines was succeeded, in the southern part of the island, by CHRISTOPHE, or HENRY I., who put an end to his own life in 1820, in order to save himself from the vengeance of his subjects. In the mean time in the northern part of the island a republic had been established upon the death of Dessalines, under the presidency of PETION, a rival of Christophe. He was succeeded by J. P. BOYER, who, upon the death of Christophe, in 1820, seized his dominions, and thus became master of the entire island. In 1842 a revolution broke out, and PRESIDENT BOYER was compelled to flee to Jamaica; and in 1844 the inhabitants of the Spanish portion of the island rose, overpowered their Haytian oppressors, and formed themselves into the Republic of *Santo Domingo.*

After various individuals had for short periods occupied the executive chair of the Haytian Republic, the election fell upon general SOLOUQUE, who, in the latter part of the year 1849 ascended the throne as Emperor, with the title of FAUSTIN I. Solouque persisted, after his elevation from the presidential to the imperial dignity, in laying claim to the sovereignty of the San Domingo portion of the island, which led to much difficulty, and at last to a revolution, in which Solouque was deposed, and compelled to take flight to Europe in 1859. He was succeeded by PRESIDENT GEFFRARD, who is now at the head of the administration.

The coinage of Hayti apparently consists of the dollar of 100 centimes, which is worth about twenty-five cents of United States currency, and its subdivisions, the half, or piece of 50 centimes, and the pieces of 25, 12, and 6 centimes. "The subdivision is not mathematically correct, but there is more precision in that particular than in weight and fineness."* There is also a copper coin of two centimes, as will appear presently.

17. S. 1814. Twelve centimes. Obv. Martial emblems, and a

* Manual of Coins and Bullion.

tree, surmounted by a liberty-cap. Rev. "12*c.," encircled by a serpent. "REPUBLIQUE D'HAYTI."......"AN XI." (Eleventh year of the Republic.)

18 to 24. S. 1817. Pieces of twenty-five and twelve centimes, of PETION. All of the same type. Obv. Head of the president. "A PETION, PRESIDENT."......"AN 14." Rev. Martial emblems, and a tree surmounted by a liberty-cap. "REPUBLIQUE D'HAYTI," and the denomination.

25 to 31. S. 1818–1833. Dollars, and pieces of 50, 25, and 12 centimes, of J. P. BOYER. All of the same type. Obv. Head of the president. "J. P. BOYER, PRESIDENT," and the year of the Republic, (as "An 27"). Reverse same as Nos. 18 and 24. (See Plate XXVII. No. 2.)

32. C. 1831. Two centimes. Obv. A fasces surmounted by a liberty-cap. "LIBERTE EGALITE."......"AN 28." Rev. "DEUX CENTIMES, 1831," inscribed between two branches of palm. "REPUBLIQUE D'HAYTI."

35 and 36. Cut dollar and piece, of TRINIDAD. (See page 382.)

37 to 44. Cut money of various islands. (See page 382.)

BRITISH POSSESSIONS.

45 to 50. S. 1822. Pieces of one-quarter, one-eighth, and one-sixteenth, of the Spanish dollar. All of the same type. Obv. The arms of Great Britain. "GEORGUS IV D. G. BRITANNIARUM REX F(idei) D"(efensor). Rev. An anchor and a crown, with the denomination. ("IV., VIII.," or "XIV.") "COLONIAR. BRITAN. MONET."......"1822."

FRENCH POSSESSIONS.

55 and 56. C. 1825–1828. Ten and five centimes, of CHARLES X. Obv. Bust of Charles, *laureated.* "CHARLES X ROI DE FRANCE." Rev. "10" or "5 CENT.," inscribed within a wreath of laurel. "COLONIES FRANCAISES," and the date.

WINDWARD ISLANDS: MARTINIQUE, ETC.

57 to 60. S. 1731–1732. Small pieces, of LOUIS XV. All of the same type. Obv. Bust of the king *laureated.* "LUD. XV D. G. FR. ET NAV. REX." Rev. "ISLES DU VENT."......"1731–1732," and the three *fleurs de lis.*

DANISH POSSESSIONS.

63 and 64. S. 1763–1765. Pieces of twenty-four skilling, of Frederick V., King of Denmark. Obv. The royal monogram, crowned. "D. G. DAN. NOR. VAN. GOT. REX." (See *Denmark.*) Rev. A ship, beneath which is the date. "XXIIII SKILL. DANSKE. AMERICANSK M"(ynt).

65 and 66. S. 1767. Pieces of twelve skilling, of Christian VII. Same types as Nos. 66 and 67.

67 to 71. S. 1816–1837. Pieces of 20, 10, and 2 skilling. Obv. A crowned shield, bearing the arms of Denmark. Rev. (of No. 70.) "XX SKILLING DANSK AMERIKANSK MYNT, 1816," inscribed in six lines.

72. S. 1859. Twenty cents, of Frederick VII. Obv. Head. "FREDERICK VII KONGE AF DANMARK."......"1859." Rev. A vessel under sail. "DANSK VESTINDISK MONT."...... "20 CENTS." Edge grained. (See Plate XXVII. No. 3.)

73. S. 1859. Ten cents, of same. Obverse same as preceding. Rev. A sugar-cane. "DANSK VESTINDISK MONT."......"10 CENTS."

74. S. 1859. Five cents, of same. Same type as No. 72.

75. S. 1859. Three cents, of same. Obv. Same as No. 72, without the date. Rev. "3 CENTS, 1859." "DANSK VESTINDISK MONT." Edge plain.

76. B.S. 1859. One cent, of same. Obv. Crowned shield, bearing the arms of Denmark. "FREDERIK VII KONGE AF DANMARK." Rev. "1 CENT.," inscribed between two branches of oak, crossed. "DANSK VESTINDISK MONT."......"1859."

AFRICA.

SIERRA LEONE.

This colony was founded in 1787, on the western coast of Africa, by a company acting under a charter from the British government. Silver coins were struck for it in 1791 and 1796, consisting of the dollar, of 100 cents, or ten *macutas;* the half dollar, and the pieces of twenty and ten cents, or one *macuta.* In weight these correspond pretty nearly to the usual dollar standard (418 grains), but fall much behind in the standard of fineness. A half dollar assayed at this mint was found to be only 838 thousandths fine; value about forty-eight cents.* Copper coins were struck at the same time, the denominations being the one-penny piece and the one-cent piece—the latter being the half of the former. It is doubtful whether there has been any coinage for this colony since the time above mentioned (1796).

77 to 79. S. 1791–1796. Dollar, half dollar, and ten-cent piece. All of the same type. Obv. A lion. "SIERRA LEONE COMPANY."...... "AFRICA." Rev. Two hands clasped in friendship. Above and beneath the hands are inscribed "100." (One hundred cents.) "ONE DOLLAR PIECE."......"1791." (The half dollar is inscribed "*Half dollar piece,*" and the macuta "*ten cent piece.*") (See Plate XXVII. No. 4.)

80 to 84. C. 1791. One-penny and one-cent pieces. All of the same type as the silver coinage. The "one-cent piece," No. 82, appears to have been much larger than the other two pieces of the same date, which makes two varieties of that coin.

REPUBLIC OF LIBERIA.

This Republic was founded in 1820 by the American Colonization Society, as a colony of free blacks, and the enterprise, though at first laboring under great disadvantages, has been eminently successful. The capital is at MONROVIA. The government is modeled after that of the United States, the senate consisting of six members, and the house of representatives of twenty-eight. It was declared an independent State in 1847, and immediately inaugurated a coinage of copper, consisting of the pieces of one and two cents, which is the only regular coinage of the country.

86 and 87. C. 1847. Pieces of two and one cent. Same type. Obv. A head of Liberty, with the liberty-cap; upon the latter is impressed a star. "REPUBLIC OF LIBERIA." Rev. A palm-tree. "TWO CENTS," or "ONE CENT," and the date. The inscriptions or legends on both sides are impressed, in sunken letters, into a raised rim, similar to that on the huge copper two-penny pieces of England.

* Manual of Coins and Bullion.

MAURITIUS.

This island, situated in the Indian Ocean, was under the dominion of the French up to the year 1810; in that year it was captured by the British, and has since remained in their possession.

In 1810 a silver piece of ten livres was struck by the French government for this and the adjoining Island of Bourbon. These were about 833 thousandths fine, and weighed 414 grains; value about 96 cents—thus placing the colonial livre at *half* the value of the national.

89 and 90. S. 1810. Ten livres. Obv. The French eagle, surmounted by a crown. "ISLES DE FRANCE ET BONAPARTE." Rev. "DIX LIVRES," inscribed between two branches of laurel.

ISLAND OF ST. HELENA.

92. C. 1821. Half penny. Obv. A shield, surmounted by a helmet, upon which is a lion carrying a crown, and supported by two lions *rampant*, each carrying a flag. Rev. "ST. HELENA, 1821. HALF PENNY," inscribed within a wreath of laurel. A particular interest attaches to this coin from the fact that the first NAPOLEON spent the last days of his life in exile upon the island which it represents.

HAWAIIAN ISLANDS.

It will be something of a stride for the imagination to transport itself from the west coast of Africa, across oceans and continents, to the Sandwich Islands, but such is the present necessity; and then we have but little to show, our "collection" of Hawaiian coins amounting only to duplicates of one piece, the cent, or "one-hundredth." This, be it known, however, is the only coinage of that region. They have the American system of moneys, and use United States coins, with the exception of this piece, which is coined there. The legends and inscription are in the language of the country. On the obverse (see Nos. 94 and 95) is a full-face bust of the king, attired in uniform, with the legend "KAMEHAMEHA III KO MOI," and the date. On the reverse is the inscription "HAPA HANERI" (one-hundredth), inclosed in a wreath of laurel, and the legend "AUPUNI HAWAII."

ORIENTAL COINS.*

The coinage of Oriental countries, with one or two exceptions, bear no devices, and as a detailed catalogue or description of the very complete collection of the coins of this character contained in the Cabinet would be very uninteresting, to say the least, we have adopted the alternative of laying before the reader certain rules and explanations by which he may the more readily distinguish such coins as are impressed with Oriental characters, for which a knowledge of the language is not requisite.

Almost the only character inscribed upon Oriental coins is the Arabic, variously modified; in Java and Morocco, the letters are drawn as rudely as possible; in Turkey and Egypt, with more precision; in Persia they are in the flowing *taleek*, which appears to bear something of the relation to the *niskhi*, or strict Arabic, that our Italic letters do to the Roman. The universality of this character on Eastern moneys is due to the extension and domination of the Mohammedan faith.

But a person may be versed in Arabic and Persian, as he finds them in books, and yet not be able to read these inscriptions. The reasons are the following:—*first*, the letters are not in the form of

1

printing, but of writing; as, for instance, the dashing character (fig. 1.) so conspicuous on all Turkish, Egyptian, and Barbary coins (except Morocco), is, in type, the preposition في *in*, or *at*. As this character affords a good clew to those classes of coin, it is to be again noticed. The second reason is that the arrangement of the words is often irregular or fanciful. For example, if we instance a Turkish silver coin, we find that if the inscription on the reverse were altered from Arabic to English script, it would appear nearly as in fig. 2. It is meant to read "*Struck at Constantinople*, year 24 of the Sultan's reign, which

* For this article we are largely indebted to Mr. Du Bois, Assistant Assayer, and the "Manual of Coins and Bullion."

commenced 1223 of the hegira." Again, a sicca rupee of Calcutta will be found still more at variance with our ideas of order. Fig. 3 represents the reverse side; that is, "*Struck at Morshedabad in the* 19*th year of the happy accession to the throne.*" Stars or rosettes are frequently put in by way of ornament.

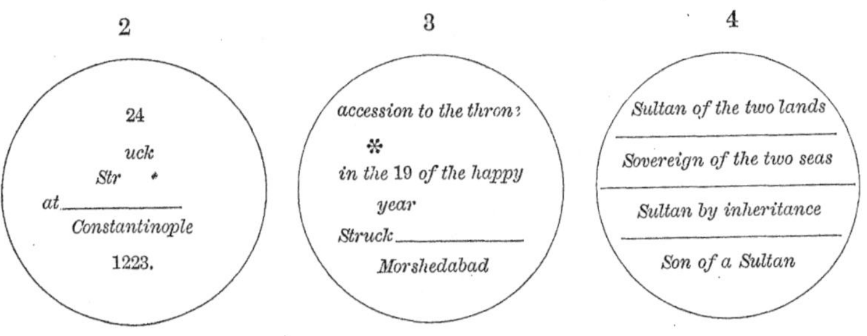

This irregularity (as *we* call it) is still more embarrassing in Persian coins; but, not to multiply such examples, one must be given in which the inscription is in good consecutive order—the reverse of a silver coin of Tripoli is shown as an instance (fig. 4). This inscription was formerly very common on Turkish coins; it is now confined to those of Tunis and Tripoli.

Proceeding to identify the coinage of different countries, the reader will take notice that the character already given, equivalent to the preposition *in* or *at*, is found on all coins of Turkey and of States really or nominally dependent on that empire. The *toghra*, or monogram of the sultan, is generally on those coins, but the dash universally; its place in the inscription is thus explained: "Struck *in* Constantinople," Egypt, Tripoli, or otherwise, as the case may be. This mark affords a general distinction between the moneys *west* and *east* of the Euphrates. Supposing it to be found on any given specimen, the possessor will desire to know to what particular State it belongs. For this purpose he has only to acquaint himself with the word indicating the place of coinage, which, be it observed, is always directly under the elongated preposition—sometimes a little entangled with it. The following are the characters proper to the respective Ottoman mints:—

ENGLISH NAME.	CHARACTER ON THE COIN.	TYPOGRAPHIC FORM.	EQUIVALENT IN OUR LETTERS.
Constantinople	اسلامبول	اسلامبول	ISLAMBOUL.*
do.	قسطنطنيه	قسطنطنيه	KOSTANTINIEH.
Egypt	مصر	مصر	MISR.
Tripoli	طرابلس	طرابلوس	TRABLOUS.
Tunis	تونس	تونس	TUNIS.
Algiers	جزاير	جزاير	JEZAIR.

Some allowance is to be made for variations, as the engravers use the license of penmen; but the above will be satisfactory guides in all cases.

Having thus ascertained the place of coinage, an interesting point remains, to decide the date and reign. The date is always that of the hegira, or Mohammedan era, and (with one exception) is in Arabic figures. These are as follows:—

1	2	3	4†	5	6	7	8	9	0
١	٢	٣	۴	۵	٦	٧	٨	٩	٠

These are written from left to right (according to the European order), but letters and words in Arabic run in the opposite direction. The method of arriving at the date of the coin (for most Ottoman coins bear two dates, that of the hegira and of the sultan's reign) is as follows: Having first ascertained the year of the hegira in which the sultan ascended the throne (which appears upon all the

* The usual name for Constantinople in the East is Stamboul, an easy corruption of the original Greek name. The Turks appear to have intended a play upon this word, and at the same time to commend the Mohammedan religion, by stamping on their coins *Islamboul*, which means "the fullness of the true faith." (See *Marsden*, 409.) This title was last used in the reign of Selim III., which commenced 1203 (A.D. 1789).

† The figure for 4 is sometimes in the form of our 3, reversed, especially on Ottoman coins.

coins of Turkey), upon another portion of the coin the year of his reign will be found; this being added to the former, gives the date of the coin according to the year of the hegira, which is readily transformed to the Christian date.

The accession of the sultans for the past century has been as follows:—

Mahmoud I.	A.H. 1143*	A.D. 1730
Othman III.	" 1168	" 1754
Mustapha III	" 1171	" 1757
Abdul Hamid	" 1187	" 1774
Selim III	" 1203	" 1789
Mustapha IV.	" 1222	" 1807
Mahmoud II.	" 1223	" 1808
Abdul Mejid.	" 1255	" 1839

The coins of Morocco are the exception to the foregoing explanations. They may be known by this unique characteristic; the date is that of the hegira, but the figures are European. All other coins which do not bear the distinguishing marks already stated, but are in the Arabic or Persian character, belong either to Hindostan, Java, or Persia.

The coins of Hindostan, of which we speak more at large further on, are coined at the mints of Calcutta, Madras, and Bombay. Those of Calcutta bear the name of the neighboring City of Morshedabad; those of Madras are stamped as of Arcot; and those of Bombay as of Surat. The imprints of the mint are found in the lower portion of the reverse; they are as follows:—

ENGLISH NAME.	CHARACTER ON THE COIN.	TYPOGRAPHIC FORM.	EQUIVALENT IN OUR LETTERS.
Morshedabad	مرشداباد	مرشداباد	MORSHEDABAD.
Arcot	ارکات	ارکات	ARCOT.
Surat	سورت	سورت	SURAT.

* The Mohammedan year is lunar, and therefore shorter than ours about eleven days. This makes a difference of one year in every thirty-three.

Some of these coins are dated, others not; but the dates are not to be depended upon. The gold pagodas and silver fanams of the south of India may always be known by their shape, being small and lumpy.

The coins of the Dutch East India Company in Java bore Arabic impressions previous to the restoration in 1816; they may be known by the anomaly of bearing a Christian date, and in European figures.

The coins of Persia may generally be recognized by the heavy semicircular characters in close succession, which bear an unmeaning aspect to the American eye; the date (when not omitted) is in exceedingly small characters.

I.—OTTOMAN EMPIRE.

There is no system of money so uncertain and fluctuating as that of Turkey (called the *Ottoman Empire*, after its founder, *Othman*). The piastre, or *ghersh* (otherwise spelt *grouch**), which is the unit, was worth, in 1764, (reign of Mustapha III.), sixty cents in our money, but in less than three-quarters of a century it was so far depreciated in value that, in 1830, it was worth only three cents intrinsically, although in commerce it was at eighteen to the Spanish dollar, or a fraction over five cents to the piastre.

The gold coins of Turkey are, the pieces of 100 piastres, at 915 thousandths fine, and 111 grains weight; value $4.37.4; and the *yirmilik*, of twenty piastres, the *onlik* of ten, and the *altunli beshlik*, of five piastres, at the fineness of twenty carats, or 833 thousandths; the largest weighing twenty-four and one-half grains Troy.

The silver coins are, the pieces of twenty piastres, at 828 thousandths fine, and 371½ grains weight; value eighty-two cents; and the five piastre, and its half, and the piece of one piastre, with its half and quarter, the latter consisting of ten *paras*. Besides these they also have the pieces of 6, 3, 1½ piastres, and the single *para*. The pieces of 1½ piastres and upward are forty-three and forty-four per cent. of silver, the others are much lower.

Our series of Ottoman coins is unusually extensive and complete,

---

* Marsden derives it from the German *groshen*.

through the aid of John P. Brown, Esq., now, and for many years, dragoman to the American Legation at Constantinople. The suite consists of 123 pieces, of which twenty-seven are gold, the remainder silver (mostly base) and copper. The earliest date is that of Murad I., who died in 1389. The coins of the present sultan, Abdul Medjid, conclude the series.

II.—EGYPT.

This country was reduced to the condition of a Turkish province in 1517, but at the present day, through the vigorous administration of its pacha, this dependence has been rendered merely nominal; since 1839 it has existed as a vice-royalty and fief of the Ottoman Porte. Its coins always bear the name of the sultan of Turkey; and the system of moneys is the same in both countries, both using the *piastre* as a unit.

The gold coins of Egypt are the pieces of 100, 50, 20, 10, and 5 piastres. The last two or three seem inconveniently small, and remind us forcibly of the "California quarters." The principal coin is nearly equal in value to our half eagle; hence the Egyptian piastre, in gold, is worth five cents.

In 1801 the silver piastre of Cairo was worth twenty cents of our money, less than that of Constantinople, which was then worth twenty-six cents. Under the new system of Mehemet Ali, which is based upon the Austrian standards, the *real*, equivalent to the Austrian rix dollar, is rated at twenty piastres, making the silver piastre worth 5.02 cents. There are six denominations of silver coins, 20, 10, 5, 1, $\frac{1}{2}$, and $\frac{1}{4}$ piastre; the piastre or unit is divided, nominally, into forty paras. The coins of Egyptian caliphs of the middle ages, and the still more ancient pieces of the Ptolemies, are mentioned under the head of "Greek Monarchies."

III.—TRIPOLI.

This country, one of the Barbary States, is nominally a regency of the Ottoman Empire. It formerly had a distinct coinage, in no respect assimilated to that of the sultan, except that it bore his name and titles in the impression, to the exclusion of those of the reigning bashaw. The coins were of little commercial importance, and of still less value as specimens of art, but at the present day, being extremely scarce on this side of the ocean, they are proportionably curious.

The mint law, or rather the instruction of the bashaw to his coiners, as to the alloy and composition of the moneys, was, as in most Turkish countries, a State secret, and the issue of coin as often an expedient to raise money for the government as to provide a currency for the people. A considerable parcel of coin having been struck at the mint, public criers proclaimed the value at which it must be received; and the people were compelled, under severe penalties, to accept the coin at its arbitrary valuation, until the issue in the possession of the bashaw had been expended, when the money was suffered to fall to its intrinsic value.

A notable instance of this policy was that of a pretended gold coin, issued by Youssuf Bashaw. In 1827, pieces called *adlea,* having a gold exterior, and weighing about forty grains Troy, were forced upon the people as the equivalent of a dollar. In a few days they declined to the one-thirtieth of that amount, which was considered to be their real value. These oppressive measures of Youssuf were the principal cause of the revolution which led to his overthrow and abdication in 1832.

The gold coin of Tripoli has for a long time disappeared, even rom its own capital city. The latest date is A.H. 1233 (A.D. 1820), though the dies with this date were said to have been continued in use until 1829, with a view to impose an inferior coin into circulation.

Of the silver or *billon* coin, there are two series of modern date. The first is that of Youssuf Bashaw, of the twenty-fifth year of Sultan Mahmoud II. (1832), consisting of the *ghersh* or piastre, and its divisions. The weight of the ghersh was $2\frac{1}{3}$ *meticals;* the alleged fineness was one-third, but our assays prove an habitual endeavor at one-fourth. The second series is that of Nedgib, his successor, consisting of the *utchlik* of $1\frac{1}{5}$ piastres, or 120 paras, and its divisions. The utchlik weighs $3\frac{1}{3}$ meticals, and its fineness is about the same as the ghersh. It therefore appears that the value of the piastre was increased; Youssuf's was worth ten cents in our money, that of Nedgib twelve and one-half cents; nearly the same as in Tunis.

At the present day no money is coined in Tripoli, their currency being chiefly derived from Turkey.*

IV.—TUNIS.

This country is nominally a dependency of Turkey, and allegiance is acknowledged, as in Egypt and Tripoli, by the inscription of the sultan's name and titles upon the coin, without mention of the reigning bey. The system of money is entirely distinct from that of the mother country.

While this regency is reported to have made considerable advances in civilization, it must be owned that the coinage is an exception; its fluctuations of value and baseness of composition show that it belongs to Barbary. The coins are scarcely seen in our part of the world, and are but slightly noticed in standard treatises.

The old piastre of Tunis (say of Selim III.) was of the intrinsic value of twenty-five cents, or one-fourth of a Spanish dollar. In 1828 the bey ordered a new coinage, of which the piastre was to pass for one-fifth of a dollar; but its real value was not more than fourteen cents. The coins have since declined somewhat, so that at present the piastre is scarcely worth thirteen cents. In fact, the coinage is regulated by no declared standard, but varies according to the secret instructions of the government.

The arbitrary value set upon the piastre of 1828 gave rise, as might have been expected, to a profitable speculation for private coiners beyond the Mediterranean, as well as for the bey himself. Quantities of counterfeit Tunisian piastres—if it be right to stigmatize them as such, since they were fully equal to the bey's in value—were coined in Europe, and introduced into Tunis; where, being exchanged at the rate of five to the dollar, they had the effect of driving good foreign coins out of circulation, and obliged the government to annul its decree. The piastres then fell to their true valuation, and

---

* Letter of M. J. Gaines, Consul at Tripoli, to the Treasury Department, May 21, 1859.

so continue, except that the course of trade sometimes attaches to them a variable rate in commerce. For example, a failure in the crops of corn, oil, etc., will reduce the piastre to seventy or eighty French centimes, or thirteen to fifteen cents of the United States; but when the harvests are abundant, the value (against foreign money) rises to seventeen cents.

V.—ALGIERS,

In the north of Africa, was formerly a Turkish regency, but had a system of coins distinct from the mother country. In 1830 it came under the dominion of the French, and has since been supplied with a coinage executed by that power. The coins belonging to the old system are seldom or never seen in this region, especially at the present time. We have but five specimens in the Cabinet, one of gold, three of silver, and one of copper. These are of little importance, except as curiosities; they bear inscriptions in Oriental characters, but no devices. (See Nos. 20 to 24.)

VI.—MOROCCO.

This country is one of the Barbary States, in the north of Africa, and is usually complimented with the prefix of Empire.

The coins of the neighboring country of Spain are current here, but Morocco has also a coinage of her own, executed in a truly barbarian style. The monetary system is as follows: six *filse* (copper) are equal to one *blankeel*, formerly a coin, but now imaginary; four blankeels make one silver ounce, *ukiah* or *dirhem;* and ten of these are equal to one *miscal*, a money of account. A Spanish dollar of the Peninsula passes for fifteen ounces; a *pillar* or Spanish-American dollar is held at sixteen. (This is purely a commercial distinction; intrinsically, one dollar is as good as the other.) A Peninsular dollar is also equal to one and one-half miscals. There was formerly a dollar or *real* coined in Morocco, of full value; but it is now almost out of circulation. The only gold coin is the *buntagui*, equal to two dollars.

Many years ago, a service of gold plate was sent by the king of

Spain as a present to the sultan. His religion did not permit him to accept it; but, not willing altogether to decline the courtesy, he sent it back with a request that it might be made into coin. The Spanish monarch accordingly converted it into half doubloons, or eight-dollar pieces, impressed with Moorish characters, but with the designation "Struck at Madrid." These are now very scarce, having generally been carried away to other countries, as curiosities.

VII.—PERSIA, BOKHARA, AND GEORGIA.

In this series we include only modern pieces, coined within a century past, those of an ancient date being noticed in another place. The two latter sections are of little importance to any except the curious, but the former will require a more extended notice.

Previous to the reign of Fatha Ali, which commenced in 1797, the most usual coins of Persia were the gold rupee, or *mohur*, and the silver rupee, or ten *shahee*. These corresponded pretty nearly with the India coinage, of the same era. There were other pieces, of which the ducat or *ashrafi* was the most important, and of which there is a notice as early as 1724. This was of the European ducat or sequin weight, being three-fourths of a *miscal*, which is the normal money-weight of Persia.* Amid the various changes in the coinage, it has retained its place and character, though now known by the name of *toman*. In the long reign of Fatha Ali, extending to 1834, there were some changes in the monetary system. During the earlier years the toman was issued weighing ninety-four Troy grains. From 1814 to 1824 the toman seems to have been reduced to seventy-one and one-quarter grains, or about one miscal in weight. The ducat was then a distinct coin.

Of the silver coinage in his reign, the *sahib-koran* or *real*, until 1807 inclusive, weighed 159 grains. In the next year it was reduced to 143 grains, or two miscals, and so continued, probably, to the close of his government.

---

* The miscal is variously rated at seventy-one to seventy-five and one-half Troy grains; probably it is accurate enough to assume seventy-two, which is exactly three dwts.

In 1834 Mohammed Shah, grandson of Fatha Ali, succeeded to the throne. He reduced the weight of the *toman* to fifty-three and three-quarters grains, so that it corresponds with the former ducat. The toman and its half are now the only gold coins: of the silver, the *sahib-koran* now weighs eighty-three grains; its half, the *penebad*, in proportion; the copper coins are the *shahee* and its half.

The present relations of the coins are as follows: ten shahees equal one penebad; two of these, one sahib-koran; ten of these last, one toman. Persian coins seldom stray into this quarter of the world.

VIII.—CUFIC COINS.

Under this technical title (originating from the town of *Cupah*, where was the first mint of the successors of Mohammed), collectors generally place all the coins of Arabic inscription of the middle ages. They form an extremely rare and curious series, not much studied as yet in our Western world. The earliest is the silver *dirhem* of Walid, the famous caliph of Damascus, A.D. 713. There are pieces of Haroun Alraschid, (see *Division XV.*, "*Selections*,") Almahdi, and other caliphs of Bagdad, various caliphs and Mameluke sultans of Egypt, princes of *Diarbekir* and Mosul, and Tartar conquerors of Persia, down to A.D. 1316. There are thirty pieces in this suite, of which six are gold, the remainder silver and copper.

IX.—HINDOSTAN.

The coins of this country, almost wholly under British dominion and familar to us by course of trade, may be noticed more at large.

Gold Coins.—1. Mohur of the East India Company. Struck at Calcutta in the name of the Mogul emperor, Shah Alum; dated in his year 19, or A.D. 1789.

2, 3. Half and quarter mohur, of the same.

4. Mohur of Bombay. Persian legend on one side, and English on the other. No date.

5. One-third mohur. Same.

6. Piece of two pagodas. Southern India.

7. Star pagoda, of Madras.

8. Farouki, or pagoda, of Tippoo Saib. Southern India.

Silver Coins.—9, 10, 11, 12. Sicca rupees, of the Great Mogul, Shah Jehan, dethroned A.D. 1660. Different types. Nearly fine silver. Legends in the Persian-Arabic character.

13, 14. Old octagonal Mahratta rupees. Hindoo legends.

15, 16. Old sicca rupees, of the Mogul Empire.

17, 18, 19. Square rupees. Old Mogul dynasty.

20, 21. Half rupee and eighth, of the Punjab region.

22 to 28. Sicca rupees of Northern India. Eighteenth century.

29. Mahratta rupee; circular.

30, 31. Rupees of Delhi; latter part of the Mogul dynasty.

32, 33, 34. Two rupees and half, of petty princes in Northern India; inferior silver.

35. Rupee, of Cashmere.

36, 37. Rupees of Calcutta, or Morshedabad. Coined by the East India Company in the name of the Mogul Emperor, Shah Alum. Persian legends. The edges are reeded, the lines inclining.

38, 39, 40. Rupee, half, and quarter. Same type as preceding, with perpendicular lines on the edge. More recent than the last numbers.

41, 42, 43. Rupee, half, and quarter. Same type, but of reduced diameter and smooth edges, probably coined after 1818; but they all bear the date "19th of Shah Alum," corresponding to 1779.

44, 45, 46. One half, and two quarter rupees, of the East India Company, without the 19. Struck at Morshedabad.

47. Double rupee, of Arcot (Madras), dated A.H. 1172, (A.D. 1758.) The Shah Alumghir. Really coined in 1811.

48, 49, 50, 51. Two rupees, and half and sixteenth, of the Madras Presidency of the East India Company, bearing the same date and legends as No 47 in Persian-Arabic. Really coined in 1818.

52. (Left vacant for a Bombay rupee.)

53, 54. Two quarter pagodas, of Madras. Not dated, (1811.)

55. Rupee, of Cabul.

56. (Left for a rupee of William IV.)

57, 58, 59. Two, half and one quarter rupee, of William IV., 1835. Calcutta mint. Legends in English.

60, 61, 62. (Left for Victoria pieces.)

63. Piece of two annas, or one-eighth rupee. VICTORIA, 1841.

64 to 67. Small silver fanams, of Southern India.

68. Rix dollar, of Ceylon.

71. Square piece, partly of lead. Said to bear the date A.H. 100, (A.D. 722.)

72. Pice of ALADDIN MOHAMMED SHAH, A.H. 695, (A.D. 1295.)

73. Do. of MOHAMMED SHAH, A.H. 725, (A.D. 1324.)

74. Do. of MOAZIM FIRUG SHAH, 752, (A.D. 1351.)

75. Do. of NASREDDIN MOHAMMED SHAH, 796, (A.D. 1393.)

76. Do. (Square) of MOHAMMED SHAH, A.D. 1435.

77. Do. (Square) of GHIASEDDIN, A.D. 1469.

78. Do. of SEKANDER, 894, (A.D. 1488.)

The foregoing, from 72 to 78, are of the AFGHAN SULTANS of Northern Hindostan, whose dynasty was overthrown by the descendants of TIMOUR, commonly called the Great Moguls, about the middle of the sixteenth century, who maintained their seat at Delhi until the Empire was gradually wrested from them by the East India Company.

79. Double *pice*, of AKBAR, Great Mogul, 963, (A.D. 1556.)

The next pieces, 80 to 90, are old *pice*, not identified, but presumed to be of the seventeenth and eighteenth centuries.

91 to 102, are the more recent copper coins of the East India Company, from a half anna to one *pie* (or *peisah*, or *pice*, as above), with a mixture of languages in the legends—Persic, Bengalee and English.

X.—CHINA AND COCHIN-CHINA.

The great bulk of Chinese currency consists of Spanish dollars. It was formerly* the practice among Chinese traders to cut the dollars into halves, quarters, etc., for the purpose of making change; this practice produced the necessity of weighing the coins or bits whenever a transfer took place. In fact, this operation is said to accompany all exchange of metallic money in China, each merchant being provided with a pair of scales and the other necessary ap-

* Latterly, we believe, discontinued.

pliances. The native traders have also become, from long practice, adepts in distinguishing the different qualities of metal, merely from sight and touch. They have another curious custom, long in vogue, as follows: each merchant, upon receiving a new Spanish dollar, stamped it with his private mark; in this way, before the piece in question had been long in circulation among them, it acquired the *sobriquet* of "chopped dollar." The effect of this custom will be readily seen by referring to the pieces in the Cabinet. After the Spanish coins have become so much defaced as to be no longer fit for currency, they are melted and cast into an oblong bar called a *tael*. (These are usually denominated "dollar taels," to distinguish them from the *tael* of *sycee*, or pure silver—commercially fine.) These are valued respectively at $1.50 and $1.65. (See *Division XV.*, "*Selections.*")

The Chinese also have a gold bar of ten taels. This has a peculiar *wavy* appearance upon its upper surface, produced by shaking the mould in which it is cast while the metal is cooling; after the casting has been accomplished, the inscriptions are impressed upon it with small punches. The specimen in the Cabinet (see *Division XV.*, "*Selections*,") has inscribed upon it several Chinese characters, translated as follows: "SHIH TSUH"* (ten touches), referring to *quality;* commercially fine gold. Next we have the word "WING" (everlasting); and last, "ZIH-TAE" (virtuously great). The last is said to be the title of the imperial house. This is found to be 966 thousandths fine; value $235.50.

The *tael*, applied above, appears to designate the unit of Chinese money, and is the translation adopted by the Portuguese, the Chinese word being "LEUNG."

The only regular coins struck by the Chinese are the small copper and brass pieces known as "cash;" these are about equal in size to our half eagle, and have a square hole in the center, with the Chinese characters inscribed on both sides; they are used in all the petty transactions among the natives, who string them on long strings and wear them slung about the neck. The value, which is almost too insignificant to be computed, is very nearly *one-fifth* of our cent.

---

* This is upon the upper side, and is five times repeated.

From Cochin-China, we have a specimen of a more decided attempt at a regular coinage—the silver dollar. This has upon one side the Chinese dragon (from which it derives the appellation of "dragon dollar"), and upon the other, a sun, and the inscriptions in the Chinese characters; translated "*tong pao,*" (current money). The edge is reeded, the lines inclining, and both the *obverse* and *reverse* are deeply indented around the edge. The fineness is 750 thousandths, and the value 90 cts. (See *Division XV.*, "*Selections.*")

XI.—BURMAH AND SIAM.

Of Burmah we have a specimen of their ancient currency. This is merely a gravel-stone incased in brass; a forced value was placed upon it by the government. (See *Division XV.*, "*Selections.*")

The coins of Siam, of which we have a full set, are the most remarkable of any which have yet fallen under our notice. These consist of mere lumps of silver and gold, fashioned into a shape well calculated to remind one of the *restless* character of a true circulating medium. Of the gold there are three pieces, coined about the year 1830, of the respective values of $3.88, $2.10, and 60 cents; the fineness being 800 *thousandths.* The silver consists of seven pieces: the *tecal,* valued at sixty cents, and its parts—the smallest piece being worth only one-third of a cent. The *tecal,* though modern, appears to be equivalent to the ancient *tecal* or *shekel* of Western Asia; all the pieces, both gold and silver, are stamped with Siamese characters. (See *Division XV.*, "*Selections.*")

XII.—JAPAN.

This insular empire, shut out from all intercourse with mankind by its own act, has a system of metallic moneys the peculiarities of which cannot fail to interest the American reader, especially at the present time, when the attention of the commercial world is being attracted to that quarter of the globe. The Cabinet contains a full set of these coins, recently received, and which have been fully tested and examined by the Assayers of the Mint. The subjoined extracts, taken from their report to the Director of the Mint, contain all that it will be necessary to say on this subject. (See Plate XXVII. Nos. 5 and 6.)

"The series of Japanese coin consists of three sizes of gold, two of silver, and three of an alloy of inferior metals. In their shape, composition, and relation to each other, they present some striking features, which set them apart from every other system of coinage in the world.

"The principal gold coin, known as the *cobang* or *cobank*, is of an oval shape, about two and a half inches long, and half as wide. It is very thin, soft, and easily bent, having no elasticity; its appearance is that of fine gold, and its surface is marked by sundry figures not well understood as yet, although it is said that the flowery ornaments are 'the arms of the spiritual emperor,' and that a certain central cipher is the special imprint of the 'Inspector General of Money.' The weight, two specimens agreeing, is 362 thousandths of an ounce, or nearly 174 grains. Next is a gold piece of one-fourth that weight, and intended as a quarter of the preceding, called the 'gold *itzebu;*' but its form is entirely different. It is four-sided, rectangular, and very thick; three-fourths of an inch long, and half that in width. The smallest gold coin is the half itzebu, of proportional size. We have then the silver itzebu, and its quarter of the same domino shape; the larger piece weighing .280 of an ounce, or $134\frac{1}{2}$ grains. Passing to the third division, there is the 'hundred *p'senny*,' a casting of red brass, oval and thick, measuring two inches long, and a little more than half as wide, with a hole in the center. Finally, there are pieces of four, and one *p'senny* circular, with holes in the center, and scarcely to be distinguished from the well-known Chinese *cash*.

"The *composition* of these coins, a subject falling within our particular province, has been to some extent examined. The cobang and itzebu, as was observed, have the appearance of fine gold; and it is said are regarded at home as being of high quality. But it is only necessary to scratch away the surface, to discover that the Japanese understand the process of *pickling*, well known to workers in jewelry, whether in America or Asia, or even in the center of Africa. Trusting to the somewhat permanent effects of 'hard biting,' they have not even added copper to mitigate the whitening effect of silver alloy; the mixture being gold and silver, and not far from equal proportions. The cobang, two pieces assayed, gave 567½ and 568½ thousandths fine; the itzebu resulted 566. These figures indicate a designed, though probably a secret standard. The consequent intrinsic values are, according to our mint rates, and allowing for silver contained, $4.44* for the cobang, and $1.11 (nearly) for the itzebu.

"It is interesting to observe that, although so ignorant of the methods of other nations, Japan has imitated, and even exceeded them in the process of deterioration of moneys. About the beginning of the last century, the cobang, quite similar in shape and device to the present piece, weighed 272 grains, was 854 fine, and worth just ten dollars. A century later, it had fallen to 196 grains, 667 fine, and worth (including silver) five dollars and seventy-eight cents.

"The smallest gold coin has not been assayed; it evidently contains but little gold, and has therefore a forced valuation. The transition to the next piece in order, the largest silver coin, affords a fresh surprise. It is found to be of almost absolute fineness; that is, 991 thousandths, and is worth 37 cents. While this proves that the Japanese possess the art of refining, it does not explain why they debase the gold and refine the silver. The smallest silver piece is apparently not inferior in fineness.

"The foregoing details will be interesting to the numismatist and metallurgist; but the fact which remains will excite a more popular attention—it is in regard to the legal relation which these coins bear to each other. Insulated from the rest of mankind, the Japanese have proportioned gold to silver according to their own ideas of use and state of supply. The gold and silver itzebu are, as is stated, interchangeable; that is, a piece which is worth in our eyes 111 cents

* The assay conducted at the Mint, in the presence of the Ambassadors, resulted in placing the value of the present cobang at about $3.45, or, including silver, $3.57. The full value by this assay gave a fraction over $3.58, and so near to $3.60, or 90 cents to the itzebu, that it was proposed by the Japanese to make that the round estimate for purposes of commerce, which the officers of the Mint considered reasonable; and their written views, sent afterwards to the Embassy through the Treasury Department, may be considered as a settlement of that point.

(and to a Japanese, worth nearly as much as two of our gold dollars, because he supposes it to be much better gold than it is), buys no more than a piece which with us would be 37 cents. The Spanish or Mexican dollar they consider equal to three itzebu, which is three-fourths of a cobang, or $3.33. The abundance of gold, or scarcity of silver, which creates such a strange ratio, would no doubt be promptly corrected by foreign traders for the sake of the enormous profit. But, unfortunately, there is a stringent law against the exportation of coin, which makes it very difficult even to get a few pieces for assay. For our facilities in this respect, we are indebted to the perseverance of a gentleman who is interested in the collection of rare coins, and to his correspondent abroad.

"What relation the oval piece of brass, which passes for 'one hundred,' bears to the itzebu, we are not informed. It weighs only about six times as much as the piece of one p'senny, and therefore bears an arbitrary value; unless brass is there held to be vastly more valuable than an alloy of copper and lead, which appears to be the composition of the coin which stands at the bottom of the scale."

We have since received another piece, like the last, of *iron*, of which it takes 7000 to make a Spanish dollar. (See *Division XV.*, "*Selections.*")

XIII.—MALAY ARCHIPELAGO.

Of this extensive group of islands, Sumatra and Java are under the dominion of the Netherlands, and the Philippines under that of Spain. Some of the other islands are settled by the Dutch, and over others the English claim dominion.

The only coinage of any great extent for these possessions is that for the Island of Java. For this island there has been three distinct series of coins. The first was issued by the Holland, or Dutch East India Company, and was continued until the capture of their possessions by the English in 1811. This series consisted of the gold rupee and its half, and the silver rupee, with its half and quarter; they are all impressed with Oriental characters, but have a Christian date. Besides these there was a copper piece of the denomination of a *quarter stiver.* Of these there were several types: first we have two specimens of the date 1790; they both have upon one side the letters "O. V. C.;" the V. being much larger than the other letters, and so arranged as to overlap them; this side bears the date. On the other side they differ in type: the *first* having the arms of the province of Utrecht (*party per bend, proper; argent and gules*); and the other a crowned shield, bearing two lions rampant-combatant, and the legend "IN DEO EST SPES NOSTRA" (in God is our trust). We have also two other specimens of a later date, bearing upon one side a cock, with Oriental characters; one has an inscription on the reverse in Oriental characters; while the reverse of the other is distinguished by a device resembling a sun, and the year of the hegira in European figures, 1250, (A.D. 1834.)

Upon the expulsion of the Dutch in 1811, the English issued a new series of coins bearing inscriptions in Oriental characters as in the former series. In 1816 the island was restored to the Dutch; since which time a third series of coins have been issued differing very materially from the former. These consist of the gulden, and its half and quarter, with two copper pieces of the respective values of two kreutzers and quarter stiver. The gulden has upon the obverse a head of William I., King of the Netherlands, and the legend, in Dutch, "WILLAM KÖNING DER NED. G. H. V. L.;" and on the reverse, a crowned shield, bearing the arms of the Netherlands; the value "1......G;" and the inscription (beneath the shield) "NEDERLANDSCH INDIE." Legend, "MUNT VON HET KONINGRYK DER NEDERLANDEN. 1821." The smaller pieces have the same obverse, but a different reverse; the value "HALVE GULDEÑ," or "KWART GULDEN," being inscribed within a wreath of palm; above is inscribed "NEDERLANDSCH INDIE," and beneath, the date. These all have grained edges. The copper pieces have the arms upon the obverse, and the inscription "NEDERL INDIE," and the date upon the reverse. (See *Division of Oriental Coins.*)

Of other islands, we have several specimens of copper coins, as follows: Two small pieces of the same type and date (1804)—one for the Island of Sumatra, and the other for Saltana; they are both inscribed with the name of the island to which they belong. A copper piece of the Philippine Islands, bearing the arms of Spain and the legend "YEAB. (Isabel) II. D. G. HISP ET IND. R." upon the obverse, and a crowned lion upon the reverse. A small copper piece (size of a farthing), struck for one of the British islands; the inscriptions are Oriental; but the date, which denotes the year of the hegira, 1250 (A.D. 1834), is in European characters.

INDEX.

PAGE

ANCIENT COINS.

MODERN COINS.

ORIENTAL.